Martin Hughes &
Fionn Davenport

Dublin

The Top Five

1 Marsh's Library
Peruse this veritable time capsule (p95)

2 Drinking Guinness
Sup the spirit of Dublin in the Gravity Bar, Guinness Storehouse (p94)

3 Howth
Visit this traditional fishing village (p222)

4 Trinity College
Wander around and view the Book of Kells and the Long Room (p76)

5 Grafton Street
Stroll down and take the city's pulse (p74)

Contents

Published by Lonely Planet Publications Pty Ltd
ABN 36 005 607 983

Australia Head Office, Locked Bag 1, Footscray,
Victoria 3011, ☎ 03 8379 8000, fax 03 8379 8111,
talk2us@lonelyplanet.com.au

USA 150 Linden St, Oakland, CA 94607,
☎ 510 893 8555, toll free 800 275 8555,
fax 510 893 8572, info@lonelyplanet.com

UK 72–82 Rosebery Ave, Clerkenwell, London,
EC1R 4RW, ☎ 020 7841 9000, fax 020 7841 9001,
go@lonelyplanet.co.uk

France 1 rue du Dahomey, 75011 Paris,
☎ 01 55 25 33 00, fax 01 55 25 33 01,
bip@lonelyplanet.fr, www.lonelyplanet.fr

© Lonely Planet 2004
Photographs © Olivier Cirendini and as listed (p245),
2004

Printed through The Bookmaker International Ltd
Printed in China

The Authors

FIONN DAVENPORT

Writing about your home town is not as straightforward as you would think. Even after a third time of asking (for Lonely Planet anyway), Fionn is discovering that the Dublin he knows and (often) loves is not necessarily the same city visited by a curious outsider. Over the years he has learnt to see the city through their eyes, and in so doing has discovered a city that most of its residents rarely pay attention to: a city of extraordinary culture, tradition and hidden beauty. There is life beyond the hedonism of the pub, and you don't have to stray too far to appreciate it.

Fionn resides full-time in Dublin's city centre: by day, he's a mild-mannered travel writer with a bag full of notes and a head full of facts and figures; by night, he's a DJ, bringing hip-hop's blessed beats to Dublin's night owls. His ambitions at the end of 2003 are to quit smoking before the general ban comes into effect and to cure his golf swing of the cursed reverse pivot.

Fionn researched and wrote the Walking Tours, Entertainment, Shopping, Excursions and Directory chapters.

MARTIN HUGHES

Martin was born and bred in Dublin where he dithered for some five years between journalism and public relations before ditching both and hitting the road. The Celtic Tiger arrived the day after he left. Carrying on the traditions of his forebears, he left the town he loved so well. After more than three years travelling, he eventually settled in Melbourne, Australia, where he hooked up with Lonely Planet and got them to pay for his frequent trips home. He's happily freelancing these days and returns to Dublin for at least two months each year for family get-togethers and cultural catch-ups.

Martin coordinated this edition and researched and wrote the Highlights, Introducing Dublin, City Life, Arts, Architecture & History, Neighbourhoods, Eating, Drinking and Sleeping chapters.

PHOTOGRAPHER

A journalist and photographer based in Paris, Olivier Cirendini has contributed to the writing of many French-language Lonely Planet guidebooks. Apart from pen and notebooks, his cameras have always been his most faithful travel companions. After years of black and white photography he slowly allowed his world to become quadrichromatic and became a regular contributor to Lonely Planet Images.

Introducing Dublin

Dublin has long been famous for its poetry and pubs, and the knack of its people for finding fun in the most unlikely places. These days they don't have to look very far at all – Dublin has boomed and blossomed over the last decade and what was for centuries reduced to a provincial backwater is now a thriving European capital where the creative energy seems unbounded. It never lost its personality but bejaysus and begorra…Dublin's got its mojo back.

Ireland's explosive economic growth has brought fundamental changes to life in the capital. The tide of emigration has been turned, massive development has taken place and an increasingly multicultural society is emerging. Youthful endeavour jostles with a leaden traditionalism, and it's this friction that is giving Dublin its new spark.

But the basic character of the city remains unchanged. All Dubliners share a garrulous sociability and sarcastic wit, and you can't help but enjoy the energy, humour and relaxed attitude of its people. They love nothing more than engaging in banter, and you'll hear it from the bar to the beach. The word – whether it's spoken, written or even slurred – is paramount. It's part of Dublin's great tradition that has led this little place to claim no less than four Nobel laureates for literature. Its many historic museums, top-class attractions and Georgian architecture aside, it's the conviviality and legendary craic (traditional fun) that have made it into one of Europe's top destinations.

Dubliners themselves do exceptionally good tourism; they're always on hand to tell you a story, are warmly polite and even apologise when they're giving you a gentle reminder that they have to close in 10 minutes. One greeting is insufficient so they traditionally offer one thousand welcomes. They can thank you once but they'd rather say 'thanks a million'. They don't necessarily queue but they know exactly who is next.

To seek outside recognition is inherent to most small, insecure cities and so it was with Dublin throughout its history. Its most successful artists – in music, literature and the fine arts – had to be successful outside the country before they could be celebrated in their own city. But all that has changed now, and Dublin and its denizen now strut their stuff across the world stage with a charismatic swagger. It's hip. International magazines are making Dublin their cover story, and there's a palpable sense that the city is creating a new cultural heritage.

It's positively fizzing with creativity, bulging with talent, and its tremendous cultural history is seen as a benchmark rather than a burden.

Dubliners are intensely proud not just of their celebrated forbears, but of their city, although at first glance it may be difficult to see why. It's not necessarily pleasant; sometimes it's not even clean and much of the architecture can seem like a jumble. But it's got a great personality, with a soul and sociability that make it the most charismatic of cities. At its best, it's a life-affirming experience that will restore your faith in human nature.

Dublin has lots of world-class attractions, particularly historical, which are evoked with colour and flair in many of its tourist sights and activities, from walking tours exploring the sights of the 1916 Easter Rising to the Book of Kells in Trinity College. Historic treasures have recently been polished up, while gleaming new developments have transformed the complexion of this fair city. A boon to tourists is Dublin's human scale: most of the sights are clustered around the compact centre and it's a walker's delight. When it rains, you can take shelter in a convivial pub and drink the best pints of Guinness on the planet.

If you don't want to take our word for it, just look at Dublin's new international appeal. It recently reversed the age-old tradition of emigration, and has become a place to run to rather than from. Returning Dubliners bolster the numbers, as do significant ethnic communities that are bringing new styles and multiculturalism to town. Walk into any café and you're as likely to hear an Aussie, American, Chinese, Spanish or Italian accent as you are the distinctive drawl of a Dubliner. Dubliners still can't believe it but they're happy the choice of food and coffee has improved.

The country's economic revival has now become the stuff of legend. While the famous Celtic Tiger might not be roaring any more, the economy is still purring and the optimism is unfettered. Increasingly global in outlook, Dublin swung into the new millennium with a dash, poise and self-assurance that couldn't even have been imagined a decade earlier. That said, when it comes down to it, Dublin is still all about poetry, pubs and pals.

MARTIN'S TOP DUBLIN DAY

I stroll through St Stephen's Green (p89) at dawn, quacking back at the ducks while nobody is around. With the *Irish Times* for company, I tuck into a full Irish brekkie before wandering around Georgian Dublin, admiring its elegance. I feel a surge of energy as I head down Grafton St, bumping into old friends and swapping smiles with strangers. Dublin beats Kerry in the All-Ireland football final (hey! It's my *perfect* day) and Roy Keane makes his comeback for Ireland. I contemplate these prospects over a solitary pint of Guinness in the International Bar (p156). Feeling a bit light-headed, I grab a crepe at Lemon (p149) before admiring the collection in the Chester Beatty Library (p81). I pop up to Iveagh Gardens (p85) and finish reading *Ulysses* before taking a quick bus tour of the sights of dear old Dublin town. Lonely Planet picks up the tab for my dinner at Thornton's (p147), I discover a new band, hear a new historical anecdote and retire to the Stag's Head (p160) with a few friends and argue about politics. My family comes in later and I talk sense into my old man.

Essential Dublin

- Chester Beatty Library (p81)
- A stroll around Trinity College (p77)
- Pints in Mulligan's (p158)
- A tour of Kilmainham Gaol (p94)
- A GAA match in Croke Park (p115)

City Life

City Life

DUBLIN TODAY

You might find Dublin with its feet up when you arrive. It's having a little breather after 10 mad years exchanging its rags for riches and devil-may-care spending. The cityscape has been largely rebuilt, old buildings have been given the once over, unemployment is at impressive lows, the labels are in the wardrobe, the golf clubs in the boot and the holiday homes have been signed over. Oh yeah, and there's a 120m stainless steel spire in the middle of O'Connell St. It's time to light up a fag, order a pint, reflect and take stock. What? We can't smoke in the pubs anymore...Time-out.

With the Celtic Tiger era – you'll be sick of hearing that phrase – now officially declared over, Dublin's phenomenal growth has slowed down. While it still proceeds at a rate unimagined less than a decade ago, belts are being tightened and caution is being advised. The city has been utterly transformed, and it now exudes as much style and confidence as any cosmopolitan European capital. But Dubliners are now asking at what cost.

On the upside, urban renewal carries on and life is being breathed into previously dilapidated areas. The streets are lined with restaurants, cafés, bars and clubs, and new ones open every week. With plenty of money sloshing around and a youthful, exuberant population – half of Dubliners are under 30 – the arts have never been in better shape and the city continues to punch above its weight in literature, theatre, dance and even on the screen.

Dublin's also gone multicultural although many are still a little bemused that young people from continental Europe are coming to live in their hometown. Local guys couldn't be happier: more women than men continue to immigrate to the city, where the ladies already outnumber the bowzies by 20,000.

But it's by no means a bed of roses for turn-of-the-century Dublin. For a while into the boom, locals seemed almost proud of their 'big city' setbacks, but now they're just jacked off with them. The city is bursting at the seams and town planners are scratching their heads about how to address the chronic problems of traffic congestion, a lack of affordable housing, the prohibitively high cost of living, as well as rising crime and instances of antisocial behaviour like littering and drunkenness. Meanwhile Dubliners have become almost impervious to what seem like weekly revelations of corruption in both political (see the boxed text on p24) and religious high places.

Hot Conversation Topics

- Government cutbacks (or 'readjustments' as the spin doctors call them)
- Ever-rising house prices
- Inconsistent refereeing in Gaelic games
- Do I need a new phone?
- Where to get the best coffee
- The newest restaurants

A Hundred Thousand Welcomes – As Long as You're Anglo & Have a Return Ticket Home

The most major transformation in contemporary Ireland has been the reversal of the age-old tradition of emigration. In 1998, for the first time ever, more people moved to the country than left. Figures were bolstered by returning emigrants drawn back to the honey pot but Dublin has also become a destination for refugees, asylum seekers and immigrants – including significant communities from Nigeria, Romania, Bosnia and China – as well as young temporary migrants from continental Europe.

The land of 'one hundred thousand welcomes' suddenly had its claim put under the microscope. And it didn't look pretty. Verbal abuse, racially motivated attacks and the targeting of non-nationals in crime have become relatively commonplace in Dublin, and it's a shock to find the ugly head of racism in the capital of a country that owes its very survival to the willingness of other countries to accommodate its overflow.

Make no mistake about it: the vast majority of Dubliners and the media welcome newcomers and embrace the city's new multiculturalism. What's most distressing, however, is that in the rat race of contemporary Dublin they don't stand up to the thuggish, ignorant few tarnishing their reputation.

Inevitably, the boom benefited those in a position to benefit and left the rest further behind; paradoxically, the number of poor increased during a time of unprecedented national wealth. Homelessness, street crime and drug abuse are worse than they've been for decades and you only need to spend a couple of days here to see hardship beneath the glossy veneer.

Crime and lawlessness are largely being blamed on drunkenness, although at least some of it is racially motivated (see the boxed text above). Dublin's reputation as a party destination attracts droves of 'alco-tourists' who hit town for drunken weekends. The problem got so bad that many places in ultra-touristy Temple Bar have even banned stag and hen parties. But the biggest problem with public drunkenness comes from the local youth, the majority of whom begin drinking regularly before they are 16 years old. A huge increase in youth affluence has been partly to blame in creating a drink culture that far exceeds the city's pub-loving reputation, although it can't all be blamed on this generation. The 1990s saw a whopping 46% per capita increase in booze consumption throughout Ireland and it's now estimated one in five people here drink in a harmful way. The government has taken some measures to address the problem, but it's obvious that extra police and restrictions on advertising are merely band-aids and there needs to be a significant cultural shift for there to be any real difference.

Dublin is also undeniably expensive (it's the capital of the second most expensive country in the EuroZone, after Finland). It's not just tourists who are stung by the expense of the place either. Low-rise, contemporary Dublin can't accommodate all the people who want to live here and the metropolitan area has extended out to places once known simply as 'the country'. The lowest interest rates in 40 years have fuelled ever-spiralling house prices and now owning your own home in Dublin is beyond the reach of most young people (at least those without inheritance).

Having witnessed the deplorable lows of the late '80s and the overblown highs of the '90s, Dubs are now looking for the happy medium. They're once more discovering the simpler pleasures of life in this fair city – namely the community and the craic (traditional fun).

CITY CALENDAR

There's never a bad time to visit Dublin although the high season understandably runs from June to September when the days are long, the weather is usually good and the mood relentlessly upbeat. Spring and autumn are good times for a peek, when showers are softer and the crowds thinner. Winter's all cold, wet and dark although if you're after indoor pleasures you'll have them largely to yourself and you won't feel as guilty lounging in the pub. December and Christmas are remarkably high-spirited while January is the only time the city's not really itself, when it's a little quiet and cranky after the festivities and the days seem interminably gloomy.

January

NEW YEAR'S CELEBRATIONS
Countdown to midnight at Christ Church Cathedral (p91) and Dublin's biggest official bash.

FEBRUARY/APRIL
SIX NATIONS RUGBY
Ireland plays its home matches at Lansdowne Rd Stadium in Ballsbridge (p177), the highlight often being the clash with England played here every second year (2005, 2007 etc).

MARCH
ST PATRICK'S DAY
On 17 March, half a million people watch marching bands, theatre groups, puppeteers and all sorts parade through the streets of Dublin, preceded by a weekend-long, fireworks-strewn, event-ridden street party and the three-day Guinness Fleadh music festival in Temple Bar

MARCH/APRIL
DUBLIN INTERNATIONAL FILM FESTIVAL
☎ 679 2937; www.dubliniff.com
The best of Irish and world cinema is showcased at this increasingly impressive festival (see the boxed text on p176).

MAY
HEINEKEN GREEN ENERGY FESTIVAL
☎ 284 1747; www.mcd.ie
Dublin's best music festival takes place in different venues around the city and usually has an open-air concert in the grounds of Dublin Castle (p82) as a highlight.

JUNE
WOMEN'S MINI-MARATHON
☎ 670 9461
This 10km road race for charity (second Sunday in June) is the largest of its kind in the world and attracts around 35,000 runners each year.

ANNA LIVIA OPERA FESTIVAL
☎ 661 7544; www.operaannalivia.com
A week-long festival of musical melodrama at the Gaiety Theatre (p174) in mid-June, often featuring international companies.

JUNE/JULY
PRIDE
☎ 873 4932; www.dublinpride.org/theparade.html
Dublin's gay pride event has turned into a week-long festival of parties, workshops, readings and more parties at gay venues around town, although these are just to warm up for the parade that takes place – and takes over – on the last Saturday of June or the first Saturday of July.

DUBLIN JAZZ FESTIVAL
☎ 877 9001; www.jazzireland.com
Dublin dons its black polo-neck for five days as venues clear their schedules to make way for local and international jazz musos in this increasingly popular and multicultural event.

JULY/AUGUST
WITNNESS
☎ 284 1747; www.witnness.com; Fairyhouse Racecourse, County Meath; special buses from O'Connell St
For details of this summer music festival see the boxed text on p169.

AUGUST
DUBLIN HORSE SHOW
☎ 668 0866; www.rds.ie; Royal Dublin Society (RDS)
The first week of August is when Ireland's horsey set trot down to the capital for the social highlight of the year, and particularly the Aga Khan Cup, an international-class competition of often heart-stopping excitement in which six nations participate.

SEPTEMBER/OCTOBER
DUBLIN THEATRE FESTIVAL
☎ 677 8439; www.eircomtheatrefestival.com
This two-week festival is Europe's largest and showcases the best of Irish and international productions at various locations around town. In tandem with the theatre festival is a children's season at the Ark (p80) and the Dublin Fringe Festival, held in the famous Spiegel tent, which has been erected in different positions in recent years. See the boxed text on p174 for more.

OCTOBER
DUBLIN CITY MARATHON
☎ 677 8439
If you fancy a 26-mile (and a bit) running tour through the streets of the city on the last Monday of October, you'll have to register at least three weeks in advance. Otherwise, you can have a lie-in and watch the winner cross the finishing line on O'Connell St at around 10.30am.

SAMHAIN/HALLOWE'EN

Tens of thousands take to the city streets for a night-time parade, fireworks, street theatre, drinking and music to celebrate this traditional pagan festival in celebration of the dead, the end of the harvest and the Celtic new year.

DECEMBER
LEOPARDSTOWN RACES
☎ 289 3607; www.leopardstown.com

Blow your dough and your post-Christmas crankiness at this historic and hugely popular racing festival at one of Europe's loveliest courses, from 26 to 30 December.

DECEMBER/JANUARY
FUNDERLAND
Royal Dublin Society (RDS)

Dublin's traditional funfair (from 26 December to 9 January) features all kinds of stomach-turning rides and arcade games, as well as hundreds of thousands of light bulbs and millions of reasons why the kids needn't be cooped up indoors.

Only in Dublin

All-Ireland Finals (☎ 836 3222; www.gaa.ie) The climax of the year for fans of Gaelic games when the season's most successful county teams battle it out for the All-Ireland championships in hurling and football, on the second and fourth Sundays in September, respectively. The capital is swamped with fans from the competing counties, draped in their colours and swept along by their good-natured, family-orientated exuberance.

Bloomsday (☎ 878 8547; www.jamesjoyce.ie) On 16 June Dublin is the epicentre of world-wide celebrations in honour of James Joyce's novel, *Ulysses*, and the epic wanderings begun on this day in 1904 by its central character Leopold Bloom. There's normally a week-long programme of events – including excursions, performances, readings and re-created meals – although you can expect festivities to stretch right to the end of 2004, the centenary of his famous 'walking out'.

Christmas Dip at the Forty-Foot Possibly the most hardcore hangover cure known to man, this event takes place at 11am on Christmas Day at a famous swimming spot below the Martello Tower – made famous by James Joyce in *Ulysses* – in Sandycove, 9km from the centre of Dublin. A group of the very brave and certifiably insane plunge into the icy water and swim 20m to the rocks and back. With heads cleared after their frozen frolics, each heads home for Christmas lunch.

Handel's Messiah (Map pp269–71; ☎ 677 2255; Neal's Music Hall, Fishamble St) *Messiah,* George Frederick Handel's most highly esteemed piece of music and one of the most renowned works in English sacred music, was performed for the first time at the site in today's Temple Bar on 13 April 1742, an event commemorated with a special gala-style performance each year.

Liffey Swim (☎ 833 2434) Since 1924, at summer's end (late August/early September) hundreds of swimmers – or lunatics, as they're colloquially known – dive into the Sniffy Liffey for a swim through 2km of mud and murk in the centre of Dublin. There are separate handicap races for men and women, and it's fun to line the bank and watch the competitors trying not to swallow a drop. You can see it depicted in Jack B Yeats' famous *Liffey Swim* painting in the National Gallery (p86).

CULTURE
IDENTITY

Dublin's population is around one million but the Greater Dublin area, by far the most densely populated patch in the country, accounts for at least another half a mill. It's a tough task coming up with boundaries for the city these days. With the centuries-old steady stream of migrants from the rest of Ireland, coupled with the accelerated urban sprawl of recent years and the fairly recent influx of non-nationals, neither is it so easy to describe your typical Dubliner any more. But, not ones to shy away from generalisation, we'll give it a go.

The purest of the species claim to hail from generations all born within the canals, although the label 'Dubliner' perhaps has as much to do with a state of mind as a birthright these days. Dubliners pride themselves on living in one of the most easy-going capitals in the world. While there *are* class distinctions, the structure is fairly fluid and it's an unwritten social rule that no-one is better than anyone else, some just have more money than others (and play rugby instead of Gaelic games). Despite the many changes over the last decade, the unique character of Dublin remains intact, albeit thinly veiled by a little smugness that just doesn't seem to sit right.

The humanity, humour and earthiness are still there. Dubliners are warm, chatty and gregarious. They've got the gift of the gab and will put you at ease with their willingness to have a chat. They'll entertain you with their irreverent humour, alarm you with their keenness to debate and then cut you down with their razor-sharp wit. Banter is the fibre of sociability and 'slagging' (teasing) is an art form. Exchanges can sound caustic to unfamiliar ears but you'll soon see that everybody takes it in good humour. As they'll tell you, they're only having a bit of craic.

They swear like bejaysus (a lot) but no offence is intended. It's just part of an emotive, spirited and highly articulate Dubliner's vocabulary and even the snazziest dressed businesswoman might let out a squeeky 'feck' when she's running for shelter. Don't take this as an invitation to go effing and blinding around town though; after all, without the accent this is just swearing.

They're self-deprecating and love those who can laugh at themselves. They drink too much, and don't exercise enough – but, sure, isn't a bit of weight a sign of good living. They're not renowned for their natural beauty although there are plenty of stunners. Where else could you be sitting at a bar, turn to a person you mistook as your friend and say, 'honestly, can you think of a less attractive race than the Irish?', and for the handsome stranger to reply, without barely a beat, 'ah yeah, we're fairly pug (ugly) alright'?

They're sharp, savvy and crafty. There are no flies on a Dubliner, they'll tell you. And if there are, they are paying rent. Dubs are hospitable and generous; they're more likely to buy you a drink than someone from elsewhere in Ireland. After enduring a couple of centuries of emigration, they've also got a very strong social conscience. When they didn't have two coins to rub together it was because they'd given one of them to the 'poor babies in Africa'.

They're perhaps not as well mannered as they used to be – there are a lot of stroppy youngsters – but they're still a damn sight more affable than most. They'll thank the driver when they get off the bus, even when it invariably arrives late. Saying thanks isn't actually enough; most Dubliners will say thanks a million. Maybe twice. They're chivalrous; men hold doors open for women, and women don't take offence. They bless you when you sneeze and apologise when *you* are in their way. They're grateful if you're also polite, pissed off when you're not.

As you'll see they're a relaxed bunch and there are few rigid rules of etiquette or opportunities to faux pas. However, there's one thing you should remember. While Dubliners may be fiercely critical of their own city and its people, they won't stand for being reminded of their faults by any outsiders. Your best bet is to do as Dubliners do: relax, accept the good things on offer, buy drinks when it's your round, and tear strips off them once their backs are turned.

RELIGION

Almost 90% of the population is Roman Catholic although faith for some might amount to falling asleep at the back of the church at Christmas midnight mass. Amazingly for the most liberal part of the country, the capital recently bucked a national trend by increasing church attendances, a reaction perhaps to the hedonistic materialism of the 1990s when money replaced God as the object of worship for many. The wider Protestant community accounts for about 3% of the population, while a series of tiny minorities including Jews and Muslims make up the rest.

There is a huge urban/rural divide on social issues, and positions have been polarised in recent referenda with Dublin voting massively in favour of divorce and the liberalisation of abortions laws and the rural community voting staunchly against. Divorce was accepted by the slimmest margin in 1995. The abortion issue has largely been swept under the carpet. Although abortion is illegal in Ireland, a quarter of Irish women under 30 have had the procedure – a higher rate than more liberal countries such as the Netherlands. It just means Irish women add the price of the air fare to England to the emotional toll.

LIFESTYLE

On a good day, Dubliners will tell you they've got the best lifestyle on the planet – they've got history, culture, football, shopping, pubs, a sense of community and, most importantly, a bright and breezy outlook on life. On a bad day, they're miserable as sin and couldn't imagine why anyone would move to Dublin, to the traffic, the expense, the crime, the crap television and 'the fecking weather'. On these days, it seems, Dubliners are never happy unless they're never happy. Fortunately, the good days far outnumber the bad.

They have plenty of reasons to be cheerful. Some of the world's finest beverages are brewed and distilled nearby, while the water from their taps is as good as anything you'll get from a bottle. Nowadays, they've even got a restaurant culture to tempt them out of the pubs. They've started drinking wine, while a decent coffee is never more than a block or two away. They've also become better cooks and are more likely to have people over for dinner.

Trimming Tall Poppies

The Irish are often called – by themselves mostly – a nation of begrudgers, one of the reasons given for the historical exodus of many of its greatest cultural icons. Unhealthily preoccupied with parity, and armed with a savage wit, they revel in cutting down to size anyone who dares stand out from the crowd. And then, after sufficient time has elapsed – basically when the jealousy has worn off – they take proud ownership of those very same people.

Take for example the hugely successful Dublin export and Hollywood conqueror Colin Farrell. Locals delight in telling us that he's a con, a fraud, a sham and a charlatan (yes, *all* those things). That he's from a thoroughly upper middle-class background and his working-class cred is all manufactured. That he actually speaks with a posh DORT accent (see p22) but moved to workaday Irishtown to hone his authentic Dublin twang.

But they don't *really* begrudge their stars; slagging is just a local sport. They'll quickly follow up with, in the local parlance, 'ah no, fair play to him'.

The pace of life is a lot faster than it used to be but it's still a lot slower than most capitals. There are more go-getters; that old Irish habit of putting things off until tomorrow has been replaced with an entrepreneurial spirit. Although they're beginning to be influenced more by the likes of London, Dubliners aren't nearly as fad-focused as their European peers. Yoga's not the new knitting. They're mad about sport although most adults draw the line at actually participating in it. Many of them have started visiting galleries, although for some the gallery's just what they walk through on the way to or from the café. When the sun comes out, they'll tear off their shirts, lie out, get burned and spend the rest of the sunny spell indoors, peeling. When it's raining, well, they just carry on. The weekend starts on a Thursday and ends late Sunday night. Many have holiday homes in Wexford these days, weekend escapes not far from a golf course. Most have more money than they dreamed they would have. If they get bored with their idyllic lives they'll take off for a sun holiday. Life has never been better.

Or has it?

Now that the carnival is over – or, at least, that the lights have begun to dim – Dubliners are wondering why, if life's never been better, they spend hours of their time stuck in traffic jams, and don't feel safe walking in the city at night. Why more and more mothers are having to return to work to make ends meet and why young people can't aspire to buying their own home.

Dubliners get paid 17% more than the national income of €27,000, but prices are at least that much higher so many people are running just to stand still and have less time and disposable income to indulge in all their city has to offer. Young couples are mortgaging themselves to the hilt while young singles are increasingly pooling resources to get their toes on the property ladder. The health system is also in a shambles and it seems Ireland is becoming less of an inclusive society by the minute, with an ever-widening gap between the rich and the poor.

Although so-called modernism has been picking at the fabric of Dublin life, few – whatever their circumstances – would choose to live anywhere else. It's the sense of community and the rapport they'd miss most. People dropping around unannounced, and the sociability around the teapot. They'd miss Dublin because there's no other place like it on earth. They revel in their earthiness and don't put on airs and graces for anyone. 'Howya Bono,' you might hear on a stroll down Grafton St, 'yer last album was shite!'

Most Dubliners are proud of their new multiculturalism even if the new multicultures aren't necessarily proud of them. While the capital has long been more liberal-minded than the rest of the country, it has never been what you'd call cosmopolitan. The gay population had a difficult enough time pushing through the prejudices in the 1980s, and members of the travelling community (tinkers, but derogatively called 'knackers') have suffered untold abuse and discrimination over recent decades. Despite government campaigns aimed at breaking down old prejudices within the 'settled community', progress is proving very, very slow.

FOOD

Irish food is great until it's cooked, laughed generations of travellers who used to visit these shores *in spite* of the grub. They were right and it was a thing to be mocked. The cuisine was thrown together by an indifferent, almost penitent race and was best characterised by charred chops, mushy vegetables and an overreliance on an overrated tuber. But although the reputation lingers the cap no longer fits, for nowhere is Dublin's renaissance more obvious than at the table.

Ironically, although never renowned for its culinary dash, Ireland has always been blessed with a wealth of staples and specialities, and its meat, seafood and dairy produce have long been feted around the world. It was what to do with these riches that baffled generations of Irish mothers. Then, in the twilight of the 20th century, as Ireland rode the wave of its economic boom, a brigade of talented cooks and dedicated foodies went back to consult the original model for Irish cuisine. They added a pinch of this, took back a bit of that and came up with what the media quickly described as New Irish Cuisine. In truth, there was very little new about this cuisine at all; it was more a confident return to a tradition that combined the finest local ingredients with simple cooking techniques.

It aroused the taste buds of the nation, and Dublin diners in particular suddenly became more discerning and adventurous. They started banging on their tables, sending the old rubbish back to the kitchen and demanding something to savour rather than to just soak up the drink. Restaurants had to lift their games if they were going to cash in on the new culture of dining out, and cooks sought influences from all over to satisfy the adventurous appetites of their cashed-up clientele. In the space of a decade, Ireland's gastronomy was transformed. Of course, you can still find leathery meat, shrivelled fish and vegetables so overcooked that they can barely cling to the prongs of a fork – try co-author Fionn's house for starters – but you're more likely to experience simple and sophisticated fare that will make your head spin and your palate sing.

While the revolution in London's eating scene has been propelled by celebrity and style, Dublin diners are all about substance and don't care much for the frills. Locals find it hard to believe but the makeover in Dublin's food scene is as impressive as that across the water, even more when you consider that the raw materials are vastly superior to start with. Check out the Eating chapter, p129, for more.

Of course, being a contradictory old bugger, Dublin also has an inordinate number of fast-food outlets. But the new appreciation for food has permeated every level, and a host of new artisan markets, specialist food stores, bakers and cheesemongers have opened around town in recent years (see the Shopping chapter, p181).

Don't pass up the opportunity to share a home-cooked meal because it's a chance to cut right to the heart of this unique culture. Experiencing Irish cuisine isn't just about sampling sensational seafood, fine farmhouse cheeses and mountain-bred lamb. It's the warmth and conviviality around the dinner table, the chat over a cup of tea and the sizzle of the traditional Sunday roast. Hospitality is the most important condiment at the Irish table.

> ## The Joyce of Cooking
> *by James Joyce*, Finnegans Wake
>
> The more carrots you chop, the more turnips you slit, the more murphies you peel, the more onions you cry over, the more bullbeef you butch, the more mutton you crackerhack, the more potherbs you pound, the fiercer the fire and the longer your spoon and the harder you gruel with more grease to your elbow, the merrier fumes your new Irish stew.

Staples & Specialities

Although many old Dublin staples have been consigned to the scrapheap of culinary history, some have earned their longevity while others are kept around for the sake of the tourists.

The most Dublin of dishes is coddle, a working-class concoction of rashers, sausages, onions, potato and plenty of black pepper. Another specific to the capital is gurr cake, which 19th-century bakers made out of stale bread and cakes mixed with candied peel and dried mixed fruit. Because it was very cheap, it became popular with street urchins 'on the gurr' from school. The term 'gurrier' entered the Dublin dialect to describe rough tearaways.

Ireland has a rich baking tradition and soda bread (made with buttermilk and the uniquely soft Irish flour) is one of the tastes we miss most when we leave. Scones, tarts and biscuits are specialities too. Barm brack (from the Irish for 'speckled bread') is a spicy, fruity cake long associated with Hallowe'en. Various charms are traditionally baked in the brack, and the one you get decides your destiny for the following year. Discover the ring and you'll get married, bite into the penny and you'll be wealthy (which is some consolation for the cracked tooth), the pea denotes impending poverty while a little stick cheerfully prophesises domestic violence.

Soda bread is a wonderful platform for smoked salmon, and you should take every opportunity to sample the fruits of the Irish seas, be it on a platter or wrapped in batter from a traditional chipper. Of course, you should also sample the cockles and mussels of Molly Malone fame: oysters from the west coast, and Dublin Bay prawns which are actually lobsters and superlative at their best. If you get a chance, make sure to down a Dublin lawyer. Before you go getting yourself into trouble, this is a lobster dish cooked with whiskey and cream.

More well known is the national icon, Irish stew, the slow-simmered one-pot wonder of lamb, potatoes, onions, parsley and thyme (note, no carrots). In summer look out for mountain lamb from Connemara or Kerry.

Savour the dairy produce, which is some of the best you'll taste anywhere (all that rain's got to be good for something); the butter is deliciously rich and the thick and luscious cream is a joy to behold. The resurgence of cheese-making has been one of the most exciting culinary developments of recent years and Irish farmhouse cheeses win many international awards and plaudits.

Bacon and cabbage is one those dishes we wish was consigned to history but, fortunately, you won't find it nearly as much in Dublin as you would 'down the country' (elsewhere). Perhaps the most feared Irish speciality is the full Irish breakfast, the traditional fry-up of bacon, sausages, black and white pudding, eggs, tomatoes and whatever other frills the cook can fry.

City Life – Culture

FASHION

Although not necessarily renowned for its sartorial style, Dublin has contributed its fair share of big names to the world of haute couture, including John Rocha, milliner Philip Treacy, knitwear specialist Lainey Keogh, Paul Smith and Louise Kennedy. Just like their talented kin across other creative pursuits, the big fishes of Irish fashion have traditionally jumped to the larger pond of London. Thanks to the country's recent economic miracle, the most talented young designers are now able to stay at home and there's a vibrant design college in Dublin. Whether the city market and fashion conscience are big enough to stop the fashion world haemorrhaging its best people again in the future, only time will tell.

As more than half of the city's population is under 30, it's only natural that mid-priced and mass-produced fashions dominate the local market and there are dozens of local and international stores vying for this trade. British high streets predominate although there are lots of new home-grown outlets. Which fashion direction today's all-important youth will take is the million-dollar question.

Grown-up fashions are more conservative but while Carrie Bradshaw might struggle to fill a whole weekend in town she'd give it a good crack and wear out a lot of leather in the process. Fashionistas can ogle at the Prada frocks in Brown Thomas, Dublin's most stylish department store, or head to South William St in SoDa (south of Dame St), Dublin's new epicentre of cool. It's lined with bars, espresso joints and more boutiques than you could shake a gold card at, and is a great spot to find once-off Irish designer gear from hot new designers such as Tim Ryan and Deirdre Fitzgerald. There are plenty more opportunities to unblock your retail chi, including Castle Market nearby (see the Shopping chapter, p181).

Men's bespoke tailoring is rather thin on the ground. Designers have tried to instil a sense of classical style in the Dublin male although the species doesn't seem too interested – any pressed shirt and a leather shoe seems to suffice.

Street wear, particularly sneakers, are peculiarly absent, which is perhaps to do with the likelihood of rain or numbskull club bouncers who have decided a black shoe and a light-coloured sock is more acceptable than 'runners'. Ghetto cool is creeping in though, and there are a smattering of bigger-is-best street- and skatewear stores dotted about town.

At the other end of the fashion spectrum, you'll find all the knit and tweed you want at the House of Ireland.

True fashionistas will probably have already retired to the cream leather banquettes of Cocoon (☎ 679 6259; Duke Lane, Royal Hibernian Way), a pub recently taken over by Irish playboy and racing car driver Eddie Irvine and Dublin's unofficial fashion HQ.

SPORT

Dubliners are huge sports fans, whether they're shouting their team on from the sideline or a bar stool. And – being charitable – the proliferation of soccer and Gaelic Athletic Association (GAA) jerseys you'll see worn by Dubliners of every shape and size says more about this passionate support for their idols than it does for their wayward sense of fashion. Simply put, sport has a special place in the Irish psyche, and following it is by no means an exclusively male activity. Ask any adult in Dublin for their top five sporting moments and they could probably reel them off as quickly as they could remember their five closest friends.

For information on where and when to check out various sports in Dublin, see p177.

Our Top Five Dublin Sporting Moments

- Stephen Roche winning the Tour de France, Giro d'Italia and World Championship in 1987
- Ireland's soccer team beating England 1:0 in the European Championships in Stuttgart in 1986
- Dublin beating Tyrone to become All-Ireland champions in 1995, for the first time in 12 years
- Ken Docherty winning the World Snooker Championship in 1997
- (From other author) Soccer legend and genius Roy Keane sacrificing his own World Cup dream for the sake of the greater principles of truth and honesty by blowing the lid on the ineptitude and bad preparation that marked Mick McCarthy's term as Ireland manager, Saipan 2002 (see the boxed text on p19)

Gaelic Football & Hurling

The ancient Gaelic games are at the core of Irishness; they are enmeshed in the fabric of Irish life and hold a unique place in the heart of its culture. Their resurgence towards the end of the 19th century was entwined with the whole Gaelic revival and the march towards Irish independence. When the GAA was established in 1884 and clubs set up around the country, training often took the form of military exercises. The GAA is still responsible for fostering these amateur games and it warms our hearts to see that after all this time – and amid the onslaught of globalisation and the general commercialisation of sport – they are still far and away the most popular sports in Ireland.

The GAA Stands its Ground

Croke Park (p115) is the finest stadium in the country and, with a capacity of some 80,000, the fourth largest in Europe. Yet all Ireland's international matches – apart from the mickey mouse Compromise Rules contests against Australia – take place at the vastly inferior Lansdowne Rd Stadium (p177), a rusting and ramshackle old arena with a dodgy pitch and seating for just over 35,000 people (which makes it nigh on impossible to get tickets for big games).

Why don't all the big sporting events take place at Croke Park, then? Well, you see, Croke Park is consecrated Gaelic Athletic Association (GAA) turf so it is wholly off limits to 'foreign games'. Only in this case, 'foreign' basically means anything that the Brits like – American football apparently doesn't count.

The Irish Rugby Football Union (IRFU) and the clowns who run the Football Association of Ireland (FAI) should have sorted out a national stadium long ago and unfortunately, Taoiseach Bertie Ahern's recent attempts to build one (so-called Bertie's Bowl) were abandoned. While it's not up to the GAA to bail out Irish sports, it seems like madness to leave 'Croker' underutilised while the GAA slides into debt. Votes and debates on the issue within GAA have been getting closer in recent years and it seems only a matter of time before the association relents. Come on lads, you've made your point, now cop yourselves on while you can still look big about it (and let us tourists come and savour *all* your sports).

They are simultaneously the most divisive and unifying activity in Irish culture. The GAA club is at the heart and soul of every parish in the country, and its team commands passionate support from just about every man, woman and child in the community. The fiercest rivalries are often between clubs in neighbouring parishes, whose teams sometimes play within earshot of the other even in the suburbs of Dublin. But when the best players from the club teams are selected to represent their county, local rivalries are cast aside and replaced by inter-county ones as supporters unite behind their district. And then when their county is knocked out, fans will often shout for anyone else from their province.

But as fervent as this rivalry is, and as separate as the support may be, there's rarely even a cross word between opposing fans who are ultimately united in their love of the game and shared heritage. There's nothing like it anywhere else in the world. And we love it.

The most popular of the games – and therefore Ireland's most popular sport – is Gaelic football, quite obviously the greatest game on earth. It combines athleticism, speed, strength, aggression, skill, grace and intelligence. There's too much to go into here but fans would be more than happy to enlighten you at a game.

It's most similar to Aussie Rules football – and a frankly ridiculous hybrid game of Compromise Rules (where the poor Aussies are forced to play with the unfamiliar round ball) is contested between the countries every couple of years. Nevertheless, it's always good to see the amateurs stick it to the pros.

Although support for GAA is not as great in big-city Dublin as it is in rural Ireland, this is still one of the great footballing counties and has been All-Ireland champions 22 times, a record only beaten by Kerry. Success has been hard to come by in recent years, though, and Dublin have struggled to even qualify from their province of Leinster, where County Meath are traditionally their fiercest rivals.

The other main Gaelic game is hurling, a ferocious sport played with a hurley (a long stick with a flattish blade) and a *sliothar* (small, leather ball). It's the fastest field game in the world and demands superb skill, lightning speed and absolutely no fear. There are few sounds more likely to make your blood curdle – or aficionados drool – than the so-called 'clash of the ash', when the sticks of two hurlers collide at full pelt. It's a wonder Ireland didn't achieve independence sooner and that British soldiers didn't turn and run the moment they saw the locals playing hurling. Amazingly, protective helmets are *not* compulsory and, even more amazingly, serious injuries are few.

There's also an equally tough women's version called camogie, which they have begun promoting as 'chicks with sticks' to revolutionise the sport, which celebrates its centenary in 2004. The glamorous new image is a far cry from the first games when thick black tights were part of the uniform.

Hurling itself, at least some form of it, dates back to ancient history, and the mythical Celtic hero Cúchulainn was said to have been a handy left-corner forward. The 13th-century Battle of Moytura began as a hurling match, while the Celtic Brehon Laws awarded compensation to the families of those injured in hurling matches. The Normans were so unsettled by the ferocity of the game that they tried to ban it.

Dublin isn't a big power in hurling, basically because there aren't enough people tough enough or mad enough to play the game – there are plenty of both in the southern province of Munster where the game is a religion.

Gaelic games are played throughout the year, with 'the League' in the winter and the much more important 'Championship' in the summer, where county teams must qualify from their provinces, contest a fairly convoluted finals system, before the final two contest the 'All-Ireland Finals' in September, the climax of Ireland's sporting year. Finals take place at the hugely impressive national stadium, Croke Park (p115), where the hurlers compete for the McCarthy Cup on the second Sunday of September while the footballers are desperate to get their hands on the famous Sam Maguire Cup on the fourth. Dublin play their home matches at 'Croker', when its fans occupy the famous Hill 16 terrace, which was built with rubble taken from O'Connell St after the 1916 Easter Rising. See p178 for details on attending Gaelic games.

Students playing hurling, Trinity College

Although the GAA has done a terrific job nurturing Gaelic games – ably assisted in the modern era by brilliant commentators, journalists and television coverage – its biggest challenge may lie just ahead. It's widely accepted that the amateur status of the games will have to change – it's already been stretched in some quarters – and how this is handled may determine the shape of Gaelic games for the next hundred years or so. Good luck to them.

Football (Soccer)

There is also huge support for the 'world game', although Dublin fans – and the national broadcaster – are much more enthusiastic about the likes of Manchester United and Glasgow Celtic than the poor sods rolling around in the mud as part of the struggling local league. The mostly part-timers of the League of Ireland can't compete with the glamour and glitz of the English Premiership, where all the country's top footballers strut their stuff. The current crop of Dubliners playing in England includes the sensational southsiders Damien Duff (Chelsea) and Robbie Keane (Spurs).

Nevertheless, if you want to feel the excitement of actually attending a game rather than just watching it on TV, Dublin is home to five teams in the League of Ireland first division. The season runs from April to November; see p177 for more information.

Trivia fans may be interested to know that two Dublin teams in the League of Ireland contributed to the fastest hat trick in history, when Jimmy O'Connor of Shelbourne took just two minutes and 13 seconds to put three past the Bohemians' keeper in 1967.

While not many attend matches in the local league, the whole city – well apart from a few disgruntled United supporters (see boxed text below) – follows the national side keenly. When Ireland first began qualifying for major tournaments during the '80s and '90s, it felt like the whole nation closed down and squeezed into pubs to watch the matches.

Rugby Union

Although traditionally the preserve of Ireland's middle classes, rugby captures the mood of the whole island in February and March during the annual Six Nations Championships because the Irish team is drawn from both sides of the border and supported by both nationalists and unionists. In recognition of this, the Irish national anthem is no longer played at internationals, replaced by the slightly dodgy but thoroughly inoffensive 'Ireland's Call', a song written especially for the purpose.

Now, if the Irish team was more successful it might speed up the peace process and lead to national reconciliation but, wouldn't you know it, England usually spoils the party by dominating the competition. That said, the Irish have been competitive in recent years and notched up some memorable results against the old foe. International matches are played at Lansdowne Rd Stadium (p177), the home of rugby, although tickets are difficult to come by.

The restructuring of the domestic competition in recent years has led to a downgrading in the importance of club rugby but the local provincial team, Leinster, is one of the most successful in the European and Celtic Leagues. See p179 for more information.

When Egos Fly

On the eve of the 2002 football World Cup, sports-mad Ireland was staggered when Roy Keane – the Irish captain and the greatest player to ever wear a green shirt – walked out on the Irish team. He stormed off (after being sent home – it's a long story) following a row with manager, Mick McCarthy, over what he perceived as the team's amateurish approach to the tournament.

After the shock came unbridled bitterness; in broad strokes, the country's enormous band of Manchester United fans, for whom Keane was also captain, sided with the player while the rest of Ireland backed the manager and the other players. The country descended into civil war with husbands set against wives, brothers against brothers, and guidebook co-authors against guidebook co-authors.

Ireland performed valiantly to reach the second round of the tournament but the manager was forced to quit after a poor start to the following campaign. Keane spurned an invitation to rejoin the Irish ranks under a new manager, and so the divisions remain with many pro-Keaners continuing to snub the national team.

Racing

A passion for horse racing, the 'sport of kings', is deeply entrenched in Irish life and comes without the snobbery of its English counterpart. There are several picturesque racecourses – Leopardstown, Fairyhouse, The Curragh and Puncherstown – within easy driving distance of the city centre and there are good quality meetings throughout the year. If you fancy a flutter on the geegees you can watch racing from around Ireland and England on the television in bookmakers shops every day. No money ever seems to change hands in the betting, however, and every Irish punter will tell you they 'broke evens'.

Ireland has a reputation for producing world-class horses for racing and other equestrian events like showjumping, which is also very popular albeit in a much less populist kind of way.

Traditionally the poor man's punt, greyhound racing ('the dogs') has been smartened up in recent years and partly turned into a corporate outing. It offers a cheaper, more accessible and more local alternative to horse racing. See p179 for more details on both types of racing.

Golf

Ireland has long been renowned for its outstanding golf courses, particularly its links (coastal courses), but the game's popularity took off in a huge way in the 1990s. You can cheer on local boys Pádraig Harrington and Paul McGinley when they take on the other top names in European golf at the annual Smurfit European Open in late July/early August. The prestigious Irish Open was held at Dublin's Portmarnock golf course in 2003, when there was an almighty brouhaha about the club's male-only membership policy. This inequality was a big issue in recent years although Portmarnock is one of only two remaining clubs that continue to allow women to play but not become members.

MEDIA

Five national dailies, six national Sundays, stacks of Irish editions of British publications, hundreds of magazines, more than a dozen radio stations, four terrestrial TV stations and more digital channels than you could shake the remote control at…No, not New York, we're talking about Dublin, a city with a reach of just 1.5 million people.

On the face of it, there seems to be just too much media here for the market and with the Celtic Tiger limping, an almighty scrum is taking place among the players. The country's best newspaper, *the Irish Times*, almost went under in 2002 and had to shed nearly half of its workforce to stay afloat. A new newspaper, the *Dublin Daily News*, lasted only a few months before it folded, and sales of most Irish titles are falling.

The dominant local player is Independent News & Media, owned by Ireland's primo businessman, Tony O'Reilly (see the boxed text below). Its newspapers – *Irish Independent, Sunday Independent* and *Evening Herald* – are by far the biggest sellers in each market. See p239 for details of Dublin-based newspapers and magazines.

The massive overspill of British media here, particularly in relation to the saturated Sunday market, is the biggest challenge facing the Irish media. Rupert Murdoch's News International recently established an office in Dublin clearly signalling its intent. Its main titles the *Irish Sun, News of the World* and *Sunday Times* have already made significant in-roads into the Irish market and the cat will well and truly be among the pigeons should the company decide to bring out an Irish edition of its flagship daily, *The Times*.

Tony

Tony O'Reilly, Ireland's only fully fledged media tycoon and arguably it's most powerful man, got special dispensation from the Taoiseach to receive a knighthood from the British monarch in 2001. That Bertie Ahern should have agreed so swiftly, that there was relatively little fuss made about him kneeling before a British monarch, and that the honour was bestowed in the first place, all indicate just how influential his media interests are in Ireland and Britain.

Magazine publishing has boomed with the economy in recent years and the biggest new development has been the English craving for celebrity rubbing off on the local market.

There are four terrestrial TV channels in Ireland (see p39 and p242). The best thing about the state broadcaster, RTE, is its sports coverage, particularly of Gaelic games. It and the general public were protected from a major blow in 2002 when the government stepped in to effectively block a deal, in which the governing body of Irish soccer sold exclusive rights to its international games to Murdoch's Sky satellite channel. Nevertheless, Sky continues to make solid progress in bringing the multi-channel revolution to Dublin homes.

The state of local radio is much healthier. There is a huge choice incorporating talk radio, current affairs, pirate stations, progressive music channels and lots of commercial dross. If you want to take the pulse of the city, check out talk show host Joe Duffy on

Liveline (RTE 1, 1.45pm Mon-Fri) and inspiring DJ Donal Dineen (*Here Comes the Night* on Today FM, 9pm-midnight Mon-Fri). It's a peculiar combo but we stand by it.

LANGUAGE

Although Gaeilge (Irish) is the official language – and all official documents, street signs and official titles are either in Gaeilge or bilingual – it's only spoken in isolated pockets of rural Ireland known as Gaeltacht areas.

While all Dubliners must learn it at school, the teaching of Gaeilge has traditionally been thoroughly academic and unimaginative, leading most kids to resent it as a waste of time. Ask Dubliners if they can speak Irish and nine out of 10 of them will probably reply, 'ahhh cupla focal' (literally 'a couple of words') and they generally mean it. It's a pity that the treatment of Irish in schools has been so heavy-handed because many adults say they regret not having a greater grasp of it. At long last, and for the first time since the formation of the state, a new Gaeilge curriculum has recently been introduced which will cut the hours devoted to the subject but make the lessons more fun, practical and celebratory.

While most Dubliners overlooked Gaeilge, their command of English and their inventive use of vocabulary is second to none. Huge numbers of foreign-language students, particularly from continental Europe, flock to the city for study because the average Dubliner's elocution is so clear. When travelling in Italy or Spain, it's gas to hear locals speaking English with Dublin accents.

You could probably say Dubliners love the sound of their own voices, and they are genuinely interested in the way words sound as much as in their meaning. They're very articulate, are generally confident orators, and like nothing more than a good debate (preferably over a pint).

Dublin accents – for there are several – have all the traits of the typical Irish brogue, which are softened, shortened vowels, hardened consonants and discarded 'h's in the 'th' sound (the old 'tirty tree and a tird' joke). The average, or neutral, Dublin accent is possibly one of the most eloquent and easily understandable in the English-speaking world while the extremes are barely comprehensible at all. The 'real Dublin' accent is clipped, drawn out and slack-jawed. It discards consonants disdainfully, particularly the letter 't' (alright becomes origh) and is peppered with so many instances of 'fuck', 'jaysus' and 'yer wha'' that you think the speaker might be dumbstruck without them.

Dublin Slang

Dubliners are like the mad scientists of linguistics, and have an enormous lexicon of slang words from which to choose. For example, there is said to be more than 50 alternative words for 'penis', while it's quite possible they have more words to describe 'drunkenness' than the Eskimos have for 'snow'. Here are just a few doozies:

a header – mentally unstable person

banjaxed – broken down

chiseller – a young child

couldn't be arsed – couldn't be bothered

fair play/fucks to you – well done

jax – toilet

I will in me bollix – I won't

make a bags of something – mess it up

me belly tinks me trotes been cut – I'm rather hungry

minger – ugly person

rag order – bad condition

ride – have sex with

scarlet (scarleh) – blushing

shite – rubbish

shorts – spirits

slagging – teasing

trow a wobbler – have a temper tantrum

work away – go ahead, after you

yer man – that guy

yer wha'? – excuse me?!?

yoke – inserted to describe a noun when the actual word has slipped the speaker's mind

Cupla Focal

Here are a few useful phrases *os Gaeilge* (in Irish), which can help you impress the locals:

amadáin (ohm-a-dawn) – fool

cad is ainm duit? (cawd iss anim dit) – what is your name?

céad míle fáilte (kade meela fallcha) – one hundred thousand welcomes

conas a tá tú? (kunas aw taw two) – how are you?

dia dhuit (dee-a gwit) – hi

dún do chlab (doon daw klob) – shut your mouth

go raibh maith agat (gur rev moh agut) – thanks

is mise Amanda (iss misha Amanda) – my name is Amanda

ní maith liom Westlife (knee moh lum Westlife)– I don't like Westlife

ní ólfaidh mé go brách arís (knee ohl-hee mey gu brawkh u-reeshch) – I'm never ever drinking again

póg ma thóin (pogue ma hone) – kiss my arse

slainte (slawn-cha) – your health (cheers)

táim go maith (thawm gomoh) – I'm good

Yet this is infinitely preferable to the plummy accent of affluent southsiders who contort and squeeze vowels at will. Formerly known as the Dublin 4 accent, this diction has since come to be known as the 'DART accent' (or DORT as its speakers would pronounce it) because it has spread out south along the coastal railway line. It is even threatening to take over the area of Montrose where the national broadcaster, RTE, is based.

The spread of this pseudo-received accent is so alarming that Frank McNally of the *Irish Times* suggested the only way to eradicate the DART accent would be to make it compulsory in schools – it damn nearly worked for Gaeilge!

ECONOMY & COSTS

If you think Dublin is an expensive place to visit imagine what it's like for the people who live here. Ireland is the second most expensive country in the EuroZone, after Finland, a position consolidated with the introduction of the new currency in 2002 when retailers took to 'rounding up' a little too creatively.

According to Mercer, the folk who do those cost-of-living indices we often read about, Dublin is the third costliest city in the European Union (EU) after London and Copenhagen. The cost of living is twice the EU average and, what's more, with inflation at around 4%, it's only going to get more expensive in the near future.

You won't find nearly as many rip-off merchants as you do in some of the major tourist destinations of continental Europe (well, apart from in the Temple Bar area and taxi drivers from the airport) but Dublin *is* very expensive these days and you don't generally get value for money. Accommodation, meals, taxis, entertainment and shopping will all make your wallet sag and your purse pout.

How Much?

A coffee: €2

Admission to a big-name club on a Friday: €20

CD: €20

City-centre bus ticket: Up to €1.40

Colour film (36 exposure): €7.50

Petrol per litre: €0.92

Pint of Guinness: Temple Bar/city/suburbs €4.70/€3.90/€3.40

The Irish Times: €1.45

Three-course meal with wine/beer: from €30

Ticket to a GAA match: €20–35

Dublin is at the tail end of the greatest economic boom since Irish independence. In the early 1990s the economy grew so rapidly that it was dubbed the 'Celtic Tiger' because of its similarity to the tiger economies of Southeast Asia. It was kick-started by numerous foreign multinationals which made their European bases here, after being enticed by government tax incentives and the availability of a highly educated, inexpensive, English-speaking workforce. At the same time, Ireland was getting huge handouts from the EU to modernise its infrastructure and then suddenly, during the IT boom, economic growth accelerated to over 10% per year. Then the tourist industry mushroomed and further fuelled the growth. Record lows were recorded in interest, unemployment and income tax rates, while inflation was negligible.

But there was no way that the speed of expansion could be maintained and, while the boom hasn't necessarily been followed by a bust, the Central Bank of Ireland did pronounce the Celtic Tiger dead in late 2001. A rise in inflation and wages, the resurfacing of industrial strife, the virtual collapse in the IT sector and pressure on the euro have all served to undermine the country's competitiveness. Changing market conditions have served to highlight Ireland's dependence on multinational corporations and its vulnerability to world trends.

Our Two Cents Worth

The introduction of the Euro was so successful and complete in Ireland that most people seem to have bought the official and plainly daft line that the words 'euro' and 'cent' are both singular, plural and immutable. Whereas before Dubliners would use slang terms like quid, spondooliks and even smackerooonies instead of the word 'pound' they seem to be at pains to follow the official line when referring to several euro and many cent. It seems the government may have misunderstood the EU directive that each member state would use the singular form only, which was meant for officialdom and not the general populace.

While analysts and economists toss up whether this is a slow-down or the beginnings of a recession, nobody believes Dublin will go back to the dark old days of mass emigration and huge unemployment. Meanwhile, the government is hastily making cutbacks and planned frills like a sports stadium and a government jet have been scrapped. However, proposed cuts to public services reveal that there's really not much that can be cut because, despite the unprecedented boom, the health service is in crisis with almost 30,000 people already on waiting lists for treatment.

Higher wages and low interest rates led to an extraordinary boom in the property market and house prices have rocketed since 1994, making it increasingly difficult for those with even a decent income to get on the property ladder. Things could soon get even worse with local authorities considering a €10,000 levy on new houses to fund infrastructure. Although the slums that were the shame of 19th-century Dublin have disappeared, a substantial segment of the population still lives in substandard corporation-run housing estates and flats, especially on the north side. Critics say the government has squandered public money in the further beautification of some areas while virtually ignoring the needier.

It's by no means all doom and gloom; Dublin is still 'flying' and there's very little chance that the economy is going to crash to earth. Most analysts predict a soft landing, followed by another period of lower but more sustainable growth. One thing's for sure: the fantastical optimism of the 1990s has been tempered by a dose of fiscal realism and the realisation that now is a time for careful planning.

GOVERNMENT & POLITICS

The Irish political system is a parliamentary democracy, and virtually all national power rests with a government comprising of a cabinet of 14 all-powerful ministers. Whatever the government decides is approved by the Dáil (Irish parliament), which is dominated by the government. An appointed 'whip' ensures that everyone in the ruling party toes the party line when it comes to voting. The current Taoiseach (prime minister) and

Tanaiste (vice prime minister) are Bertie Ahern and Mary Harndy, leaders of the ruling Fianna Fáil and junior Progressive Democrats (PDs) parties, respectively.

The Republic's electoral system is proportional representation (PR), where voters mark the candidates in order of preference. Elections must take place at least once every five years.

Irish politics – and society at large – is largely homogenous and voters are mostly influenced by local issues and personalities rather than ideologies or national policies. You can hardly see light between the positions of the major parties and it's not unusual for supposedly left- and right-leaning parties to cosy up together to form government.

The centre-right Fianna Fáil party has a solid base of around 40% of the electorate and has dominated politics for most of the last 75 years. The second biggest party, which got smashed in the 2002 general election and seems to be virtually disappearing in Dublin, is Fine Gael. These two parties are direct descendants of the anti-treaty and pro-treaty sides in the Civil War, respectively.

The most important socialist party is centre-left Labour, which didn't fare too well in the smash-and-grab boom of the

In Terms of Irish Politics

Dáil (dawl) – Lower House

Oireachtas na Éireann (ow-rawktus na air-in) – Irish parliament

Taoiseach (tea-shok) – Prime minister

Tanaiste (taw-nashta) – Vice prime minister

Teachta Dalai (tee-ochta dawl-lee) – Deputies, members of parliament; also known as TDs

An tUachtaran (awn uk-ta-rawn) – President

1990s. Next up is the staunchly capitalist – centre-further-right if you like – Progressive Democrats which has done much better on the promise of keeping the government honest from within (it is Fianna Fáil's preferred coalition partner). Next on the ladder is the Green Party, which shed its socks-and-sandals image and managed to secure six seats in the last election. Sinn Fein, the political wing of the IRA, promotes itself as the party for all the disenfranchised and currently has five TDs. Each of its TDs takes just one-third (€29K) of their parliamentary wage and donates the balance to the party.

The constitutional head of state is the president, who is elected by popular vote for a seven-year term. While this position has little real power, the largely apolitical (at least in an Irish party sense) Mary Robinson wielded considerable informal influence over social policies when she was elected in 1990. She was succeeded by the more low-key although equally ballsy Mary McAleese, a Belfast-born Catholic nationalist. By the time you read this, you'll know whether or not she decided to run for a second term in the 2004 election.

At local level, Dublin is mainly governed by two elected bodies: Dublin City Council and Dublin County Council. The city version used to be known as Dublin Corporation ('the Corpo'), a name synonymous with inefficiency and incompetence but the new incarnation is a progressive and admired local government. Each year, it elects a Lord

Graft

Bertie Ahern, leader of Fianna Fáil and Taoiseach since 1997, has prospered by being everything his party predecessors were not. The salt-of-the-earth Dubliner loves his sports, still drinks in his old Drumcondra local and is portrayed simply as a man of the people (and, since 2003, the most eligible bachelor in town).

His most impressive achievement thus far has been to separate his party from its predecessors, whose systematic corruption has been revealed in a seemingly endless series of tribunals since 1997. At the centre of the 'graft' scandals is Charlie Haughey, who served as Taoiseach for seven years and allegedly received millions in apparent 'gifts' from prominent businesses at a time when the country was scraping along on its arse.

Despite the long-running and incredibly expensive tribunals having implicated a host of politicians and their business buddies, nobody has been brought down. The only tangible results are tribunal fatigue among the general public, and a new millionaire class of barrister.

Mayor who shifts into the Mansion House, speaks out on matters to do with the city and is lucky if half of Dublin knows his or her name by the time they have to hand back the chains.

ENVIRONMENT

Though the city doesn't suffer the air pollution that chokes some other European capitals, James Joyce's 'dear, dirty Dublin' does have its fair share of environmental concerns. Chief among these are the woeful traffic congestion and urban sprawl that have emerged in the last decade – in fact, you can combine the two because it's the car-orientated sprawl into the countryside that is concerning planners most these days.

Dublin used to spread conveniently around the arc of Dublin Bay but these days it's all over the place and the commuter belt has well and truly spilled over into neighbouring counties poorly equipped to cope. Dubliners have been fleeing the exorbitant house prices and bursting through the former city boundaries. Ireland being one of the most car-dependent societies in the world means that the vast majority of these commuters drive in and out of the city daily.

After what seemed like a decade of talking and coming up with excuses, efforts have been made to alleviate congestion and coax commuters onto public transport. At least

Taking a stroll through Phoenix Park (p111)

partial service on the much-heralded LUAS light rail should have commenced by the time you read this but some of the problems it was supposed to solve have already broadened along with the size of the metropolitan area – it's not uncommon for people to commute up to 50 miles to and from work these days.

But there are fears that the planners are never going to catch up with the problems. Ireland is far and away the fastest growing country in the EU and the population grew by a staggering 8% from 1996 to 2002. At this rate, Dublin will be home to 2.2 million and half the country's population by 2020.

However, despite the problems of this burgeoning city, Dublin is becoming more environmentally responsible and has been at the forefront of some very impressive green initiatives. In 2002 the government drew world praise for introducing a 15 cents surcharge on plastic bags, reducing their occurrence by 90% within a few months. There are plans to use similar tactics to eradicate street litter which has stained Ireland's green image in recent years – a tax is to be introduced on chewing gum, polystyrene food wrappers and cash machine receipts. The money earned from these taxes is being used to fund recycling facilities. There is also a policy of naming and shaming businesses that break litter laws.

Although not compulsory in Dublin, more and more people are using recycling bins and the council aims to be recycling 60% of household waste by 2009. However, these figures seem pretty ambitious considering that, the last we heard, thousands of Dublin residents were refusing to pay the €154 yearly bin charge and weren't going to have their refuse collected at all.

In another huge development, in 2003 Dublin got one of the most advanced water-waste treatment plants in the world. It cost €300 million and is set to dramatically improve the water quality in Dublin Bay.

Most controversially, however, the government was set to ban smoking from all restaurants and, incredibly, pubs at the beginning of 2004 as this book was being printed. There was furious debate on the subject throughout 2003 and many people laughed off the proposal as unenforceable. Did the government back down? We doubt it. Are people talking about Ireland becoming a 'nanny state'? Mmm…probably.

Arts

Arts

Dublin has always operated an enormous cultural surplus, having provided the world of arts with much more than could have been demanded from such a teeny little city. There's hardly been any let-up in the last couple of centuries and the city is still racing further and further into the black. Even by local standards, Dublin is currently in the grip of a cultural explosion and there are more poetry readings, book launches, live gigs, contemporary dance, operas, plays, films, comedy shows and club nights than you could shake a decent listings guide at, while Dubliners continue to regale the world with books, films and albums. Jees, even Irish dancing is hot these days.

LITERATURE

It's in literature that Dublin has made the greatest contribution to the world, and no other city can claim four Nobel Prize winners for literature or to have had a greater impact on the English-reading world.

The knack for creative writing goes back to the arrival of Christianity when the country became known as the land of saints and scholars. However, Dublin is most renowned for the literature it has produced from the 18th century onwards, from a time when the Irish and English languages began to cross-fertilise. Experimenting with English, using turns of phrase and expressions translated directly from Irish, and combining these with a uniquely Irish perspective on life, Irish writers have dazzled and delighted readers for centuries. British theatre critic, Kenneth Tynan, summed it up thus: 'The English hoard words like misers: the Irish spend them like sailors'.

Dublin has as many would-be sailors as Hollywood has frustrated waitresses, and it often seems like a bottomless well of creativity. The section given over to Irish writers is often the largest and busiest in any local bookstore,

Long Room, Trinity College (p76)

reflecting not only a rich literary tradition and thriving contemporary scene but also an appreciative, knowledgeable and hungry local audience. Buskers on Grafton St will recite any Irish poem upon request, and would probably go hungry if they were relying on the tourists.

Indeed, Dublin has produced so many writers and has been written about so much that you could easily plan a Dublin literary holiday. *A Literary Guide to Dublin*, by Vivien Igoe, includes detailed route maps, a guide to cemeteries and an eight-page section on literary and historical pubs. See p118 for our Literary Dublin walking tour.

OLD LITERARY DUBLIN

Modern Irish literature begins with Jonathan Swift (1667–1745), the master satirist, social commentator and dean of St Patrick's Cathedral. He was the greatest Dublin writer of the early Georgian period and is most famous for *Gulliver's Travels*, a topical social satire that has survived as a children's favourite. He was an 'earnest and dedicated champion of liberty' as he insisted in writing his own epitaph.

He was followed by Oliver Goldsmith (1728–74), author of *The Vicar of Wakefield,* and Thomas Moore (1779–1852), whose poems formed the repertoire of generations of Irish tenors. Dublin-born Oscar Wilde (1854–1900) is renowned for his legendary wit, immense talent and striking sensitivity (see p33). Bram Stoker (1847–1912) is another well-known literary figure and is most celebrated for his gothic novel *Dracula,* one of the world's most popular books. The name of the count may have come from the Irish *droch fhola* (bad blood).

Playwright and essayist George Bernard Shaw (1856–1950), author of *Pygmalion* (which was later turned into *My Fair Lady*), hailed from Synge St near the Grand Canal, while James Joyce (1882–1941), the city's most famous son and one of the greatest writers of all time (see p30), was born not far away in Rathgar.

Arts – Literature

William Butler (WB) Yeats (1865–1939) is best remembered as a poet though he also wrote plays and cofounded the Abbey Theatre. *Sailing to Byzantium* and *Easter 1916* are two of his finest poems – the latter, about the Easter Rising, ends with the famous line 'A terrible beauty is born'. His poetry is mostly tied up with his sense of an Irish heroism and the unrequited love he had for Maud Gonne.

Oliver St John Gogarty (1878–1957) is said to have borne a lifelong grudge against his friend James Joyce because of his appearance as Buck Mulligan in the latter's *Ulysses*. He was a character in his own right and his views are presented in his memoirs *As I Was Going Down Sackville Street* (1937). He had a mean streak, though, and took exception to a throwaway remark written by Patrick Kavanagh (1904–67), successfully suing the poet whom he described as 'that Monaghan boy'.

Kavanagh, from farming stock in Monaghan, walked to Dublin (a very long way) in 1934 and made the capital his home. His later poetry explored Ireland's city versus country dynamic. He was fond of the Grand Canal, along the banks of which he is commemorated, with 'just a canal-bank seat for the passer-by', as he had wished.

You can't imagine the brooding Samuel Beckett (1906–89) hanging around in this company and, while his greatest literary contributions were as a dramatist (see p33) in self-imposed exile, he did write a collection of short stories in Dublin, *More Pricks Than Kicks* (1934), about an eccentric local character. The book so irked the new Free-State government that it was banned, no doubt hastening Beckett's permanent move to Paris.

One-time civil servant Brian O'Nolan (1911–66), also known as Flann O'Brien and Myles na Gopaleen, was a celebrated comic writer and career drinker. He wrote several books, most notably *At Swim-Two-Birds* (1939), but was most fondly remembered for the newspaper columns he penned for nearly three decades before his death.

Not so Taxing Times

Although Dublin is proud as punch of its literary credentials and is willing to flaunt its genius at every opportunity, the awkward truth is that most of the city's greatest writers — including Wilde, Beckett and Joyce — got the hell out of the place after suffering censorship or receiving no support. Since the 1970s, to ensure that Ireland doesn't endure this ignominy again and to maintain the creative output, the Irish government provides tax exemptions for all artists who choose to live in Ireland, from musicians to authors. Creative folk have flocked to these shores ever since, although of course it's for the people, the kinship and the earthiness of the place that they did so much.

He was eclipsed – at least in the drinking stakes – by novelist, playwright, journalist and quintessential Dublin hell-raiser, Brendan Behan (1923–64), who led a short and frantic life. In 1953, Behan began work as a columnist with the now defunct *Irish Press*, and over the next decade wrote about his beloved Dublin, using wonderful, earthy satire and a keen sense of political commentary that set him apart from other journalists. A collection of his newspaper columns was published under the title *Hold Your Hour and Have Another* (see also p33.)

James Joyce

Of course, utmost among Dublin writers is James Joyce (1882–1941), the author of *Ulysses*, the greatest book of the 20th century. Although Joyce left town at the earliest opportunity, he continued living here through his imagination and literature. Dubliners are immensely proud of Joyce although most people have never read him; many who have tried to read *Ulysses* have found it impenetrable – 'James Joyce's *Ulysses*? Ah yeah, great preface!'.

Born in Rathgar in 1882, the young Joyce had three short stories published in an Irish farmers' magazine under the pen name Stephen Dedalus in 1904, the year he fled town with the love of his life, Nora Barnacle. He spent most of the next 10 years in Trieste, Italy, where he wrote prolifically but struggled to get published. His career was further hampered by recurrent eye problems and he had 25 operations for glaucoma, cataracts and other conditions.

The first major prose he finally had published was *Dubliners* (1914), a collection of short stories set in the city, which included the three stories he had written in Ireland. Publishers began to take notice, and his autobiographical *A Portrait of the Artist as a Young Man* (1916) soon followed. In 1918 the US magazine *Little Review* started to publish extracts from *Ulysses* but notoriety was already pursuing his epic work and the censors prevented publication of further episodes after 1920.

Passing through Paris on a rare visit to Dublin, he was persuaded by Ezra Pound to stay a while in the French capital. He 'came to Paris for a week and stayed 20 years'. It was a good move for the struggling writer for, in 1922, he met Sylvia Beach of the Paris bookshop Shakespeare & Co who finally managed to put *Ulysses* (1922) into print. The publicity of its earlier censorship ensured instant success.

Buoyed by the success of the inventive *Ulysses*, Joyce went for broke with *Finnegans Wake* (1939), 'set' in the dream-scape of a Dublin publican. Perhaps not one to read at the airport, the book is a daunting and often obscure tome about eternal recurrence. It is even more complex than *Ulysses* and took the author 17 years to write.

In 1940 WWII drove the Joyce family back to Zürich where the author died the following year.

Ulysses

Ulysses is the ultimate chronicle of the city, in which Joyce intended to 'give a picture of Dublin so complete that if the city suddenly one day disappeared from the earth it could be reconstructed in my book'. It is set here on 16 June 1904 – the day of Joyce's first date with Nora Barnacle – and follows its characters as their journeys around town parallel the voyage of Homer's *Odyssey*.

The experimental literary style makes it difficult to read – in fact it's often called one of the 'great unread works of the English language' – although there's much for even the slightly bemused reader to relish. It ends with Molly Bloom's famous stream of consciousness discourse, a chapter of eight huge, unpunctuated paragraphs. Because of its sexual explicitness, the book was banned in the US and the UK until 1933 and 1937, respectively.

Testament to the book's enduring relevance and extraordinary innovation, it has inspired writers of every generation since. Joyce admirers from around the world descend on Dublin every year on 16 June to celebrate Bloomsday and retrace the steps of its central character, Leopold Bloom. If you're here in 2004, the centenary of the fictitious stroll, you can expect every day to be Bloomsday (head to Dublin Tourism offices or see www.dublintourism.ie for details).

THE CONTEMPORARY SCENE

The most successful and most Dublin of Dublin writers in recent times has been Roddy Doyle (1958–) who captured the mood, wit and vernacular of the times perfectly in his easy-reading Barrytown trilogy, *The Commitments* (1987), *The Snapper* (1990) and *The Van* (1991). But it wasn't until he wrote the semi-autobiographical *Paddy Clarke Ha Ha Ha*, winner of the Booker Prize in 1993, that the literary world took him terribly seriously. His writing has moved on steadily and admirably, turning new corners with every project. He tackled domestic violence in *The Woman Who Walked into Doors* (1997), a social history in *A Star Called Henry* (2000), and nonfiction with his *Rory & Ita* (2002), essentially an interview with his parents. He also wrote a brilliant and bleak four-part drama series for RTE called *The Family* that was light on laughs and heavy on social commentary.

John Banville (1945–) is perhaps the best known local writer in international literary circles. He was short-listed for the Booker Prize with *The Book of Evidence* (1989) and returned to his flowery, eloquent best with *Shroud* (2002). John McGahern (1934–) is perhaps more popular and influential within Ireland. He's been kicking around for a long time and obtained long-overdue recognition with his Booker-nominated *Amongst Women* (1990).

Jennifer Johnston (1930–) was the most well-known female writer from Dublin in the second half of the 20th century. She made her name with *Shadows on Our Skin* (1977) and continues in vigorous form with *This is Not a Novel* (2002) which, of course, is a very good novel. The 'come here and I'll tell you a story' style of prodigious Dublin writer Maeve Binchy (1940–) has seen her outsell many of the greats of Irish literature including Beckett and Behan, and her long list of bestsellers includes *Circle of Friends* (1990) and *Tara Road* (1999).

That Dublin's extraordinary literary past doesn't stifle aspiring writers is down to people like Dermot Bolger (1959–), a talented writer, editor, publisher and tireless promoter of new talent. His *The Journey Home* (1990) is one of our favourite novels. Colum McCann (1965–) maintains Ireland's greatest literary tradition, expatriation, and his best novel is probably *This Side of Brightness* (1998). Colm Tóibín (1955–) was born in Enniscorthy in County Wexford but lives in Dublin (and his birthplace is almost part of the capital these days anyway). He took four years to find a publisher for his first novel *The South* (1990) and has gone on to become a hugely successful novelist and scholar. Joseph O'Connor (1963–), Sinéad's little brother, burst onto the scene with *Cowboys & Indians* (1991) and has delivered a string of popular novels, none better than *The Star of the Sea* (2002), a tale of life on board a 19th-century famine ship. Another

contemporary notable is Jamie O'Neill (1962–), whose *At Swim, Two Boys* (2001) is the great Irish gay novel (attentive readers will have recognised the pun on Flann O'Brien's book).

Nuala O'Faolain, former opinion columnist for the *Irish Times,* 'accidentally' wrote an autobiography when a small publisher asked her to write an introduction to a collection of her columns. Her irreverent, humorous and touching prose struck a chord with readers and the essay was republished as *Are You Somebody?* (1996), and then followed up with *Almost There – the onward journey of a Dublin Woman* (2003), which both became international bestsellers.

There seems to be an endless supply of young writers prepared to follow their illustrious predecessors, and a quick scan through the lists of newcomers reveals that Dublin and Irish fiction is in terrific shape – even if they're not getting the fanfare and razzmatazz that accompanies new publications by young authors in neighbouring London. Two of the most recent stars to emerge from literary Dublin are Keith Ridgway and Claire Kilroy, whose debut novels *The Parts* (2003) and *All Summer* (2003) have been turning more than pages.

Seamus Heaney (1939–) was born in Derry but now lives mostly in Dublin. He is the bard of all Ireland and evokes the spirit and character of the country in his poetry. He won the Nobel in 1995, and the humble wordsmith compared all the attention to someone mentioning sex in front of their mammy. *Opened Ground – Poems 1966–1996* (1998) is our favourite book.

Dubliner Paul Durcan (1944–) is one of the most reliable chroniclers of changing Dublin. He won the prestigious Whitbread Prize for Poetry in 1990 for *'Daddy, Daddy'* and is a funny, engaging, tender and savage writer. Poet, playwright and Kerryman, Brendan Kennelly, is an immensely popular

character around town. He lectures in Trinity College and writes a unique brand of poetry that is marked by its playfulness, as well as historical and intellectual impact. Eavan Boland is a prolific and much-admired writer best known for her poetry. She combines Irish politics with an outspoken feminism, and *In a Time of Violence* (1995) and *The Lost Land* (1998) are two of her most celebrated collections.

If you're interested in finding out more about poetry in Ireland in general, visit the website of the excellent *Poetry Ireland* (www.poetryireland.ie), which showcases the work of new and established poets.

Recommended Reading

At Swim-Two-Birds (1939; Flann O'Brien) By the late satirical columnist and regarded by many as the great Dublin novel. It's funny and absurd and uses inventive wordplay in telling the story within a story of a student novelist.

Circle of Friends (1990; Maeve Binchy) By the queen of Irish popular fiction, ably captures the often hilarious peculiarities of the lives of two hapless country girls in the 1940s, who come to Dublin in search of romance.

Down by the River (1997; Edna O'Brien) By the London-based novelist who had the honour of having her *The County Girls* (1960) banned, this is a sensationalist novel based on the controversial true story of a 14-year-old Dublin girl who was raped and went to England for an abortion.

Amongst Women (1990; John McGahern) Focuses on a rough old Republican whose story is told through his three daughters. It's essentially a study of the faults and comforts of humanity and an exploration of family ties, told by an exceptionally skilled author who combines a gentle tone with an unfailing eye for the human condition.

At Swim, Two Boys (2001; Jamie O'Neill) A beautifully crafted masterpiece that has drawn comparisons to Joyce and Beckett for the language and characterisation. Essentially it's a coming-of-age tale of gay youth set against the backdrop of revolutionary Dublin circa 1916. It's ambitious, absorbing and absolutely brilliant.

The Book of Evidence (1989; John Banville) Written by the former literary editor of the *Irish Times*, this consists of the prison memoir of Freddie Montgomery on trial for the brutal murder of a female servant. It's a terrific and elaborate piece of literary, philosophical and political fiction.

Paddy Clarke Ha Ha Ha (1993; Roddy Doyle) A bawdy story which follows the childish adventures of 10-year-old Paddy in the fictitious working-class world of Barrytown in north Dublin. It won Doyle the Booker Prize in 1993.

The Ginger Man (1955; JP Donleavy) A high-energy foray around Dublin from the perspective of an Irish-American scoundrel. It received the Catholic Church's 'seal of approval' by being banned in Ireland for many years.

The Informer (1925; Liam O'Flaherty) The classic book about the divided sympathies that plagued Ireland during its independence struggle and the ensuing Civil War. Set in the Dublin underworld, this enthralling revolutionary drama was successfully brought to the big screen by the legendary John Ford.

My Left Foot (1954; Christy Brown) The story of the author's life growing up with cerebral palsy, which he overcame to become an accomplished painter and writer. This autobiography was later expanded into the novel *Down all the Days* (1970) which formed the basis of the acclaimed film *My Left Foot*.

A New Book of Dubliners (1989) A fine collection of Dublin-related short stories written by authors including James Joyce, Oliver St John Gogarty, Liam O'Flaherty, Samuel Beckett and Flann O'Brien.

Finbar's Hotel (1996) A collection of short stories or a serial novel about a soon-to-be-demolished Dublin landmark, occupied by the imaginations of seven of Dublin's favourite authors. Fans of the likes of Roddy Doyle, Jennifer Johnston, Joseph O' Connor and Dermot Bolger will have fun trying to work out who wrote what.

The Dancers Dancing (1999; Éilis Ní Dhuibhne) The story of four Dublin teenagers who visit a Gaeltacht area in Donegal and an illuminating meditation on class, history, politics and the Irish language in modern Irish society.

The Journey Home (1990; Dermot Bolger) Depicts the underside of modern Irish society with a pacy, absorbing narrative and beautifully crafted characters and scenarios. The tourist board would probably have it banned if it had its way.

One Day as a Tiger (1997; Anne Haverty) Short listed for the Whitbread First Novel Award, this is about a brilliant young historian who returns to his family's sheep farm where a genetically modified sheep impacts on his imagination. It's a charming and comic portrayal of rural Ireland.

THEATRE

Dubliners have a unique affinity with theatre; it seems to course through their veins. Perhaps this explains why dramatists Oliver Goldsmith, Oscar Wilde and George Bernard Shaw conquered the theatre world in London even before there was such an entity as Irish drama. While Dublin has a long association with the stage – the first theatre was founded here in 1637 – it wasn't until the late 19th century Celtic Revival Movement and the establishment of the Abbey Theatre that Irish drama really took off.

Perhaps the first renowned Dublin playwright was Oliver Goldsmith (1730–74) who enjoyed much success with *The Good Natur'd Man* (1768) and *She Stoops to Conquer* (1773) before his early death. Language enthusiasts might like to know that another London favourite, Richard Brinsley Sheridan (1751–1816), gave us the word 'malapropism' after the misguided character Mrs Malaprop from his play *The Rivals* (1775).

The infinitely quotable Oscar Wilde (1854–1900) left Dublin for London after studying at Trinity and caused a sensation with his uproarious, challenging plays such as *The Importance of Being Earnest* (1895) and *An Ideal Husband* (1895). However, his most important and vigorous work is *The Ballad of Reading Gaol* (1898) which he wrote while serving a prison sentence for being a progressive homosexual in a backward time. Wilde paid a heavy toll for the harsh prison conditions and the ignorance of Victorian society, dying bankrupt not long after his release.

Fellow Trinity alumnus John Millington Synge (1871–1909) was one of the first to create headlines at Dublin's Abbey Theatre, established in 1904 by WB Yeats and Lady Gregory to stage Irish productions and stimulate the local scene. In stark contrast to Wilde, Synge's plays focused on the Irish peasantry, whose wonderful language of bawdy witticisms and eloquent invective he transposed into his plays. His honest portrayal of the brutality of rural life in his most famous drama, *The Playboy of the Western World* (1907), resulted in rioting when it first opened at the Abbey. Sadly for Irish drama, Synge died of Hodgkin's disease within two years aged just 38.

Sean O'Casey (1880–1964), from the working-class north inner city, didn't even become a full-time writer until his 40s but made up for the slow start with a brilliant burst in which he wrote the powerful trilogy on patriotism and life in Dublin's slums, *Shadow of a Gunman* (1923), *Juno and the Paycock* (1924) and *The Plough and the Stars* (1926). The latter also caused riots in the Abbey Theatre when it was first staged and it's a wonder WB Yeats and Co could afford the insurance to carry on.

Brendan Behan (1923–64) was another immensely talented Dublin playwright whose creative fire was quenched much too early. A die-hard Republican, he shot to prominence with his autobiographical accounts of his time in prison in Dublin and England, in the play *The Quare Fellow* (1954) and the tale *Borstal Boy* (1958). His masterpiece was *The Hostage* (1958), a devastatingly satirical play about an English soldier being ransomed by the IRA. He struggled to cope with the fame his talent brought, and his alcoholism – and the image of celebrity hell-raiser that he tried to live up to – delivered his early demise.

It hardly seems possible that he could have shared the same era as Dublin-born Samuel Beckett (1906–89). Although Beckett spent most of his adult life in Paris and wrote much of his work in French, he is still thought of as an Irish playwright perhaps because it was as much his rejection of Irish culture that drove him as a longing for anything else. His greatest works are associated with the bleakness and self-examination that occurred in continental Europe following WWII, from which he himself spent a good time on the run. Many consider his *Waiting for Godot* (1953) to be the modernist theatrical masterpiece. Beckett got the nod from the Nobel committee in 1969 and literary Dublin got another feather in its well-plumed cap.

Catching the Classics

The Abbey today – or the National Theatre of Ireland as it announces itself at every opportunity – is nowhere near as controversial or dynamic as it was when Yeats and Lady Gregory called the shots. In its first decades, productions caused riots and Yeats himself scaled the stage to admonish the audience after it went wild at the sight of a nationalist flag among prostitutes in Sean O'Casey's *The Plough and the Stars* in 1926.

In contrast the gloomy concrete facade and dismal interior of the current Abbey, opened in 1966 after the original was destroyed by fire, is vigorously dispiriting. Despite this, Dubliners are still immensely fond of the place. In 2002 there was furious debate about a proposal to move it from its original city centre spot out into the redeveloped Docklands. A decision was finally taken to stay put and the complex will be dramatically redeveloped some time in the future.

For now, while the Abbey may no longer be the progressive or groundbreaking force of old, it is a vital repository of Irish drama tradition and offers visitors not-to-be-missed opportunities to see dutiful and highly polished productions of some of Ireland's greatest plays.

CONTEMPORARY DUBLIN THEATRE

Irish theatre is still sincerely and refreshingly self-absorbed, which means it offers visitor a direct short cut into the heart of Irish culture. After a mid-century descent into the dol drums – when Irish society stagnated and was therefore a less interesting study – the theatr underwent something of a renaissance in the early 1990s, thanks largely to a reinvigorate establishment and a host of new companies that were prepared to push the boundarie with challenging and thought-provoking contemporary plays as well as new spins on ol classics.

It's slowed again in the last couple of years, perhaps reflecting a society readjusting afte the excesses of the 1990s and the inevitability that some of these progressive, avant-gard companies have crossed over into the establishment. Rough Magic, one of the most success ful independent companies of recent years, specialises in bringing new works to Ireland an new Irish writers to the stage. Prominent among this new crop is Declan Hughes, whos seminal *Shiver* (2003) about two couples in post-boom Dublin was perhaps the first piec about this new society.

Brian Friel and Tom Murphy are the country's leading establishment playwright Neither is from Dublin although most of their work is premiered there, often in the Gat Theatre. But the most exciting stuff is being written by the likes of Conor McPherso whose enormously successful *The Weir* won an Olivier award in 1999; the Anglo-Iris Martin McDonagh, who collected four Tonys for his Broadway smash hit *The Beaut Queen of Leenane* (1998), which premiered in Dublin; Mark O'Rowe, who presented a electrifying picture of gangland Dublin in his award-winning *Howie the Rookie* (199 and also co-wrote the film *Intermission* starring Colin Farrell; and Eugene O'Brie whose *Eden* is regarded by many as the best work to come out of Dublin in recer years.

Dublin's small but choice international and fringe festivals take place in late Septembe early October (see p10), the perfect time to take the city's pulse. See p173 for more o Dublin's theatres.

MUSIC

Music is another area where Dublin gives a lot more than it takes, and you'll see that it intrinsic to the local lifestyle. There are rock gigs most nights, traditional sessions in ju about every pub frequented by tourists, name DJs spinning steelies in clubs all over tow and background music in all the new pubs (aarrghhh!). Meanwhile you can hardly wal down Grafton St without stubbing your toe on the next international superstars buskir their way to a record contract. One thing's for certain, you'll have the music of Dubl ringing in your ears long after your gig here is done.

TRADITIONAL & FOLK

Dublin's not the best place in Ireland to sav-our a traditional session although, thanks to the tourist demand, it's a lot better than it was 10 years ago. Traditional music was in the doldrums in the middle of the 20th century and at risk of dying out altogether as Ireland raced to become modern and just like everyone else. That it has been revived is thanks to pioneers who updated the way it was played (in ensembles rather than the customary *céilidh* – communal dance – bands), the habit of pub sessions (introduced by returning migrants) and the econom good times which encouraged the Irish to celebrate their culture rather than trying to re licate international trends. Of course, it also got help from a little show called *Riverdan* (see p42). It has also been disproportionately influential on other music styles, not lea

Top Five Most Underrated Dublin Albums

- *24 Star Hotel*, Mundy
- *The Last Man in Europe*, The Blades
- *A Feeling Mission*, Harvest Ministers
- *Understand*, Brian
- *The Way We Were*, A House

Arts – Music

34

n American Country & Western which is said to be a fusion of Mississippi Delta blues
nd Irish traditional tunes.

Although city slickers often scoff at traditional music, these days the city reverberates
o its tune. Granted, much of it is trad-lite (a bogus 'howya boys and girls' variety put on
or the tourists) but there are also a few organised gigs, impromptu pub sessions and even
treet performers.

The most famous traditional band – and arguably the original 'band' – is the Chieftains,
which was formed in 1963 and is still going strong after four decades. The most loved band
n the capital, although more folksy than
raditional, is the Dubliners, fronted by the
istinctive gravel voice and grey beard of
onnie Drew, whose photograph should
ppear above the word Dublin whenever
's printed. Luke Kelly (1940–84) was an-
ther hugely popular member of this band
nd his solo version of 'Scorn not his Sim-
licity' is one of the saddest, most beautiful
ongs ever recorded. Another band whose
areer has been stitched into the fabric of
)ublin life is the Fureys, comprising four
rothers originally from the travelling
ommunity (no, not like the Wilburies)
long with guitarist Davey Arthur. And if
's rousing renditions of Irish rebel songs
ou're after, you can't go past the Wolfe
ones.

Since the 1970s, various bands have
ried to blend traditional with more
rogressive genres with mixed success.
he first band to pull it off was Moving
learts, led by Christy Moore who went on
o become the greatest Irish folk musician
ver. Political agitator, storyteller, guitar
layer and poet, Christy is the man to span all eras and an hour or two in his company
s an essential experience. Get *Ride On* or *Christy Moore – The Collection* for an aural
our of Irishness.

One of the best Irish albums from the last 20 years is the superb collection *A Woman's
leart,* which kick-started the careers of some of the country's finest female vocalists in-
luding Dublin sisters and solo performers Mary and Frances Black, and Eleanor McEvoy.
ugging on their coat-tails are a new crop of young women, including local lass Gemma
layes, a former Grafton St busker who is winning international fans and plaudits with her
ew and punchier folk style.

While traditional music continues to be popular in its own right both in Ireland and
road, it also continues to provide the base for successful new genres. The ravishingly
eautiful Corrs, from neighbouring County Louth, have been very successful with their
lend of trad and pop while a wonderful product of contemporary Ireland has been the
fro-Celt Foundation, which fuses African rhythms and electronic beats with Irish tradi-
onal to great effect.

OPULAR MUSIC

the traditional music stakes, Dublin only survives on the reputation of the rest of Ireland –
's with rock music that it really kicks arse. Perhaps inspired by Belfast's Van Morrison
nd the blossoming London scene, it was in the late 1960s that the city's musicians began
organise themselves.

It was young black Dubliner, Phil Lynott, bass-playing front man with Thin Lizzy, who
ut Dublin on the music map. The hard-rocking, twin-guitar engine outfit formed in 1969

but didn't make their breakthrough until the album *Jailbreak* (1975). Their finest hour, literally, was *Live & Dangerous* (1978), one of the greatest live albums ever recorded. Thin Lizzy's music aged better than their charismatic and hard-living lead singer, whose life and creativity were blighted by drug use and physical deterioration – he died in 1986.

During the punk explosion of the mid-1970s, Bob 'for fuck's sake' Geldof and the Boomtown Rats carried the mantle for Dublin, strutting their way to centre stage with hit singles 'Rat Trap' and 'I Don't Like Mondays'. By the time the band had begun to wane, Geldof had moved onto more important matters like organising the world's biggest gig, Live Aid, to provide humanitarian aid to Ethiopian famine victims.

In 1976, a young drummer stuck a note on his school notice board looking for fellow pupils who were interested in forming

a band. The band became U2. Even on their debut album, *Boy* (1980), Bono's impassioned vocals, the Edge's emotional guitar and Larry and Adam's driving rhythm set this band apart. They produced a string of brilliant albums before going mega with *The Joshua Tree* (1987). And mega they've remained due to their numerous reinventions and in spite of Bono's posturing. If you're not already familiar with early U2, get yourself acquainted. The live *Under a Blood Red Sky* (1983) is very special. In their decades-spanning career, U2 have gone in and out of favour in Dublin but they've continued to live in the capital through thick and thin. Fair play to them.

While Bono and the boys were posing in their clip for the single 'Gloria' in gritty Ringsend *(October)*, local three-piece The Blades were building up a fanatical live following. Unfortunately, it never translated to commercial success for their album *Last Man in Europe* (1985) and we never got to see what charismatic front man, Paul Cleary, was really capable of doing.

The Blades failed partly because of record company indifference – if they'd hung around for U2's *The Joshua Tree,* they could have benefited from the scramble by the majors to sign the next big Dublin thing. It never came. Sinéad O'Connor wasn't exactly what they were looking for but she made them sit up and take notice all the same. The raw emotion on *The Lion and the Cobra* (1985) makes it a fine offering.

The Nuts & Bolts of Traditional Music

Despite misconceptions, the harp isn't widely used in traditional music. (It *is* the national emblem but that probably has more to do with the country traditionally being run by pulling strings.) The bodhrán (pronounced 'bow-rawn') goatskin drum is much more characteristic although it makes for a lousy symbol. The uillean pipes, played with a bellows squeezed under the elbow, provides another distinctive sound although you're not likely to see them in a pub. The fiddle isn't unique to Ireland but it is one of the main instruments in its indigenous music, along with the flute, tin whistle, accordion and bouzouki (a version of the mandolin). Music fits into five main categories (jigs, reels, hornpipes, polkas and slow airs) while the old style of singing unaccompanied versions of traditional ballads and airs is called *sean-nós*.

There was a great live scene in Dublin in the 1990s. Bands like A House, Something Happens, Four of Us, Aslan, Stars of Heaven, Fat Lady Sings, Harvest Ministers and Hothouse Flowers could have been huge in another time. OK, maybe not the Hothouse Flowers but you get our gist. Anyway, guitar-based rock was out and the vacuum was filled by…we can hardly bare to mention it…boy bands.

But even when it came to manufactured pop Dublin excelled, thanks chiefly to manager extraordinaire Louis Walsh. First off the school bus in 1993 were Boyzone, a sappy five-piece from Dublin, headed by Ronan Keating who has gone onto a hugely successful international solo career. He also created Westlife who – although it means sod all any more recently matched the Beatles' record with seven consecutive No 1 hits in Britain. Walsh also manages the Irish/Zambian, totally foxy R&B diva, Samantha Mumba.

On a serious note, however, Dublin's tradition of singer-songwriters is in great shape with Damien Rice, David Kitt, returned ex-pat Mark Geary and adoptee Mundy the best of the current crop. The majors don't like rock-pop Mundy much but both his albums are excellent. Very new boys Paddy Casey and Mark McLaughlin are also worth keeping an ear out for. If you'd visited Dublin a few years ago, you might have seen Tipperary-born Gemma Hayes busking. Now she's the leading lady of Irish rock, albeit a fairly folksy version. Her debut *Night on My Side* (2002) is terrific. The magnificent Divine Comedy, which basically comprises Derry-born Neil Hannon, settled into Dublin recently and has lifted the local average with brilliantly baroque pop and heavily orchestrated mini-epics. For us, the best albums were *Liberation* (1993) and *Promenade* (1994) but we're still paying avid attention. Glen Hansard is the sole musical survivor of Alan Parker's *The Commitments* (1991), which briefly brought soul to the city. His band, The Frames, have been going for donkey's years and while they've failed to make a splash internationally, their power pop is huge on the local scene. The live album, *Set List* (2003), captures them at their best.

In late 2003, all the hype was about the handsome and eminently marketable The Thrills and their Mercury-nominated debut album *So Much for the City* (2003), a laid-back, dreamy soundtrack to summer that pays homage to the retro music of west coast USA. We don't get it though – it just sounds dippy. Stay-at-home merchants, the quirkily popping The Chalets are also turning heads and are likely to record something soon.

Pony Club (formerly Bawl), led by Mark Cullen, are a great local band in the old mould, and combine wonderful melodies with confronting lyrics. *Home Truths* (2001) is a reminder, in these overhyped, haphazardly halcyon days, that Dublin is in fact still inhabited by real people.

Dublin DJs

Billy Scurry Simply the best techno DJ in the city. Back in the early '90s he set the tone for the e-fuelled revolution in the city's dancing habits and has never looked back. A true Dub, totally unaffected by fame and reputation, he plays his records in a seamless, perfect way, pulling the crowd this way and that for hours on end.

DJ Mek The best hip-hop DJ this country has ever produced. A scratch and mix genius, he has the unique ability (in Ireland anyway) not to get lost in his technical prowess (which is virtually infinite) and keep the party going. (He once ate a can of beans on stage and then proceeded to scratch like he was farting. Sensational.)

Johnny Moy Another superb techno DJ. Back in the 1990s, he was invited to play the legendary Hacienda Club in Manchester. He started well, got the crowd going and then, halfway through his set, let the track fade out. Silence for nearly 20 seconds as everyone looked around going 'what the fuck?'. Then came the explosive sound of The Jam's 'Going Underground'. The crowd went absolutely mental. A moment of pure genius that took iron balls to pull off.

DJ Tu-Ki Part of the new crop of hip hop DJs and a part of Mek's inner circle. In 2003 he was the very first Irish DJ to make it to the finals of the World DMC Championships, the *crème de la crème* for hip-hop DJs throughout the world. (Beck's DJ is a former winner.) Needless to say, he's a wizard on the wheels of steel.

DJ Arveene Another new kid on the block; a freestyle DJ who packs his bag with techno, house, hip-hop, hardcore rock, punk, soul and pop, which he mixes, scratches and cuts to keep the party going. Great fun, great skill and perfect to dance to.

VISUAL ARTS

Although they started off brilliantly – think of the gold and bronze works in the National Museum and the Book of Kells – Irish artists never really delivered on their early promise, and in recent decades, the country has been more famous for its art heists than artists. Russborough House in County Wicklow has been robbed three times since 1974, with Vermeer, Goya and Gainsborough all among the victims.

Beyond one impressionist who settled and died in Dublin, Jack B Yeats, and the surrealist Francis Bacon who wanted nothing to do with the city after he left it aged 16, Dublin has contributed little to the world of art. Or perhaps just little compared to its other artistic endeavours.

But even this apparent cultural fallibility has been revised in recent years with 20th century Irish art more than tripling in value since 1990. While it was probably under rated beforehand, this revaluation no doubt has more to do with the wealth of Irish collectors, their rediscovery of indigenous art and their hunger for a piece of heritage.

The National Gallery (p86) has an extensive Irish School collection, much of it chronicling the personages and pursuits of the Anglo-Irish aristocracy. Garrett Murphy (1680–1716) and James Latham (1696–1747) were respected portrait painters of their day. Nathaniel Hone (1831–1917), an important 19th-century landscape artist, was born in Ireland and returned to Dublin after a lengthy stint working in France.

Roderic O'Conor (1861–1940) was the first Irish painter to make a splash. He was dubbed the Irish Van Gogh because he grasped the Dutch genius' revolution and matched his vibrant, exuberant and extraordinary strokes. He too was drawn to France and never returned to his homeland. Dublin-born William Orpen (1878–1931) became well known for his depictions of Irish life and his *Portrait of Gardenia St George with Riding Crop* (1912) holds the distinction of being the most expensive Irish painting ever sold at auction, fetching UK£1.8 million. He just pipped his contemporary, Belfast-born John Lavery.

National Gallery (p86)

The most original and famous of the Irish painters was Jack B Yeats (1871–1957), the first impressionist painter from the British Isles. Like his big brother, poet WB, Jack was a champion of the Celtic Revival Movement. He mastered a range of painting techniques but is best known for setting down thick and broad strokes of pigment in a bold and gutsy spin on impressionism. This style provided a self-confident art for the newly independent Ireland created after the formation of the Irish Free State in 1922. The characters he drew were often strong, isolated and solitary – and every stroke seems to reveal his deep love for all things Irish. The National Gallery has a specific gallery devoted to his work, and a visit here should be one of the highlights of your trip to Dublin. Among our favourites are *The Liffey Swim* (1923), *Man of Destiny* (1946) and *The Singing Horseman* (1949).

Most modern Irish artists turned their backs on the nationalism that so defined the world of Yeats. The abstract painters, Mainie Jellett (1896–1943) and Evie Hone (1894–1955) are considered two of the greatest innovators of modern Irish art. The self-taught Louis LeBrocquy (1916–) is one of the foremost Irish painters of the 20th century. While his works aren't necessarily innovative – they borrow heavily from Picasso, Manet and others – they are unique in their Irishness. He is most famous for his depictions of the travelling community in the 1940s in a series known as the *Tinker Paintings*.

Today, Dublin is at the forefront of a new Irish artistic revolution which has seen a fundamental transformation in the infrastructure

Top Five Galleries

- National Gallery (p86)
- Hugh Lane Gallery (p103)
- RHA Gallagher Gallery (p89)
- Douglas Hyde Gallery (p77)
- Temple Bar Gallery & Studios (p80)

and culture of visual arts. There is now a thriving network of part-funded and fully commercial galleries in the city, and a buoyant, dynamic local scene. Although it doesn't have nearly the vitality, celebrity or popular appeal of the London scene, the Irish market is big and busy for its size and increasingly international in its outlook. Some of the key Dublin-based artists to look out or include: Corkonian Dorothy Cross whose luminescent *Ghost Shop* (1999) was temporarily moored in Dublin Bay; video artist James Coleman; Shane Cullen who carved the 11,500 words of the 1998 Anglo-Irish Treaty in his vast sculptural work *The Agreement* (2002); and Graham Knuttel, whose paintings are instantly identifiable for their distinctive bold, stylised figures.

Francis Bacon

Dubliners like to tell you that Francis Bacon, the foremost British painter of his generation, was actually Irish although it's a pretty tenuous claim to call him one of their own.

Born in Dublin – of English parentage – in 1909, Bacon was thrown out of home at the age of 16 when his parents discovered he was actively homosexual. In that great Irish artistic tradition, Bacon split as soon as he could and turned his back on his narrow-minded hometown forever, pointedly denying his roots thereafter. He flitted about Berlin and Paris before settling in London in 1928 where he developed his distinctive, distorted, violent and utterly captivating style.

Critics dismissed him as a warped caricaturist, and it is true that his best-known works are distortions of other painters' creations – Velázquez' *Portrait of Innocent X* became Bacon's most celebrated series *The Screaming Popes* (1949–55) – but there is no denying his extraordinary ability to paint isolation, pain and suffering, major themes of post-WWII iconography and of homosexuality in repressed times.

His notoriously debauched lifestyle was nearly as well publicised as his genius. Although remarkably productive, he destroyed many of his canvases and relatively little of his work survives. Precious little is on display in Dublin – no doubt the way he would have wanted it – although the Hugh Lane Gallery (Municipal Gallery of Modern Art; see p103) did acquire the contents of the London studio where Bacon worked for three decades until his death in 1992. It has been faithfully reconstructed here in perhaps the most oddly compelling art exhibit in Dublin.

CINEMA & TV

TV

In such a sociable city as Dublin, you're not likely to sit indoors and watch TV for the duration of your holiday. And it's a good job because it's on the box that you see how small Ireland really is, and an hour or two watching Irish TV could blow Dublin's reputation for being culturally cutting-edge.

RTE, the national broadcaster, is best summed up thus. Its best comedy (a programme called *After the Game*) is produced by the sports department; in one of the few programmes it tried to make on its own (a cross between *Big Brother* and *Survivor* called *Cabin Fever*), the boat sank in the Irish Sea and contestants had to swim for their lives; and thirdly, it turned down the enormously successful comedy drama series *Father Ted,* a gentle and hilarious poke at conservative Ireland, which was then commissioned by Britain's Channel 4. Perhaps the most Irish TV programme ever – featuring the best Irish writers, cast, director and crew of their generation – and it only got made because a British company had the balls to take a risk. Tut-tut RTE. No wonder much of Dublin's best talent continues to live in London.

Dublin viewers might have gone bonkers over recent decades if their viewing choices hadn't been broadened by the availability of the English channels from BBC, ITV and Channel 4, which are all receivable along the east coast. More than half of the programmes on RTE are either repeats or can be seen on the British channels.

While there's not exactly a list of RTE classics for you to track down, there are some good documentaries. *From a Whisper to a Scream* and the more conservative *Make 'em Laugh* plot the history of Irish music and comedy, respectively. From the outsider's perspective, the most interesting show currently in its schedule is the popular and long-running soap *Fair City*, which depicts working-class life in the city. You might be surprised to turn on the TV at 6pm (or the radio at noon or 6pm) to hear a minute of slow, sombre gonging. This is the Angelus, a national minute-long call to prayer that has been broadcast every day since radio and TV began in Ireland.

Another distinction for the national broadcaster is the *Late Late Show* (Friday 9.30pm) which began in July 1962, a year after television was first broadcast here, and is the longest-running chat show in the world. Up until 1999, it was hosted by the inimitable Gay Byrne and its history is intertwined with the shaping of modern Ireland. The most important people and events have featured on what was once compulsive and often controversial weekend viewing. For nostalgia's sake catch it while you can because the show is suffering a slow and painful (for loyal viewers) death in the hands of the solidly wooden Pat Kenny. Death by a thousand splinters, if you like.

In 2003, the commercial channel TV3 started the *Eamon Dunphy Show* to compete against the *Late Late* on Friday night. The battle of the useless goes on in earnest...

FILM

While Ireland hasn't much of a film-making tradition – largely because the British cinema industry drained much of its talent and creative energies – it has contributed more than its fair share of glorious moments to the silver screen as well as a disproportionate number of its biggest stars.

The Irish Film Board was set up in 1981 in the government's two-pronged attempt to stimulate the local industry. Big international productions – like *David Copperfield, In the Name of the Father* and *Reign of Fire* – were tempted here with generous tax incentives in order to spread expertise among Irish crews, while money was pumped into the local scene so Dublin could get a chance to play itself once in a while rather than just appearing as some big screen double. The first part of the plan certainly worked, although local output has not been all the government had hoped. There are plans to shelve the tax incentive at the end of 2004, which may have bleak consequences for the industry.

> ### Top Five Films
> - *My Left Foot*
> - *A Man of No Importance*
> - *The Snapper*
> - *I Went Down*
> - *Intermission*

Or it may not. Ireland – or more accurately 'Oirland' (a sappy we're-poor-but-happy version so loved by plastic paddies abroad) – has long inspired film-makers and hardly a year goes by without some major Hollywood stars sashaying into the country, murdering the accent, and allowing every second two-bit actor in Dublin to brag about having 'made a fillem with Meryl Streep'.

Notables such as Orson Welles and Jimmy Stewart got their first big breaks in Dublin's Gate Theatre and, although they were far from being Irish, locals will tell you that these leading lights would never have shone had it not been for their Dublin experience.

Of course, Ireland has plenty of famous actors and directors of its own. Two of the biggest, Liam Neeson and Stephen Rea, both cut their acting teeth on the boards of the Abbey Theatre, a scene second-generation Irishman Aidan Quinn couldn't break into so went back to his birthplace, Chicago. Anglo-Irish star Daniel Day-Lewis lives just outside Dublin.

> ### Beckett on Film
>
> In a rare and commendable coming together, the Gate Theatre, Irish Film Board, RTE and several other companies made a film anthology of Samuel Beckett's 19 plays, including adaptations of some wonderful theatrical productions. Highlights of the extraordinarily ambitious project include David Mamet directing John Gielgud and Harold Pinter in *Catastrophe*, inimitable Dublin duo Johnny Murphy and Barry McGovern in *Waiting for Godot* and Julianne Moore taking direction from Neil Jordan in *Not I*. But arguably the gem is *Krapp's Last Tape*, with the dream team of John Hurt and the director Atom Egoyan. You can get the lot on DVD at www.beckettonfilm.com.

Some of the best and most famous Irish-themed films of recent years were directed by Dubliner Jim Sheridan (*In the Name of the Father, My Left Foot* and *The Field*) while the patchy Neil Jordan (*Michael Collins, The Butcher Boy*) has also chipped in with a couple among his high-budget blockbusters. Quickly making a name for himself is another Dublin director, Damien O'Donnell, whose debut *East is East* (2000) was one of the best 'British' films in recent years. Look out for the follow-up *Heartlands* (2003). The embarrassingly young Kirsten Sheridan (1977–), Jim's daughter, made a pretty good fist of *Disco Pigs* (2001), a strange coming-of-age flick.

Other native thespians include Gabriel Byrne (*Miller's Crossing, The Usual Suspects*)

Recommended Viewing

About Adam (2000; Gerry Stembridge) Set in contemporary Dublin, an agreeable tale that focuses on one man's ability to woo three sisters by appealing to what each woman wants in a man (apparently, sometimes more than a Dublin accent). It features local actor Stuart Townsend and US sensation Kate Hudson.

Dead Bodies (2003; Robert Quinn) A dark and stylish thriller set in contemporary Dublin against the backdrop of a general election. It's a terrific debut from the first-time director and features serial Irish bad guy, Gerard McSorley among a terrific cast.

The Dead (1987; John Huston) Based on a short story from James Joyce's *Dubliners*, *The Dead* focuses on a dinner party in Dublin at the end of the 19th century and specifically the thoughts of one of the partygoers. Difficult task for Huston in his last film, and he *almost* pulls it off.

I Went Down (1997; Paddy Breathnach) A quirky comedy caper with two characters borrowed from Quentin Tarantino's rogues gallery, which works particularly well with the Irish humour and sensibility. It stars one of our favourite actors, Brendan Gleeson, and is Ireland's all-time highest grossing film.

The Snapper (1993; Stephen Frears) A made-for-TV movie about how a Dublin family copes when their daughter gets 'up the pole' and won't tell anyone who the father is. Our choice of the Barrytown trilogy, which also included *The Commitments* and *The Van*. Full of slang, humour and pathos, it is Dublin to the core and absolutely brilliant. Colm Meaney is outstanding as the father.

A Man of No Importance (1994; Suri Krishnamma) Stars the brilliant Albert Finney as a repressed bus conductor trying to come to terms with his own homosexuality in 1960s Dublin while at the same time staging an amateur production of Oscar Wilde's *Salome*. Melancholy and beautiful, it feels like a poem.

Intermission (2003; John Crowley) A raucously funny, compellingly gritty and brilliantly scripted drama about a host of eccentric characters in pursuit of love. The cast features the cream of local talent, including Cillian Murphy, Colin Farrell and Colm Meaney.

The Magdalene Sisters (2002; Peter Mullan) A confronting and uncompromising film based on the true story of four young 'sinners' who were sent to one of the infamous Magdalene asylums in Dublin in the 1960s, where they suffered abuse by the nuns who ran the place (inhumanity still being investigated by the state). It's as moving as it is bleak.

The General (1998; John Boorman) A portrayal of Ireland's most notorious and enigmatic crime boss who, during the early 1990s when he was the pinnacle of gangland Dublin, was seen as much as a folk hero as a thug. Aptly, the film is horrific and disconcertingly funny, while Brendan Gleeson and Jon Voight are terrific in the leads.

Michael Collins (1996; Neil Jordan) This biopic of the man who delivered Irish independence and was assassinated during the 1922 civil war is an epic tale and a great film with pride and passion. The only downside is Jordan's shameful revision of history, specifically his portrayal of Eamon de Valera as a weak and pathetic collaborator in Collins' murder.

Veronica Guerin (2003; Joel Schumacher) Stars Cate Blanchett in a true story about an investigative journalist who is murdered after delving too deeply into the roots of the escalating drug problem that was pulling Dublin asunder in the mid-1990s. It's a little too Hollywood, with excess scenes of domestic bliss, but a powerful tale nonetheless.

My Left Foot (1989; Jim Sheridan) The best film made in and about Dublin in modern history. Based on the life story of Christy Brown, an Irish writer/artist with cerebral palsy, the stirring and triumphant film is made by the astonishing performance of Daniel Day-Lewis who didn't leave his character on set for the duration of the shoot, even forcing crew to carry him around.

When Brendan Met Trudy (2001; Kieron Walsh) A likable, light-hearted romance based in Dublin that apes scenes from old movies (there's a clue in the title) to add an extra layer for anyone who feels stiffed by the superficiality of a feel-good flick.

who might have been a priest if he hadn't been kicked out of the seminary for smoking; the hilarious Colm Meaney (who *made* the film versions of Roddy Doyle's Barrytown trilogy); the equally funny Brendan Gleeson (star of *The General* and the best film to come out of Ireland in the last decade, *I went Down*); the brilliant Johnny Murphy (who played Joey 'the Lips' Fagan in Alan Parker's *The Commitments* – Dubliners never want to hear the song 'Mustang Sally' again); the Cusack acting dynasty (the late father Cyril and his daughters Sinéad, Niamh and Sorcha); Brenda Fricker (who won an Oscar for her role in

My Left Foot); and the most recent export Colin Farrell (who burst his way to stardom with his sensational performance in *Tigerland*).

But perhaps the most exciting developments in Irish film in recent years is the quality of the new writers. Gerry Stembridge wrote the sprightly romantic comedy *About Adam* Roddy Doyle the quirky *When Brendan Met Trudy* (2001) and Derek Landy the out-of-the-blue hit of recent years, *Dead Bodies* (2003), which features lots of Dublin landmarks. Most attention has been directed to Dublin theatre writer Mark O'Rowe who wrote the gangster movie *I Went Down* and the blistering *Intermission,* the offering from and about Dublin starring megastar Colin Farrell and soon to be megastar, Cork's Cillian Murphy.

COMEDY

Ireland has always had an embarrassment of comedy riches, which is hardly surprising for a nation happy to laugh at itself as much as make fun of others. Even before there was a comedy scene in Dublin, raconteurs were filling hotel ballrooms and the city was exporting its talent around the world. Now that there is a scene, there's just no stopping them and Irish performers are the toast of comedy the world over. Our highly subjective list of historical highlight from the capital's comedy includes the greatest storyteller of them all, Dave Allen; the pioneering and brilliant stand-up Sean Hughes; and the late Dermot Morgan, a superb satirist who enjoyed huge success late in his career as Father Ted. Of the current crop doing stand-up in Dublin, we wouldn't miss an opportunity to see Father Ted co-star Ardal O'Hanlon, Barry Murphy or Tommy Tiernan.

DANCE

There's good and bad news. Yes, *Riverdance* and its various mutations like Lord of the Tight Pants are still going strong, stomping their way around the world, but the *good* news is that you're far less likely to be bombarded with the hand-by-the-sides phenomenon in Dublin than just about anywhere else in the world. Now don't get us wrong; we've got nothing against the modernisation of Irish dancing – it reflects the new dynamism in Irish culture – but it's just that after almost a decade of hype we're kind of hoping it can move on from the blockbuster.

Broadway hits and multiple international touring companies are a far cry from the dusty halls of rural Ireland where the tradition of Irish dancing was preserved on life support throughout the last century. Formerly the dancing was only performed at *céilidhs* and accompanied by traditional bands with musicians in green waistcoats.

Riverdance

For a while in the early 1990s it seemed like Ireland was the permanent host of the Eurovision Song Contest because it won the kitschy, conservative and compellingly ridiculous competition so often. RTE, the national broadcaster, needed to fill a slot between the end of the performances and the commencement of voting at the recording of the show in Dublin, and theatre composer Bill Whelan was asked if he could come up with something to keep the 300 million viewers entertained during the intermission.

Holy bejaysus! The subsequent seven minutes shook the world with an electrifying fusion of modern and traditional Irish dance, pounding feet and swirling music, primeval impulses and sophisticated tastes. An enraptured audience left their seats, gasped, caught their breath and roared for more – Irish dancing had been reinvented and *Riverdance* was born. The subsequent single topped the Irish charts for 18 weeks, and the first full-length version of the show opened in Dublin in 1995 to thunderous acclaim.

The etiquette was rigidly strict, fun was discouraged, and it seemed like most of the dancers were there under duress rather than to celebrate a tradition that has been around in some form since at least the 16th century. But not any more – thanks to a moment of inspiration (see the boxed text on this page); the roots of Irish dancing have been given a good soaking and the tradition is blossoming once again. While still true to the jigs and reels of its past, the dancing has evolved into something more tribal, vital and – and we can still hardly believe it – sexy.

Up until fairly recently, Irish dancing was virtually the only dancing in Ireland, although this situation is no longer as Dublin has become a destination for touring companies, while city venues are putting on their own shows and local companies creating their own.

Architecture

Architecture

Dublin raced into the third millennium with most of its finest architecture intact and with a rate of development not seen since the height of its Georgian heyday, when the city was regarded as one of the finest in Europe. Most of the public architecture of boom town (see p48) has generated a wonderful sense of energy and adventure about renaissance Dublin. Of course some mistakes have been made in the mad recent rush to build, but Dubliners have learned from the mistakes of their recent past (see p47) and are more architecturally savvy these days. They demand higher standards of design for their most deserving city and local authorities haven't let them down.

Although there's been a lull in activity in the last couple of years, it's a good opportunity for planners to take stock and refocus on the old problems, such as housing and transport.

MEDIEVAL DUBLIN

For architectural evidence of the pre-Norman settlers you will have to look further afield than the capital, which has been rebuilt far too many times. Dublin's tangled history has left very few survivors, even from Norman days, and what is left is either fragmentary or has been heavily reconstructed.

The imposing Dublin Castle (p82) – or the complex of buildings that are known as Dublin Castle – bears little resemblance to the fortress that was erected by the Anglo-Normans at the beginning of the 13th century and more to the neoclassical style of the 17th century. However, there are some fascinating glimpses of the lower reaches of the original, which you can visit through a tour (see p71 for more details).

Although Christ Church (p91) and St Patrick's (p96) Cathedrals, finished in the 12th century, were heavily rebuilt in Victorian times, there are some original features, including the crypt in Christ Church, which has a 12th-century Romanesque door. St Audoen's Church (p96) dates from 1190 and it too has a few Norman odds and ends, including a late 12th-century doorway.

Designs on Dublin

There are two terrific websites that enable you to keep an eye on Dublin's development. Reflecting City (www.reflectingcity.com) offers virtual tours of all the major urban renewal areas, while Archéire (www.irish-architecture.com) is a comprehensive site covering all things to do with Irish architecture and design. For more information on the buildings listed in this chapter, see the individual listings in the index.

THE ANGLO-DUTCH PERIOD

After the restoration of Charles II in 1660, Dublin embarked upon almost a century and a half of unparalleled growth as the city raced to become the second most important in the British empire. The grandest example of 17th-century architecture and indeed Dublin's first classical building is the hugely impressive Royal Hospital Kilmainham (1680; p96), which was designed by William Robinson as a home for invalid soldiers. Comprising a vast, cobbled courtyard in the centre of a quadrangular building with arcades, it was given a stunning makeover in the 1980s and now houses the Irish Museum of Modern Art (IMMA).

Similar in stature – and now also in shape, size and function – the Royal Barracks (Collins Barracks; 1701; p108) was built by Thomas Burgh as the first purpose-designed military barracks in Europe. The awesome square could accommodate six regiments, and the barracks was the oldest to remain in use until the National Museum commandeered the premises to stock its decorative arts.

Robinson moved from the mammoth to the miniature when he built the enchanting Marsh's Library (1701; p95), which was the first public library in Ireland and has remained virtually untouched.

GEORGIAN DUBLIN

Dublin's architectural apogee can roughly be placed in the period spanning the rule of the four English Georges, between the accession of George I in 1714 and the death of George IV in 1830. The greatest influence on the shape of modern Dublin throughout this period was the Wide Street Commissioners, appointed in 1757 and responsible for designing civic spaces and the framework of the modern city. Their efforts were complemented by Dublin's Anglo-Irish Protestant gentry who, flush with unprecedented wealth, dedicated themselves wholeheartedly towards improving their city.

Their inspiration was the work of the Italian architect Andrea Palladio (1508–80), who revived the symmetry and harmony of classical architecture. When the Palladian style reached these shores in the 1720s, the architects of the time tweaked it and introduced a number of, let's call them, 'refinements'. Most obvious were the elegant brick exteriors and decorative touches, such as coloured doors, fanlights and ironwork, which broke the sometimes austere uniformity of the form. Consequently, Dublin came to be known for its 'Georgian style'.

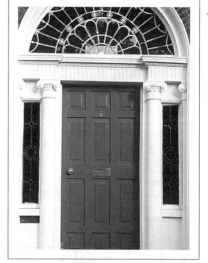

The architect is credited with the introduction of this style to Dublin's cityscape was Sir Edward Lovett Pearce (1699–1733), who first arrived in Dublin in 1725 and turned heads with the building Parliament House (Bank of Ireland; 1728–39; p75). It was the first two-chamber debating house in the world and the main chamber, the House of Commons, was topped by a massive Pantheon-style dome.

Pearce also created the blueprint for the city's Georgian town houses, the most distinguishing architectural feature of Dublin. The local version typically consists of four storeys, including the basement, with symmetrically arranged windows and an imposing, often brightly painted front door. Granite steps lead up to the door, which is often further embellished with a delicate leaded fanlight. The most celebrated examples are on the south side of the city, particularly around Merrion and Fitzwilliam Sqs (Map pp266–8), but the north side has some magnificent streets, including North Great George's and Henrietta Sts (Map pp264–5). The latter features two of Pearce's originals (at Nos 9 and 10) and is still Dublin's most unified Georgian street. Mountjoy Sq (Map pp264–5), the most elegant address in 18th-century Dublin, is currently being renewed after a century of neglect.

German architect Richard Cassels (Richard Castle; 1690–1751) hit town in 1728. While his most impressive country houses are outside Dublin, he did design Nos 85 and 86 St Stephen's Green (1738), which were combined in the 19th century and renamed Newman House (p88). Nos 80 and 81 were later altered to create Iveagh House, now the Department of Foreign Affairs (p90). The Rotunda Hospital (1748; p106), which closes off the top of O'Connell Street, is also one of Cassels' works. As splendid as these buildings are, it seems he was only warming up for Leinster House (1745–51; p85), the magnificent country residence built on what was then the countryside and is now the centre of government.

Dublin's boom attracted such notable architects as the Swedish-born Sir William Chambers (1723–96), who designed some of Dublin's most impressive buildings, though never actually bothered to visit the city. The north side benefited most from his genius: the chaste and elegant Charlemont House (Hugh Lane Gallery; 1763; p103) lauds over Parnell Sq, while his most stunning and bewitching work is the Casino at Marino (1755–79; p114).

Georgian Plasterers

The handsome exteriors of Dublin's finest Georgian houses are often matched by superbly crafted plasterwork within. The fine work of Michael Stapleton (1770–1803) can be seen in Trinity College (p77), Ely House (Map pp266-8) near St Stephen's Green and Belvedere House in north Dublin (p102). The La Franchini brothers, Paolo (1693–1770) and Filippo (1702–79), are responsible for the outstanding decoration in Newman House on St Stephen's Green (p88). But perhaps Dublin's most famous plastered surfaces are in the chapel at the heart of the Rotunda Hospital (p106). Although hospitals are never the most pleasant places to visit, it's worth it for the German stuccodore, Bartholemew Cramillion's gem of rococo plasterwork.

Across the river, Chambers designed the Examination Hall (1779–91) and the Chapel (1798), which flank the elegant 18th-century quadrangle of Trinity College, known as Parliament Sq (p77). However, Trinity's most magnificent feature, the old Library Building (1712; p78) with its breathtaking Long Room, had already been designed by Thomas Burgh.

It was towards the end of the 18th century that Dublin's developers really kicked into gear, when the power and confidence of the Anglo-Irish Ascendancy seemed boundless. Of several great architects of the time, James Gandon (1743–1823) stood out, and he built two of Dublin's most enduring and elegant neoclassical landmarks, Custom House (1781–91) and Four Courts (1786–1802). They were both built on the quays so afford plenty of space in which to admire them.

Gandon's greatest rival was Thomas Cooley (1740–84), who died too young to fill his full potential. His greatest building, the Royal Exchange (City Hall; 1779), was butchered to provide office space in the mid-19th century, but returned to its breathtaking splendour in a stunning 2000 restoration.

REGENCY & VICTORIAN

There is precious little 19th-century architecture, which is a reflection of the city's sharp decline. Francis Johnston (1760–1829) was unfortunate to miss out on the boom, which ended with the Act of Union 1801. His most famous building is the General Post Office (GPO; 1814; p103) on O'Connell St, although he's also well known for something he didn't do. When Parliament House was sold in 1803, on the proviso that it could never again be used for political assembly, Johnston was hired to adapt the building and he surreptitiously maintained the architectural integrity of the House of Lords. Cheers, Frank.

A rare Victorian highlight is the stunning series of curvilinear glasshouses at the National Botanic Gardens (p116), which were designed mid-century by the Dublin iron-master Richard Turner (1798–1881) and restored in 1995.

After Catholic Emancipation in 1829, there was a wave of church building, and later the two great Protestant cathedrals of Christ Church (p91) and St Patrick's (p96) were reconstructed. In a space between two Georgian houses on St Stephen's Green, Cardinal Newman commissioned his professor of fine arts at Newman University, John Hungerford Pollen (1820–1902), to create the splendidly ornate and incongruous Newman University Church (1856; p89), which was done in a Byzantine style simply because the cardinal was none too keen on the Gothic that was all the rage at the time.

Most of the public funds from the mid-18th to late-20th century were spent on providing sanitation and housing, and for the most part Dublin's architecture and infrastructure deteriorated. Perhaps a reflection on where priorities lay during this time, one of the best examples of high-Victorian architecture – and the one we've seen most of – is the magnificent Stag's Head pub (1895; p160) in Dame Ct, which has a dazzling interior of panelling, arcading, mirrors and stained glass.

MODERN ARCHITECTURE

The beginning of the 20th century was more about destroying notable buildings than erecting them; the GPO, Custom House and the Four Courts all became collateral damage in Ireland's rocky road to independence.

Coincidentally, one of Dublin's most majestic constructions – and the last great British building here – was the Royal College of Science (1904–22, p84), which was actually finished off after independence. It was massively and lavishly refurbished in the late 1980s to become the Government Buildings, and it was dubbed 'Taj MaHaughey' after the controversial Taoiseach of the time.

Sampling Sam Stephenson

One of the architects who designed the Electrical Supply Board (ESB) offices that broke up Dublin's 'Georgian Mile' – and a name synonymous with the 'rape of the city' in the 1970s and '80s – was Sam Stephenson who, to be fair, owes much of his notoriety to being in the right place (*in* with the government) at the wrong time (a government that happened to be more than a little dodgy). His two most infamous buildings are the Central Bank of Ireland (1975; Map p269-71) and the Dublin Corporation Offices (Phase I, 1976; Map pp266-8) at Wood Quay, neither of which he was allowed to complete for various reasons.

The Central Bank of Ireland is a bold geometric presence towering over today's Temple Bar. Although innovatively designed, its brutal bulkiness was controversially at odds with the low-rise old city it occupied. Furthermore, the building was left incomplete because brazen project managers exceeded the height limit and the roof had to be removed.

Even more vilified were the Dublin Corporation Offices he designed for Wood Quay. His original plan was for four squat towers descending towards the river and linked by a glass atrium but, not long after construction began, the remains of the Viking city were discovered, and so began several years of hurried excavations, court cases and much palaver. The corporation eventually went ahead with its plans – the archaeological treasure was sealed and the bunkers built – but bottled out halfway through and, compounding the damage, only completed half the plan. In the mid-1990s an extension was added to the original building, which proved popular among the public and critics alike. It's certainly easier on the eye, although we think it looks a bit like a camel.

The Dublin Airport terminal (1940; p228) was built by a consortium of architects and comprised a curved, Art Deco building that embraced incoming passengers. But it wasn't until Busáras Station (1953; Map pp264-5) that modernity really began to express itself in Dublin – amid howls of protest from a population unimpressed with its expense and stark appearance. It was designed by the influential Michael Scott, and is noteworthy for its pioneering glass facades and wave canopy roof. Locals still love it and loathe it in equal measure, but you have to admire its vigour and personality. A major revamp, mostly internal, will be completed by the end of 2004.

The tallest most denigrated structure is the shamefully shabby Liberty Hall (1965; Map pp264-5) on the quays. *This* is probably why the city shunned skyscrapers. Paul Koralek's bold and brazen Berkeley Library (1967; p78), in the grounds of Trinity College, is the most interesting construct to come out of 1960s Dublin.

The poorly regulated building boom of succeeding decades paid no attention to the country's architectural heritage and destroyed more than it created. There were no noble causes to blame this time around, just sheer stupidity. In the most notorious case of

Temple Bar

The state transport company spent much of the 1980s buying up the properties of Temple Bar (p79) to eventually clear them and build a huge bus depot. In the meantime, it rented out the properties it already owned to artists, musicians and cultural groups, and the area soon became Dublin's alternative, bohemian quarter. The community rallied against the proposed depot and convinced the government to launch the Temple Bar initiative instead. It was the flagship project of Dublin's year as European City of Culture in 1991 and in some ways marks the beginning of the capital's rebirth.

While many Dubliners preferred the area when it was ramshackle, genuinely boho and slightly edgy – before it became a holding pen for stag parties and hen nights – it's a hugely successful model of urban renewal thanks in part to the young Group 91 Architects who provided the frame for the project. Among the best new features are two public spaces (Meeting House Sq and Temple Bar Sq) and a curved street (Curved St!), while the Millennium Bridge opens up a splendid new vista of Eustace St.

While the quaint, brightly coloured tourist facades are inevitable, serious attempts have been made to retain the precinct's alternative vibe and many exceptional structures have been stitched into its grain. As you wander through, look out in particular for the interior of the Irish Film Centre (1992; p175), the Gallery of Photography (1996; p80), National Photographic Archives (1996; p80) and the Ark (1995; p80).

cultural vandalism, in 1970 the state-owned Electricity Supply Board (ESB) demolished 16 Georgian houses on Lower Fitzwilliam St to build its headquarters, breaking a unique mile-long Georgian streetscape. Adding insult to injury, after just 30-odd years the company is in the process of selling the building and shifting out to the suburbs.

The 1980s were a miserable time to be in Dublin: the city was in the jaws of a depression and seemed to be disintegrating into 100 shades of grey. The Temple Bar area was being left to waste away (see the boxed text above), and according to Frank McDonald, environment correspondent of the *Irish Times*, there wasn't a single private apartment available for sale in the centre of Dublin back then. In 2003 there were some 13,000 apartments and the city is *still* one of the lowest density capitals in Europe.

BOOM TOWN

Ireland's explosive growth during the 1990s was mostly focussed on its capital, where the tower cranes punched the sky triumphantly. Naturally enough, considering the breakneck speed of the developments, some opportunities were wasted. The International Financial Services Centre (IFSC; Map pp264-5), while mostly completed around the turn of the century, was conceived back in the late 1980s when Dublin was still desperate to appear modern. It is huge, it sparkles and it is remarkably unremarkable. The most interesting feature of the complex – a cylindrical timber-clad apartment block – is hidden away in the heart of the behemoth.

The Spire

The most controversial piece of modern architecture is the Spire (Monument of Light; 2003; p106) on O'Connell St, the heart of Dublin. A 120m-tall hollow cone that tapers from 3m wide at the base to 15cm wide at the top, it is by far the highest structure in the city. It's absolutely ridiculous, but it works. And your eye can't help but be drawn up and down its reflective brushed steel surface, which looks different in every light. Fortunately, it illuminates in dull, overcast conditions.

For the duration of the construction, a massive crane was parked outside the famous Clery's & Co department store. When the Spire was unveiled and the crane eventually removed, Dubliners took to singing, 'I can see Clery's now the crane has gone'.

More successful developments around Dublin include the Waterways Visitor Centre (1994; p100), which is colloquially known as the 'box in the docks' because the steel-framed, white-panelled structure appears to float. The Millennium Wing (2001; p86) of the National Gallery is a superb example of civic architecture, and has a compelling sculpted Portland stone facade and a tall, light-filled atrium.

Another terrific civic development is the Boardwalk (2001; Map pp269-71), a 450m-long promenade along the Liffey, which complements the new bridges, makes a feature of the river, and provides for a pleasant, occasionally even sunny, stroll away from the noise and the traffic fumes of the northern quays.

Entire areas have been earmarked for redevelopment, creating different centres around the city. One of the most ambitious is taking place around the previously dilapidated Smithfield market area (p107), which now has a stunning plaza (2000) and an old chimney that was converted into an observation tower and offers up fabulous views of historic Dublin. Flanking the square is a series of lofty lighting masts topped by gas braziers, which evoke a sense of the area's medieval past.

Another area being given a major makeover is the Grand Canal Docks (Map pp266-8), where historic warehouses are being restored and massive new residential and recreational development is underway. It is already the site of the striking 16-floor Charlotte Quay Apartments (1998), the tallest residential building in the country. The U2 Tower – so-called because the band's recording studio will occupy the top two floors – is a wild-looking, 60m twisted high-rise block slated for completion around 2007. The area is no doubt on the up (though it's a terrifying thought that U2 will still be recording by then).

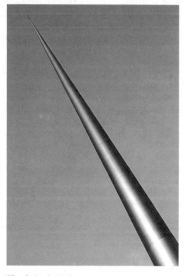

The Spire (p106)

Thankfully, work has also finally begun on the transformation of Dublin's most important and most neglected strip, O'Connell St (Map pp264-5), with the construction of a pedestrianised plaza beneath the Spire (see the boxed text on p48), a reduction in traffic lanes, and the provision of various street furniture with the likes of cafés, booths and shelter to make the street more user-friendly. You should start to see a major difference around here by 2005.

Bridges

In recent years, the city has literally and figuratively tried to bridge the gap between the north and south sides of Dublin by building several new crossings, remodelling or restoring others and illuminating them all at night.

The beautifully arched Ha'penny Bridge (1816; Map pp269-71) is *the* symbol of Dublin and got its popular name from the toll that used to be paid to cross the river. Prices have gone up so much in the last decade that one wag suggested we call it the 'four euro twenty cent bridge'. Next along is the distinctive O'Connell Bridge (1798 & 1880; Map pp269-71), as wide as it is long. Green and grand Grattan Bridge (1874; Map pp269-71) has ornate cast-iron lamps and is one of our favourites. It was recently widened and will soon feature a book market.

Of the new crossings, the simple, sturdy and elegant Millennium Footbridge (2000; Map pp269-71) impresses, while the James Joyce Bridge (2003; Map pp262-3) certainly catches the eye. The latter was the work of celebrated Spanish architect Santiago Calatrava and is a gleaming, white, futuristic construction with splayed arches (which local kids immediately took to sliding down, sending everyone into a tizz). It's supposed to 'set a standard for the new development of the area', but we reckon it looks absurdly out of place. Calatrava has been commissioned to build another bigger and even bolder bridge in the docklands, which should be open by early 2005.

In the meantime, yet another pedestrian bridge is being built near Custom House, one that will be able to swing open for maritime traffic. It will be the 16th bridge in the city.

Some of the most impressive works of recent times have been the superb restoration and redevelopments of wonderful buildings, such as the Royal Hospital Kilmainham (p96) Collins Barracks (p108), City Hall (p81) and Dublin Castle (p82).

The Guinness Brewery also commissioned a spectacular refit of its original Fermentation House (1904; p94) – reputedly the first steel-framed, multistorey building in the British Isles – an undertaking that some years ago would instead have seen the building torn down but for the prohibitive costs of demolition. It now houses the Guinness Storehouse (visitor centre 2001), which is designed around a pint-shaped atrium and topped with the circular, glass panelled Gravity Bar where you have awesome panoramic views of the city (which you can see through the bottom of the glass when you've finished your complementary pint).

Debate goes on about whether or not Dublin would benefit from skyscrapers and it's possible that some will be erected down by the Docklands area, where they wouldn't interfere with famously low-rise Dublin. There doesn't seem to be a call for them in the centre anyhow, as the trend of recent years has seen offices moving out. The only residential high-rises, seven notorious blocks of flats in Ballymun in Dublin's north, began to be demolished in 2003.

The slowdown in the growth of the economy has probably come at a good time for Dublin to take a breather, and for Dubliners to have another long, hard look at how their city is shaping up. Architectural integrity is a watchword these days, but only time will tell how well aesthetics and the needs of the burgeoning city are reconciled.

1 *Dame St at night (p79)*
2 *Guinness at O'Donoghue's (p161)*
3 *Street musicians on Grafton St (p75)*

1 *Dublin Castle (p82)* 2 *The Spire, O'Connell St (p106)* 3 *Central Bank of Ireland (p47)* 4 *Stained-glass windows, Christ Church Cathedral (p91)*

1 Custom House (p102)
2 St Patrick's Cathedral (p96)
3 Georgian doorways near Merrion Sq (p85) 4 Trinity College (p77)

1 Glasnevin Cemetery (p115)
2 James Clarence Mangan bust, St Stephen's Green (p90) 3 Fountain, Iveagh Gardens (p85) 4 Oscar Wilde statue, Merrion Sq (p89)

1 *Grand Canal (p99)* 2 *Formal garden, Irish Museum of Modern Art (p96)* 3 *Mountjoy Sq (p101)* 4 *Morning jog in Phoenix Park (p111)*

History

HISTORY

More than just about any other city we know, Dublin wears its history on its sleeve. The historical events and figures that so clearly and profoundly shape the modern capital are evoked on every street, etched on every surface, commemorated on every plinth and retold in every story.

Dubliners themselves are highly passionate scholars of their own history – and we mean their *own* history. Perhaps because it continues to have such a strong bearing on modern life, it's near impossible for any two Irish people to agree on the details of any one historical episode. However, they'll instantly unite against an outsider's version, and there are much greater contradictions between Irish and English historical accounts of events that took place here. Take Oliver Cromwell for example. An Irish text would describe him as an English parliamentarian who raped, pillaged and plundered his way through Ireland – a complete and utter bastard. If you picked up an English history book on the other hand you might learn that Cromwell defeated the Royalists in the English Civil War and *apparently* used to holiday in Ireland.

Government Buildings (p84)

On your travels, don't be surprised if you hear different spins on the same subjects and bear in mind that *everybody* has a bias – some are just cleverer at hiding it than others. See if you can spot ours.

THE RECENT PAST

Dublin hit the new millennium flying: the Celtic Tiger gave a last thundering roar and there was one more dazzling year of ostentatious consumption before the big cat went hoarse and talk of cutbacks and belt-tightening punctured the festive air. This is by no means to suggest that the capital is facing a return to the dark days of unemployment and emigration – widely believed to have been banished forever; rather in the last few years Dublin has been forced to return to a little reality.

The city's recent past can pretty much be summed up by the 120m-high Millennium Spire on its main and most central thoroughfare, O'Connell St. The monument was conceived in 1999 when reaching for the sky seemed like a level-headed proposition to some Dubliners. It was unveiled in 2003 when the mood called for something still hugely impressive but perhaps 25% lower.

TIMELINE	8000 BC	4000 BC	500 BC
	The first humans arrive in Ireland, after the last Ice Age ends	Farming introduced to Ireland	Celtic people begin to settle in Ireland

FROM THE BEGINNING

EARLY FOOTPRINTS & CELTIC HIGHWAYS

Stone-Age farmers who arrived in Ireland around 4000 BC provided the country's genetic stock and lay the foundations of its agricultural economy. During the following Bronze Age, in addition to discovering and crafting metals to stock the future National Museum, they also found time to refine their farming techniques and raise livestock.

Iron-Age warriors from Eastern Europe, known as the Celts, arrived around 500 BC and divided Ireland into provinces and myriad districts ruled by chieftains. Their society was ruled by Brehon Law, the tenets of which still form the basis of Ireland's ethical code today. Roads connecting these provinces converged at a ford over the River Liffey called Áth Cliath (Ford of the Hurdles) and the settlement that grew up at this junction was to give Dublin its Irish name, Baile Áth Cliath (Town of the Hurdle Ford).

THE COMING OF CHRISTIANITY

As legend has it, Christianity came to Ireland in 432 in the form of St Patrick who began converting the locals to the religion of Rome, and baptising them himself at the site where St Patrick's Cathedral now stands. The new creed was firmly entrenched by the 6th century when monastic settlements flourished around a tidal pool in the estuary of the River Poddle known as Dubh Linn (Black Pool), from which the city took its English name.

Monasteries became hugely important centres of learning and were, in effect, Europe's first universities. They supported a golden age of Gaelic Christianity when stunning works of art such as the Book of Kells and Ardagh Chalice were produced. No doubt this creative burst was helped along by the monks' new-found expertise at brewing ale.

THE VIKINGS

The Celts had it easy for around a millennium and the monasteries thrived in the relative peace of the time. That changed in the 9th and 10th centuries with the arrival of the Vikings, the first to urbanise Dublin in any significant way. Raids from the north had become a fact of Irish life, with Norse longboats attacking monasteries and settlements along the coast and rivers and making off with whatever loot – and local women – they could carry.

To aid them in their plundering ways the Vikings built a harbour (or *longphort*) on the banks of the Liffey in 837. Although a Celtic army forced them out some 65 years later, they returned in 917 with a massive fleet, established a stronghold (or *dun*) by the black pool at Wood Quay (behind Christ Church Cathedral), and dug their heels in.

Happy Birthday Dublin

Perhaps figuring that Dubliners needed cheering up after the economic doom and gloom of the 1980s, city fathers decided to celebrate Dublin's millennium in 1988, which marked the *approximate* time when the Vikings set up camp.

They went back to plundering the countryside but also laid down guidelines on plot sizes and town boundaries for their town of 'Dyflinn', which became the most prominent trading centre in the Viking world. But their good times came to an end in 1014 when an alliance of Irish clans led by Brian Ború decisively whupped them at the Battle of Clontarf, forever breaking the Scandinavian grip on the eastern seaboard. Rather than abandoning the place in defeat, however, the Vikings liked Dublin so much that they decided to stay and integrate.

432 AD	837	1014	1169
St Patrick begins to convert the Irish to Christianity	Vikings set up harbour	Brian Ború defeats the Vikings in Battle of Clontarf	Arrival of the Normans, led by Strongbow

THE NORMANS

During a century or so with no new foreign invaders to repel, the restless Irish clans fough among themselves. The Normans, former Vikings themselves, had completed their con quest of Britain by the mid-12th century but had showed little interest in following thei distant cousins to Ireland. That all changed after the King of Leinster invited them over t help sort out his own squabbles.

When the Anglo-Normans arrived in 1169, led by Richard de Clare (better known a Strongbow), they were so taken with the place that they decided to stay. They took Dubli the following year, and essentially kept it for the following 750 years. Strongbow inherite the kingship of Leinster – of which modern Dublin is capital – and made himself at home The English king, Henry II, soon sent his own army over to keep an eye on Strongbow an his consorts who, he reckoned, were 'more Irish than the Irish themselves'.

The Anglo-Normans set about reconstructing and fortifying the captured city. In 117: construction began on Christ Church Cathedral and 20 years later, work began on S Patrick's Cathedral a few hundred metres to the south. Dublin soon became a pilgrimag city, particularly because it housed the *bacall Íosa* (staff of Jesus).

Henry II's son, King John, commissioned the construction of Dublin Castle in 120 '...for the safe custody of our treasure...and the defence of the city'. As capital of the Eng lish 'colony' in Ireland, Dublin expanded. Trade was organised and craft guilds developed although membership was limited to those of 'English name and blood'.

For all their might, the Anglo-Normans' dominance was limited to a walled area sur rounding what today is loosely Greater Dublin and was then called 'the Pale'. Beyond th pale – a phrase that entered the English language to mean 'beyond convention' – Irelan remained unbowed and unconquered.

As Dublin grew bigger so did its problems, and over the next few centuries misery seemed to pile upon mishap. In 1317 Ireland's worst famine of the Middle Ages killed of thousands and reduced some to cannibalism. In 1348 it was decimated by the Black Death the devastating recurrence of which over the following century indicates the terrible squalo of medieval Dublin.

In the 15th century, the English extended their influence beyond the pale by cleverl throwing their weight behind the dominant Irish lords. The atmosphere was becoming markedly cosier as the Anglo-Norman occupiers began to follow previous invaders by integrating into Irish culture.

THE TUDORS & THE PROTESTANT ASCENDANCY

Henry VIII ascended to the throne in 1509 and soon put a stop to that by snubbing the lord and decreeing absolute royal power over Ireland. In 1534 the most powerful of Leinster' Anglo-Normans, 'Silken' Thomas Fitzgerald, renounced his allegiance to Henry VIII an launched a rebellion against Dublin Castle. He could hardly have estimated the ferocit with which Henry came after him: a huge army was dispatched to confiscate his lands an the young Fitzgerald was hanged, drawn and quartered the following year. Henry ordere the surrender of all lands to the English Crown and, three years later, after his spat wit Rome, he dissolved all the monasteries and all Church lands passed to the newly constitute Anglican Church. Dublin was declared an Anglican City and relics such as the *bacall Íos* were destroyed.

Elizabeth I (1533–1603) was crowned in 1558 and her rule was marked by repeated an ruthless efforts to finally bring the Irish to heel. The Crown met with most resistance from the province of Ulster, which became the last outpost of the Irish chiefs. The Irish fought dog gedly under the lead of Hugh O'Neill, the Earl of Tyrone, but were defeated in 1603. O'Neil

1204	1317	1348	1534
Construction of Dublin Castle is commissioned	Ireland's worst famine of the Middle Ages	Black Death arrives in Ireland for the first time	'Silken' Thomas Fitzgerald's rebellion put down and Henry VIII orders the surrender of all lands to the English Crown

chieved a Pyrrhic victory of sorts, refusing to surrender until Elizabeth had died. The chiefs led the country in what came to be known as the Flight of the Earls. This defeat sounded the death knell for Gaelic Ireland and the country was set for total Anglicisation.

After Elizabeth's reign, the country was colonised through Plantation. Loyal Protestants from England and Scotland were awarded the rich agricultural, confiscated lands of Ulster, which sowed the seeds of the bitter divisions that blight the province to this day. Unlike previous invaders, the Tudors never integrated.

Although most of the Irish were now disenfranchised and reduced to a state of near misery, Dublin prospered as the bulwark of English domination and became a bastion of Protestantism. A chasm developed between the 'English' city and the Irish countryside where there was continuing unrest and growing resentment. After winning the English Civil War, the battle-happy Cromwell came to Ireland to personally reassert English control and while Protestant Dublin was untouched, Cromwell's troops murdered, raped, looted and burned their way up and down the eastern coast.

GEORGIAN DUBLIN & THE GOLDEN AGE

After 1660 when Charles II (1630–85) was restored to the English Crown, Dublin embarked upon a century of unparalleled development and essentially waved two fingers to the rest of Ireland which was being brought to its grubby Catholic knees. In 1690 the rest of Ireland backed the losing side once more when it took up arms for the Catholic king of England James II (1633–1701), who was ultimately defeated by the Protestant William of Orange at the Battle of the Boyne, not far from Dublin, in 1690.

William's victory ushered in the punitive Penal Code, which stripped Catholics of most basic rights in a single, sweeping legislative blow. Again however, the country's misfortune proved the capital's gain as the city was flooded with landless refugees willing to work for a pittance. The end of the century also saw an influx of Huguenot weavers, who settled in Dublin after fleeing anti-Protestant legislation in France and established a successful cloth industry that helped fuel the city's growth.

With plenty of cash to go around and an eagerness to live in a city that reflected their new-found wealth, the Protestant nobility overhauled Dublin. Speculators bought up swathes of land and commissioned substantial projects of urban renewal, including the creation of new streets, the laying out of city parks and the construction of magnificent new buildings and residences (see p45).

It was impossible to build in the heart of the medieval city, so the nouveau riche moved north across the river, creating a new Dublin of stately squares surrounded by fine Georgian mansions. The elegantly made-over Dublin became the second city in the British Empire and the fifth largest in Europe.

> ## Top Five Books on Dublin History
>
> - *Dublin – One Thousand Years*, Stephen Conlon
> - *Dublin – A Celebration*, Pat Liddy
> - *44 – A Dublin Memoir*, Peter Sheridan
> - *Dublin Made Me*, CS 'Todd' Andrews
> - *Encyclopaedia of Dublin*, Douglas Bennett

Dublin's teeming, mostly Catholic slums soon spread north in pursuit of the rich, who turned back south to grand new homes around Merrion Sq, St Stephen's Green and Fitzwilliam Sq. In 1745, when James Fitzgerald, the earl of Kildare, started construction of Leinster House, his magnificent mansion south of the Liffey, he was mocked his foolish move into the wilds. 'Where I go society will follow,' he confidently predicted and was soon proved right. Today Leinster House is used as the Irish Parliament and is in modern Dublin's centre.

1603	1605	1660	1690
Irish chiefs are defeated, leading to the Flight of the Earls	Start of Plantation, in which the English colonise Ulster and assume ownership of land	Charles II restored to the Crown and Dublin's resurgence begins	Battle of the Boyne

DUBLIN'S DECLINE & CATHOLIC EMANCIPATION

The constant migration from the countryside into Dublin meant that by the end of the 18th century, the capital had a Catholic majority. Influenced by the principles of the French Revolution of 1789, many influential Irish figures began to foment revolt against English rule. Rebellion was in the air at the turn of the century, starting with the abortive French-backed invasion by Dubliner Wolfe Tone and the United Irishmen in 1798 and the idealistic insurgence led by Robert Emmet (1778–1803) in 1803 (see the boxed text below).

It was only a matter of time before Dublin's bubble burst and the pin came in the form of the 1801 Act of Union, which dissolved the Irish parliament and reintroduced direct rule from Westminster. Many of the upper classes fled to London and the dramatic growth that had characterised Dublin in the previous century came to an almost immediate halt, and the city fell into a steady decline.

While Dublin was licking its wounds, a Kerry lawyer by the name of Daniel O'Connell (1775–1847) launched his campaign to recover basic rights for Catholics, achieving much with the Catholic Emancipation Act of 1829. The 'Liberator', as he came to be known, became the first Catholic lord mayor of Dublin in 1841.

History – From the Beginning

Robert Emmet

In 1803 Robert Emmet (1778–1803), a Corkman educated at Trinity College, organised just one of the idealistic and romantic but ill-conceived and badly planned rebellions for which occupied Ireland was renowned. He was tried for treason, hanged and buried in a secret location, but before reaching his expiry date Emmet guaranteed his immortality by delivering one of the most eloquent and rousing speeches in Irish history. 'When my country takes her place among the nations of the earth, then shall my character be vindicated, then may my epitaph be written' is its most famous line and the Irish still debate whether or not it's time to write his epitaph (while spoil sports raise the question: who was the amazing note-taker who recorded his 4000 words?).

THE FAMINE & ENGLAND'S SHAME

Rural Ireland had become overwhelmingly dependent on the easily grown potato. When it was hit by potato blight in 1845, it was the beginning of the country's greatest disaster. The crops failed dismally for the next three years; 1847, the third consecutive year, was apocalyptic and has been remembered through the ages as 'Black 47'. The human cost was cataclysmic: more than one million people died from disease and starvation while more again fled the country, preferring to take their chances on 'coffin ships' riddled with disease than remain in their god-forsaken homeland. The damage was compounded by the shamefully *laissez faire* attitude of the British government and the landlords who continued to extract rents and export food *out* of the country while incarcering the poor in workhouses and prisons for defaulting on their rents.

As Britain continued to rule with an iron fist, opposition to its rule hardened. The famine, the deaths and the mass exodus changed the social and cultural structure of Ireland profoundly and left a scar on the Irish psyche that cannot be overestimated.

Although Dublin escaped the worst effects of the famine, its streets and squares became overcrowded with desperate migrants. Wealthier citizens began moving southwards to the more salubrious suburbs along the coast, made accessible by Ireland's first railway line which was built in 1834 to connect the city and present-day Dun Laoghaire. The flight from the city continued for the next 70 years and many of the fine Georgian residences became slum dwellings. By 1910 it was reckoned that 20,000 Dublin families each occupied a single

1695	1759	1798	1801
Penal laws prohibit Catholics from buying property	Guinness Brewery founded	Unsuccessful United Irishmen rebellion, led by Wolfe Tone	Act of Union precipitates Dublin's demise

room. Booze had long been a source of solace for Dubliners but alcohol abuse became a huge social problem.

THE BLOSSOMING OF NATIONAL PRIDE

Early-20th-century Dublin was staunchly divided along sectarian lines and, although Catholics were still partly second-class citizens, a burgeoning Catholic middle class provided the impetus for Ireland's march towards independence.

It was the dashing figure of Protestant landlord Charles Stewart Parnell (1846–91), from County Meath, that first harnessed the broad public support for Home Rule. Elected to Westminster in 1875, the 'Uncrowned King of Ireland' campaigned tirelessly for land reform and a Dublin parliament.

He appeared to have an ally in British prime minister, William Gladstone, who lightened the burden on tenants by passing Land Acts enabling them to buy property. He also agreed on Ireland's need for some form of self-government, although British opposition was galvanised following the murder in 1882 of two high-ranking English officials in the Phoenix Park by an obscure revolutionary group called the 'Invincibles'. Gladstone tried to pass the Home Rule Bill three times between 1886 and 1895 but it was defeated in the House of Lords each time (after which the Lords' ability to kill a bill was limited to three times).

Parnell himself suffered a swift fall from grace after it was made public that he had been having an affair with a married woman, Kitty O'Shea. Castigated by the Church and the morally indignant, he was ditched as leader of his own party. He fought unstintingly to regain his reputation but died of pneumonia within two years of the scandal. Dublin seemed to forgive him and turned out in droves for his funeral.

In the twilight of the 19th century there was a move to preserve all things Irish. The Gaelic Athletic Association (GAA) was set up in 1884 to promote Irish sports while Douglas Hyde and Eoin McNeill formed the Gaelic League in 1893 to encourage Irish arts and language. The success of the Gaelic League paved the way for the Celtic Revival Movement, spearheaded by WB Yeats and Lady Gregory who founded the Abbey Theatre in 1904.

THE STRUGGLE FOR INDEPENDENCE

Irish culture was thriving at the start of the 20th century but the country was still in Westminster's headlock, and peaceful efforts to free itself from British rule were thwarted at every juncture. Dublin had the worst slums in Europe, and the emergence of militant trade unionism introduced a socialist agenda to the struggle for self-determination.

In 1905 Arthur Griffith (1871–1922) founded a new political movement known as Sinn Féin (We Ourselves), which sought to achieve home rule through passive resistance rather than political lobbying. It urged the Irish to withhold taxes and its MPs to form an Irish government in Dublin.

Meanwhile, trade union leaders Jim Larkin and James Connolly agitated against low wages and corporate greed. This culminated in the Great Lockout of 1913 (see the boxed text on p66), which was marked by state-sponsored violence and the establishment of the Irish Citizen Army (ICA) by Connolly to defend the striking workers. Things were hotting up in Dublin.

In 1914 Westminster passed a Home Rule bill but suspended its implementation for the duration of WWI. Bowing to pressure from the Protestant-dominated north where 140,000 members of the newly formed Ulster Volunteer Force (UVF) swore to resist any efforts to weaken British rule, the bill made provisions for the partition of Ireland. In response, nationalists in the south established the Irish Volunteer Force (IVF) but when WWI broke

1829	1841	1845–51	1875
Daniel O'Connell achieves Catholic emancipation	O'Connell becomes first Catholic lord mayor of Dublin	Great Potato Famine	Parnell elected to parliament

out, the majority of them enlisted in the British Army thinking they would return to an independent Ireland.

Some 180,000 Irish volunteers fought, including many committed nationalists who thought they would help Ireland in the long run by aiding Britain now. By the end of the Great War, almost 50,000 Irish citizens had died.

'Big Jim' Larkin & the Great Lockout of 1913

Of all the statues on O'Connell St, the most dramatic is that of James 'Big Jim' Larkin (1876–1947), the leading figure of the Irish labour movement and the driving force behind the greatest showdown between employers and workers in Dublin's history.

It began on 21 August 1913, when 100 employees of the Tramways Company were dismissed for being members of Larkin's Irish Transport & General Workers' Union (ITGWU), which had been a thorn in the side of the Dublin Employers Federation since its foundation in 1909. William Martin Murphy, media tycoon and owner of the Tramways Company, was eager to crush them once and for all.

At precisely 10am on 26 August – the opening day of the busiest festival of the social calendar, the Dublin Horse Show – ITGWU workers pinned their union badges on and 'downed tools', leaving crowded trams stranded and the city in commotion. Larkin made a rousing speech from a window of Liberty Hall, urging the crowd to fight for their 'bread and butter', and promising to address a huge meeting on O'Connell St on 28 August even though it had been banned.

Dublin waited keenly to see if Larkin would keep his promise; the street was crowded with workers and lined with hundreds of police. A bearded man suddenly appeared on the balcony of Murphy's own hotel, removed the false beard and spoke to the crowd. Larkin had kept his promise and the crowd went wild. He was immediately arrested – later imprisoned for a month – while the police launched a ferocious baton charge on the crowd, injuring more than 200.

A month later almost 30,000 workers were locked out for refusing to sign a pledge against the ITGWU. The next February after a harsh winter marked by police brutality, dreadful suffering and fights with 'scab' workers, the strike was called off. Although Murphy claimed victory, trade unionism became a vital force in Irish labour relations and Larkin is fondly remembered as the champion of the people. Murphy, on the other hand, urged the British government to execute James Connolly, hero of the 1916 Easter Rising, in his newspaper the *Irish Independent* and helped create a martyr that turned the tide of public opinion towards revolution.

THE 1916 EASTER RISING

The more radical factions within Sinn Féin, the IVF and the ICA saw Britain's difficulty as Ireland's opportunity, and planned to rise up against the Crown on Easter Sunday, 1916. In typical fashion, the rhetoric of the rebellion was far superior to the planning.

When the head of the IVF, Eoin McNeill, got wind of the plans, he published an advertisement in the newspaper cancelling the planned 'manoeuvres'. The leaders rescheduled the revolution for the following day but word never spread beyond the capital, where a motley band of about a thousand rebels assembled and seized strategic buildings. The main garrison was the General Post Office (GPO), outside which the poet and school teacher Pádraig Pearse (see the boxed text opposite) read out the Proclamation of the Republic.

The British Army didn't take the insurgence seriously at first but after a few soldiers were killed, they sent a gunboat down the Liffey to rain shells on the rebels. After six days of fighting the city centre was ravaged and the death toll stood at 300 civilians, 130 British troops (many of whom were Irish) and 60 rebels.

The rebels, prompted by Pearse's fear of further civilian casualties, surrendered and were arrested. Crowds gathered to mock and jeer them as they were led away. Initially, Dubliners resented them for the damage they had caused in their futile rising. Then, in a cruel and monumental miscalculation, Britain executed all the leaders at Kilmainham Gaol.

1882	1884	1890s	1904
Phoenix Park murders	Gaelic Athletic Association (GAA) is established	Celtic Revival Movement intensifies pride in all things Irish	Abbey Theatre is established by WB Yeats and Lady Gregory

Pádraig H Pearse & the Blood Sacrifice

It is doubtful that the leaders of the Rising thought they could achieve anything more than a symbolic victory. One of its ringleaders, the poet and devoted patriot Pádraig Pearse, was convinced of the need for 'blood sacrifice'. During the oration at the funeral of another Irish rebel, O'Donovan Rossa, he said, 'Life springs from death, and from the graves of patriotic men and women spring living nations.' Pearse was a visionary with his head in the clouds, not a military man, and the ragtag brigade that turned up for the Rising couldn't have had much of an idea of what he was banging on about. Each of the signatories of the proclamation would have known that by putting their name to that document they were virtually condemning themselves to certain death when the insurrection failed.

Among those shot was 18-year-old Willie Pearse whose main crime was being the brother of Pádraig. James Connolly, the hero of the working man, was severely injured during the Rising and then detained at the military hospital in Dublin Castle. At dawn on 12 May, he was taken by ambulance to Kilmainham Gaol, carried on a stretcher into the prison yard, strapped into a chair and executed by firing squad. This was too much for Dublin to bear; the British had made a fatal mistake and passive sympathy for the rebels turned to passionate support.

THE WAR OF INDEPENDENCE

In the 1918 general election, the radical Sinn Féin won three-quarters of the Irish seats. Its members thumbed their noses to Westminster, declared independence and in May 1919 established the first Dáil Éireann (Irish Assembly) in Dublin's Mansion House. The assembly was led by Eamon de Valera, who had been spared the firing squad in 1916 because of his US birth (so killing him would have been a public relations disaster). This was effectively a declaration of war.

Mindful that they could never match the British on the battlefield, Sinn Féin's military wing – made up of Irish Volunteers now renamed the Irish Republican Army (IRA) – began attacking arms dumps and barracks in guerrilla strikes. The British countered by strengthening the Royal Irish Constabulary (RIC) and introducing a brutal, unforgiving auxiliary force made up of returning WWI servicemen known as the Black and Tans (after the colour of their uniforms).

They met their match in Michael Collins, the IRA's commander and a master of guerrilla warfare. Although the British knew his name, Collins masterfully concealed his identity and throughout the war was able to freewheel around the city on his bicycle like he didn't have a care in the world.

On 10 November 1920, Collins learned that 14 undercover British intelligence operatives known as the 'Cairo Gang' had just arrived in Dublin. The following morning, he had his own crack squad ('the Apostles') assassinate each one of them as they lay in their beds.

Furious and unrestrained, the British retaliated that afternoon by opening fire on the crowd at a hurling match at Croke Park. Ten spectators and the captain of the Tipperary

Women of the Revolution

The 1916 Proclamation was a radical document for its day, and called for equal rights between men and women (Britain only gave women full suffrage in 1928). Two key reasons for this were Countess Markievicz (1868–1927) and Maud Gonne (1865–1953), two Englishwomen who inspired a generation of revolutionaries. Committed republican and socialist Countess Markievicz was a military leader of the 1916 Easter Rising and went on to become a minister in the first government. Maud Gonne was also a staunch republican who is perhaps better known as WB Yeats' gorgeous muse (and desperately unrequited love).

1904	1913	1916	1919–21
16 June is immortalised in James Joyce's *Ulysses*	Jim Larkin leads workers in the Great Lockout	Easter Rising	War of Independence

hurling team, Michael Hogan, were killed (the main stand at Croke Park is named after Hogan). 'Bloody Sunday', as it became known, served to quash any moral doubts over the often brutal tactics adopted by the IRA.

The fighting was worst in the province of Munster, particularly west Cork and other rural areas, where the legendary 'flying columns' achieved notable success with their hit-and-run tactics. Dublin was comparatively calm although ambushes and street shootings were frequent, and the heavy military presence raised tensions. In May 1921, Irish rebels struck a blow against the British civil service when they burned down the Custom House. Although obviously a military act, tens of thousands of hesitant Dublin taxpayers rejoiced at the burning of the tax records.

The struggle reached a stalemate and as foreign pressure was brought to bear on British Prime Minister Lloyd George to resolve the issue one way or the other, a truce was signed on 11 July 1921. Unknown to the British government, the IRA had been on the verge of collapse.

CIVIL WAR

The terms of – and the circumstances surrounding – the Treaty that ended the War of Independence make up the single most divisive episode in Irish politics, one that still breeds prejudice, inflames passions and shapes the political landscape of the whole island.

De Valera sent a reluctant Michael Collins over to London to head the party, a move which made little sense considering Collins' inexperience and the loss of his most valuable asset, his anonymity. Some believe that de Valera knew that only limited independence was on the table and wanted to disassociate himself from it.

After months of argument and facing the threat of, in the words of Lloyd George, an 'immediate and terrible war', Collins and the Irish team signed the Anglo-Irish Treaty on 6 December 1921. Instead of establishing the Irish Republic for which the IRA had fought, it created an Irish Free State, effectively a British dominion. But much worse from a nationalist perspective, it paved the way for the partitioning of Ireland. Although Collins was dissatisfied with the deal, he hoped it would be the 'first real step' towards a republic. Nevertheless, he foresaw trouble and remarked prophetically, 'I've just signed my own death warrant.'

De Valera vehemently opposed the Treaty and the two erstwhile comrades were pitted against one another in pro-Treaty and anti-Treaty camps. Although the Dáil narrowly ratified the Treaty and the electorate accepted it by a large majority, Ireland slid into Civil War in June 1922. It began when Anti-Treaty IRA forces occupied Dublin's Four Courts and were shelled by pro-Treaty forces led by Collins. Ironically, the capital suffered far more during the Civil War than it had during the War of Independence a year earlier.

One of the many tragedies of the Civil War was the assassination of Collins by anti-Treaty forces in his home county of Cork on 22 August. Many more deaths followed with the Dáil introduction of a mandatory death sentence for any IRA member caught in possession of a gun. Robert Erskine Childers – whose yacht, the *Asgard,* had brought arms for the republican cause to Howth in 1914 – was executed for possessing a revolver given to him by Collins. After 11 months and about 3000 deaths (including 77 state executions), de Valera ordered the IRA to drop their arms.

THE IRISH REPUBLIC

Ireland finally entered a phase of peace. Without an armed struggle to pursue – at least not one pursued by the majority – the IRA became a marginalised force in independent Ireland

1920	1921	1922	1936
First Bloody Sunday, when British forces kill 11 people in a reprisal at Croke Park	Anglo-Irish Treaty leads to the partition of the island into the Irish Free State and Northern Ireland	Civil War breaks out; Michael Collins is killed	After refusing to disarm, the IRA is outlawed

nd Sinn Féin fell apart. In 1926, de Valera created a new party, Fianna Fáil (Soldiers of Destiny), which has dominated Irish politics ever since.

Over the following decades, Fianna Fáil gradually eliminated most of the clauses of he Treaty with which they had disagreed (including the oath). In 1932, a freshly painted Dublin hosted the 31st Eucharistic Congress, which drew visitors from around the world. The Catholic Church began to wield disproportionate control over the affairs of the state; contraception was made illegal in the 1930s and the age of consent was raised from 16 to 7. In 1936, when the IRA refused to disarm, de Valera had it banned.

The Victor's Version

Eamon de Valera (1882–1975) went on to have a long political career as Taoiseach and president, and he more than anybody shaped the conservative and predominantly Catholic nature of 20th-century Ireland. He left public life only in 1973, aged 91, the oldest head of state in the world.

The 'long fellow', as he was affectionately known, was idolised during his life when the majority of people sided with him over the divisive issue of the Treaty. Ludicrously, Michael Collins was seen by many, if not most, as a traitor. Now, even if your father was chairman of the Fianna Fáil party, you'd have to concede that Collins was the greatest figure in Irish history. This imbalance has been redressed in recent decades although some people have gone too far with the backlash, including Neil Jordan in his epic film *Michael Collins* who took it upon himself to revise history and depict de Valera as a weasel and a sneak.

Although Ireland remained neutral during WWII – as a way of pushing its independence – Dublin's north strand was hit by a 500lb German bomb on 31 May 1941, killing more than 40 and injuring 90.

Despite having done much of the groundwork, Fianna Fáil lost out to its rivals Fine Gael, descendants of the original Free State government, on declaring the state a republic in 1949.

THE STROLL TO MODERNISATION

Sean Lemass succeeded de Valera as Taoiseach in 1959 and set about fixing the Irish economy, which he did so effectively that the rate of emigration soon halved. While neighbouring London was swinging in the '60s, Dublin was definitely swaying. Youngsters from rural communities poured into the expanding city and it seemed like the good times were never going to end. But, almost inevitably, the economy slid back into recession.

On the 50th anniversary of the 1916 Easter Rising, Nelson's Pillar on O'Connell St was partially blown up by the IRA and crowds cheered as the remainder was removed the following week. Republicanism was still prevalent and a new round of the 'troubles' were about to flair up in the north. Dublin was hardly touched by the sectarian tensions that would pull Northern Ireland asunder over the next three decades, although 25 people died after three loyalist car bombs exploded in the city in 1974.

Ireland joined the forerunner to the European Union (EU) in 1973 and got a significant leg-up from its coffers over the following decades. Pope John Paul II popped over for a few days in 1979 and more than one million people flocked to Phoenix Park to hear him say Mass. Political instability and an international recession forced the country deeper into the doldrums in the early 1980s and high emigration returned. But perhaps the two greatest factors holding Ireland back at this stage were the stranglehold of the ultra-conservative Catholic Church and the crookedness of many of its elected officials.

1937	1949	1973	1974
Irish constitution renames the country Eire and prioritises Roman Catholicism as the majority religion	Republic of Ireland declared	Ireland joins the EEC (later renamed the EU)	Three loyalist car bombs explode in Dublin, killing 25 people

CONTEMPORARY IRELAND

In the 1990 presidential election, the political shoo-in was brought down by a fairly minor scandal and Mary Robinson, a lawyer with liberal, leftist tendencies, swept to victory as part of a largely apolitical rainbow coalition. She helped shake the parochialism out of the Irish and made them feel like they were part of a young and modern nation.

In 1992, Taoiseach Charlie Haughey resigned in a phone tapping scandal, which proved to be only the tip of an iceberg of corruption involving him and many of his cronies that is still being mined through various tribunals.

The same year brought the infamous 'X Case', when a young Dublin woman who was impregnated after being raped by a family friend was stopped by the High Court from going to England to have an abortion. The Supreme Court ruled against this cruel constraint enraging Ireland's right-wing element and the all-powerful Church, which alienated many of its moderates through its fanaticism on the issue. In the following years, the Church was disgraced after a cavalcade of scandals involving sexual abuse, paedophilia, cover-ups a bishop's child and untold exposés of gross hypocrisy.

Sean McBride

Maud Gonne's son, Sean McBride (1904–88), was one of the most extraordinary characters of 20th-century Ireland. In his long career, he was the trusted teenage messenger of Michael Collins, an anti-Treaty fighter in the Civil War, chief of staff of the IRA in the mid-1930s, a successful Dublin barrister, foreign minister in the government that declared Ireland a republic, an esteemed statesman and diplomat, a cofounder of Amnesty International (and its chairman for 14 years) and a joint Nobel Peace Prize winner in 1974. He eventually ran out of steam in Dublin in 1988.

Abortion is still illegal here although women are – thanks only to a referendum – free to receive information about it and to travel to England for the procedure, a slightly hypocritical state of affairs to say the least. In a 1995 referendum, divorce was accepted by the skinniest possible margin.

No doubt helped along by this progressive thinking and the shedding of old ways, the country's economic fortunes changed dramatically paving the way for the so-called Celtic Tiger and the greatest transformation of Dublin since Georgian times.

1990	1990s	1992	2001
Mary Robinson is elected president	Irish economy booms like never before	Charlie Haughey resigns in a phone-tapping scandal, and the 'X Case' polarises people on the issue of abortion	Celtic Tiger era is declared over

Neighbourhoods

Neighbourhoods

Despite its remarkable reputation, Dublin city is actually quite small and compact. It ha a clear focus and is a walker's delight. While pub-life might be the biggest draw for some there are many superb sights that will leave even committed teetotallers feeling a littl light-headed, particularly if they're into Irish history and culture. The vast majority of th sights are conveniently clustered around the city centre, while the ones that demand a littl legwork are genuinely worth the effort.

To make the city even more navigable, we've broken it down into nine hefty portions six of which are on the south side of the River Liffey where the vast majority of Dublin' tourist life is lived. Around Grafton St covers the area surrounding Dublin's main recrea tional thoroughfare, Temple Bar is its designated tourist heart and SoDa its cutting edge Georgian Dublin is a large sprawling area surrounding Merrion Sq and St Stephen's Green containing many of Ireland's national mu-

seums. Kilmainham & the Liberties, to the west of the city centre, are laden with sights and character but light on social opportunities. Beyond the Grand Canal are the inner southern suburbs, which are exactly the opposite.

On the north side of the Liffey, Around O'Connell Street encompasses most of the inner north, while Smithfield & Phoenix Park takes in the northwest. Beyond the Royal Canal are workaday Dublin, which has a host of very impressive sights. Further out still, in both directions, are seaside suburbs that are well worth a look (see the Excursions chapter, p209).

ITINERARIES

One Day

Start your express tour on **O'Connell St** (p101). Here you'll see the juxtaposition of Dublin old and new with the **Spire** (p106) and the **General Post Office** (GPO; p103), where the modern nation began. Walk across the Liffey, through **Trinity College** (p77), up **Grafton St** (p67 and left along and past **St Stephen's Green** (p89) for an eyeful of Georgian Dublin. After an earl lunch on Lower Baggot St, before the office workers break, head to the museums aroun **Leinster House** (p85) for a quick dip into Irish culture. Spend the rest of your day soaking u the atmosphere of a traditional Irish pub, preferably **Doheny & Nesbitt's** (p160).

Three Days

Devote a morning to the wonderful **Chester Beatty Library** (p81). Check out the restored **City Ha** (p81) and wander through the grounds of **Dublin Castle** (p82) while you're in the neighbourhood Cross Dame St for a treat at the **Queen of Tarts café** (p131). **Christ Church Cathedral** (p91) is nearby, as i **St Patrick's** (p96), if you can handle two churches in a row. You're inching closer to the **Guinnes Storehouse** (p93) if you fancy paying homage to Dublin's finest drink and seeing a panorama c Dublin from its glassed **Gravity Bar** (p93). You're also heading in the direction of the evocativ **Kilmainham Gaol** (p94), a must if you have *any* interest in Irish history. Head to the north sid on your third day, clocking the **Four Courts** (p110) and then wandering through **Smithfield** (p107 hich is a blend of historical working-class character and 21st-century pizzazz. You could roll along the relatively new Boardwalk along the Liffey, and head up O'Connell St again, to arnell Sq, and specifically the **Dublin Writers Museum** (p103) and the **Hugh Lane Gallery** (p103). Head ack south side to hip and happening **SoDa** (p80) for dinner and drinks.

ne Week

f you've got the luxury of a week you can afford half an hour to queue for a ticket to see e magnificent **Book of Kells** (p76). Savour the unforgettably Irish experience of a Gaelic match t **Croke Park** (p115). If you're young and up for some wild drinking, head to Temple Bar at ny time of the day or week. If you're, eh, not…take in the cultural sights of Dublin's tour- t quarter during the day and its nocturnal delight on a week night only. You should also avour some music, either a traditional session or a gig recommended in Hot Press (p240). pend one of your days visiting the cluster of sights just beyond the Royal Canal, namely the AA museum (p115), a walking tour of **Glasnevin Cemetery** (p115) and the bewitching **Casino at Marino** 114). Walk along the quays or take the bus to **Phoenix Park** (p107) and see Dubliners at play. xplore the seaside suburbs of **Howth** (p222), **Malahide** (p224) and **Dalkey** (p225), all within easy each of the centre by DART (see p232 for alterations to DART weekend services).

RGANISED TOURS

us

ublin Bus (Map pp264–5; ☎ 872 0000; www lublinbus.ie, 59 Upper O'Connell St) runs variety of tours.

You can join the **Dublin City Hop-on Hop-off City** ur (adult/child €12.50/6; ☯ 9.30am-4.30pm; ½hr), which runs every 15 minutes, at any f the 16 designated stops covering the city entre's major attractions. Admission prices) the sights are not included.

The **Ghost Bus Tour** (adult €22; ☯ 8pm Tue- ri, 7pm & 9pm Sat & Sun; 2hr) is a popular ur of graveyards and haunted places.

The **Coast & Castles Tour** (adult/child €20/10; ☯ 10am; 3hr) takes in the National Botanic ardens in Glasnevin, the Casino at Ma- no, Malahide and Howth.

The **South Coast Tour** (adult/child €20/10; ☯ 11am & 2pm; 3¾hr) brings you along e stretch of coastline between Dun aoghaire and Killiney.

The national bus company, **Bus Éireann** usáras; Map pp264–5; ☎ 836 6111; www useireann.ie; about €25), specialises in ay trips to major attractions near the apital, including Glendalough, Powers- ourt and Newgrange (see Excursions hapter, p201).

VILD COACH TOURS

hese award-winning tours are run by **Aran** urs (☎ 280 1899; www.wildcoachtours om). Prices include admission.

Departing from the Gresham Hotel, e **Wild Powerscourt Tour** (adult/child €20/16; ☯ 1.30pm Mar-Sep, Sat & Sun only Oct-

Feb; 4½hr) covers Sandycove and Power- scourt house and gardens.

Wild Wicklow Tour (adult/child €28/25; ☯ 9am; 8½hr) leaves from Dublin Tourism, Suffolk St, and goes down the coast to Avoca Handweavers, Glendalough and Sally Gap.

Top Five – Dublin for Free

- National Museum (p87)
- Chester Beatty Library (p81)
- National Gallery (p86)
- Natural History Museum (p87)
- Tour of Glasnevin Cemetery (p115)

Carriage

You can pick up a horse and carriage with a driver/commentator at the junction of Grafton St and St Stephen's Green. Half-hour tours cost up to €40 and the carriages can take four or five people. Tours of different lengths can be negotiated with the drivers.

Macabre

In recent years there has been a growth of tours that focus on Dublin's more sinister past, both real and invented. Aside from the very popular ghost bus tour run by Dublin Bus (see above), the below is worth checking out, as is the Zozimus Experience (p74).

The evening **Walk Macabre Tour** (☎ 087-677 1512; www.ghostwalk.cjb.com; admission €9; ☯ 7.30pm; 1¼hrs) is as much a show as a walk through the spooky corners of Georgian Dublin, departing from St Stephen's Green main gate.

Musical

The **Dublin Musical Pub Crawl** (☎ 478 0191; www
.musicalpubcrawl.com; adult/student €10/8;
🕑 7.30pm daily May-Oct, Fri & Sat Nov &
Feb-Apr; 2½hrs) focuses on Irish traditional
music: two musicians demonstrate the various styles and explain the music's history in a
number of pubs in Temple Bar. The tour leaves
from Oliver St John Gogarty's pub (p158).

Self-Paced

Accredited guides can be contacted via the
tourist board (☎ 602 4000). They cost an average of €100 per day for an English-speaking
guide and €125 for other languages. A reputable firm that hires out guides is **Meridien
Tours** (☎ 677 6336; 26 South Frederick St).

Train

Railtours Ireland (☎ 856 0045; www.railtours
.ie; tours €30–125) goes to virtually every
must-see sight in the country in a range of
half and full-day trips.

Walking
HISTORICAL

The **1916 Rebellion** (☎ 676 2493; www.1916
rising.com; adult/child €10/free; 🕑 11.30am
& 2.30pm Mon-Sat, 1pm Sun, no 2.30pm
tour Mar & Oct; 1½hr) departs from the International Bar (p156) and is an irreverent
and entertaining tour of historical Dublin
with the best guides in the city.

The **Zozimus Experience** (☎ 661 8646; www
.zozimus.com; admission per person €10;

🕑 around 9pm May-Oct, 7pm Nov-Apr)
is a hugely entertaining (street) tour that
leaves from the gates of Dublin Castle or
an exploration of Dublin's superstitious
and seedy medieval past. The costume
guide recounts stories of murders, great
escapes and mythical events.

LITERARY

The **James Joyce Centre** (☎ 878 8547; 35 North
Great George's St; adult/concession/children
aged under 12 €10/9/free; 🕑 2.15pm Mon,
Wed & Fri Jun-Sep; 1hr) organises walking
tours of north Dublin, focusing on sites associated with James Joyce.

Dublin Literary Pub Crawl (☎ 454 0228; www
.dublinpubcrawl.com; adult/student €10/8;
🕑 7.30pm Mon-Sat, noon & 7.30pm Sun
Apr-Nov, 7.30pm Thu-Sat, noon & 7.30pm
Sun Dec-Mar; 2½hr) Starting at the Duke
pub (p156), this offers an entertaining walk-
and-performance led by two actors around
pubs with literary connections. A drink at
each stop may lead to a fuzzy memory at
the end when there's a competition relating to the tour. This award-winning tour is
very popular, so be sure to get to the pub by
7pm to buy tickets. Also available at Dublin
Tourism Centre (p243).

Water

Viking Splash Tours (Map pp266–8; ☎ 707 6000;
www.vikingsplashtours.com; 64-65 Patrick
St, Dublin 8; adult/child from €14/8; 10 tours
daily; 1¼hr) has witty tours of Viking Dublin
in reconditioned WWII amphibious boat-
buses ending in the Grand Canal basin.

SOUTH OF THE LIFFEY

You're likely to spend an inordinate amount of your time on the south side, the most salubrious surrounds of inner Dublin where you'll find most of its tourist attractions, along
with its best shops, most memorable restaurants, liveliest pubs and most elegant Georgian
squares.

AROUND GRAFTON STREET

Drinking p129; Eating p107; Shopping p161; Sleeping p179
The heart of affluent Dublin, Grafton St is a quaint pedestrianised thoroughfare lined with
four-storey Georgian buildings. It snakes its way from the cobblestones of Trinity College to
the lawns of St Stephen's Green, and it's here that you'll find Dublin's snazziest shops, street
life and *joie de vivre*.

Named after the 17th-century Duke of Grafton who owned much of these parts, Grafton St
proper starts from the area known as College Green, the centre of the city since Viking times.
Across its traffic-gnarled expanse are the elegant facades of Trinity College, one of world's most
prestigious universities, and the Bank of Ireland, built to house Ireland's first parliament. A

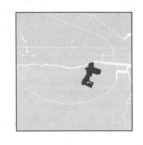

atue of Molly Malone (Map pp272–3) leads us, bosoms first, ⊃ the pedestrianised street, which *is* Grafton St for locals.

It has been a fashionable precinct for more than 200 years, nd was a major traffic artery until 1982 when the cars were riven out and the pedestrians paraded in. It's crowded hroughout the day with a constant flow of locals taking the cenic route from A to B and out-of-towners taking the city's ulse. The sun breaks through the clouds, catching the flower ellers and setting the street ablaze with seasonal colours. Few eople ever seem to be in a rush and smiles are never far from heir faces. An assortment of street performers sets the mood, roviding the soundtrack for a memorable stroll. On any given ay, you might bump into a string quartet, a straggly haired rock band, lone folk singers with uitars, a whistling South American troupe or a shaven-headed street urchin chancing his rm with an auld ballad. There's a poet who'll recite whatever poem you want for a couple of uros, the occasional moving statue and a guy making bird noises. The buskers compete with he beggars to keep your eyes and hard-earned from the swish shops lining the street.

The jewel in its retail crown is Brown Thomas (p184), the swankiest department store in own. Its window displays in December are as important to a Dubliner's idea of Christmas as an old man with a white beard. Further along is the main branch of Bewley's Oriental Café (p131), the most famous meeting spot in Dublin, which, while tarted up recently, still bears a stunning facade, cosy Victorian interior and some of its old character.

The fun doesn't stop after dark because this strip is criss-crossed by lively streets teeming with historical old pubs, sophisticated bars and great places to eat, so there's always comings and goings on Dublin's favourite street.

Top Five – Around Grafton Street

- The Book of Kells (p76)
- A wander through Trinity College (p77)
- Shopping on Grafton St (p183)
- Sociable pubs off Grafton St (p156)
- The Douglas Hyde Gallery (p77)

BANK OF IRELAND Map pp269–71

☎ 671 1488; College Green; ⏱ 10am-4pm Mon-Fri, 0am-5pm Thu

acing Trinity College across College Green, his sweeping Palladian pile was built to house the Irish parliament and was the first urpose-built Parliament House in the world. he original building, the central colonnaded ection that distinguishes it, was designed by ir Edward Lovett Pearce in the first half of the 8th century.

When the parliament voted itself out of existence through the 1801 Act of Union, the building was sold under the condition that he interior would be altered to prevent it ever again being used as a debating chamber. t was a spiteful strike at Irish parliamentary spirations, but while the central House of Commons was remodelled and offers little int of its former role, the smaller House of .ords chamber survived and is much more nteresting. It has Irish oak woodwork, a mahogany longcase parliament clock and a ate-18th-century Dublin crystal chandelier. he tapestries date from the 1730s and depict the Siege of Derry (1689) and the Battle of the Boyne (1690), the two Protestant victories over Catholic Ireland. In the niches are busts of George III, George IV, Lord Nelson and the Duke of Wellington. There are **tours of the House of Lords** (admission free; ⏱ 10.30am, 11.30am & 1.45pm Tue), which include a talk as much about Ireland and life in general as the building itself.

Also part of the complex, and reached via the sedate Foster Place, is the **Bank of Ireland Arts Centre** (p75), which hosts a variety of cultural events, including classical concerts and regular free lunchtime recitals and poetry readings. It also features an eight-minute film about banking and Irish history called the **Story of Banking** (☎ 671 2261; adult/concession €1.50/1; ⏱ hourly 10am-3pm Tue-Fri). An exhibition features a 10kg silver-gilt mace that was made for the House of Commons and retained by the Speaker of the House when the parliament was dissolved. It was later sold by his descendants and bought back from Christies in London by the Bank of Ireland in 1937.

BOOK OF KELLS & THE LONG ROOM Map p78

☎ 608 2320; East Pavilion, Library Colonnades, Trinity College; adult/concession €7/6; ☼ 9.30am-5pm Mon-Sat, noon-4.30pm Sun, 9.30am-4.30pm Sun Jun-Sep

One of Ireland's greatest treasures, the magnificent Book of Kells, is an illuminated copy of the gospels created by monks around 800. The artists, probably from St Columba's Monastery on the remote island of Iona in Scotland, used valuable dyes on vellum to create stunningly intricate drawings and texts that continue to impress 12 centuries later. The manuscript contains the four New Testament gospels, written in Latin, as well as prefaces, summaries and other text. It is distinguished by the superbly decorated opening letters of each chapter and extensive, complex, smaller illustrations between the lines. The 680-page (340-folio) book was rebound in four calfskin volumes in 1953.

Fleeing ferocious Viking raids, the monks shifted to Ireland at the beginning of the 9th century and brought their masterpiece with them. They settled in Kells, County Meath, after which the book is known. It was stolen in 1007, then rediscovered three months later buried underground. Some time before the dissolution of the monastery, the metal shrine, or *cumdach*, was lost, possibly taken by looting Vikings who wouldn't have valued the text itself. About 30 of the beginning and ending folios (double-page spreads) are also missing. It was brought to the college for safekeeping in 1654.

Before you see the book itself, savour the preceding exhibitions, which put the treasure in its geographical, historical, academic, artistic and cultural context. They also give you the opportunity to see the extraordinary detail of the work and help you appreciate the craftsmanship that went into its creation. Once you reach the display case, hover a while until there's an opening, jump in and shuffle around until you've seen all the contents of the cabinet. Two volumes of the Book of Kells are usually on display, one showing an illuminated page, the other showing text. Alongside these are the almost as impressive AD 807 *Book of Armagh* and AD 675 *Book of Durrow*, all part of an exhibition called 'The Book of Kells: Turning Darkness into Light'. The pages of each book are turned once every three months (although you can see all of the images in various marketable forms in the shop).

Up stairs from the star attraction is the highlight of Thomas Burgh's building, the magnificent 65m Long Room with its barrel-vaulted ceiling. It's lined with shelves containing 200,000 of the library's oldest books and manuscripts, along with busts of eminent scholars, a 14th-century harp and an original copy of the *Proclamation of the Irish Republic*, read out by Pádraig Pearse at the beginning of the 1916 Easter Rising.

Around half a million people come to see the Book of Kells each year, and half-hour queues are common in summer. Arrive early if you can.

In Statuary Terms

One of the most endearing qualities of Dubliners is their penchant for humanising statues and monuments by giving them irreverent nicknames. As soon as a new one goes up there are dozens of contenders for its unofficial name, with the winner being adopted into the local vernacular within months.

The jury is still out on the Spire (p106), although the 'stiletto in the ghetto' is an early favourite. The 'skewer in the sewer' is another that disparages the current state of O'Connell St. The 'rod up to God' is popular, although our favourite is simply 'Milligan' after the deceased goon, Spike, whose father was Irish and who took Irish citizenship.

In a nearby side street, Dublin's most famous son, James Joyce, stands with head slightly cocked and his hand leaning on a walking stick (Map pp264–5). He's fondly regarded as the 'prick with the stick'. The writer loved his rhyming word play, so he probably would have approved. The Anna Livia statue, depicting Joyce's spirit of the Liffey, was removed in recent years to make way for the Spire. The universally vilified sculpture featured a hideous female figure lying in water and was known as the 'floozy in the Jacuzzi'. Plans are to install the carbuncle in Collins Barracks (p108).

Dublin's next most famous scribe, Oscar Wilde, is remembered in Merrion Sq (p85) as the 'fag on the crag', while the poet Patrick Kavanagh is portrayed in contemplative mood alongside his beloved Grand Canal (p99), sitting on the 'bench with the stench'.

On the north side of the Ha'penny Bridge, a bronze sculpture of two women sitting on a bench with shopping bags at their feet is known as 'the hags with the bags' (Map pp269–71), while the new Boardwalk (p49) was christened the 'plank by the bank'. At the end of Grafton St, Molly Malone is depicted, with an impressive cleavage, pushing her famous wheelbarrow filled with cockles and mussels (Map pp272–3). She's known locally as the 'tart with the cart'. And you'll recognise *Crann an Ór* outside the Central Bank of Ireland (Map pp269–71) if you look for the 'golden goolie'.

DOUGLAS HYDE GALLERY Map p78

☎ 608 1116; Arts & Social Sciences Bldg, Trinity College, entrance on Nassau St; admission free; ⏰ 11am-6pm Mon-Wed & Fri, 11am-7pm Thu, 11am-4.45pm Sat

This is one of the country's leading contemporary galleries, and hosts regularly rotating shows presenting the works of top-class Irish and international artists across a wide range of media – well worth checking out.

DUBLIN EXPERIENCE Map p78

☎ 608 1688; Arts & Social Sciences Bldg, Trinity College; adult/student €4.20/3.50; ⏰ hourly 10am-5pm mid-May–Oct

Trinity College's *other* attraction is this 45-minute audiovisual introduction to the city, which takes place in a lecture hall in the bowels of the opposite building, transformed with a few papier-mâché boulders placed in front of the screen. It is saccharine, clichéd, historically skewed, amateurish, takes itself too seriously and features exceedingly annoying actors trying to sound like Dublin taxi drivers. Keep walking.

MONUMENTS OF COLLEGE GREEN Map pp269–71

The area between the Bank of Ireland and Trinity College contains barely a blade of grass these days but is still known as College Green. Today it's a tangle of traffic and dashing pedestrians, and home to a number of statues. In front of the bank is Henry Grattan (1746–1820), distinguished parliamentary orator. Nearby is a modern memorial to the patriot Thomas Davis (1814–45). Where College St meets Pearse St, another traffic island is topped by a 1986 sculptured copy of the Steyne (the Viking word for stone), which was erected on the riverbank in the 9th century to stop ships from grounding and removed in 1720.

TRINITY COLLEGE Map p78

☎ 677 2941; admission free; ⏰ 8am-10pm; walking tours ☎ 608 1724; admission €8.50 including Book of Kells; ⏰ 10.15am-3.40pm Mon-Sat, 10.15am-3pm Sun mid-May–Sep

Ireland's most prestigious university is both a calm and cordial retreat from the bustle of contemporary Dublin and home to one of its greatest attractions, the Book of Kells (see p76). On a summer's evening, when the crowds thin and the chatter subsides, there are few more delightful places in the world to be.

Established by Elizabeth 1 in 1592 on land confiscated from the Augustinian priory, Trinity was the English monarch's attempt to provide an alternative to higher education on the Continent and stop Protestant youth from being 'infected with popery'. Despite its bigoted beginnings, Trinity went on to become one of Europe's outstanding seats of learning, producing notable graduates the likes of Jonathan Swift, Oscar Wilde and Samuel Beckett to name just a literary few.

It remained completely Protestant until 1793. But even when the university relented and began to admit Catholics, the Church forbade it. Until 1970, any Catholic who enrolled here could consider themselves excommunicated. Although hardly the bastion of British Protestantism that it once was – most of its 13,000 students are Catholic – it is still a popular choice for British students. Women were first admitted to the college in 1903, earlier than at most British universities.

The 16-hectare site is now in the centre of the city, but when it was founded it was described as being 'near Dublin' and was bordered on two sides by the estuary of the Liffey. Nothing now remains of the original Elizabethan college, which was replaced in the Georgian building frenzy of the 18th century. The elegant **Regent House entrance** on College Green was built between 1752 and 1759, and is guarded by statues of the writer Oliver Goldsmith (1730–74) and the orator Edmund Burke (1729–97). The railings outside the entrance are a popular meeting spot. The walking tours depart from here and leave every 40 minutes.

Through the entrance are the Front and Parliament Sqs, dominated by the 30m-high **Campanile**, designed by Edward Lanyon and erected from 1852 to 1853 on what was believed to be the centre of the monastery that preceded the college. Students who pass beneath it when the bells toll will fail their exams, according to legendary superstition. To the north of the Campanile is a statue of George Salmon, the college provost from 1886 to 1904, who fought bitterly to keep women out of the college. He carried out his threat to permit them in 'over his dead body' by dropping dead when the worst happened. To the south of the Campanile is a statue of historian WEH Lecky (1838–1903).

North of the square is the **Chapel** (☎ 608 1260; admission free; organised tours only), designed by William Chambers and completed in 1799. It has some fine plasterwork

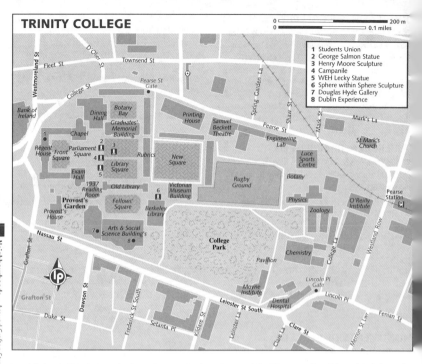

TRINITY COLLEGE

| | 0 | 200 m |
| | 0 | 0.1 miles |

1 Students Union
2 George Salmon Statue
3 Henry Moore Sculpture
4 Campanile
5 WEH Lecky Statue
6 Sphere within Sphere Sculpture
7 Douglas Hyde Gallery
8 Dublin Experience

by Michael Stapleton, Ionic columns and painted, glass windows, and has been open to all denominations since 1972. Next is the **Dining Hall**, which was originally built by Richard Cassels in the mid-18th century. The great architect must have had an off-day because the vault collapsed twice and the entire structure was dismantled 15 years later. The replacement was completed in 1761, but extensively restored after a fire in 1984.

On the grassy expanse of Library Sq are a 1969 sculpture by British sculptor Henry Moore (1898–1986) and two large Oregon maples. On the north side is the 1892 Graduates' Memorial Building, in an area known as Botany Bay.

On the far east of the square, the red-brick **Rubrics building** dates from around 1690, making it the oldest building in the college. It was extensively altered in an 1894 restoration, and then underwent serious structural modifications in the 1970s. Behind this is New Sq, featuring the highly ornate **Victorian Museum Building** (☎ 608 1477; New Sq; admission free; ☻ by prior arrangement only), which houses a Geological Museum. The Doric-fronted **Printing House** was also designed by Richard Cassels.

While it's a pleasant stroll checking out these buildings, the real attractions are

housed in Thomas Burgh's splendid, early-18th-century **Old Library**, which contains Trinity's two gems, the Book of Kells and the Long Room (p76). Despite Ireland's independence, the 1801 Library Act entitles Trinity College Library to a free copy of every book published in Britain. Housing this bounty requires nearly 1km of extra shelving every year and the collection amounts to around five million titles, which are stored at various facilities around town.

Beside the Old Library on Fellow's Sq is the brutalist and brilliant **Berkeley Library** designed by Paul Koralek in 1967. It has been hailed by the Architectural Association of Ireland as the best example of modern architecture in Ireland. It's fronted by Arnaldo Pomodoro's sculpture *Sphere Within Sphere* (1982–83). George Berkeley, the distinguished Irish philosopher, studied at Trinity when he was only 15 years old. His influence spread to North America, where Berkeley, California and its university, are named after him.

Next around the square is the Arts & Social Science Building, which houses the underwhelming Dublin Experience (p77), an alternative entrance and the Douglas Hyde Gallery (p77).

Continuing back towards the main entrance, after the Reading Room is the late-18th-century Palladian **Examination Hall**, which like the chapel opposite – which it closely resembles – was the work of William Chambers and features plasterwork by Michael Stapleton. It contains an oak chandelier rescued from the Irish Parliament (now the Bank of Ireland).

Towards the eastern end of the complex **College Park** is a lovely place to lounge around on a sunny day and occasionally catch a game of cricket, a bizarre sight in Ireland. Keep in mind that there's another gate located in the southeast corner of the grounds, which provides a handy shortcut to Merrion Sq (p85).

TEMPLE BAR

Drinking p129; Eating p107; Shopping p161; Sleeping p179

Dublin's prime tourist precinct is a maze of cobbled streets dotted between Dame St and the river, and running roughly from Trinity College to Christ Church Cathedral. There are lots of interesting sights, fashionable boutiques and worthy places to stay along here but the area's main draws are pubs, restaurants and no-holds barred hedonism, attracting visitors in their tens of thousands and awarding Temple Bar its reputation as one of Europe's liveliest entertainment districts (see the Entertainment chapter, p135).

Fishamble St, the oldest street in Dublin, dates back to Viking times and marks the western boundary of Temple Bar. Brass symbols in the pavement direct you towards a mosaic laid out to show the ground plan of the sort of Viking dwelling excavated here in the early 1980s. The land was acquired by William Temple (1554–1628) after Henry VIII dissolved the monasteries in 1537 and turfed out the Augustinian friars. The narrow lanes and alleys date from the early 18th century when Temple Bar became a disreputable area of pubs and prostitution.

In 1742 Handel conducted the first performance of his *Messiah* in the Neal's Music Hall (see p11), behind Kinlay House (on Lord Edward St), now part of a hotel that bears the composer's name. In the 19th century it developed a commercial character with small craft and trade businesses. On Parliament St, down to the quays from Dublin Castle (p82), the Sunlight Chambers (named after a brand of soap; Map pp269–71) has a beautiful frieze showing the Lever Brothers' view of the world and soap: men make clothes dirty, women wash them.

The area fell into decline in the first half of the 20th century along with most of central Dublin. In the 1960s the government planned to turn it into a massive bus depot. While it was acquiring the remaining properties, many of the condemned buildings were leased on short-term contracts to artists, artisans and community groups. Temple Bar then took shape as Dublin's bona fide cultural quarter, an idea seized upon by the government in the 1990s (see the boxed text on p48). Its rundown buildings and streets were revitalised, derelict buildings demolished and new squares built. Among the cultural gems of the quarter are the progressive Project Arts Centre (p174), Temple Bar Gallery & Studios (p80) and Irish Film Centre (IFC; p135). The new Millennium Bridge opens up a fetching vista of Eustace St, to match Crown Alley and the atmospheric Merchant's Arch, which opens splendidly onto the Ha'penny Bridge.

In some ways the area has been ruined by the success of its renewal. In attempts to recreate a Left Bank atmosphere where artists' studios stood alongside cosy cafés and small boutiques selling ethnic artefacts, developers succumbed to the powerful draw of the mammon and created an overly commercialised quarter full of overpriced restaurants serving indifferent food, tacky souvenir shops and – with one or two exceptions – characterless bars that are more like meat markets than decent Dublin hostelries. During the day and on weekday evenings, it's a pleasantly lively – but expensive – place to be. Most Dubliners give it a wide berth at weekends when it overflows with drunks, the atmosphere is alcopop-charged and the nickname Temple Barf seems justified. The **Temple Bar Information Centre** (Map pp269–71; ☎ 671 5717; 18 Eustace St) publishes a guide and has specific details on the area.

Top Five – Temple Bar

- National Photographic Archives (p80)
- A photograph of the Ha'penny Bridge (p49)
- Lingering by day
- A summer movie in Meeting House Sq (p175)
- The Ark (p80)

THE ARK CHILDREN'S CULTURAL CENTRE Map pp269–71

☎ 670 7788; 11a Eustace St; admission free;
⏰ 9.30am-4pm Tue-Fri, 10am-4pm Sat

Aimed at youngsters between the ages of four and 14, the enormously popular – and perpetually booked out – Ark runs activities aimed at stimulating children's interests in science, the environment and the arts. The centre has an open-air stage for summer events.

GALLERY OF PHOTOGRAPHY

Map pp269–71

☎ 671 4653; Meeting House Sq, Temple Bar;
admission free; ⏰ 11am-6pm Mon-Sat

Dublin's best photographic gallery hosts regular temporary exhibitions from contemporary local and international photographers in its light and airy three-level space. The exceptionally well-stocked shop is a terrific place for a browse.

HEY DOODLE, DOODLE Map pp269–71

☎ 672 7382; 14 Crown Alley; admission €6.50;
⏰ 11am-6pm Tue-Sat, 1-6pm Sun

Budding young ceramicists get their chance to display their talents at one of the city's more interesting kids venues. Kids pick a piece of pottery, paint it whatever way they like, and pick it up a week later after it's been fired and glazed. The odd adult has been spotted with a paintbrush in hand too. It gets busy at weekends, and group bookings must be made in advance.

NATIONAL PHOTOGRAPHIC ARCHIVES Map pp269–71

☎ 671 0073; Meeting House Sq, Temple Bar; admission free; ⏰ 11am-6pm Mon-Sat, 2-6pm Sun

Anyone interested in photography and Irish history should make a beeline for this wonderful resource, which hosts regular themed exhibitions from its huge collection of pics from 19th-century Ireland to today. Many of the images are also catalogued on computer, and you search by time and place in the library, assisted by friendly and accommodating staff.

ORIGINAL PRINT GALLERY Map pp269–71

☎ 677 3657; Black Church Studio, 4 Temple Bar; admission free; ⏰ 10.30am-5.30pm Mon-Sat, 2-5pm Sun

This gallery specialises in original, limited-edition prints including etchings, lithographs and silk-screens mostly by Irish artists.

TEMPLE BAR GALLERY & STUDIOS Map pp269–71

☎ 671 0073; 5 Temple Bar; admission free; 10am-6pm Mon-Sat, 2-6pm Sun

This huge gallery showcases the works of dozens of up-and-coming Irish artists at a time and is the best place to see cutting-edge Irish art across a range of media. Artists studios are also part of the complex, but these are off-limits to casual visitors.

SoDa

Drinking p129; Eating p107; Shopping p161; Sleeping p179

More famous than Temple Bar with those in the know these days, SoDa is Dublin's cutting edge cultural quarter and…what, you've never heard of SoDa? SoDa! South of Dame St? Where you been?

OK, it's a totally made-up name. And without you no such area exists. When we were trying to break Dublin up into distinct, bite-sized entities we got tired of the heading 'South of Dame St' and hit upon SoDa as the perfect title to describe this up-and-coming quarter, which is regenerating all on its own and without the publicity spin of the civic authorities. Sure, you might get some quizzical looks from locals the first few times you mention SoDa, but what price to pay for being part of history? For leaving a piece of yourself forever in Dublin? In years to come, you'll be sitting around listening to people talk about Dublin. Been there, done that, you'll think. And then they'll mention SoDa and you can say, 'hey I named that place!'.

Even if you don't adapt the name – and leave us hanging like fools – you've got to get into this great part of Dublin. It's one of the few parts of the city that *hasn't* been earmarked for regeneration, yet it has grown organically and presents an invigorating mix of old and new, local and international, trendy and grungy.

It was from the area around Dublin Castle that the city first grew, at the dark pool (dubh linn) that formed at the confluence of the Rivers Liffey and Poddle. The Poddle still trickles below Dublin Castle, first built by the Anglo-Norman invaders in the early 13th century. Dublin originally developed west of the castle but expanded eastwards during the Georgian era. Sandwiched between medieval and Georgian Dublin, SoDa – see how natural it is? – has long fallen between two stools. It's neither very old nor very elegant, although the bits beside the Liberties tend to be old, while the bits towards Grafton St are that bit more elegant, as exemplified by the magnificent 18th-century Powerscourt Townhouse.

But these days, it doesn't need to court either because SoDa is making 'alternative' a personality. It's here you'll find Dublin's single best attraction in the Chester Beatty Library, groovy markets, alternative shops, atmospheric old pubs, the best ethnic eats, and some of the hippest bars and liveliest music venues. From superstylin' South William St to convivial Camden St, explore SoDa now before the developers take over.

CHESTER BEATTY LIBRARY Map pp266–8

☎ 407 0750; www.cbl.ie; admission free; ☺ 10am-5pm Mon-Fri, 11am-5pm Sat, 1-5pm Sun, closed Mon Oct-Apr

Housed in the Clock Tower at the back of Dublin Castle is the world-famous Chester Beatty Library, the finest museum in Ireland and, in our opinion, one of the best in Europe. It is home to the collection of New York mining magnate Alfred Chester Beatty (1875–1968), a kindly paternal figure who took Dublin as his adopted home and was made Ireland's first honorary citizen in 1957. An avid traveller and collector, Beatty was fascinated by different cultures, and amassed more than 20,000 manuscripts, rare books, miniature paintings, clay tablets, costumes and any other *objets d'art* that caught his fancy and could tell him something about the world. Fortunately for visitors to Dublin, he was also a man of exceedingly good taste.

The collection is spread over two levels. On the ground floor you'll find a compact but stunning collection of artworks from the Western, Islamic and East Asian worlds. Highlights include the finest collection of Chinese jade books in the world and illuminated European texts featuring exquisite calligraphy that stand up in comparison with the Book of Kells. Audiovisual displays explain the process of bookbinding, paper-making and print-making.

The second floor is a wonderful exploration of the world's major religions through decorative and religious art, enlightening text and a cool cultural-pastiche video at the entrance. The collection of Qur'ans dating from the 9th to the 19th centuries (the library has over 270 of them) is considered by experts to be the best example of illuminated Islamic texts in the world. There are also outstanding examples of ancient papyri, including renowned Egyptian love poems from the 12th century, and some of the earliest illuminated gospels in the world, dating from around AD 200. The collection is rounded off with some exquisite scrolls and artwork from China, Japan, Tibet and Southeast Asia, including the two-volume Japanese *Chogonka Scroll*, painted in the 17th century by Kano Sansetu.

As if all of this wasn't enough for one visit, the library also hosts temporary exhibits that are usually not to be missed. Not only are the contents of the museum outstanding, but the layout, design and location are also unparalleled, from the ubiquitous café and gift shop to the Zen rooftop terrace and the beautiful landscaped garden out the front. These features alone would make this an absolute Dublin must-do.

CITY HALL Map pp269–71

☎ 672 2204; www.dublincorp.ie/cityhall; Cork Hill; admission to building free, exhibition adult/concession €4/2; ☺ 10am-5.15pm Mon-Sat, 2-5pm Sun

One of the architectural triumphs of Dublin's recent boom was the magnificent restoration of City Hall, originally built by Thomas Cooley as the Royal Exchange between 1769 and 1779, and botched in the mid-19th century when it became the offices of the local government. In the 2000 restoration, the internal walls were cleared and the building was returned to all its gleaming Georgian glory. The rotunda and its ambulatory form a breathtaking interior, bathed in natural light from enormous windows to the east. A vast marble statue of former mayor and Catholic emancipator Daniel O'Connell stands here as a reminder of the building's links with Irish nationalism (the funerals of Charles Stewart Parnell and Michael Collins were both held here). Dublin City Council still meets here on the first Monday of the month, gathering to discuss the city's business in the Council Chamber, which was the original building's coffee room.

The striking vaulted basement hosts a multimedia exhibition entitled 'The Story of the Capital', which traces the history of the city from its earliest beginnings to its rosy future. There's more info here than even the most nostalgic expat could take in, and exhibits are a little text heavy, but it's all slickly presented and the audiovisual displays are informative and easy to absorb.

DUBLIN CASTLE Map pp269–71

☎ 677 7129; www.dublincastle.ie; Cork Hill, Dame St; adult/concession €4/3; ☺ 10am-5pm Mon-Fri, 2-5pm Sat & Sun

Although the stronghold of British power here for 700 years, Dublin Castle today is principally an 18th-century creation more accurately described as a palace than a castle. The original Anglo-Norman fortress was built on Viking foundations early in the 13th century and the Record Tower survives intact. It was subject to a siege by 'Silken' Thomas Fitzgerald in 1534 (see p62), virtually destroyed by a fire in 1684 and the setting for some momentous scenes during Ireland's battle for independence. It was officially handed over to Michael Collins on behalf of the Irish Free State in 1922, when the viceroy is reported to have rebuked Collins on being seven minutes late. Collins replied 'we've been waiting seven hundred years you can wait seven minutes'. The castle is now used by the Irish government for meetings and functions, and can only be visited on a guided tour of the State Apartments and excavations of the former Powder Tower.

If you were hoping to relieve yourself before taking the tour, unfortunately the large public conveniences beside the tourist shop are reserved for people 'who have used the restaurant'. Furthermore, you're urged not to ask for the security code as refusal may offend. One hundred thousands welcomes indeed! Punch in 2207 and if the mean-spirited management has changed the code, give them a good tongue lashing.

As you walk in to the grounds from the main Dame St entrance, there's a good example of the evolution of Irish architecture. On your left is the Victorian **Chapel Royal** (occasionally part of the Dublin Castle tours), decorated with over 90 heads of various Irish personages and saints carved out of Tullamore limestone. The interior is wildly exuberant, with fan vaulting alongside quadripartite vaulting, wooden galleries, stained glass and lots of lively looking sculpted angels. Beside this is the **Norman Tower**, which has 5m-thick walls and now houses the **Garda Museum** (☎ 668 9998; admission free; ring the bell), which follows the history of the Irish police force. It doesn't have all that much worth protecting, but the views are fab. On your right is the Georgian **Treasury Building**, the oldest office block in Dublin, and behind you,

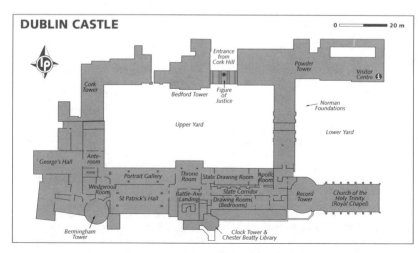

Dublin Castle (opposite)

yikes, is the uglier-than-sin **Revenue Commission-ers Building** of 1960.

Heading away from that eyesore, you ascend to the Upper Yard. On your right is a figure of Justice with her back turned to the city, an appropriate symbol for British justice, reckoned Dubliners. Next to it is the 18th-century **Bedford Tower**, from which the Irish Crown Jewels were stolen in 1907 and never recovered. Opposite is the entrance to the tours.

The 45-minute guided tours (departing every 20 to 30 minutes depending on numbers) are pretty dry, seemingly pitched at tourists more likely to ooh and aah over period furniture than historical anecdotes. You get to visit the State Apartments, many of which are decorated in dubious taste. There are beautiful chandeliers (ooh!), plush Irish carpets (aah!), splendid rococo ceilings, a Van Dyck portrait and the throne of King George V. You also get to see St Patrick's Hall where Irish presidents are inaugurated and foreign dignitaries toasted, and the room in which the wounded James Connolly was tied to a chair while convalescing after the 1916 Easter Rising, brought back to health to be executed by firing squad.

The highlight is a visit to the subterranean excavations of the old castle, discovered by accident in 1986. They include foundations built by the Vikings (whose long-lasting mortar was made of ox blood, egg shells and horse hair), the hand-polished exterior of the castle walls that prevented attackers from climbing up the walls, the steps leading down to the moat and the trickle of the historic River Poddle, which once filled the moat on its way to joining the Liffey.

DUBLIN CIVIC MUSEUM Map pp272–3
☎ 679 4260; 58 South William St; admission free;
✆ 10am-6pm Tue-Sat, 11am-2pm Sun
Still finding its feet a little, this tribute to old Dublin occupies the impressive 18th-century City Assembly House and is worth a visit if you're going past. The jumbled displays form a very mixed bag, from Viking objects to a tram model. The highlight is the stone head of Lord Nelson toppled from its column on O'Connell St by the Irish Republican Army (IRA) in 1966. Plans are afoot to share the splendid space with outside exhibitions, which should make it a more rewarding visit in the future.

IRISH-JEWISH MUSEUM Map pp260–1
☎ 453 1797; 4 Walworth Rd; admission free; ✆ 11am-3.30pm Tue, Thu & Sun May-Sep, 10.30am-2.30pm Sun only Oct-Apr; bus 16, 19 & 122 from Trinity College
Housed in an old synagogue, this museum recounts the history and cultural heritage of Ireland's small but prolific Jewish community. It was opened in 1985 by the Belfast-born, and then Israeli president, Chaim Herzog. The various memorabilia includes photographs, paintings, certificates, books and other artefacts.

POWERSCOURT TOWNHOUSE SHOPPING CENTRE Map pp272–3
☎ 679 4144; 59 South William St
This elegant Richard Cassels–designed townhouse was built between 1771 and 1774, and boasts some fine plasterwork by Michael Stapleton among its features. The stylish shopping centre you see today was created in two recent restorations, the most recent in 2000. See the Shopping chapter (p161) for more.

SHAW BIRTHPLACE Map pp266–8
☎ 475 0854; 33 Synge St; adult/concession €6/5;
✆ 10am-1pm & 2-5pm Mon-Sat, 11am-5pm Sun Easter-Oct; bus 16, 19 & 122 from Trinity College
Close to the Grand Canal, the birthplace of playwright George Bernard Shaw is now a restored Victorian home that is interesting even to nonliterary buffs because it provides an insight into the domestic life of the 19th-century's middle classes. Shaw's mother held musical evenings in the drawing room, and it is likely that her son's store of fabulous characters was inspired by those who attended.

WHITEFRIARS CARMELITE
CHURCH Map pp266–8
☎ 475 8821; 56 Aungier St; admission free; ☺ 8am-6.30pm Mon, Wed-Fri, 8am-9.30pm Tue, 8am-7pm Sat, 8am-7.30pm Sun; bus 16, 19 & 122 from Trinity College

If you find yourself mulling over the timing of a certain proposal – or know someone who needs some prompting – pop along to this church, which contains the remains of none other than St Valentine, donated by Pope Gregory XVI in 1835. The Carmelites returned to this site in 1827, when they re-established their former church that had been seized from them by Henry VIII in the 16th century. In the northeastern corner is a 16th-century Flemish oak statue of the Virgin and Child, which is believed to be the only wooden statue to have escaped destruction during the Reformation.

GEORGIAN DUBLIN

Drinking p129; Eating p107; Shopping p161; Sleeping p179

East of Grafton St is where much of moneyed Dublin works and plays, amid the magnificent Georgian splendour thrown up during Dublin's 18th-century prime. When James Fitzgerald, the earl of Kildare, built his mansion south of the Liffey, he was mocked for his foolhardy move into the wilds. 'Where I go society will follow,' he confidently predicted and was soon proved right. Today Leinster House is used as the Irish Parliament and is in the epicentre of Georgian Dublin.

The area around Kildare St is the administrative core of the country as well as a repository for its treasures, housed in the likes of the National Museum, National Gallery and Natural History Museum. The most celebrated emblems of the times are the magnificent Merrion and Fitzwilliam Sqs, surrounded by buildings that still retain their original features. This was the original stomping ground of Ireland's protestant ascendancy, and the many plaques on the buildings remind us that it was behind these brightly coloured doors that the likes of Oscar Wilde and William Butler Yeats hung their hats.

St Stephen's Green

Top Five – Georgian Dublin

- Atmospheric old boozers (p160)
- National Gallery (p86)
- Natural History Museum (p87)
- National Museum (p87)
- Iveagh Gardens (p85)

The streets running off these squares house the offices of some of the country's most important businesses. When there's even a hint of sunshine, workers pour out into the various parks or follow the lead of poet Patrick Kavanagh and lounge along the banks of the Grand Canal (p99). The south side's greatest park, and the centrepiece of Georgian Dublin, is St Stephen's Green, beautifully landscaped and dotted with statuary that provides a veritable who's who of Irish history. When they clock off, those same workers head to the wonderfully atmospheric and historical pubs of Baggot St and Merrion Row for a couple of scoops and unwinding banter. There are also plenty of smart restaurants, including several of Dublin's best.

FITZWILLIAM SQUARE Map pp266–8

Southeast of St Stephen's Green, Fitzwilliam Sq is the smallest and the last of Dublin's great Georgian squares, completed in 1825. It's also the only one where the central garden is still the private domain of the square's residents. William Dargan (1799–1867), the railway pioneer and founder of the National Gallery, lived at No 2, and the artist Jack B Yeats (1871–1957, see p37) lived at No 18. Look out for the attractive 18th- and 19th-century metal coal-hole covers. The square is a centre for the medical profession by day and a notorious prostitution beat at night.

GOVERNMENT BUILDINGS Map pp266–8
☎ 662 4888; www.irlgov.ie/taoiseach; Upper Merrion St; free guided tours 10.30am-3.30pm Sat, tickets from National Gallery ticket office

This gleaming Edwardian pile was the last building (almost) completed by the British before they were booted out, and opened as the Royal College of Science in 1911. When the college vacated in 1989, disgraced Taoiseach

Charlie Haughey and his government moved in and spent a fortune refurbishing the complex. Among Haughey's needs, apparently, was a private lift from his office that went up to a rooftop helipad and down to a limo in the basement. The 40-mintute tour takes you through the Taoiseach's office, the cabinet room, the ceremonial staircase with a stunning stained-glass window designed by Evie Hone (1894–1955) for the 1939 New York Trade Fair, and many fine examples of modern Irish arts and crafts.

Approximately across the road from here and now part of the Merrion Hotel (p200), 24 Upper Merrion St is thought to be the birthplace of the Duke of Wellington, who downplayed his Irish origins and once said 'being born in a stable does not make one a horse'. It is also possible that the cheeky bugger was born in Trim, County Meath.

VEAGH GARDENS Map pp266–8

8.15am-6pm Mon-Sat, 10am-6pm Sun May-Sep, 8.15am-dusk Oct-Apr

Although no longer Dublin's best-kept secret, these lovely gardens still get a lot less crowded than nearby St Stephen's Green. They were designed by Ninian Niven in 1863 as the private grounds of Iveagh House, and include a rustic grotto, cascade, fountain, maze and rosarium.

LEINSTER HOUSE – IRISH PARLIAMENT Map pp266–8

☎ 618 3000, tour information 618 3271; www.irlgov ie/oireachtas; Kildare St; ☺ observation gallery usually 2.30-8.30pm Tue, 10.30am-8.30pm Wed, 10.30am-5.30pm Thu Nov-May

All the big decisions are made – or at least are seen to be – at Oireachtas na Éireann (Irish parliament). It was built by Richard Cassels in the Palladian style between 1745 and 1748, and was considered the forerunner of the Georgian style that became the norm for Dublin's finer residences. Its Kildare St facade looks like a town house (which inspired Irish architect James Hoban's designs for the US White House), whereas the Merrion Sq frontage was made to resemble a country mansion.

The first government of the Irish Free State moved in from 1922, and both the Dáil (lower house) and Seanad (senate) still meet here to discuss the affairs of the nation and gossip at the exclusive members bar. The 60-member Seanad meets for fairly low-key sessions in the north-wing saloon, while there are usually more sparks and tantrums when the 166-member Dáil bangs heads in a less interesting room that was formerly a lecture theatre added to the original building in 1897. Parliament sits for 90 days a year, and you get an ticket to the observation gallery of the lower or upper house from the Kildare St entrance on production of identification. Pre-arranged free guided tours are available weekdays when parliament is in session.

The obelisk in front of the building is dedicated to Arthur Griffith, Michael Collins and Kevin O'Higgins, the architects of independent Ireland.

MANSION HOUSE Map pp272–3
Dawson St

Built in 1710 by Joshua Dawson – after whom the street is named – this has been the official residence of Dublin's mayor since 1715, and was the site of the 1919 Declaration of Independence and the meeting of the first parliament. The building's original brick Queen Anne style has all but disappeared behind a stucco facade added in the Victorian era.

MERRION SQUARE Map pp266–8

Perhaps the most prestigious in Dublin, Merrion Sq was laid out in 1762 and is flanked on three sides by elegant Georgian houses with colourful doors, peacock fanlights, ornate door knockers and, occasionally, foot-scrapers, used to remove mud from shoes before venturing indoors. One former resident, WB Yeats (1865–1939), was less impressed and described the architecture as 'grey 18th century'. The square is bordered on its remaining side by the National Gallery (p86) and Leinster House (p85), and filled with an immaculately manicured park that teemed with destitute rural refugees when it was used as a soup kitchen during the famine.

Another famous resident was Oscar Wilde, who left of his own accord, while the British Embassy at No 39 was burned out in 1972 in protest against the events of Bloody Sunday in Derry, Northern Ireland, when 13 civilians were killed by the British army.

Damage to fine Dublin buildings hasn't always been the prerogative of vandals, terrorists or protesters. East Merrion Sq once continued into Lower Fitzwilliam St in the longest unbroken series of Georgian houses in Europe. Despite this, in 1961 the Electricity Supply Board (ESB) knocked down 26 of them to build an office block (see p47). The **Royal Institute of the Architects of Ireland** (☎ 676 1703; www.riai.ie; 8 North Merrion Sq; admission free; ☺ 9am-5pm Mon-Fri) is rather more respectful of its Georgian address and hosts regular exhibitions.

NATIONAL GALLERY Map pp266–8

☎ 661 5133; www.nationalgallery.ie; Merrion Sq West; admission free; ☺ 9.30am-5.30pm Mon-Wed & Fri-Sat, 9.30am-8.30pm Thu, noon-5.30pm Sun

A stunning Caravaggio and a whole room full of Ireland's pre-eminent artist Jack B Yeats are the highlights from this fine collection, amassed by the state since 1854. Its original collection of 125 paintings has grown, mainly through bequests, to over 12,500 artworks, including oils, watercolours, drawing, prints and sculptures. The new ultramodern and utterly splendid **Millennium Wing** was added in 2002. It provides two floors of galleries for visiting exhibitions, a centre for the study of Irish art and a multimedia room that lets you track down any painting in the gallery. The new wing also provides a more central entrance to the Gallery on Clare St, but as impressive as it is, you can't help thinking that all this new space wasn't necessary – they could have whittled down the permanent exhibition and focussed on quality rather than quantity.

The building itself was designed by Francis Fowke, whose architectural credits also include London's Victoria & Albert Museum. On the lawn in front of the main entrance is a statue of the Irish railways magnate William Dargan, who organised the 1853 Dublin Industrial Exhibition at this spot; the profits from the exhibition were used to found the gallery. The entire building comprises 54 galleries, housing over 11,000 works that are divided by history, school, geography and theme. There are four wings: the original Dargan Wing, the Milltown Wing (added between 1899 and 1903), the Beit Wing (added 1964 to 1968) and the Millennium Wing. There's a free colour-coded floor plan, and there are free guided tours at 3pm on Saturday and 2pm, 3pm and 4pm Sunday.

The collection spans from the 14th to the 20th centuries and includes all the major Continental Schools. Obviously there is an emphasis on Irish art, and among the works to look out for are William Orpen's *Sunlight*, Roderic O'Conor's *Reclining Nude* and *Young Breton Girl*, and Paul Henry's *The Potato Diggers*. But the highlight, and one you should definitely take time to explore, is the **Yeats Museum**. This is devoted to, and has more than 30 paintings by, Jack B Yeats, a uniquely Irish impressionist and arguably the country's greatest artist (see p37). Some of his finest moments are *The Liffey Swim, Men of Destiny* and *Above the Fair*.

The absolute stand-out of the European schools is Caravaggio's sublime *The Taking of Christ*, in which the troubled Italian genius attempts to light the scene figuratively and metaphorically (he is portrayed holding the lantern on the far right). The masterpiece lay undiscovered for over 60 years in a Jesuit house in nearby Leeson St, and was found accidentally by the chief curator of the gallery, Sergio Benedetti, in 1992. Fra Angelico, Titian and Tintoretto are all in this neighbourhood. Facing Caravaggio, way down the opposite end of the gallery, is *A Genovese Boy Standing on a Terrace* by Van Dyck. In between, old Dutch and Flemish masters line up but all defer to Vermeer's *Lady Writing a Letter*, which is lucky to be here having been stolen by Dublin gangster Martin Cahill in 1992, as featured in the film *The General*.

The French section contains Jules Breton's famous 19th-century *The Gleaners*, along with works by Monet, Degas, Pisarro and Delacroix, while Spain chips in with an unusually scruffy *Still Life with Mandolin* by Picasso, as well as paintings by El Greco, Goya and an early Velázquez. There is a small British collection with works by Reynolds, Hogarth, Gainsborough and Turner. One of the most popular exhibitions occurs only in January when the gallery hosts its annual display of watercolours by Joseph Turner. The 35 works in the collection are best viewed at this time due to the particular quality of the winter light.

Dublin for Children

Dublin is one of Europe's more child-friendly cities. Provisions are made for children in hotels and restaurants, and there are several dedicated attractions to keep them entertained. Some of the sites (The Ark, p80; Dvblinia, p93; Hey Doodle, Doodle, p80; and the Natural History Museum, p87) are right in the centre. Others (Dublin Zoo, p109; Phoenix Park Visitor Centre, p111) are a short bus ride away, while the likes of Newgrange Farm (p215) is further out and take a little more planning. Several grown-up attractions like the National Museum (p87) and the National Gallery (p86) also put on children's activities. Don't forget the city's smaller parks and gardens, which are traffic-free oases where young children can crawl and run to their hearts' content.

NATURAL HISTORY MUSEUM

Map pp266–8

☎ 677 7444; www.museum.ie; Merrion St; admission free; ☯ 10am-5pm Tue-Sat, 2-5pm Sun

Weird and wonderful, this window into Victorian times has barely changed since Scottish explorer Dr David Livingstone opened it in 1857. The creaking interior is crammed with some two million stuffed animals, skeletons and other specimens from around the world, ranging from West African apes to pickled insects in jars. Some are freestanding, others behind glass, but everywhere you turn the animals of the 'dead zoo' are still and staring.

Compared to the multimedia, interactive this and that of virtually every modern museum, this is a beautifully preserved Victorian charm. It is usually full of fascinated kids, but it's the adults who seem to make most noise as they recoil like pinballs between displays. The Irish Room on the ground floor is filled with mammals, sea creatures, birds and butterflies all found in Ireland at some point, including the skeletons of three 10,000-year-old Irish elk that greet you as you enter. The World Animals Collection, spread across three levels, has the skeleton of a 20m-long fin whale found beached in County Sligo as its centrepiece. Evolutionists will love the line-up of orang-utan, chimpanzee, gorilla and human skeletons on the first floor. Other notables include the extinct Australian marsupial the Tasmanian tiger (mislabelled as a Tasmanian wolf), a giant panda from China, and several African and Asian rhinoceroses. The wonderful Blaschka Collection comprises finely detailed glass models of marine creatures whose zoological accuracy is incomparable.

NATIONAL LIBRARY & GENEALOGICAL OFFICE Map pp266–8

☎ 603 0200; www.nli.ie; Kildare St; admission free; ☯ 10am-9pm Mon-Wed, 10am-5pm Thu & Fri, 10am-1pm Sat

Next door to Leinster House (p85), the National Library was built from 1884 to 1890 at the same time as the National Museum and to a similar design by Sir Thomas Newenham Deane. Its extensive collection has many valuable early manuscripts, first editions, maps and other items of interest. Parts of the library are open to the public, including the domed reading room where Stephen Dedalus expounded his views on Shakespeare in Ulysses. Check in your bags at security for a look-see, although you won't expound anything at all in the stiflingly hushed atmosphere.

There's a Genealogical Office (☎ 603 0200; ☯ 10am-4.45pm Mon-Fri, 10am-12.30pm Sat) on the second floor, where you can obtain information on how best to trace your Irish roots (see the boxed text below).

NATIONAL MUSEUM Map pp266–8

☎ 677 7444; www.museum.ie; Kildare St; admission free, guided tours €1.50; ☯ 10am-5pm Tue-Sat, 2-5pm Sun, guided tours at 11am, 12.30pm, 2pm & 3pm

Established in 1877, the National Museum occupies a superb purpose-built building next door to the Irish parliament, and is one of Dublin's star attractions. It is home to Europe's finest collection of Bronze and Iron-Age gold artefacts, the most complete collection of medieval Celtic metalwork, fascinating prehistoric and Viking artefacts, and a few interesting items relating to Ireland's fight for independence. If you don't mind groups, the themed tours will help you appreciate these riches.

The **Treasury** is perhaps the most famous part of the collection, and its centrepieces are Ireland's two most famous crafted artefacts, the **Ardagh Chalice** and the **Tara Brooch**. The 12th-century Ardagh Chalice is made of gold, silver, bronze, brass, copper and lead. It measures 17.8cm high and 24.2cm in diameter and, put simply, is the finest example of Celtic art ever found. The equally renowned Tara Brooch was crafted around AD 700 primarily in white bronze, but with traces of gold, silver, glass, copper, enamel and wire beading, and was used as a clasp for a cloak. It was discovered on a beach in Bettystown, County Meath, in 1850, but later came into the hands of an art dealer who named it after the hill of Tara, the historic seat of the ancient high kings. It doesn't have quite the same ring to it, but it was the Bettystown Brooch that sparked a revival of interest in Celtic jewellery that hasn't let up to this day. There are many other pieces that testify to Ireland's history as the land of saints and scholars.

Virtually all of the treasures are named after the location in which they were found. It's interesting to note that most of them were discovered not by archaeologists' trowels but by bemused farmers out ploughing their fields, cutting peat or, in the case of the Ardagh Chalice, digging for spuds.

Elsewhere in the Treasury is the exhibition **Ór-Ireland's Gold**, featuring stunning jewellery and decorative objects created by Celtic artisans in the Bronze and Iron Ages. Among them are the Broighter Hoard, which includes a 1st-century-BC large gold collar unsurpassed anywhere in Europe and an extraordinarily delicate gold boat. There's also the wonderful Loughnasade bronze war trumpet, which dates from the 1st century BC. It is 1.86m long and made of sheets of bronze riveted together, with an intricately designed disc at the mouth. It produces a sound similar to the Australian didgeridoo, though you'll have to take our word for it. Running alongside the wall is a 15m log boat, which was dropped into the water to soften it, abandoned and then pulled out 4000 years later, almost perfectly preserved in the peat bog.

On the same level is the **Road to Independence** exhibition, which features the army coat worn by Michael Collins on the day he was assassinated (there's still mud on the sleeve). In the same case is the cap purportedly also worn by Collins on that fateful day, complete with a bullet hole in its side. Somehow, we think if the authorities had any confidence in this claim, the exhibit wouldn't be on the floor of the cabinet without even a note.

Upstairs, if you can cope with any more history, is **Medieval Ireland 1150–1550** and **Viking Age Ireland**, which features exhibits from the excavations at Wood Quay – the area between Christ Church Cathedral and the river.

NEWMAN HOUSE Map pp266–8

☎ 475 7255; 85-86 St Stephen's Green; adult/ concession €4/3; ☼ guided tour only, noon, 2pm, 3pm & 4pm Tue-Fri Jun-Aug

Cardinal Newman established the Catholic University of Ireland here in 1865, in one of the finest examples of Georgian architecture currently open to the public. The school provided education to the likes of James Joyce, Pádraig Pearse and Eamon de Valera, who would otherwise have had to submit to the Protestant hegemony of Trinity College if they wanted to receive higher education at home. Newman House is still part of the college, which later decamped to the suburb of Belfield and changed its name to University College Dublin (UCD).

The house comprises two exquisitely restored town houses. No 85, the granite-faced original, was designed by Richard Cassels in 1738 for parliamentarian Hugh Montgomery, who sold it to Richard Chapel Whaley MP in 1765. Whaley wanted a grander home, so he commissioned another house next door at No 86.

Aside from Cassels' wonderful design, the highlight of the design is the plasterwork, perhaps the finest in the city. For No 85, the artists were the Italian stuccodores Paulo and Filipo LaFranchini, whose work is best appreciated in the wonderfully detailed Apollo Room on the ground floor. The plasterwork in No 86 was done by Robert West, but it is not quite up to the high standard of next door.

When the newly founded, Jesuit-run Catholic University of Ireland took possession of the house in 1865, alterations were made to some of the more graphic plasterwork, supplying the nude figures with 'modesty vests'.

During Whaley's residency, the house developed certain notoriety, largely due to the activities of Whaley's son Buck, a notorious gambler and hell-raiser who once walked all the way to Jerusalem for a bet and somehow connived to have himself elected to parliament at the tender age of 17. During the university's tenure, however, the residents were a far more temperate lot. The Jesuit priest and wonderful poet Gerard Manley Hopkins lived here during his time as Professor of Classics from 1884 until his death in 1889. Hopkins' bedroom is preserved as it would have been during his residence, as is the classroom where the young James Joyce studied while obtaining his Bachelor of Arts degree between 1899 and 1902.

NEWMAN UNIVERSITY CHURCH Map pp266–8

☎ 478 0616; 83 St Stephen's Green; admission free; ⏰ 8am-6pm

Next to Newman House, this neo-Byzantine charmer was built in the mid-18th century (Cardinal Newman didn't care too much for the Gothic style of the day). Its richly decorated interior was mocked at first but has since become the preferred surroundings for Dublin's most fashionable weddings.

NO 29, LOWER FITZWILLIAM ST

Map pp266–8

☎ 702 6165; www.esb.ie; adult/student €3.50/1.50; ⏰ 10am-5pm Tue-Sat, 2-5pm Sun

In an effort to at least partly atone for its sins against Dublin's Georgian heritage – it broke up Europe's most perfect Georgian row to build its headquarters (see p47) – the Electricity Supply Board (ESB) preserved and restored this home to give an impression of genteel family life in the city at the beginning of the 18th century. From the rat traps in the kitchen basement to the handmade wallpaper and Georgian cabinets, the attention to detail is impressive, but the tours are disappointingly dry.

OSCAR WILDE HOUSE Map pp266–8

☎ 662 0281; www.amcd.ie/oscar; 1 North Merrion Sq; admission €2.50; ⏰ tours 10.15am & 11.15am Mon, Wed & Thu

In 1855 the surgeon William Wilde and his wife 'Speranza' Wilde moved to 1 North Merrion Sq with their one-year-old son Oscar, whose genius would later be stimulated by the famous literary salon hosted here by his mother. The family lived in the house right through Oscar's education at nearby Trinity. In 1994 the house was taken over by the American College Dublin. The first two floors have been restored to what might have been their appearance in Oscar's day and can be visited via guided tour.

Across the road, just inside the railings of Merrion Sq park, is a flamboyant statue of the man himself. It is crafted from a variety of precious stones, and is an aptly colourful depiction of Wilde wearing his customary smoking jacket and reclining on a rock. Wilde may well be sneering at Dublin and his old home, although the expression may have more to do with the artist's attempt to depict the deeply divided nature of the man. From one side, he looks to be smiling and happy while on the other he looks gloomy and preoccupied. Atop one of the plinths, daubed with witty one-liners or Wildean throwaways, is a small green statue representing Oscar's pregnant mother.

ROYAL HIBERNIAN ACADEMY (RHA) GALLAGHER GALLERY Map pp266–8

☎ 661 2558; www.royalhibernianacademy.com; 25 Ely Pl; admission free; ⏰ 11am-5pm Mon-Wed, Fri & Sat, 11am-9pm Thu, 2-5pm Sun

At the end of a serene Georgian street, you'll find this large and well-lit gallery, which is one of the city's most prestigious exhibition spaces for modern and contemporary Irish and international artists. The RHA Annual Exhibition is held here each May, and features works submitted by artists from all over the country.

ROYAL IRISH ACADEMY Map pp272–3

☎ 676 2570; 19 Dawson St; admission free; ⏰ 10am-5.30pm Mon-Thu, 10am-5pm Fri (closed May 2004)

Next door to the Mansion House is the seat of Ireland's pre-eminent society of letters, whose 18th-century library houses many important documents, including an extensive collection of ancient manuscripts such as the *Book of Dun Cow*, the oldest surviving Irish manuscript; the *Cathach of St Columba*; and the entire collection of 18th-century poet Thomas Moore.

ST STEPHEN'S CHURCH Map pp266–8

☎ 288 0663; Upper Mount St; admission free; ⏰ for services only, 11am Sun & 11.30am Wed, 11am Fri Jul-Aug; bus 5, 6, 7, 8, 10, 44, 47, 48 & 62 from city centre

Built in 1825 in Greek Revival style and commonly known as the 'pepper-canister' on account of its appearance, St Stephen's is one of Dublin's most attractive and distinctive churches, and looks particularly fetching at twilight when its exterior lights have just come on. It occasionally hosts classical concerts, but don't go out of your way to see the interior.

ST STEPHEN'S GREEN Map pp266–8

As you listen to the geese, ducks and waterfowl splish-splashing about the ponds, consider that the nine elegantly landscaped hectares of St Stephen's Green once formed a common for public whippings, burnings and hanging. These days, the green provides a favourite lunch-time escape for workers, a breath of fresh air for the city and a relaxing stroll for visitors.

The buildings around the square date mainly from the mid-18th-century, when the green was landscaped and became the centrepiece of Georgian Dublin. The northern side was known as the Beaux Walk and it's still one of Dublin's most esteemed stretches, home to Dublin's original society hotel, the Shelbourne (p200). Nearby is the tiny Huguenot Cemetery, established in 1693 by French Protestant refugees.

Railings and locked gates were erected in 1814 when an annual fee of one guinea was charged to use the green. This private use continued until 1877 when Sir Arthur Edward Guinness pushed an act through parliament opening the green to the public once again. He also financed the central park's gardens and ponds, which date from 1880.

The main entrance to the green today is beneath **Fusiliers' Arch** (Map pp272–3), at the top of Grafton St. Modelled to look like a smaller version of the Arch of Titus in Rome, the arch commemorates the 212 soldiers of the Royal Dublin Fusiliers who were killed fighting for the British in the Boer War (1899–1902).

Across the road from the western side of the green are the 1863 **Unitarian Church** (Map pp266–8; ☎ 478 0638; St Stephen's Green; admission free; ⏰ 12.30-2.30pm Mon-Fri) and the early 19th-century **Royal College of Surgeons** (Map pp272–3), which has one of the finest facades on St Stephen's Green. During the 1916 Easter Rising, the building was occupied by rebel forces led by Countess Markievicz (1868–1927). The columns are scarred from the bullet holes.

Among the statues and memorials dotting the green, there's one of the Countess in the southeast corner. Since it was Guinness money that created the park you see today, it's only right that Sir Arthur should be present, and there's an 1892 statue of him on the western side of the park. Just north of here, outside the railing, is a statue of Irish patriot Robert Emmet (1778–1803), born across the road where Nos 124 and 125 stand. His actual birthplace has been demolished. The statue was placed here in 1966 and is a replica of an Emmet statue in Washington, DC. There is also a bust of poet James Clarence Mangan (1803–49) and a curious 1967 statue of WB Yeats by Henry Moore. The centre of the park has a garden for the blind, complete with signs in Braille and plants that can be handled. There is also a statue of the Three Fates, presented to Dublin in 1956 by West Germany in gratitude for Irish aid after WWII. In the corner closest to Shelbourne Hotel is a monument to Wolfe Tone, the leader of the abortive 1796 invasion. The vertical slabs serving as a backdrop to Wolfe Tone's statue have been dubbed 'Tonehenge'. At this entrance is a memorial to all those who died in the famine.

On the eastern side of the green is a **children's playground** and to the south there's a fine old bandstand, erected to celebrate Queen Victoria's jubilee in 1887. Musical performances often take place here in the summer. Near the bandstand is a bust of James Joyce, facing Newman House (p88) of University College Dublin, where Joyce was once a student. Also on this side is **Iveagh House**. Originally designed by Richard Cassels in 1730 as two separate houses, they were bought by Benjamin Guinness in 1862 and combined to create the family's city residence. After independence the house was donated to the Irish State and is now home to the Department of Foreign Affairs.

Of the many illustrious streets fanning from the green, the elegant Georgian **Harcourt St** has the most notable addresses. Edward Carson was born at No 4 in 1854. As the architect of Northern Irish Unionism, he was never going to be the most popular figure in Dublin but he did himself no favours as the prosecuting attorney during Oscar Wilde's trial for homosexuality. George Bernard Shaw lived at No 61.

KILMAINHAM & THE LIBERTIES

Drinking p129; Eating p107; Shopping p161; Sleeping p179

Light on entertainment but laden with sights, these areas are among the oldest in Dublin. Their future seems to have been put on hold for much of the last century, but it's the historical wealth and significance of these areas that draw tourists from far and near.

On the fringes of the Liberties, the oldest part of Dublin, you'll find splendid sights like Christ Church (p91) and St Patrick's (p96) Cathedrals and the magnificent Marsh's Library (p95), while deep in the heart of the area, surrounded

by working-class Georgian architecture, is the famous Guinness Brewery (p93). Kilmainham, further west, has less character than the Liberties but more Dublin characters happy to strike up conversation with any Johnny Foreigner. It also has some heavyweight tourist sights in the awesomely atmospheric Kilmainham Gaol (p94), inexorably linked with Ireland's slow and painful slog towards independence, and the hugely impressive Royal Hospital Kilmainham (p96), which today houses the Irish Museum of Modern Art.

In medieval times, when Dublin was only a twinkle in a developer's eye, the sprawling area known as the Liberties lay outside the city walls and was so-called because it was self-governing and free of many of the tithes and taxes of Dublin proper. That the two major cathedrals of Christ Church and St Patrick's were built here is testament to its medieval importance. In some ways, it became the engine room for Dublin's growth, a centre of industry and trade, into which migrants flocked looking for employment. Around 10,000 Huguenot refugees from France flooded into the area from the mid-17th century, introducing silk and linen weaving, which transformed the area and had a profound effect on the city as a whole. The Liberties prospered, standards of living increased and a fierce community pride emerged. The boom busted when Britain imposed high levies on Irish produce from the late 18th century and Irish manufacturers lost out to cheaper imports. Tens of thousands of weavers were put out of work, gangs went about attacking people wearing foreign fabrics and the Liberties descended into squalor.

The Liberties has never really recovered and is still one of the inner city's most deprived areas, racked by unemployment and drug abuse. Yet it retains the passionate pride of a community that has been knitted together over many centuries, and some Dubliners are increasingly looking nostalgically towards the area as an example of their city 'in the rare auld times'. Most visitors duck in and out fairly quickly but if you have a thick skin and adventurous spirit, you should linger a while and soak up the unique atmosphere of the place.

Top Five – Kilmainham & the Liberties

- Kilmainham Gaol (p94)
- Guinness Storehouse (p93)
- Christ Church Cathedral (p91)
- Marsh's Library (p95)
- Royal Hospital Kilmainham (p96)

Neighbourhoods – Kilmainham & the Liberties

CHRIST CHURCH CATHEDRAL Map pp266–8

Church of the Holy Trinity; ☎ 677 8099; www.cccdub.ie; Christ Church Pl; adult/concession €5/2.50 'invited donation'; ☿ 9.45am-5pm

Christ Church Cathedral is the heart of medieval Dublin and a uniquely atmospheric place around which Dubliners have come to ring in the New Year since time immemorial. It is also a widely recognisable symbol of the city and one of its most photogenic sights (you'll get the best pics looking up at it from the quays).

An earlier wooden church was built by the Vikings in 1038, but its secular clergy was replaced in 1163 by Archbishop Laurence O'Toole (patron saint of Dublin) who installed Augustinian monks. Soon after the Normans blew into town in 1169, Strongbow made an agreement with the Archbishop to construct a new stone cathedral that would symbolise their joint glory. The work wasn't completed until late in the 12th century, by which time both were long dead.

Above ground, the north wall, the transepts and the western part of the choir are almost all that remain from the original. It has been restored several times over the centuries and, despite its apparent uniformity, is a hotchpotch of different styles ranging from Romanesque to English Gothic.

Until the disestablishment of the Church of Ireland in 1869, senior representatives of the Crown all swore their allegiance here. The church's fortunes, however, were not guaranteed. By the turn of the 18th century its popularity waned along with the district as the upper echelons of Dublin society fled north, where they attended a new favourite, St Mary's Abbey. Through much of its history, Christ Church vied for supremacy with nearby St Patrick's Cathedral, but both fell on hard times in the 18th and 19th centuries. Christ Church was virtually derelict – the nave had been used as a market and the crypt had earlier housed taverns – by the time restoration took place. Whiskey distiller Henry Roe donated the equivalent of €30 million to save the church, which was substantially rebuilt from 1871 to 1878. Ironically, both the great Church of Ireland cathedrals are essentially outsiders in a Catholic nation today, dependant on tourist donations for their very survival.

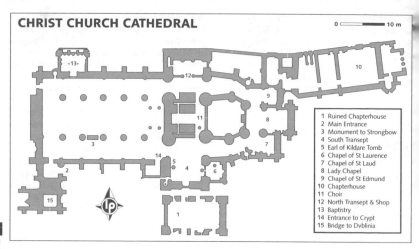

CHRIST CHURCH CATHEDRAL

0 _____ 10 m

1 Ruined Chapterhouse
2 Main Entrance
3 Monument to Strongbow
4 South Transept
5 Earl of Kildare Tomb
6 Chapel of St Laurence
7 Chapel of St Laud
8 Lady Chapel
9 Chapel of St Edmund
10 Chapterhouse
11 Choir
12 North Transept & Shop
13 Baptistry
14 Entrance to Crypt
15 Bridge to Dvblinia

Neighbourhoods – Kilmainham & the Liberties

From its inception, Christ Church was the State Church of Ireland, and when Henry VIII dissolved the monasteries in the 16th century, the Augustinian priory that managed the church was replaced with a new Anglican clergy, which still runs the church today.

From the southeastern entrance to the churchyard you walk past ruins of the chapterhouse, which dates from 1230. The entrance to the cathedral is at the southwestern corner and as you enter you face the northern wall. This survived the collapse of its southern counterpart but has also suffered from subsiding foundations (much of the church was built on a peat bog) and, from its eastern end, it leans visibly.

The southern aisle has a monument to the legendary Strongbow. The armoured figure on the tomb is unlikely to be of Strongbow (it's more probably the earl of Drogheda), but his internal organs may have been buried here. A popular legend relates that the half-figure beside the tomb is of Strongbow's son, who was cut in two by his loving father when his bravery in battle was suspect.

The southern transept contains the superb baroque tomb of the 19th earl of Kildare, who died in 1734. His grandson, Lord Edward Fitzgerald, was a member of the United Irishmen and died in the abortive 1798 Rising (see p64). The entrance to the Chapel of St Laurence is off the south transept and contains two effigies, one of them reputed to be of either Strongbow's wife or sister.

An entrance by the south transept descends to the unusually large arched crypt, which dates back to the original Viking church. Curiosities in the crypt include a glass display-case housing a mummified cat in the act of chasing a mummified mouse, frozen in pursuit inside an organ pipe in the 1860s. Also on display are the stocks of the old 'liberty' of Christ Church, when church authorities meted out civil punishments to wrongdoers. The Treasury exhibit here includes rare coins, the Stuart coat of arms and gold given to the church by William of Orange after the Battle of the Boyne. From the main entrance, a bridge, part of the 1871–78 restoration, leads to Dvblinia (p93).

Evensong at the Cathedrals

In a rare coming together, the choirs of St Patrick's Cathedral and Christ Church Cathedral both participated in the first-ever performance of Handel's *Messiah* in nearby Fishamble St in 1742, conducted by the great composer himself. Both houses of worship carry on their proud choral traditions, and visits to the cathedrals during evensong will provide enchanting and atmospheric memories. The choir performs evensong in St Patrick's at 5.45pm Monday to Friday (not on Wednesday in July and August), while the Christ Church choir competes at 5.30pm on Sunday, 6pm on Wednesday and Thursday, and 5pm Saturday. If you're going to be in Dublin around Christmas, do not miss the carols at St Patrick's and call ahead early for tickets (☎ 453 9472).

DVBLINIA Map pp266–8

☎ 679 4611; adult/concession €5.75/4.75; ☺ 10am-
5pm Apr-Sep, 11am-4pm Mon-Sat, 10am-4.30pm Sun
Oct-Mar

Inside what was once the Synod Hall, which
was added to Christ Church Cathedral during
its late-19th-century restoration, this is a lively
and kitschy attempt to bring medieval Dublin
to life using models, music, streetscapes and
interactive displays. The ground floor has wax
models of 10 episodes in Dublin's history, explained in a choice of five languages through
headsets as you wander around. Up one floor
there's a large selection of objects recovered
from Wood Quay, the world's largest Viking
archaeological site, as well as a huge model
of 11th-century Dublin. There are also models
of the medieval quayside and of a cobbler's
shop. On the top floor is the 'Medieval Fayre',
featuring merchants wares, a medicine stall, an
armourer's pavilion, a confessional booth and
a bank. Finally, you can climb neighbouring St
Michael's Tower and peek through its grubby
windows for views over the city to the Dublin
hills. There is also a pleasant café and the
inevitable souvenir shop.

Your ticket gets you into Christ Church Cathedral free, via the link bridge. More precisely,
you don't have to feel guilty about not leaving
a donation.

GUINNESS STOREHOUSE & ST
JAMES'S GATE BREWERY Map pp262–3

☎ 408 4800; www.guinness-storehouse.com; St
James's Gate; adult/child/concession/student over
18/family €13.50/3/6.50/9/28; ☺ 9.30am-5pm; bus
21A, 78 & 78A from Fleet St

Mecca for beer lovers, the Guinness Storehouse in the heart of the famous St James's
Gate Brewery is an all-singing, all-dancing extravaganza combining sophisticated exhibits,
spectacular design and a thick, creamy head of
marketing hype. In many ways the brewery is
the spiritual centre of Dublin; the famous dark
beer is probably more closely associated with
the city than Joyce. The stout is made in Dublin's oldest district and it's been responsible
for fuelling this unique culture for more than
two centuries, so it's no wonder the brewery
is such a powerful draw.

Heading westwards beyond Christ Church,
you'll end up in the area known as the Liberties
and the historic 26-hectare St James's Brewery,
which stretches along St James's St and down
to the Liffey. On you way you'll pass No 1 Thomas St, where Arthur Guinness used to live,
across the road from the 40m-tall **St Patrick's
Tower**, built around 1757 and the tallest surviving windmill tower outside the Netherlands.

When Arthur started brewing in Dublin in
1759, he couldn't have have had idea that
his name would become synonymous with
Dublin around the world. Or could he? Showing extraordinary foresight, he had just signed
a lease for a small disused brewery under the
terms that he would pay just £45 annually
for the next 9000 years, with the additional
condition that he'd never have to pay for the
water used.

In the 1770s when other Dublin brewers
fretted about the popularity of a new English
beer known as porter – which was first created
when a London brewer accidentally burnt his
hops – Arthur started making his own version.
By 1799 he decided to concentrate all his efforts on this single brew. He died four years
later, aged 83, but the foundations for world
domination were already in place.

At one time a Grand Canal tributary was cut
into the brewery to enable special Guinness
barges to carry consignments out onto the
Irish canal system or to the Dublin port. When
the brewery extensions reached the Liffey in
1872, the fleet of Guinness barges became a
familiar sight. Pretty soon Guinness was being
exported as far afield as Africa and the West
Indies. As the barges chugged their way along
the Liffey towards the port, boys used to lean
over the wall and shout 'bring us back a par-
rot'. Dubliners still say the same thing to each
other when they're going off on holiday.

As an employer, the company reached its
apogee in the 1930s, when there were over
5000 people working here, making it the largest employer in the city. For nearly two centuries it was also one of the best places to work,
paying 20% more than the market rate and offering a comprehensive package of subsidised
housing, health benefits, pension plans, longer
holidays and life insurance. In the 19th century,
young women of marrying age in Dublin were
advised by their mothers to get their hands on
a Guinness man as he'd be worth more than
most alive or dead! Today, however, the brewery is no longer the prominent employer it once
was; a gradual shift to greater automatisation
has reduced the workforce to around 600.

One link with the past that hasn't been
broken is the yeast used to make Guinness,
essentially the same living organism that has
been used since 1770. Another vital ingredient is a hop by the name of fuggles, which
used to be grown exclusively around Dublin

but is now imported from Britain, the US and Australia (everyone take a bow).

The brewery is far more than just a place where beer is manufactured. It is an intrinsic part of Dublin's history and a key element of the city's identity. Accordingly, the quasi-mythical stature of Guinness is the central theme of the brewery's museum, the **Guinness Storehouse,** which opened in 2000 and is the only part of the brewery open to visitors.

While inevitably overpriced and overhyped, this paean to the black gold is done exceptionally well. It occupies the old Fermentation House, built in 1904. As it's a listed building the designers could only adapt and add to the structure without taking anything away. The result is a stunning central atrium that rises seven storeys and takes the shape of a pint of Guinness. The head is represented by the glassed **Gravity Bar,** which provides panoramic views of Dublin to savour with your complimentary pint.

Before you race up the top, however, you might want to check out the museum for which you've paid so handsomely. Actually, it's designed as more of 'an experience' than a museum. It has nearly four acres of floor space featuring a dazzling array of audiovisual, interactive exhibits that cover most aspects of the brewery's story and explain the brewing process in overwhelming detail.

On the ground floor, a copy of Arthur Guinness' original lease lies embedded beneath a pane of glass in the floor. Up through the various exhibits, including 70-odd years of advertising, you can't help feeling that the wholly foreign-owned company has hijacked the mythology Dubliners attached to the drink, and it has all become more about marketing and manipulation than mingling and magic.

The climax, of course, comes when you emerge onto the circular Gravity Bar for your complimentary Guinness. It may well be the most technically perfect pint of Guinness you'll ever have – and the views are breathtaking – but if you're like us, you'll probably be more excited about getting back down to earth and having a pint with real Dubliners.

KILMAINHAM GAOL Map pp262–3
☎ 453 5984; Inchicore Rd; adult/child €5/2;
⏱ 9.30am-5pm Apr-Oct, 9.30am-4pm Mon-Sat, 10am-5pm Sun Nov-Mar; bus 23, 51, 51A, 78 & 79 from Aston Quay

If you have *any* interest in Irish history, particularly the struggle for independence, you will be shaken and stirred by a visit to this infamous, eerie prison. It was the stage for many of the most tragic and heroic episodes in Ireland's recent past, and the list of its inmates reads like a who's who of Irish nationalism. Solid and sombre, its walls absorbed the barbarism of British occupation and recount them in whispers to every visitor.

It took four years to build and the prison opened – or rather closed – its doors in 1796, when the first reluctant guests were led in. The Irish were locked up for all sorts of misdemeanours, some more serious than others. A six-year-old boy spent a month here in 1839 because his father couldn't pay his train fare, and during the famine it was crammed with the destitute who had been imprisoned for stealing food and begging. But it is most famous for incarcerating 120 years of Irish nationalists, from Robert Emmet in 1803 to Eamon de Valera in 1923. All of Ireland's botched uprisings ended with the leaders' confinement here, usually before their execution.

It was the treatment of the leaders of the 1916 Easter Rising that most deeply etched the gaol into the Irish consciousness. Fourteen of the rebel commanders were executed in the exercise yard, including James Connolly who was so badly injured at the time of his execution that he was strapped to a chair at the opposite end of the yard, just inside the gate. The places where they were shot are marked by two simple black crosses. The

Guinness Storehouse

executions turned an apathetic nation on a course towards violent rebellion.

The gaol's final function was as a prison for the newly formed Irish Free State, an irony best summed up with the story of Ernie O'Malley who managed to escape from the gaol when incarcerated by the British but was locked up again by his erstwhile comrades during the Civil War. This chapter is somewhat played down on the tour. Even the passing comment that Kilmainham's final prisoner was the future president, Eamon de Valera, doesn't reveal that he had been imprisoned by his fellow Irish citizens. The gaol was finally decommissioned in 1924.

Visits are by guided tour and start with a stirring audiovisual introduction, screened in the former chapel where 1916 leader Joseph Plunkett was wed to his beloved just 10 minutes before his execution. The lively, thought-provoking (but too crowded) tour takes you through the old and new wings of the prison, where you can see former cells of famous inmates, read graffiti on the walls and immerse yourself in the atmosphere of the execution yards.

Incongruously sitting outside in the yard is the *Asgard*, the ship that successfully ran the British blockade to deliver arms to nationalist forces in 1914. It belonged to, and was skippered by, Erskine Childers, father of the future president of Ireland. He was executed by Michael Collins' Free State army in 1922 for carrying a revolver, which had been a gift from Collins himself. There is also an outstanding museum dedicated to Irish nationalism and prison life. History fans should allow at least half a day for a visit.

KILMAINHAM GATE Map pp262–3

The Kilmainham Gate was designed by Francis Johnston (1760–1829) in 1812 and originally stood, as the Richmond Tower, at the Watling St junction with Victoria Quay, near the Guinness Brewery. It was moved to its current position opposite the prison in 1846 as it obstructed the increasingly heavy traffic to the new Kingsbridge station (now Heuston station), which opened in 1844.

MARSH'S LIBRARY Map pp266–8

☎ 454 3511; www.marshlibrary.ie; St Patrick's Close; adult/child €2.50/2; ☼ 10am-12.45pm & 2-5pm Mon & Wed-Fri, 10.30am-12.45pm Sat (groups of more than 10 have to book in advance); bus 50, 50A & 56A from Aston Quay, or 54 & 54A from Burgh Quay

Virtually unchanged in three centuries, this magnificently preserved scholars library is only around the corner from St Patrick's Cathedral and one of the highlights of a visit to the city. Few think to scale its ancient stairs to see its beautiful, dark oak bookcases, each topped with elaborately carved and gilded gables, and crammed with books. To savour the atmosphere of three centuries of learning, to slow into synch with the tick-tocking of the 19th-century grandfather clock, listen to the squeaky boards and record the scent of leather and learning. It's amazing how many people visit the cathedral and overlook this gem – they're mad, they don't deserve a holiday.

Founded in 1701 by Archbishop Narcissus Marsh (1638–1713) and opened in 1707, the library was designed by Sir William Robinson, the man also responsible for the Royal Hospital Kilmainham. It's the oldest public library in the country, and contains 25,000 books dating from the 16th to the early 18th centuries, as well as maps, manuscripts (including one in Latin dating back to 1400) and a collection of *incunabula* (books printed before 1500). In its one nod to the 21st century, the library's current 'keeper', Dr Muriel McCarthy, is the first woman to hold the post.

Apart from theological books and bibles in dozens of languages, there are tomes on medicine, law, travel, literature, science, navigation, music and mathematics. One of the oldest and finest books is a volume of *Cicero's Letters to His Friends* printed in Milan in 1472. The most important of the four main collections is the 10,000-strong library of Edward Stillingfleet, bishop of Worcester.

Most of Marsh's own extensive collection is also here and there are various items that used to belong to Jonathon Swift, including his copy of *History of the Great Rebellion*. His margin notes include a number of comments vilifying Scots, of whom he seemed to have a low opinion. He also held a low opinion of Archbishop Marsh, whom he blamed for holding him back in the church. When Swift died in 1745, he was buried in St Patrick's Cathedral, near his former enemy (see p96).

Like the rest of the library, the three alcoves, in which scholars were once locked to peruse rare volumes, have remained virtually unchanged for three centuries. The skull in the furthest one doesn't, however, belong to some poor forgotten scholar – it's a cast of the head of Stella, Swift's other half. The library's also home to Delmas Conservation Bindery, which repairs and restores rare old books, and makes an appearance in Joyce's *Ulysses*.

ROYAL HOSPITAL KILMAINHAM & IRISH MUSEUM OF MODERN ART (IMMA) Map pp262–3

☎ 612 9900; www.modernart.ie; Military Rd; admission free; ☼ 10am-5.30pm Tue-Sat, noon-5.30pm Sun; bus 24, 79 & 90 from Aston Quay

IMMA is the country's foremost gallery for contemporary Irish art, although it takes second billing to the majestic building in which it is housed. The Royal Hospital Kilmainham was built in 1680–84 as a retirement home for veteran soldiers, a function it fulfilled until 1928, after which it was left to languish for half a century before being saved in a 1980s restoration.

The inspiration for the design came from James Butler, duke of Ormonde and Charles II's viceroy, who had been so impressed by Les Invalides on a trip to Paris that he commissioned William Robinson to knock up a Dublin version. What the architect designed was Dublin's finest 17th-century building and the highpoint of the Anglo-Dutch style of the day. It consists of an unbroken range enclosing a vast, peaceful courtyard with arcaded walks. A chapel in the centre of the northern flank has an elegant clock tower and spire. This was the first truly classical building in Dublin and marked the beginning of the Georgian boom. Christopher Wren began building the London's Chelsea Royal Hospital two years after work commenced here.

The spectacularly restored hospital was unveiled in 1984, on the 200th anniversary of its construction. The next year it received the prestigious Europa Nostra award for its 'distinguished contribution to the conservation of Europe's architectural heritage'. A **heritage itinerary** (adult/concession €3.50/2; tours only 10am-5.30pm Tue-Sat, noon-5.30pm Sun Jun–end Sept) shows off some of the building's treasures, including the Banqueting Hall, with 22 specially commissioned portraits, and the stunning baroque chapel, with papier-mâché ceilings and a set of exquisite Queen Anne gates. Also worth seeing are the fully restored formal gardens.

In 1991 it became home to IMMA and the best of modern and contemporary Irish art. The blend of old and new works wonderfully, and you'll find contemporary Irish artists such as Louis Le Brocquy, Sean Scully, Richard Deacon, Richard Gorman and Dorothy Cross featured here. The permanent exhibition also features paintings from heavy hitters Pablo Picasso and Joan Miró, and is topped up by regular temporary exhibitions. There are **free guided tours** (☼ 2.30pm Wed, Fri & Sun), and there's a good café and bookshop on the grounds.

ST AUDOEN'S CHURCHES Map pp262–3

☎ 677 0088; Cornmarket, High St; adult/concession €2/1.25; ☼ 9.30am-4.45pm Jun-Sep

St Audoen, the 7th-century bishop of Rouen and patron saint of Normandy, was such a big hit in Dublin that he had two churches named after him, both just west of Christ Church Cathedral. The more interesting of the two is the **Church of Ireland**, the only medieval parish church in the city that's still in use. It was built between 1181 and 1212, although a 9th-century burial slab in the porch suggests that it was built on top of an even older church. Its tower and door date from the 12th century and the aisle from the 15th century, but the church today is mainly a product of its 19th-century restoration.

As part of the tour, you can explore the ruins as well as the present church, which has funerary monuments that were beheaded by Cromwell's purists. Through the heavily moulded Romanesque Norman door you can also touch the 9th-century 'lucky stone' that was believed to bring good luck to business.

St Anne's Chapel, the visitors centre, houses a number of tombstones of leading members of Dublin society from the 16th to the 18th centuries. At the top of the chapel is the tower, which houses the three oldest bells in Ireland, dating from 1423. Although the church's exhibits are hardly spectacular, the building itself is beautiful and a genuine slice of medieval Dublin.

The church is entered from the north of High St through **St Andrew's Arch**, which was built in 1240 and is the only surviving reminder of the city gates. The adjoining park is pretty but attracts many unsavoury characters particularly at night.

Joined onto the Protestant church is the newer Catholic **St Audoen's**, an expansive church, in which Father 'Flash' Kavanagh used to read Mass at high speed so that his large congregation could head off to more absorbing Sunday pursuits, such as football matches.

ST PATRICK'S CATHEDRAL Map pp266–8

☎ 475 4817; www.stpatrickscathedral.ie; St Patrick's Close; adult/concession/family €4/3/8; ☼ 9am-6pm Mon-Fri, 9am-6pm Sat Mar-Oct, 9am-5pm Sat Nov-Mar, for worship only 10.45am-12.30pm & 2.30-4.30pm Sun; bus 50, 50A & 56A from Aston Quay or 54 & 54A from Burgh Quay

Situated on the very spot that St Patrick rolled up his sleeves and baptised Irish converts, this is one of Dublin's earliest Christian sites and its

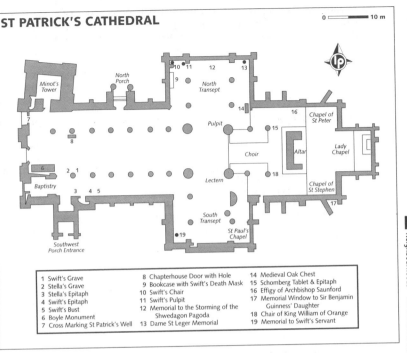

ST PATRICK'S CATHEDRAL

0 — 10 m

Minot's Tower

North Porch

North Transept

10 11 12 13

9

14

Pulpit

16 Chapel of St Peter

7

8

15

Choir

Altar

Lady Chapel

6

2 1

Baptistry

3 4 5

Lectern

18

Chapel of St Stephen

17

South Transept

St Paul's Chapel

19

Southwest Porch Entrance

1 Swift's Grave
2 Stella's Grave
3 Stella's Epitaph
4 Swift's Epitaph
5 Swift's Bust
6 Boyle Monument
7 Cross Marking St Patrick's Well

8 Chapterhouse Door with Hole
9 Bookcase with Swift's Death Mask
10 Swift's Chair
11 Swift's Pulpit
12 Memorial to the Storming of the Shwedagon Pagoda
13 Dame St Leger Memorial

14 Medieval Oak Chest
15 Schomberg Tablet & Epitaph
16 Effigy of Archbishop Saunford
17 Memorial Window to Sir Benjamin Guinness' Daughter
18 Chair of King William of Orange
19 Memorial to Swift's Servant

most hallowed chunk of real estate. Although a church has stood here since the 5th century, this building dates from the turn of the 12th century and has been altered several times, most notably in 1864 when it was saved from ruin and, some might say, overenthusiastically restored. The interior is as calm and soothing as the exterior is sombre, and it's crammed with interesting curios, monuments and memorials. The picturesque St Patrick's Park, adjoining, was a crowded slum until it was cleared in the early 20th century.

It's likely that St Patrick's was intended to replace Christ Church as the city's cathedral but the older church's stubborn refusal to be usurped resulted in the two cathedrals being virtually a stone's throw from one another. Separated only by the city walls (with St Patrick's outside), each possessed the rights of cathedral of the diocese. While St Pat's isn't as photogenic as its neighbour (it doesn't get the clicks, if you like), it does have as interesting a history and perhaps more impressive associations.

It too was built on unstable ground, with the subterranean River Poddle flowing beneath its foundations, and because of the high water table it does not have a crypt. The cathedral had been built twice by 1254 but succumbed to a series of natural disasters over the following century. Its spire was taken out in a 1316 storm, while the original tower and part of the nave were destroyed by fire in 1362 and rebuilt immediately after.

Its troubles were to be more than structural, however. Following Henry VIII's 16th-century hissy fit and the dissolution of the monasteries, St Patrick's was ordered to handover all of its estates, revenues and possessions. The chapter was imprisoned until they *agreed* to the hand over, the cathedral's privileges were revoked and it was demoted to the rank of parish church. It was not restored to its previous position until 1560.

Further indignity arrived with Cromwell in 1649, when the nave was used as a stable for his horses. In 1666 the Lady Chapel was given to the newly arrived Huguenots and became known as the French Church of St Patrick. It remained in Huguenot hands until 1816. The northern transept was known as the parish church of St Nicholas Without (meaning outside the city), essentially dividing the cathedral into two distinct churches.

Such confusion led to the building falling into disrepair as the influence of the deanery and chapter – previously charged with the church's maintenance – waned. Although the church's most famous dean, Jonathan Swift (who served from 1713 to 1745) did his utmost to preserve the integrity of the building, by the end of the 18th century it was close to collapse. It was just about still standing when the benevolent Guinness family stepped in to begin massive restoration in 1864.

Fittingly, the first Guinness to show an interest in preserving the church, Benjamin, is commemorated with a statue at the main entrance to the cathedral. Immediately inside to your left is the oldest part of the building, the baptistery, which was probably the entrance to the original building. It has original floor tiles and a medieval stone font, which is still in use. Inside the cathedral proper, you come almost immediately to the graves of Jonathan Swift and his long-term companion Esther Johnson, better known as Stella. The Latin epitaphs are both written by Swift, and assorted Swift memorabilia here includes a pulpit and death mask.

Chancing One's Arm

In 1492 a furious argument erupted in St Patrick's Cathedral between the Earls of Kildare and Ormonde, whose troops swiftly squared up to one another. When strong words were about to lead to blows, the Earl of Ormonde barricaded himself into the chapterhouse, which was then part of the southern transept of the cathedral. Kildare, having counted to 10 and eager to end hostilities, cut a hole in the door and stuck his arm through it, exposing himself to danger while inviting Ormonde to shake hands. Peace was restored, Ormond kept his limb and the expression 'chancing your arm' entered the English language. The hole is still in the door, which is displayed in the cathedral as a symbol of reconciliation.

Beginning clockwise around the cathedral, you can't miss the huge Boyle Monument, erected in 1632 by Richard Boyle, earl of Cork. It stood briefly beside the altar until, in 1633, Dublin's viceroy, Thomas Wentworth, earl of Strafford, had it shifted from its prominent position because he felt he shouldn't have to kneel to a Corkman. Boyle took his revenge in later years by orchestrating Wentworth's impeachment and execution. A figure in a niche

at the bottom left of the monument was the earl's son Robert who went on to become a noted scientist and discovered Boyles' Law which sets out the relationship between the pressure and the volume of a gas.

In the opposite corner, there is a cross on a stone slab that once marked the position of St Patrick's original well, where the patron saint of Ireland rolled up his sleeves and got to baptising the natives. Towards the north transept is displayed a door that has become a symbol of peace and reconciliation, and comes with a good yarn (see the boxed text below).

The north transept contains various military memorials to the Royal Irish Regiments, while the northern choir aisle has a tablet marking the grave of the Duke of Schomberg, a prominent casualty of the Battle of the Boyne in 1690. Swift provided the duke's epitaph caustically noting on it that the duke's own relatives couldn't be bothered to provide a suitable memorial. On the opposite side of the choir is a chair used by William of Orange when he came to the cathedral to give thanks to God for his victory over the Catholic James II during the same battle.

Passing through the south transept, which was once the chapterhouse where the Earl of Kildare chanced his arm (see the boxed text to the left), you'll see magnificent stained-glass windows above the funerary monuments. The south aisle is lined with memorials to prominent 20th-century Irish Protestants including Erskine Childers, president of Ireland from 1973 to 1974, whose father was executed by the Free State during the Civil War. The son never spoke of the struggle for Irish history because on the eve of his death, his father made him promise never to do anything that might promote bitterness among Irish people.

On your way around the church, you will also take in the four sections of the relatively new permanent exhibition, Living Stones, which explores the cathedral's history and contribution to the culture of Dublin. The cathedral managers are also hoping to provide **tours of Minot's tower** (approx €7.50, limited to groups of eight) some time in the future so it will be worth phoning ahead if you're interested.

ST WERBURGH'S CHURCH Map pp266–8
☎ 478 3710; Werburgh St; donations welcome;
🕙 10am-4pm Mon-Fri; phone, or see the caretaker at 8 Castle St to see inside

Lying west of Dublin Castle, St Werburgh's Church stands upon ancient foundations probably from the 12th century), but was rebuilt several times during the 17th and 18th centuries. The church's tall spire was dismantled after Robert Emmet's rising in 1803, for fear that future rebels might use it as a vantage point for snipers. Interred in the vault is Lord Edward Fitzgerald, who turned against Britain, joined the United Irishmen and was a leader of the 1798 Rising. In what was a frequent theme of Irish uprisings, compatriots gave him away and his death resulted from the wounds he received when captured. Co-incidentally, Major Henry Sirr, the man who captured him is buried out in the graveyard. On the porch you will notice two fire pumps that date from the time when Dublin's fire department was composed of church volunteers. The interior is rather more cheerful than the exterior, although the church is rarely used today.

BEYOND THE GRAND CANAL

Drinking p129; Eating p107; Shopping p161; Sleeping p179

Two canals encircle central Dublin: the older Grand Canal to the south and the newer Royal Canal to the north (see p113). True Dubliners, it is said, are born within the confines of the canals.

Built to connect Dublin with the River Shannon in the centre of Ireland, the Grand Canal makes a graceful 6km loop around south Dublin and enters the Liffey at Ringsend, through locks that were built in 1796. The large Grand Canal Dock, flanked by Hanover and Charlotte Quays, is now used by windsurfers and canoeists and is the site of major new development. Here you'll find the Waterways Visitor Centre (p100), which illustrates the gleaming new development of the area that, for now, sits side by side with the workaday, historical and even quaint auld Dublin of Ringsend and Irishtown. At the northwestern corner of the dock is Misery Hill, once the site of public executions. It was the practice to bring the corpses of those already hung at Gallows Hill, near Upper Baggot St, to this spot, to be strung up for public display for anything from six to 12 months.

The canal hasn't been used commercially since 1960, but some stretches are attractive and enjoyable to stroll or cycle along. The poet Patrick Kavanagh was particularly enamoured with the 2km stretch from Mount St Bridge west to Richmond St, which has grassy, tree-lined banks and – as you might have guessed – a cluster of pubs. Among Kavanagh's compositions is the hauntingly beautiful *On Raglan Road*, which was put to music by Van Morrison. In another, he requested that he be commemorated by 'a canal bank seat for passers-by'. His friends obliged with a seat beside the lock on the southern side of the canal. A little further along on the northern side you can sit down by Kavanagh himself, cast in bronze, comfortably lounging on a bench and staring at his beloved canal.

Top Five – Beyond the Grand Canal

- Villagey Ranelagh
- Waterways Visitor Centre (p100)
- Pearse Museum (p100)
- Rathfarnham Castle (p100)
- A walk along the canal

Beyond the Grand Canal and into the southern outer-reaches of Dublin are inner suburbs that have developed along the main roads into the city. Lively Rathmines is a predominantly student area that has some decent bars and restaurants. Relaxed Ranelagh is steadily moving upmarket, with an influx of moneyed 'culchies' (a disparaging term for Irish people from outside of Dublin), although it has some terrific places to eat, an atmospheric pub or two and – for the time being at least – a cosy village atmosphere. Moving further to the east, you enter 'Dublin 4', two words synonymous with money and affectation. Elegant and embassy-laden Ballsbridge has some terrific places to eat, many top-end hotels, galleries and the famous Lansdowne Rd Stadium (p177), where international rugby and football (soccer) matches are played.

NATIONAL PRINT MUSEUM Map pp260–1

☎ 660 3770; Garrison Chapel, Beggar's Bush, Haddington Rd; adult/concession €3.20/1.90; ☺ 10am-5pm Mon-Fri, noon-5pm Sat & Sun; bus 7, 8 & 45 from city centre, DART Grand Canal Dock

You don't have to be into printing to enjoy this quirky little museum, where personalised guided tours are offered in a delightfully casually way. First you can watch a video relating to printing and its place in Irish history. Then take a wander amid the smell of ink and metal and through the various antique presses that are still worked for small jobs by a couple of retired printers doing it for the love of the craft. The guides are excellent and can tailor the tours to suit your special interests – for example anyone interested in history can get a detailed account of the difficulties encountered by the rebels of 1916 when they tried to get the proclamation printed. Upstairs, there are lots of old newspaper covers recording important episodes in Irish history over the last century.

PEARSE MUSEUM

☎ 493 4208; St Enda's, Grange Rd, Rathfarnham; admission free; ☺ 10am-5pm, 10am-5.30pm May-Aug, 10am-4pm Nov-Jan; bus 16 from O'Connell St

Occupying the house in which nationalist poet and 1916 martyr Pádraig Pearse established his experimental Gaelic school, St Enda's (which focused on Irish language and sports), this museum is devoted to one of Ireland's greatest visionaries and comprises audiovisual guides, books, an informative personalised tour and exhibits that include Pearse's original writing desk. A visit is a must for anybody interested in the events surrounding Irish independence, while the beautiful grounds, gardens and grottos make it a pleasant excursion for everyone else.

RATHFARNHAM CASTLE

☎ 493 9462; Rathfarnham Rd, Rathfarnham; ☺ 9.30am-5.30pm May-Oct; adult/concession €2/1; bus 16 from O'Connell St

This castle (more accurately, a fortified house) was originally built by Adam Loftus, the archbishop of Dublin, in the late 16th century and is most interesting as a restoration in progress. Several of the rooms – including 18th-century interiors by William Chambers – have been returned to their original splendour, while others are clearly struggling under the ravages of time. The guides have an infectious enthusiasm for the project.

ROYAL DUBLIN SOCIETY SHOWGROUND Map pp260–1

☎ 668 9878; Merrion Rd, Ballsbridge; bus 7 from Trinity College

Founded in 1731, the Royal Dublin Society (RDS) horse show was involved in the establishment of the National Museum, Library, Gallery and Botanic Gardens. The showground is used for various exhibitions throughout the year, but the main event is the **Dublin Horse Show**, which reflects the society's agricultural background. It takes place in the first week of August and includes a prestigious international showjumping contest among other events.

WATERWAYS VISITOR CENTRE Map pp266–8

☎ 677 7510; Grand Canal Quay; adult/concession €2.50/1.25; ☺ 9.30am-5.30pm Jun-Sep, 12.30-5.30pm Wed-Sun Oct & May; DART to Grand Canal Quay

Upstream from the Grand Canal Docks, this interpretive centre – colloquially known as the 'box in the docks' because of its situation and

---

The 'Sniffy Liffey' & the Great Divide

It's relatively shallow, not very wide, it occasionally pongs and is usually a colour ranging from brown to pea-green . . . it's the dear auld River Liffey, cherished by Dubliners. Although much cleaner than it once was, at low tide you can appreciate the origins of its nickname; but even if there was no eau de Liffey, locals would still fondly regard it as the 'Sniffy Liffey'.

Its greatest contribution to Dublin life has been as a physical, psychological and social divide between – in the broadest possible strokes – the southern 'haves' and northern 'have-nots'. After a few days exploring both sides, you'll see that rich and poor live cheek by jowl on both banks, but this doesn't stop the rivalry, which is sometimes passionate but more often just the source of an endless supply of jokes. It's very childish really, and not to be encouraged. What's the difference between Batman and a northsider? Batman can go into town without Robbin'. What do you call a northsider in a suit? The Accused. How do you know ET was a northsider? Because he looked like one.

Ner-ner-ner-ner-na.

shape – explores the history and personality of Ireland's canals and waterways through models (if they're working), audiovisual displays and panels. If you are here in summer and are wondering why it needs to employ a security guard, it's to keep local kids from storming up to the centre's roof and using it as a diving platform into the basin. Sometimes the kids content themselves with diving off the shed on the bridge, terrorising those on board the Viking Splash Tours (p74) that pass beneath.

NORTH OF THE LIFFEY

The north side has endured a reputation for being the poorer half of the city, better known in recent decades for social ills and drug-related problems than the shopping and sights of its southern neighbour. It's as gritty as the south side is glitzy, and its people are as down-to-earth as some of their southern neighbours are pretentious. There are also plenty of attractions to see, both old and new, and pockets of the inner north side like Smithfield are already shining examples of urban renewal. But it's the sense of traditional Dublin that makes the north side unique. As Jimmy Rabbite said in *The Commitments* (1991), 'the Irish are the blacks of Europe, Dubliners are the blacks of Ireland, and northsiders are the blacks of Dublin…so say it loud – I'm black and I'm proud!' His audience was as bemused as you probably are, but the general gist of what we're saying is that the north side's greatest feature is that it has soul and vitality.

AROUND O'CONNELL STREET

Drinking p129; Eating p107; Shopping p161; Sleeping p179

The imperially wide O'Connell St is the centre of Dublin and its most historically important thoroughfare, where the 1916 Easter Rising was centred and where many momentous episodes have been played out.

Putting the best spin on it, this area provides glimpses of old Dublin through historical boozers, the Clery's & Co department store (p191), prestigious theatres, the venerable Gresham Hotel (p205), St Mary's Catholic pro-Cathedral (p107) and numerous cultural sights. But leaving nostalgia aside, O'Connell St has fallen into a heap of ugly shops, fast-food outlets and amusement arcades, where gangs of drunken louts frequently menace at night and litterbugs foul by day. Authorities, at long last, are overhauling the street and there are plans to make it more user-friendly (though a 120m-tall steel centrepiece wasn't exactly what we had in mind).

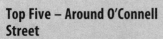

Top Five – Around O'Connell Street

- Dublin Writers Museum (p103)
- A stroll along the Boardwalk (p102)
- Hugh Lane Gallery (p103)
- The Spire (p106)
- James Joyce Centre (p104)

It became Dublin's main street in 1794, when O'Connell Bridge was built and the city's axis shifted east. The north side was the residential area of choice at the start of the Georgian period, but when the hoi polloi got too close, the aristocracy doubled back over the Liffey and settled the new areas surrounding Leinster House (p85). The Georgian squares named after Parnell and Mountjoy fell into rapid decline and were partly converted into slum dwellings. Although much more neglected, they still display a certain dishevelled charm and are gradually being restored. O'Connell St leads north to the large Parnell Sq, which is flanked by museums, public buildings and some fine, if rather run-down, Georgian residences. It is here you'll find the Dublin Writers Museum (p103), Hugh Lane Municipal Gallery of Modern Art (p103), the prestigious Gate Theatre (p174), the distinctive Rotunda Hospital (p106) and the relief of the Garden of Remembrance (p103).

Mountjoy Sq, northwest of O'Connell St, was *the* most elegant square in Dublin. Out of sight, it also became the most neglected square in Dublin over the next two centuries when it became a prime example of urban decay. It's most famous former resident was the playwright Sean O'Casey who set his masterpiece *The Shadow of a Gunman* here.

Parnell St has become a popular area with Dublin's new ethnic communities, particularly from Africa. As the epicentre of the city's new multiculturalism, it should be coloured in with the customs and traditions of new Dubliners over coming years.

The north quays of the River Liffey have undergone some transformations over recent decades. During the 1980s, many buildings were left derelict and crumbling, and it looked like the area between the magnificent Georgian landmarks of the Four Courts (p110) and Custom House (p102) might tumble into the river altogether. Fast forward to 2004 and there's a snazzy new continental-style boardwalk running alongside the river; the hip Morrison Hotel on Ormond Quay; the Ha'Penny Bridge has been given a polish; the sturdy and stylish Millennium Bridge leads into a brand new street; and Bachelor's Walk has, at least, been patched up.

We hate to say it but, for now, there aren't many reasons to visit this area after dark, although hopefully this will change in coming years.

BELVEDERE HOUSE Map pp264–5
6 Great Denmark St; closed to the public
Great Denmark St runs northeast to Mountjoy Sq and passes the 18th-century Belvedere House at No 6. This has been used as the Jesuit **Belvedere College** since 1841, and none other than James Joyce studied here between 1893 and 1898, describing it later in *A Portrait of the Artist as a Young Man*. The building is renowned for its magnificent plasterwork by the master stuccodore Michael Stapleton and for its fireplaces by the Venetian artisan Bossi, but the only chance you'll get to admire these features is if you enrol for a class at this secondary school. The plasterwork isn't *that* special.

Meetin' in Monto

The area immediately east of O'Connell St used to be Dublin's most notorious red-light district until 1925 when the city decided that such shenanigans were inappropriate so close to the main Catholic church. All the brothels were closed down and Catholic girls marched through the streets attaching holy pictures to the doors of former dens of disrepute.

CUSTOM HOUSE Map pp264–5
☎ 888 2538; Visitor Centre, Custom House Quay; admission €1; ☺ 10am-12.30pm & 2-5pm Mon-Fri, 2-5pm Sat & Sun (closed Mon, Tue & Sat Nov–mid Mar)
This was the first great building by 18th-century Dublin's pre-eminent architect, James Gandon, and was constructed just past Eden Quay at a wide stretch in the River Liffey between 1781 and 1791. When it was being built, angry city merchants and dock workers from the original Custom House further up river in Temple Bar were so menacing that Gandon

sometimes appeared on the building site wielding a sword rather than a hard hat. He was supported by the era's foremost property developer, Luke Gardiner, who saw the new Custom House as a major part of his scheme to shift the axis of the city eastwards from medieval Capel St to what was then Gardiner' Mall (now O'Connell St).

It's a colossal, neoclassical pile that stretches for 114m along the River Liffey. It can only be taken in and admired from the south side of the river, although its fine detail deserves closer inspection. Arcades, each with seven arches, join the centre to the end pavilions and the columns along the front have harps carved in their capitals. Motifs allude to transportation and trade, including the four rooftop statues of Neptune, Mercury, Plenty and Industry, destroyed when the building was gutted in a five-day fire during the independence struggle in 1921 and replaced in 1991. (The interior was extensively redesigned after 1921 and again in the 1980s Below the frieze are heads representing the gods of Ireland's 13 principal rivers. The sole female head above the main door represents the River Liffey. The cattle heads honour Dublin's beef trade, and the statues behind the building represent Africa, America, Asia and Europe. The building is topped by a copper dome with four clocks and, above that, a 5m-high statue of Hope.

Beneath the dome, the **Visitor Centre** features a small museum on Gandon and the history of the building.

Just outside the Custom House, on Custom House Quay, is a remarkable set of life-size bronze figures, a **memorial to the victims of the Famine** (1845–49) made by Rowan Gillespie in 1997. The piece powerfully evokes the drama of Ireland's greatest single tragedy.

DUBLIN WRITERS MUSEUM Map pp264–5

☎ 872 2077; www.writersmuseum.com; 18 North Parnell Sq; adult/child/concession/family €6/3.50/5/6.50; ☼ 10am-5pm Mon-Sat, 10am-6pm Jun-Aug, 11am-5pm Sun

There's a sense of occasion entering this museum of Dublin's literary greats. The beautiful gallery upstairs houses busts and portraits of the city's most famous writers, but it's the ground-floor displays of their letters, photographs and other memorabilia that are of most interest. Exhibits include Samuel Beckett's phone (with a button for excluding incoming calls, of course), a letter from the 'tenement aristocrat' Brendan Behan to his brother, and a first edition of Bram Stoker's *Dracula*. Admission includes taped guides in English and other languages, which have the annoying habit of repeating quotes with actor's voices. The exhibits stop some three decades ago and the flat cabinet displays can literally become a pain in the neck, but this is still a fascinating wander for anyone interested in Dublin's literary lore.

The building, comprising two 18th-century houses, is worth exploring on its own. Dublin stuccodore Michael Stapleton decorated the upstairs gallery. The Gorham Library next door to it is worth a peek and there's also a calming Zen garden. The museum café is a pleasant place to linger, while the basement Chapter One restaurant (p151) is one of the north side's best.

While the museum focuses on the dearly departed, the **Irish Writers Centre** (☎ 872 1302; 19 North Parnell Sq) next door provides a meeting and working place for their living successors.

GARDEN OF REMEMBRANCE

Map pp264–5

Parnell Sq

This rather austere little park was opened by President Eamon de Valera in 1966 for the 50th anniversary of the Easter Rising. It is still known to some Dubs as the 'Garden of Mature Recollection', mocking the linguistic gymnastics employed by former favourite for president, Brian Lenihan, who was caught out lying in a minor political scandal and used the phrase to try and wiggle his way out of it.

The most interesting feature in the garden is a bronze statue by Oisin Kelly of the **Children of Lir**, who according to Irish legend were turned into swans by their wicked stepmother. It was probably intended to evoke the famous lines penned by WB Yeats in his poem *Easter 1916*:

'All is changed, changed utterly, A Terrible beauty is born.'

GENERAL POST OFFICE (GPO)

Map pp264–5

☎ 705 7000; www.anpost.ie; O'Connell St; ☼ 8am-8pm Mon-Sat

As the headquarters of the 1916 Easter Rising, the GPO is the most important landmark in the history of Irish independence and has become the focal point for everything from official parades to personal protests. Pádraig Pearse, James Connolly and the other five leaders of the Easter Rising proclaimed Ireland a republic from its steps and then braced themselves for a week of bombardment from the British military. The huge building, designed by Francis Johnston and opened in 1818, was gutted during the battle (virtually every building in Lower O'Connell St was destroyed). The facade features a huge Ionic portico, which spans the five central bays and is topped by three statues representing Fidelity, Hibernia and Mercury. The frieze is heavily carved, and that's not counting the various pockmarks and bullet holes it still bears from the 1916 clash. It was reopened in 1929.

In the spacious and light-filled interior there's a beautiful bronze statue, the *Death of Cuchulainn* (1935), depicting the legendary hero of Ulster, whose spirit was evoked in the poetry of Pádraig Pearse. He was an awesome warrior slain at the age of 27 after being tricked into an unfair fight. Even as he lay dead, nobody dared approach the body for fear and it wasn't until ravens landed on him that they were convinced he was dead. The statue is dedicated to those who died in the rising. Also inside is a series of Communist noble worker-style paintings depicting scenes from the Easter Rising. There are also lots of people going about the everyday business of buying stamps and posting letters. Finally, among all the flags hanging in here, notice that the Union Jack is hung behind the counter and out of reach; it had to be moved there because people kept setting it alight.

HUGH LANE GALLERY Map pp264–5

Municipal Gallery of Ireland; ☎ 874 1903; www.hughlane.ie; 22 North Parnell Sq; admission free to permanent collection, Francis Bacon exhibition adult/child €7/3.50, free before noon Tue; ☼ 9.30am-6pm Tue-Thu, 9.30am-5pm Fri-Sat, 11am-5pm Sun; bus 3, 10, 11, 13, 16, 19 & 22 from city centre

This splendid gallery has a fine collection of paintings by French impressionists and 20th-century Irish artists. It is housed in the equally

Hugh Lane

It's hardly surprising that wealthy Sir Hugh Lane (1875–1915) was miffed by the Irish and decided to bequeath his paintings to some other nation, as he was treated with less respect than he felt he deserved in his own land. Born in County Cork, he began to work in London art galleries from 1893 and five years later set up his own gallery in Dublin. He had a connoisseur's eye and a good nose for the directions of the market, which enabled him to build up a superb and valuable collection, particularly strong in impressionists.

Unfortunately for Ireland, neither his talents nor his collection were much appreciated, and in exasperation he turned his attention to opportunities in London and South Africa. Irish rejection led him to rewrite his will and bequeath some of the finest works in his collection to the National Gallery in London. Later he relented and added a rider to his will leaving the collection to Dublin but failed to have it witnessed, thus causing a long legal squabble over which gallery had rightful ownership. He was just 40 years old when he went down with the ill-fated *Lusitania* in 1915 after it was torpedoed by a German U-boat off the southern coast of Ireland.

splendid Charlemont House, built by William Chambers in 1763, and home to the gallery since 1933. Artists featured in the permanent exhibition include Manet, Degas, Vuillard, Monet, and Irish painters Roderic O'Conor, Jack B Yeats, Louis le Brocquy and Brian Maguire.

The gallery was founded – with no help from the government – in 1908 by Hugh Lane, the wealthy nephew of Lady Gregory (WB Yeats' patron). The lack of official funding was the subject of one of WB Yeats' most vitriolic poems *September 1913*. Lane was a passenger on the ill-fated *Lusitania* and died in 1915 (see the boxed text above). There followed a bitter wrangle over the Lane Bequest between the gallery he founded and the National Gallery in London. The collection was eventually split in a complicated 1959 settlement that sees some of the paintings moving back and forth. Until November 2005 the gallery has Manet's *Eva Gonzales*, Pissarro's *Printemps*, Berthe Morisot's *Jour d'Eté* and the most important painting of the entire collection, and one of our favourites of all time, Renoir's *Les Parapluies*.

The gallery's newest permanent exhibit is the superbly presented, full-scale recreation of the studio of the painter Francis Bacon (1909–92), who was born in Dublin but left as a teenager. Before examining the 'deeply ordered chaos' of the studio where the immensely talented and troubled painter toiled for the last 30 years of his life, watch the 10-minute profile of him with Melvyn Bragg. The exhibition features some 80,000 items madly strewn about the place, including slashed canvasses, the last painting he was working on, tables piled with materials, walls daubed with colour samples, portraits with heads cut out, favourite bits of furniture and many assorted piles of crap. It's a teasing and tantalising, riveting and ridiculous masterpiece. While the gallery tries to talk up Bacon's Irishness a little bit, in truth the artist couldn't stand the place (see the boxed text left).

JAMES JOYCE CENTRE Map pp264–5

☎ 878 8547; www.jamesjoyce.ie; 35 North Great George's St; adult/concession/children aged under 12 €5/4/free; ⏰ 9.30am-5pm Mon-Sat, 12.30-5pm Sun, 1hr tours of north Dublin adult/concession €10/9 2.15pm Mon, Wed & Fri; bus 3, 10, 11, 13, 16, 16a, 19, 19A & 22 from city centre

North Great George's St was a fashionable address in 18th-century Dublin but, like so much of the north side, fell on hard times when the Act of Union turned the city into a backwater. James Joyce's family lived in north Dublin for a time and he would have been familiar with the street. Denis Maginni taught dance in the front room of this house early in the 20th century. Hardly remarkable, except for the fact that it left quite an impression on Joyce who featured it several times in *Ulysses*. In CS Andrews' *Dublin Made Me*, Maginni is described as 'egregious and ludicrous. Every afternoon he strolled up O'Connell St in silk hat, morning coat, lavender waistcoat, striped trousers, silver-topped malacca cane and gold watch-chain'. Sadly, after Maginni's departure the house fell into disrepair. In 1982 the house was taken over by Senator David Norris, a charismatic Joycean scholar and gay-rights activist, who restored the building and converted it into a centre for the study of Joyce and his books.

The centre's not just texts and papers for Joycean scholars; there's a regular programme of events (especially in 2004, the centenary of Bloom's journey around Dublin), films and lectures, walking tours of Joyce's haunts, photographs, relics and fascinating facts. Anyone who hasn't read what most consider the greatest novel of the 20th century can take heart in the fact that neither did Nora Barnacle, oyce's lifelong partner. Not only did she not read *Ulysses*, she tried to get Joyce to give up writing altogether!

While here, you can also admire the fine plastered ceilings, some of which are restored originals while others are meticulous reproductions of Michael Stapleton's designs. Senator Norris ought a long time, unrewarded, for the preservation of Georgian Dublin, and it's wonderful to see others have followed his example – the street has been given a much needed acelift and now boasts some of the finest Georgian doorways and fanlights in the city.

MONUMENTS OF O'CONNELL STREET Map pp264–5

eland's main street, and its front line in the battle for independence, is lined with statues of the good and the great from its history. At the southern end is a large bronze monument to the 'Liberator', Daniel O'Connell (Map pp269–71; 1775–1847) that was completed in 1880. The four winged figures at the base represent O'Connell's defining features of patriotism, courage, fidelity and eloquence. Two of them bear the scars of bullet holes from the 1916 Easter Rising. Above this a drum surrounded by figures is supposed to represent the man's labours and triumphs. Dubs began to refer to the street as O'Connell St soon after the monument was erected, but its name was only officially changed after independence.

Daniel O'Connell statue, O'Connell St

Heading away from the river, the central pedestrian area is home to a variety of statuary, including a monument to William Smith O'Brien (1803–64), leader of the Young Ireland Party. Outside the GPO, Jim Larkin (1876–1947), a trade union leader and organiser of the general strike of 1913, is depicted with hands outstretched urging workers to rise up for their rights.

The street's most famous historical monument was a Doric pillar topped by a statue of Admiral Nelson that was erected in the centre of Dublin in 1815 and predated Trafalgar Sq's famous Nelson's Column by 32 years. By way of celebrating the 50th anniversary of the 1916 Easter Rising, the IRA blew up the symbol of British imperialism and knocked Nelson off his perch. An aspect of the demolition that never ceases to amuse Dubliners is that while the IRA explosion deftly toppled the admiral and caused no other damage, the charges set by the Irish army to demolish the remaining pedestal blew out virtually every window in O'Connell St! Nelson's stone head survives in the Dublin Civic Museum (p83).

Next up and difficult to miss is the Spire (p106), to make room for which a sculpted figure (1988) of Joyce's spirit of the Liffey, Anna Livia, was removed. Thank heavens for small mercies, as it was the ugliest sight in the city and reviled by Dubliners who used it as a rubbish bin and frequently put dishwashing liquid in its fountains. It is in storage for the time being, but will probably resurface at Collins Barracks (p108) in coming years.

Watching quietly from the side, on the pedestrianised North Earl St, you must wonder what the detached figure of James Joyce would make of all of this. And what it would say about 21st-century Dublin that the best it could do on a street lined with historical figures was to erect something very high and shiny.

Further on is the figure of Father Theobald Mathew (1790–1856), who was known as the 'apostle of temperance' – there can't have been a tougher gig in Ireland. He led a spirited campaign against 'the demon drink' in the 1840s and converted hundreds of thousands to teetotalism.

The top of the street is completed by a statue of Charles Stewart Parnell (1846–91), the 'uncrowned king of Ireland' who was an advocate of Home Rule and became a political victim of Irish intolerance. Despite this, it's Parnell who gets the most imposing monument.

105

NATIONAL WAX MUSEUM Map pp164–5

☎ 873 6340; Granby Row, Parnell Sq; adult/child €7/4;
🕙 10am-5.30pm Mon-Sat, noon-5.30pm Sun; bus 3,
10, 11, 13, 16, 19 & 22 from city centre

No matter how naughty or misbehaving, no kid – or guidebook researcher – should be forced to endure this tired and depressing collection of wax moulds featuring the usual offerings of fairy tales, rock stars and the inevitable chamber of bloody horrors. There are lots of Irish historical figures, cultural figures, TV personalities and sports stars that your kid will probably have no idea about, and an unusual life-size replica of Leonardo da Vinci's *Last Supper*. We're not into wax but you never know, if your little one has a penchant for kitsch, it might be a worthwhile shelter on a rainy day.

ROTUNDA HOSPITAL Map pp164–5

☎ 873 0700; Parnell Sq; 🕙 visiting hours 6-8pm

Irish public hospitals aren't usually attractions, by any stretch of the imagination, but this one makes for an interesting walk-by or an unofficial wander inside if you're interested in Victorian plasterwork. It was the first maternity hospital in the British Isles – and once the world's largest – and was established by Dr Bartholomew Mosse in 1748 at a time when the burgeoning urban population was enduring shocking infant mortality rates.

It shares its basic design with Leinster House (p85) because the architect of both, Richard Cassels, used the same floor plan to economise. He added a three-storey tower into which Mosse intended to charge visitors to help fund the hospital. He also laid out pleasure gardens, which were fashionable among Dublin's high society for a time, and built the Rotunda Assembly Hall to raise money. The hall is now occupied by the Ambassador Theatre (p168), and the Supper Rooms house the Gate Theatre (p174).

Inside, the public rooms and staircases give some idea of how beautiful the hospital once was, and they lead to one of Dublin's largely hidden gems, the sumptuous **Rotunda Chapel**, built in 1758, and featuring superb coloured plasterwork by German stuccodore Bartholomew Cramillion. The Italian artist Giovanni Battista Capriani was supposed to supplement the work but his paintings were never installed, which is probably just as well because you can't imagine how this little space would have looked with even more decoration. If you intend visiting, you have to bear in mind that this is still a functioning hospital and you must be very quiet when

coming to see the chapel. It's not terribly we signposted inside and is often locked outsic of visiting hours (although if you ask kindly look like you're in desperate need of a praye somebody will let you in).

THE SPIRE Map pp164–5

Soaring 120m over O'Connell St, it's impossib to miss this gigantic knitting needle that wa erected here in homage to Ireland's most re ognisable export, the humble – but surprising warm and eminently sensible – Aran sweate Ah no, the Spire isn't meant to commemora anything, save perhaps the notion in 199(Dublin that the sky was the limit. But it's n just an ornament; it *is* apparently the highe sculpture in the world and, sarcasm aside, it a hugely impressive feat of architectural eng neering (see the boxed text on p48).

From a base of only 3m in diameter, soars over 120m into the sky and tapers into 15cm-wide beam of light. It was the brainchi of London-based architect Ian Ritchie and meant to be the centrepiece in a programm aimed at regenerating O'Connell St. As an i dication of what many Dubliners think of th street, local wags came up with alternativ names for the Spire, such as the 'gleamir tower of pizza land', the 'tip' and the 'stiletto the ghetto'. When indicating that somethir isn't likely, some locals have taken to sugges ing there was a better chance of 'Bertie Ahe shimmying bollock naked up the Spire'.

ST GEORGE'S CHURCH Map pp164–5

Hardwicke Pl; closed to the public; bus 11, 16 & 41
from city centre

If you're on the north side, the steeple of th deconsecrated church may catch your eye. Th church was built by Francis Johnston from 18(in Greek Ionic style, and the 60m-high steep was modelled on that of St Martin-in-the-Fielc in London. Although this was one of Johnston finest works and the Duke of Wellington wa married here, the church has been sorely n glected (probably because it's Church of Irelar and not Roman Catholic, it has to be said). Th bells that Leopold Bloom heard in *that* boc were removed, the ornate pulpit was carve up and used to decorate Thomas Read's pu (p159), and the spire is in danger of crumblin It's especially disappointing considering th is Taoiseach Bertie Ahern's own constituenc The venue is now used as the Temple Theat nightclub (p173). Now, if it had been an histor boozer on Bertie's doorstep…

ST MARY'S ABBEY Map pp269–71

☎ 872 1490, Meeting House Lane; adult/concession 1.50/1; ⌚ 10am-5pm Wed & Sun mid-Jun–mid-Sep

All that remains open of this Cistercian abbey is the chapterhouse, which only gives you a glimpse of what was once the most powerful and wealthy monastery in Ireland. Built in 1180, the abbey played a dominant role in Irish church politics until Henry VIII ordered the dissolution of the monasteries in 1537. Only three years earlier 'Silken' Thomas Fitzgerald, the most important of Leinster's Anglo-Norman lords, had renounced his allegiance to Henry in the chapterhouse, which had been a popular meeting place for rebels conspiring against the English monarch. There's a small exhibition and a model of what the abbey looked like in medieval times.

ST MARY'S CHURCH Map pp264–5

Mary St; closed to the public; bus 11, 16 & 41 from city centre

Designed by William Robinson in 1697, this is the most important church to survive from that period (although not in use). John Wesley, founder of Methodism, delivered his first Irish sermon here in 1747 and it was the preferred church of Dublin's 18-century social elite. Many famous Dubliners were baptised in its font and Arthur Guinness was married here in 1793.

ST MARY'S PRO-CATHEDRAL

Map pp264–5

☎ 874 5441; Marlborough St; admission free; ⌚ 8am-6.30pm

Dublin's most important Catholic church was built between 1816 and 1825. It was originally intended to occupy the site where the GPO stands, but the local Protestant community went nuts about the idea of it having such a prominent position so it was built in a much less conspicuous side street, away from the main thoroughfare. In fact, it's so cramped for space around here that you'd hardly notice the church's six Doric columns, which were modelled on the Temple of Theseus in Athens, much less be able to admire it. The interior is fairly functional, and its few highlights include a carved altar by Peter Turnerelli and the alto relief representation of the Ascension by John Smyth. The best time to visit is 11am on Sunday when the Latin mass is sung by the Palestrina Choir, with whom Ireland's most celebrated tenor, John McCormack, began his career in 1904.

The 'pro' in the title implies, roughly, that it is an 'unofficial cathedral'. More accurately it was built as a sort of interim cathedral to be replaced when sufficient funds were available. Church leaders never actually got around to it, and it seems odd that the capital of this most Catholic of countries doesn't have a befitting place of worship.

The design of the church is shrouded in some mystery. In 1814 John Sweetman won a competition held to find the best design for the church, a competition that had actually been organised by his brother William. It's not certain whether John actually designed the building, since he was living in Paris at the time and may have bought the plans from the French architect Auguste Gauthier, who designed the similar Notre Dame de Lorette in northern France. The only clue as to the church's architect is in the ledger, which lists the builder as 'Mr P'.

SMITHFIELD & PHOENIX PARK

Drinking p129; Eating p107; Shopping p161; Sleeping p179

Smithfield is a go-go these days as Dublin's newest hotspot, and it's an intoxicating blend of the old and the very new in architecture, food, atmosphere, sights and entertainment.

The area has been synonymous with markets since the 17th century and, in recent decades, a bustling horse fair where deals were sealed with a spit in your hand. The centrepiece of the new redevelopment is a huge plaza, for which some 400,000 antique cobblestones were removed, hand cleaned and relaid alongside new granite slabs to provide a thoroughly modern feel without sacrificing the traditional beauty of the place. In 2000 the city unveiled its new civic space to universal acclaim. Even the horsetraders seemed impressed when they came on the first Sunday of the next month, crowding the square as normal. The authorities had conniptions. All that shit and shenanigans on their lovely new plaza?! Open-air concerts were more what they had in mind. They tried to ban the fair, but the horsetraders didn't take a blind bit of notice and kept turning up. A compromise was finally reached, and the market shifted a few blocks north to the grounds of Grangegorman, a former mental hospital.

St Stephen's Green

This uneasy dynamic between old and new is what makes Smithfield so enticing. It's be exemplified in the starkly contrasting architecture surrounding the plaza, where Georgian pil rub shoulders with tiny Victorian red-brick terraces, and run-down council flats stand chee by jowl with slick 21st-century adaptations. You can also see it on the streets, where your gurriers sit on corners eyeing up bewigged barristers. If you want a drink you can superstyle at the Morrison Hotel (p206), roll up to the Cobblestone (p163) for *craic agus ceoil* (tradition

Top Five – Smithfield & Phoenix Park

- The fusion of old and new
- Collins Barracks (p108)
- The 'mummies' of St Michan's (p112)
- Old Jameson Distillery (p110)
- The wilds of Phoenix Park (p111)

fun and drinking), or sidle down to the Dic Bar (p163) for some cutting edge tunes an attitude. For eats you can sample a tradition Dublin coddle at Paddy's Place (p151) or th latest in international fusion at Kelly & Pin (p151). The city is pushing the whole villag within-a-city concept way too hard but th is urban renewal in action, baby, and it's a exciting time to be here.

There are terrific views from the clever converted Smithfield chimney and a slic presentation on the 'hard shtuff' at the Ol Jameson Distillery (p110), while 'mummies' await in the vaults of St Michan's Churc (p112). A little further west and you'll come to the decorative arts section of the Nation Museum (p87), now housed in the stunningly restored Collins Barracks (p108).

Beyond this, we run out of city and into Phoenix Park (p111), the largest city park i Europe. A wonderful place to kick back or explore, the park also provides shelter for th Irish president (p111), as well as hundreds of animals at the historic Dublin Zoo (p109).

ÁRAS AN UACHTARÁIN Map p112

☎ 617 1000; Phoenix Park; admission free; ☒ guided tours between 9.40am-4.20pm Sat; bus 10 from O'Connell St or 25 & 26 from Middle Abbey St

The residence of the Irish president is a Palladian lodge that was built in 1751 and enlarged a couple of times since, most recently in 1816. It was home to the British viceroys from 1782 to 1922, and then to the governors-general until Ireland cut ties with the British Crown and created the office of president in 1937. Queen Victoria stayed here during her visit in 1849 when she appeared not to even notice the famine. The candle burning in the window is an old Irish tradition meant to guide 'the Irish diaspora' home.

Tickets for the one-hour tours can be collected from the Phoenix Park Visitor Centre (p112), where you'll see a 10-minute introductory video before being shuttled to the Áras itself to inspect five state rooms and the president's study. If you can't make it on a Saturday, just become elected president of your own country or become a Nobel Laureate or something, and then wrangle a personal invite.

ARBOUR HILL CEMETERY Map pp260–1

Arbour Hill; admission free; ☒ 9am-4.30pm Mon-Sat, 9.30am-noon Sun; bus 25, 25A, 66, 67 & 90 from city centre

Just north of Collins Barracks, this small cemetery is the final resting place of all 14 of the executed

leaders of the 1916 Easter Rising. The buri ground is plain, with the 14 names inscribed stone. Beside the graves is a cenotaph bearin the Easter Proclamation, a focal point for offic and national commemorations. The front of th cemetery incongruously but poignantly co tains the graves of British personnel. Here, in th oldest part of the cemetery, as the gravestone toppled they were lined up against the boun ary walls where they still stand solemnly toda

THE CHIMNEY Map pp262–3

☎ 817 3820; Smithfield Village; adult/concession €5/3.50; ☒ 10am-5pm Mon-Sat, 11am-5.30pm Sun; bus 67, 67A, 68, 69, 79 & 134 from city centre

As part of the ongoing development of th Smithfield area, an old distillery chimne (nicknamed 'the flue with the view', built b Jameson's in 1895, has been converted int Dublin's first and only 360-degree observ tion tower. A glass lift shuttles you to the to where you get unique views of historic nor Dublin. The commentary is excellent from th knowledgeable and humorous guide, which a good job because Dublin's no oil painting

COLLINS BARRACKS Map pp262–3

☎ 677 7444; www.museum.ie; Benburb St; admissio free; bus 25, 25A, 66, 67 & 90 from city centre

No wonder the British army were so relucta to pull out of Ireland, when they were occup ng this magnificent space. This is the oldest army barracks in Europe and was recently spruced up to house the National Museum's collection of decorative arts. The building – the museum bit can wait – was designed by Thomas Burgh and completed in 1701. Its central square held six entire regiments and is a truly awesome space, surrounded by arcaded colonnades and blocks linked by walking bridges.

Any city would be hard pressed to come up with a museum to match the surroundings, and the decorative arts don't exactly get the heart pumping. That said, the museum has done an exceptional job of presenting an impressive, if hardly remarkable, collection featuring fashion, furniture, weaponry, folk life, silver, ceramics and glassware.

The exhibitions offer a pretty good bird's-eye view of Ireland's social, economic and military history over the last millennium through exquisitely designed displays, interactive multimedia and a brilliant adaptation of the buildings often-cramped interiors. The Curator's Choice exhibition is a terrific introduction bringing together such disparate objects as a 2000-year-old Japanese ceremonial bell and the gauntlets worn by King William of Orange at the Battle of the Boyne in 1690. Museum buffs might also relish the chance to see how curators go about the process of research, restoration and conservation in a section called the Museum at Work. Other examples of the exhibits on show – to whet your appetite or otherwise – are a life buoy from the *Lusitania*, an 18th-century bone crucifix, gorgeous 19th-century wine glasses, a 13th-century Chinese porcelain vase, the great seal of the Irish Free State, an assortment of St Brigid's Crosses and 16th-century German beer drinking vessels. There's an ambitious exhibition titled 'The Way We Wore' – 350 years of Irish clothing and jewellery, and there are regular temporary exhibitions on subjects such as Irish glass or famous personages.

DUBLIN ZOO Map pp260–1

☎ 677 1425; www.dublinzoo.ie; Phoenix Park; adult/concession/family €11/7/32; ⏰ 9.30am-6pm Mon-Sat, 10.30am-6pm Sun May-Sep, 9.30am-4pm Mon-Fri, 9.30am-5pm Sat, 10.30am-5pm Sun Oct-Apr; bus 10 from O'Connell St or 25 & 26 from Middle Abbey St

Established in 1830, the 12-hectare Dublin Zoo is one of the oldest in the world, and as thrilling or depressing as any other old zoo trying to drag itself into the 21st century. A 2000 expansion, the Savannah-style African Plains, comprises a large lake and woodland that doubled the size of the zoo and has made it a much more pleasant place for the larger residents and for visitors to stroll around. The zoo is well known for its lion-breeding programme, which dates back to 1857, and includes among its offspring the lion that roars at the start of MGM films. You'll see these tough cats, from a distance, on the African Plains.

The zoo has several hundred different species ranging from owls to hippos, most of which are housed in the old-fashioned part of the complex, including a 'World of Primates' section and 'Fringes of the Arctic' where similar animals have been grouped together as part of the zoo's modern restructuring. The one thing they haven't managed to fix, however, is the depression that seemingly afflicts the polar bears, who seem rightly incapable of coming to terms with the narrow confines of their world, a far cry from the northern tundra.

Still, the zoo has gone to great lengths to make it visitor-friendly, and the presence of new babies or animals on breeding loans from other zoos will surely generate a couple of 'oohs' and 'aahs' from the kids. There are also plenty of children's activities including a Meet the Keeper programme, which has events approximately every half-hour from 11am to 3.30pm, where children get to feed the animals and participate in other activities. Our favourite section is the City Farm, which brings you within touching distance of chickens, cows, goats and pigs, the luckiest animals here. There's also a zoo train and a nursery for infants.

Although there are places to eat, they're not very good and you'd be much better off bringing a picnic but, for God's sake, don't feed the animals.

FARMLEIGH HOUSE Map p112

☎ 815 5900; www.farmleigh.ie; Phoenix Park; admission free; ⏰ 10.45am-5pm for 30min house tours Sat, Sun & bank holidays Easter-Oct; bus 10 from O'Connell St or 25 & 26 from Middle Abbey St

Situated in the northwest corner of Phoenix Park, this enormous and opulent mansion is the state's official Bed & Breakfast, where visiting dignitaries rest their very important heads – at least in theory. The truth is that after spending more than €52 million on purchasing and restoring the house, it was used to provide accommodation for just three weeks in the first two years since it was opened in mid-2001. It has drawn savage criticism from some commentators who consider it money wasted on an already ugly house.

Regardless, the open days have been enormously popular with locals who, as tax payers, reckon it's as much their pad as anyone else's. The estate takes up 79 acres and there are many beautiful features. The main house is a bit blowsy and overblown but it's a pleasant enough example of Georgian–Victorian architecture. The real highlight is the garden, where regular shows are held. There is also an extensive programme of cultural events in summer, ranging from food fairs to classical concerts. Because the property is used for state business, schedules may change and you should telephone in advance.

FOUR COURTS Map pp262–3
☎ 872 5555; Inn's Quay; admission free

Impossible to miss if you're up this end of town, James Gandon's (1743–1823) masterpiece is a mammoth complex stretching 130m along Inns Quay. Construction on the Four Courts began in 1786, soon engulfing the Public Offices (built a short time previously at the western end of the same site), and continued until 1802. By then it included a Corinthian-columned central block connected to flanking wings with enclosed quadrangles. The ensemble is topped by a diverse collection of statuary. The original four courts – Exchequer, Common Pleas, King's Bench and Chancery – branch off the central rotunda.

The Four Courts played a brief role in the 1916 Easter Rising, without suffering damage, although it wasn't so lucky during the Civil War. When anti-Treaty forces seized the building and refused to leave, Free State forces led by Michael Collins shelled it from across the river. As the occupiers retreated, the building was set on fire and many irreplaceable early records were burned. These were the opening salvos in the Irish Civil War. The building wasn't restored until 1932.

Visitors are allowed to wander through, but not to enter the courts or other restricted areas. In the lobby of the central rotunda you'll see bewigged barristers conferring and police officers handcuffed to their charges waiting to enter court.

HENRIETTA ST Map pp264–5
Bus 25, 25A, 66, 67, 90 & 134 from city centre

Henrietta St dates from the 1720s and was the first project of Dublin's pre-eminent Georgian developer, Luke Gardiner. It was designed as an enclave of prestigious addresses, where Gardiner himself lived at No 10, and remained

one of Dublin's most fashionable streets until the Act of Union 1801. It's still looking a little forlorn these days after spending much of the 20th century as tenement housing, where up to 70 tenants were crammed into each four storey house. Some of the residences are in disrepair, yet it's sill a wonderful insight into the evolution of Georgian residential architecture, and features mansions of varying size and style.

KING'S INNS Map pp264–5
☎ 874 4840; www.kingsinns.ie; Henrietta St; ☼ only members & their guests; bus 25, 25A, 66, 67, 90 & 134 from city centre

Home to the Dublin legal profession, King's Inns occupy a classical building that was built by James Gandon between 1795 and 1817 (Francis Johnston chipped in with the cupola). In 1541, when Henry VIII staked his claim to be King of Ireland as well as England, the lawyers society took the title of King's Inns and moved to this home, where Irish barristers are still trained.

OLD JAMESON DISTILLERY Map pp262–3
☎ 807 2355; Bow St; adult/concession €7/5.75; ☼ 10am-5.30pm; bus 67, 67A, 68, 69, 79 & 134 from city centre

This enormous museum is devoted to Irish whiskey and, while it's probably a little too slick and sanitised for the serious fan, it does provide an excellent introduction to the history and culture of the essential Irish spirit. The museum occupies a section of the old distillery, which kept the capital in whiskey from 1780 to 1971 (after which the remaining distillers moved to a new ultramodern distillery in Middleton, County Cork). The museum can only be visited by guided tour, which runs every 35 minutes. It starts with a short film and then, with the aid of models and exhibitions, explains everything you ever wanted to know about Irish whiskey, from its fascinating history to how it's made and why it differs from Scotch etc. At the end of the tour, you'll be invited into the Jameson Bar for a dram of complementary whiskey. Stay alert and make sure to volunteer for the tasting tour, where you get to sample whiskies from all around the world and train your palate to identify and appreciate the differences between each.

At the end of the tour, you're deposited in the shop, which was kinda the whole point of the tour in the first place you reckon. If you do want to bring a bottle or two home, make sure

Where Whiskey Got its Name

When whiskey was first made by the monks they called it *uisce beatha* (the water of life; pronounced ish-ka ba-ha). Non–Irish speakers, particularly parched English soldiers stationed in Ireland, couldn't get their tongues around the words (even before they'd had a few) and, perhaps misled by the local accents, anglicised it to 'whiskey'. The first thing that sets the Irish and Scotch versions apart is the spelling. In Ireland, it's 'whiskey' and in Scotland it's 'whisky', but not even the cleverest barman will be able to tell which one you're after.

ou buy one that you can't get in your local tore. There are some 100 brands of Irish whisey (not all sold here) but only three – Jame-on, Bushmills and Tullamore Dew – are widely vailable. Our tip is Red Breast, pure pot still, he way all Irish whiskey used to be made, alhough the swashbuckling Power's is numero no in Ireland and difficult to get elsewhere. ou can also get a rare distillery reserve with our name printed on the label – kind of tacky ut neat, the way we like our whiskey.

There's also a good café and restaurant on he premises.

PHOENIX PARK Map p112

us 10 from O'Connell St or 25 & 26 from Middle Abbey St

Comprising 709 hectares, Phoenix Park is one of the world's largest city parks and Dublin's herished playground. It dwarfs New York's entral Park (which stretches to a mere 337 ectares) and is larger than all of the major ondon parks put together. There are gardens nd lakes, a host of sporting facilities, the econd-oldest public zoo in Europe, a visitor entre, a castle, the Garda Síochána (police) eadquarters, various government offices, he residences of the US ambassador and the ish president, and even a herd of some 300 eer. The name is probably a corruption of onn uisce (clear water), rather than anything o do with the legendary bird.

From the Anglo-Norman invasion up to 537, it was part of the lands owned by the nights of Jerusalem, keepers of an important riory on what is now the site of the Royal lospital Kilmainham. After King Henry VIII disolved the monasteries, the lands passed into he hands of the king's viceroys. In 1671 the Duke of Ormonde, James Butler, introduced herd of fallow deer, 1000 pheasants and ome partridge and turned it into a royal deer

park, soon enclosed by a wall. It remained the preserve of the British Crown and its Irish court until 1745, when the viceroy, Lord Chesterfield, threw it open to the public.

The first of the park's great mansions was Newtown House, built in 1668 as the home of the Phoenix Park Ranger. It was demolished in 1751 to build a new residence, which now makes up the central section of Áras an Uachtaráin (Offices of the President).

In an episode that set back the cause of Irish Home Rule, the British chief secretary for Ireland, Lord Cavendish, and his assistant were murdered outside what is now the Irish president's residence in 1882, by an obscure Irish nationalist group called the Invincibles. Lord Cavendish's home is now called Deerfield, and is used as the US ambassador's residence.

Near the Parkgate St entrance to the park is the 63m-high **Wellington Monument** obelisk, which took almost 50 years to build because the Duke fell from favour during its construction. It was finally completed in 1861. Nearby is the **People's Garden**, dating from 1864, and the bandstand in the Hollow. Just north of the Hollow is Dublin Zoo. Chesterfield Ave separates the Hollow and the zoo from the Phoenix Park Cricket Club of 1830 and from Citadel Pond, usually referred to as the Dog Pond.

Going northwest along Chesterfield Ave, which runs right through the park, you'll see the **Áras an Uachtaráin** (p108), where the Irish president lives and might be brewing a pot of tea for some famous foreign dignitary as you pass. On the left, the **Papal Cross** marks the site where Pope John Paul II preached to 1¼ million people in 1979 and drove around waving to the crowds in what was best described as a Tic-Tac box with wheels.

In the centre of the park the **Phoenix Monument**, erected by Lord Chesterfield in 1747, looks so unlike a phoenix that it's often referred to as the Eagle Monument. To the northwest of the monument stand the **Phoenix Park Visitor Centre** and **Ashtown Castle** (see p112). The southern part of the park has many football and hurling pitches; although they actually occupy about 80 hectares (200 acres), the area is known as the Fifteen Acres. To the west, the rural-looking **Glen Pond** corner of the park is extremely attractive.

At the northwestern end of the park near the White's Gate entrance are the offices of **Ordnance Survey Ireland** (OSI; ☎ 802 5300; www .osi.ie), the government mapping department. This building was originally built in 1728 by Luke Gardiner, who was responsible for the

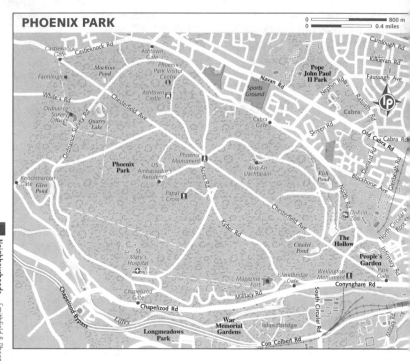

PHOENIX PARK

architecture in O'Connell St and Mountjoy Sq in north Dublin. In the building's map shop (☎ 802 5349; ⏱ 9am-4.45pm Mon-Fri) you can buy all of the OSI maps for any of the 26 counties of Ireland.

Back towards the Parkgate St entrance is the **Magazine Fort** (closed to the public) on Thomas's Hill. Like the nearby Wellington Monument, the fort was no quick construction, the process taking from 1734 to 1801. It provided useful target practise during the 1916 Easter Rising, and was raided by the IRA in 1940 when the entire ammunition reserve of the Irish army was nabbed, but recovered a few weeks later.

PHOENIX PARK VISITOR CENTRE & ASHTOWN CASTLE Map p112
☎ 677 0095; adult/concession/family €2.75/1.25/7; ⏱ 10am-5pm Apr-Sep; bus 37 & 29 from Middle Abbey St

This centre occupies what were the stables of the papal nunciate, and explores the wildlife and history of the park through film and two floors of exhibits. You will also be taken on a tour of the adjacent four-storey Ashtown Castle, a 17th-century tower-house that was concealed inside

the later building of the papal nunciate and wa only 'discovered' when the latter was demol ished in 1986. Box hedges surrounding th tower trace the ground plan of the lost build ing. Children keen on all things furry will lov the Great Slumber Party exhibition upstairs, walk-through tunnel that looks at the sleepin habits of animals such as foxes and badgers.

ST MICHAN'S CHURCH Map pp262–3
☎ 872 4154; Lower Church St; adult/concession €3.50/2.50; ⏱ 10am-12.45pm & 2-4.45pm Mon-Fri, 10am-12.45pm Sat; bus 134 from city centre

Macabre remains are the main attraction at this church, which was founded by th Danes in 1096 and named after one of the saints. The oldest architectural feature is th 15th-century battlement tower; otherwise th church was rebuilt in the late 17th century considerably restored in the early 19th centur and again after the Civil War.

The interior of the church, which feels mor like a courtroom, is worth a quick look as yo wait for your guide. It contains an organ fron 1724, which Handel may have played for th first-ever performance of his *Messiah*. Th organ case is distinguished by the fine oa arving of 17 entwined musical instruments n its front. A skull on the floor on one side of he altar is said to represent Oliver Cromwell. On the opposite side is the Stool of Repentnce, where 'open and notoriously naughty vers' did public penance.

The tours of the underground vaults are he real draw, however. The bodies are aged between 400 and 800 years old, and have been preserved by a combination of methane as coming from rotting vegetation beneath he church, the magnesium limestone of the masonry, which absorbs moisture from the air, and the perfectly constant temperature. The corpses have been exposed because the coffins in the vaults were stacked on top of one another and some toppled over and opened when the wood rotted. Among the 'attractions' is an 800-year-old Norman crusader who was so tall that his feet were lopped off so he could fit in a coffin. The guide sounds like he's been delivering the same, albeit fascinating, spiel for too long, but you're definitely glad you're not alone down there.

BEYOND THE ROYAL CANAL

Drinking p129; Eating p107; Shopping p161; Sleeping p179

Constructed from 1790, when the usefulness of such waterways was already on the wane, the Royal Canal was a total commercial flop. It was founded by Long John Binns, a director of the Grand Canal who quit the board in a huff after condescending remarks were made over his profession as a shoemaker. He established the Royal Canal principally for revenge, but it never made money and he became a bit of a laughing stock. Adding insult to injury, his waterway came to be known as the 'Shoemaker's Canal'. In 1840 the canal was sold to a railway company and the rail tracks still run alongside much of the canal's route.

St Stephen's Green

The towpath makes a relaxing walk through the heart of the city. You can join it beside Newcomen Bridge at North Strand Rd, just north of Connolly Station, and follow it to the suburb of Clonsilla and beyond, more than 10km away. The walk is particularly pleasant beyond Binns Bridge in Drumcondra. At the top of Blessington St, a large pond, used when the canal also supplied drinking water to the city, attracts water birds.

Beyond the Royal Canal lie the working-class and authentic auld Dublin suburbs of Glasnevin, Phibsborough, Marino and Drumcondra, which is still the stomping ground of the Taoiseach Bertie Ahern. The area is dominated by the mighty Croke Park (p115), headquarters of Gaelic games. There are also a host of compelling sights, including the architecturally magnificent Casino at Marino (p114), the historic Glasnevin Cemetery (p115) and the soothing National Botanic Gardens (p116).

> ## Top Five – Beyond the Royal Canal
>
> - Watching a match at Croke Park (p115)
> - The free tour of Glasnevin Cemetery (p115)
> - Casino at Marino (p114)
> - National Botanic Gardens (p116)
> - GAA Museum (p115)

BRAM STOKER DRACULA EXPERIENCE

☎ 805 7824; www.thebramstokerbraculaexperience .com; Bar Code, Westwood Club, Clontarf Rd; adult/ child €7/4; ☽ noon-10pm Fri-Sun; bus 20, 20B, 27, 27B, 29A, 31, 31A, 32, 32A, 32B, 42, 42A, 42B, 43, 127, 129 & 130 from Lower Abbey St, DART to Clontarf
Bram Stoker was born and raised in the pretty seaside suburb of Clontarf, so it makes perfect sense that the local fitness club should be home to a brand-new museum dedicated to the author's life and, particularly, to his most memorable creation. The sight of Dublin's suburbanites struggling to fend off the effects of age and gravity on a Stairmaster may be scary enough, but Bram Stoker's imagination was just that little bit more extreme. The tour through his fictional world mightn't keep you awake at night, but it's pretty effective nonetheless, as each of the various rooms have been created to stimulate maximum discomfort and fear. The journey begins in a Time Tunnel to Transylvania, and

A Splash of Irish Art

Apart from the major galleries mentioned throughout this chapter (see the index), Dublin boasts many private galleries, arts centres and corporate exhibition areas.

Kerlin Gallery (Map pp272–3; ☎ 670 9093; Anne's La, South Anne St; admission free; ☺ 10am-5.45pm Mon-Fri, 11am-4.30pm Sat) Along with the RHA Gallagher Gallery (p89), this is the Shangri-la for Irish artists, conclusive proof that one's reached the big leagues.

Graphic Studio Gallery (Map pp269–71; ☎ 679 8021; Cope St, Temple Bar) Only work by new Irish artists gets exhibited at this place.

Rubicon Gallery (Map pp272–3; ☎ 670 8055; 10 St Stephen's Green) This is one of the city's more prestigious galleries, and has constantly changing exhibitions by local and international talent.

Solomon Gallery (Map pp272–3; ☎ 679 4237; top floor, Powerscourt Townhouse Shopping Centre, 59 South William St) Strictly contemporary work is shown in this bright, airy gallery.

Taylor Galleries (Map pp272–3; ☎ 676 6055; 16 Kildare St) Spread across three floors of a fine Georgian building, the big guns of the Irish contemporary art world are shown in permanent exhibition, while rotating exhibits feature the work of those who'd love to join them.

transports suspecting visitors to such delightful destinations as Renfield's lunatic asylum and the bowels of Castle Dracula, where a meeting with the sharp-toothed one awaits. We won't ruin the fun by telling you how it was all put together; suffice to say that technology and the warped imagination of the designers have combined to startling effect. There is also an exhibit dedicated to the life of Bram Stoker.

CASINO AT MARINO

☎ 833 1618; off Malahide Rd, Marino; adult/child/student €2.75/1.25/1.25; ☺ 10am-5pm May & Oct, 10am-6pm Jun-Sep, noon-4pm Sat & Sun Feb-Apr & Nov-Dec, noon-5pm Apr, closed Jan; bus 20A, 20B, 27, 27B, 42, 42C & 123 from city centre, DART to Clontarf Rd Station

No, not that kind of casino; perhaps it's the images of blackjack and slot machines that make so many visitors overlook this bewitching 18th-century architectural folly, which is a *casino* in the Italian sense of the word, as in a 'house of pleasure' or summer home. It was built for the Earl of Charlemont (1728–99), who returned from his grand European tour with a huge art collection and a burning passion for the Italian Palladian style of architecture. He appointed the architect Sir William Chambers to build the casino, a process that spanned three decades and was never really concluded because the earl frittered away his fortune.

Externally, the building's 12 Tuscan columns, forming a temple-like facade, and huge entrance doorway suggest that it encloses simple single open space. Only when you g inside do you realise what a wonderful extrava gance it is. The interior is a convoluted maz planned as a bachelor's retreat but eventuall put to a quite different use. Flights of fanc include carved draperies, ornate fireplace chimneys for central heating disguised as roo urns, downpipes hidden in columns, beautiful parquet floors built of rare woods and a spa cious wine cellar. All sorts of statuary adorn th outside, the amusing fakes being the most en joyable. The towering front door is a sham, an a much smaller panel opens to reveal the inter ior. The windows have blacked-out panels t disguise the fact that the interior is a comple of rooms rather than a single chamber. Entr is by guided tour only, and the last tour is 4 minutes before closing.

When the earl married, the casino becam a garden retreat rather than a bachelor's quar ters. The casino was designed to accompan another building where he intended to hous the art and antiquities he had acquired durin his European tour, so it's perhaps fitting tha his town house on Parnell Sq, also designe by Sir William Chambers, is now the Municipa Gallery of Modern Art (p167).

Despite his wealth, Charlemont was a com paratively liberal and free-thinking aristocra He never enclosed his demesne and allowe the public to use it as an open park. Nor wa he the only eccentric in the area at that time. I 1792 a painter named Folliot took a dislike to the earl and built Marino Crescent at the bot tom of Malahide Rd purely to block his view f the sea. Bram Stoker (1847–1912), author of *Dracula*, was born at 15 Marino Crescent.

After Charlemont's death his estate, crippled by his debts, quickly collapsed. The art collection was dispersed and in 1870 the town house was sold to the government. The Marino estate followed in 1881 and the casino in 1930, though it was in a decrepit condition when the government acquired it. Not until the mid-1970s did serious restoration begin, and it still continues. Although the current casino grounds are a tiny fragment of the original Marino estate, trees around the building help to hide that it's now surrounded by a housing estate.

CROKE PARK & GAA MUSEUM
Map pp264–5

☎ 855 8176; www.gaa.ie; New Stand, Croke Park, Clonliffe Rd; museum only adult/child/concession/family €5/3/3.50/13, museum & stadium tour €8.50/6/5/21; ⏰ 9.30am-5pm Mon-Sat, noon-5pm Sun Apr-Oct, 10am-5pm Tue-Sat, noon-4pm Sun Nov-Mar; bus 3, 11, 11A, 16, 16A & 123 from O'Connell St

Uniquely important in Irish culture, the magnificent stadium at 'Croker' is home to the Gaelic Athletic Association (GAA), the governing body of Ireland's national sports. It goes without saying that this is the country's largest stadium (see the boxed text on p17); after being virtually rebuilt in recent years, it's actually the fourth largest stadium in Europe, with a capacity of some 82,000 people. And this for sports that are only played in this tiny little country! There are stadium tours available twice a day, although these are largely for hardcore GAA and sports stadia fans and are not available on match days. It's much better to get a ticket for a match, when you can watch these brilliant games, soak up the unique atmosphere and have a squizz at the arena. Hogan Stand ticket holders can visit the museum on match days.

In the 1870s, the site was developed as the 'City & Suburban Racecourse', but was bought by the GAA in 1913 and immediately renamed Croke Park in honour of the association's first patron, Archbishop Croke of Cashel. Since its foundation it has been entwined with Irish nationalism. The famous Hill 16, which is traditionally where the hardcore Dublin fans stand during matches, was so-called because its foundations were built with rubble taken from O'Connell St after the Easter Rising of 1916. This was also the site of the first Bloody Sunday in Irish history, the greatest single atrocity of the War of Independence (see p67).

This is one of the episodes recounted in the outstanding GAA Museum, where the history and culture of these most Irish of games is explored in fascinating, interactive style. As well as going into exhaustive detail about Gaelic games, the exhibitions feature audiovisual displays that are sure to get the hairs on the back of any GAA fan's neck to stand up, and many relics from other sports and episodes that have captured the mood of the nation. There are terminals set up where you can watch highlights from any All-Ireland football or hurling final that has been recorded, but the highlight, for us at least, is the opportunity to test one's skills with a football or a hurley and *sliothar* (small, leather ball), and imagine the glories that might have been.

GLASNEVIN CEMETERY Map pp260–1

☎ 830 1133; Finglas Rd; admission free; ⏰ 24hr, tours 2.30pm Wed & Fri; bus 40, 40A & 40B from Parnell St

Make sure your visit coincides with one of the free tours, which are provided by Dublin's most entertaining, informative and irreverent tour guide, the inimitable Lorcan Collins (also of the 1916 Rebellion tours, p66), who'll bring you around all the most interesting sights in Ireland's largest cemetery.

It was established in 1832 as a cemetery for Roman Catholics, who faced opposition when

Glasnevin Cemetery

they conducted burials in the city's Protestant cemeteries. Many monuments and memorials have staunchly patriotic overtones, with numerous high crosses, shamrocks, harps and other Irish symbols. The single most imposing memorial is the colossal monument to Cardinal McCabe (1837–1921), archbishop of Dublin and primate of Ireland.

A modern replica of a round tower holds the tomb of Daniel O'Connell, who died in 1847 and was reinterred here in 1869, when the tower was completed. Charles Stewart Parnell's tomb is topped with a huge granite rock. Other notable people buried here include Sir Roger Casement, who was executed for treason by the British in 1916 and whose remains weren't returned to Ireland until 1964; the republican leader Michael Collins, who died in the Civil War; the docker and trade unionist Jim Larkin, a prime force in the 1913 general strike; and the poet Gerard Manley Hopkins.

There's a poignant 'class' memorial to the men who starved themselves to death for the cause of Irish freedom over the last century, including 10 men in the 1981 H Block hunger strikes. The most interesting parts of the cemetery are at the southeastern Prospect Sq end. The towers were once used to keep watch for body snatchers. The cemetery is mentioned in *Ulysses* and there are several clues for Joyce enthusiasts to follow.

NATIONAL BOTANIC GARDENS

☎ 837 7596; Botanic Rd, Glasnevin; admission free; ⊙ 9am-6pm Mon-Sat, 11am-6pm Sun Apr-Oct, 10am-4.30pm Mon-Sat, 11am-4.30pm Sun Nov-Mar; bus 13, 13A & 19 from O'Connell St or bus 34 & 34A from Middle Abbey St

This 19.5-hectare treasure is a delightful blend of exoticism and tousled gentility. Although only established in 1795, the area was used as a garden long before it was christened so and the area of Yew Walk (Addison's Walk) features trees dating back to the first half of the 18th century.

The architectural highlight in the gardens is a series of curvilinear glasshouses that date from 1843 to 1869. They were created by Dubliner Richard Turner, who was also responsible for creating the Palm House at London's Kew Gardens. Within these Victorian masterpieces, you will find the latest in botanical technology, including a series of computer-controlled climates that reproduce environments from different parts of the world.

The gardens also have a palm house, which was built in 1884. Among the pioneering botanical work conducted here was the first attempt to raise orchids from seed, back in 1844. Pampas grass and the giant lily were first grown in Europe in these gardens.

Walking Tours

Walking Tours

Dublin's city centre is pretty small, and by far the best way to get to know it is by putting on a comfortable pair of shoes and hitting the pavement. At ground level you can get real sense of the city's history and heritage, but more importantly you get to observe an participate in how the city moves from day to day. You'll achieve a stronger feel for the city's distinct neighbourhoods, whose differences vary from the abrupt to the very subtle Here we have included five separate walking options that take in most of the city centre from the top of Parnell Sq South to the Grand Canal, east as far as the Grand Canal Dock on the edge of Dublin Bay, and as far west as Smithfield Terrace. Each of the walks can b done in less than three hours, but in order to get the most of the goodies along the way linger long and take your time.

THEMATIC WALKS

The three walks included here take on three of the city's major themes, beginning with Dublin's well-earned reputation as a hive of literary genius, followed by a traipse through the city's faded Viking and medieval past. Finally, there's the staggered walk that most people come to Dublin for – the pub crawl.

LITERARY DUBLIN

Dublin's rich reservoir of literary talent is such that it is the only city of comparable size in the world to have spawned four Nobel laureates for literature: George Bernard Shaw William Butler Yeats, Samuel Beckett and Seamus Heaney (born in Derry but residing in Dublin). Yet Dublin's most imposing literary shadow, considered by many to be the best author of the 20th century, never got a sniff of a Nobel cheque. Instead, James Joyce had to settle for posthumous fame and the everlasting gratitude of a city that he loved…from a distance.

Start your walk just north of the Grand Canal at the **Shaw Birthplace** 1 (p83). George Bernard Shaw (1856–1950), author of *Pygmalion* (which was subsequently hammed up and turned into the highly successful stage musical and film *My Fair Lady*), won the Nobel Prize for literature in 1925 for his play *Saint Joan*, but he donated most of the winner's cheque to the National Gallery (p86). The house, where he lived until he was 10, has been painstakingly restored to its austere Victorian best, even if there are very few original furnishings belonging to the family.

Walk north along Synge St and take a left along Grantham St until you get to Heytesbury St. Directly opposite, at **No 33** 2, is the birthplace of Cornelius Ryan,

> ### Walk Facts
>
> **Start** Shaw Birthplace, 33 Synge St
> **End** Dublin Writers Museum, Parnell Sq North
> **Distance** 3.5km
> **Duration** 2½–3 hours
> **Transport** Bus 11, 11A, 13B & 48A from Trinity College

author of *The Longest Day*, *The Last Battle* and *A Bridge Too Far*, all of which have been made into highly successful films. Retrace your steps along Grantham St and keep going until you get to the intersection with Lower Camden St. On your right, at **No 57** 3, is the birthplace of Robert Maturin (1782–1824), whose most famous book was the Gothic horror novel *Melmoth the Wanderer*. Along with Joseph Sheridan Le Fanu (*The House by the Churchyard*) and the author of *Dracula*, Bram Stoker (opposite), they form an impressive trio of masters of the horror genre. Maturin's home is now a centre of the Simon Community, a charitable organisation that helps the homeless. Across the street is the **Bleeding**

Horse 4 (p159) pub, above which lived for a time a certain Captain Bligh of *Mutiny on the Bounty* fame. Walk along Charlotte St and take a left onto Harcourt St. No 61, now the Harcourt Hotel, was **Shaw's last residence 5** before moving permanently to England in 1876. A less obvious literary link is at No 4, close to the corner with St Stephen's Green. This is the **birthplace of Sir Edward Carson 6** (1854–1935), the founder of Northern Unionism. Before devoting his life to politics he was a barrister; his most famous case was prosecuting Oscar Wilde for homosexuality in 1898.

Continue straight along West St Stephen's Green and around onto North St Stephen's Green. Take a left onto Merrion Row and continue until you reach Merrion Sq, a magnet of literary addresses. The childhood home of Oscar Wilde (1854–1900) is at **1 North Merrion Sq 7**, while WB Yeats (1865–1939) lived at **52 Merrion Sq East 8** and later, between 1922 and 1928, answered the door at **82 Merrion Sq South 9**. George (AE) Russell (1867–1935), the 'poet, mystic, painter and cooperator', worked a couple of doors down at **No 84 10**.

Take a left at the square's northern corner and walk down Nassau St alongside **Trinity College 11** (p77), the alma mater of – among many, many others – Wilde, Samuel Beckett (1906–89), Jonathan Swift (1667–1745), JM Synge (1871–1909; author of *Playboy of the Western World*; its premiere at the Abbey in 1907 actually provoked a riot for its presumed vulgarity) and Bram Stoker (1847–1912), creator of the most famous vampire of them all, *Dracula*. Stoker didn't have far to walk to go to class, as he lived at **36 Kildare St 12**, to your left off Nassau St.

Continue around past the main entrance to Trinity College and walk down Westmoreland St. Off the street to your left, on Fleet St, is the **Palace Bar 13** (p158), still the favourite haunt of journos and scribblers, including at one time Brendan Behan, who was regularly barred from here. Cross the Liffey onto O'Connell St. Take a right onto Lower Abbey St until you get to the **Abbey Theatre 14** (p173) at No 26. Founded by WB Yeats and the Irish Literary Society in 1904, it is the home of Irish national theatre. In 1955 an (accidental) fire destroyed the building and it was replaced by this monstrosity.

Walk north along Marlborough St and cross Parnell St to get to North Great George's St. On your right, at No 35, is the **James Joyce Centre 15** (p104), home of all things Joycean. Across the street is the fabulous **Cobalt Café 16** (p152), a gorgeous, elegant spot that is a must if you're in the 'hood. The James Joyce Centre couldn't be in a more fitting location, as at the top of the street, on Great Denmark St, is **Belvedere College 17** (p102), where Joyce (1882–1941) spent his thoroughly unhappy school days. Further north, at 7 Eccles St, is the **fictional home of Joyce's Leopold and Molly Bloom 18** in *Ulysses*. Apart from a plaque and a relief of Joyce's face, there's nothing to see because the house was demolished in 1982 to build an extension to the private wing of the Mater Misericordiae Hospital.

A fitting finish to this literary walk is a visit to the **Dublin Writers Museum 19** (p103), on the northern flank of Parnell Sq.

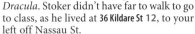

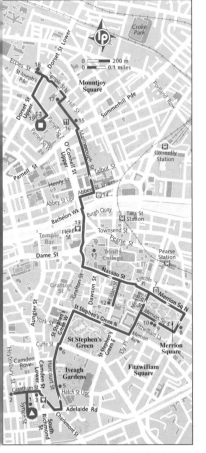

Walking Tours – Thematic Walks

VIKING & MEDIEVAL DUBLIN

Before the architectural revolution that was the 18th-century Georgian era, Dublin's medieval character had changed little since the arrival of the Normans 600 years before. Dublin was a walled fortress town, dominated by the imposing presence of a castle that governed Irish affairs and two great churches, one of which (St Patrick's, p96) stood just outside the city walls. The city has grown beyond all recognition since then, but this walk takes you to the heart of not just the medieval city, but of the Viking town that made way for it, a busy trading port whose main street was Fishamble St, just east of Christ Church Cathedral (p91). Immediately north of the cathedral, just south of the Liffey, is one of the greatest repositories of Viking artefacts in the world, but these have sadly been buried beneath two huge concrete office blocks; you'll just have to stand there and imagine what it must have been like a millennium ago.

Begin your walk at the corner of Parliament St and **Essex Gate** 1, once a main entrance gate to the city. A bronze plaque on a pillar marks the spot where the gate (also known as Buttevant's Tower) once stood. The foundations of the gate have yet to be excavated, but you can see the original foundations of **Isolde's Tower** 2 through a grill in the pavement, in front of the pub of the same name.

Veering off to your right as you walk west down Essex Gate is the curved Lower Exchange St, which follows the contours of the old walls, and was once called Blind Quay because it was out of sight of the river. Back on Essex Gate, check out the marvellous **panelled sculpture** 3 by Dublin artist Grace Weir (1996) depicting a Viking ship navigating with the aid of the constellations. The western end of West Essex St – called at various times Stable Lane, Cadogan's Alley, Smock Alley and Orange St – was widened in the 1940s and so lost its medieval curve.

At the southeastern corner of West Essex St and Fishamble St is a house that is reckoned to be the **oldest continuously inhabited home in Dublin** 4, originally built in the early 17th century but 'remodelled' in 1720.

Fishamble St was one of the most important streets of Viking and medieval Dublin. It was originally laid down in the 10th century (at twice its present length) and served as the main thoroughfare from the port to the Viking High St, the main trading street.

Walk Facts

Start Essex Gate, Parliament St
End Dublin Castle
Distance 2.5km
Duration At least 2 hours

Its name is taken from the fish stalls (known as 'shambles') that once lined the pavements. At the southern end of Fishamble St is Handel's Hotel; the building immediately to its left once housed William Neal's **Music Hall** 5, where the famous composer first performed his *Messiah* in 1742. The event is commemorated by a performance here each year, see p11.

It's impossible to ignore the huge buildings that line the western side of Fishamble St. These are the main offices of Dublin Corporation, originally built in the 1970s and immediately dubbed 'the bunkers' for their unwieldy appearance. Apart from aesthetic considerations, their construction generated a huge amount of protest as they were built on one of the most important Viking sites in the world (see the boxed text on p47). A lengthy excavation has unearthed a wealth of Viking artefacts, most of which are on display in Dvblinia (see p93).

Walk down to the quays and take a left along Wood Quay. Walk past the frontage of the Dublin Corporation Offices, cross Winetavern St and proceed along Merchant's Quay. On your left is the **Church of St Francis** 6, which is also known as Adam & Eve's after a tavern through which worshippers gained access to a secret chapel during Penal times. The next bridge you'll come to is **Father Mathew Bridge** 7, built in 1818 on the spot of the fordable crossing that gave Dublin its Irish name, Baile Átha Cliath, or 'Town of the Hurdle Ford'.

Take a left onto Bridge St. Stop for a drink at Ireland's oldest pub, on your right, the **Brazen Head** 8 (p161), which dates from 1198 (although the present building dates from 1668). Take the next left onto Cook St, where you will find the most significant remains of the medieval walls and an original gate, **St Audoen's Arch** 9, built in 1240. During the Middle Ages, Dublin was heavily protected by a double ring of walls and 32 towers and fortified gates; most of these

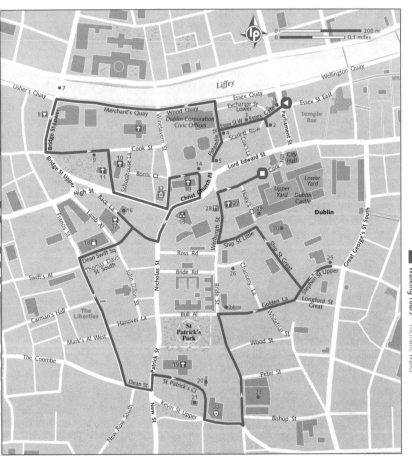

were torn down and the stone used to build elsewhere. Climb through the arch up to the ramparts, site of the twin churches of St Audoen's (p96), one a **Catholic church 10**, the other **Church of Ireland 11**. The latter, built in 1190, is the oldest parish church still in use in Dublin. Leave the little park and take a left on High St. On your left, the first corner is occupied by the former Synod Hall, now **Dvblinia 12** (p93), a museum where medieval Dublin has been interactively recreated. Turn left and walk under the Synod Hall Bridge linking it to **Christ Church Cathedral 13** (p91). Below the cathedral, on your left, is East John's Lane, and in the pavement you can see a pebble mosaic marking out the site of two **Viking dwellings 14**, a late consolation for those who had campaigned against the construction of the Dublin Corporation Offices below. Continue along the lane and take a right into the cathedral grounds. The stone ruins just inside the grounds are all that is left of a priory once attached to the main cathedral.

A visit to Christ Church Cathedral is compulsory. It is one of the city's most important landmarks and, in medieval times, the most important church inside the city walls. Once you're done, exit onto Christ Church Pl and cross over onto Nicholas St, passing the ruins of **St Nicholas Within 15**, so-called because it was within the city walls. Turn right onto Back Lane and proceed past Dublin's oldest surviving guild hall, **Tailors' Hall 16**, built between 1703 and 1707 (though 1770 on the plaque) for the Tailors Guild. It's now the headquarters of An Taisce, the National Trust for Ireland. **Mother Redcap's Tavern 17** (☎ 453 8306; Back Lane) is opposite. Back down Back Lane, turn right and head to Dean Swift Sq and the imposing structure of the old **Iveagh Market 18**, established in 1907 by Lord Iveagh of the Guinness family. There are wonderfully expressive stone faces over the arches; around the corner, the face giving a broad wink is said to be modelled on Lord Iveagh himself.

Continue down the street and take a left at the junction with Francis St. You are now in the heart of the Liberties area, so-called because medieval Dublin had a number of 'liberties' – areas outside the city jurisdiction where local courts were at liberty to administer the law. Today, Francis St is best known for its antique shops. At the bottom of the street, right will take you onto The Coombe, so called because it was once the 'coomb', or river valley, of the Poddle. Or turn left onto Dean St, named after the deanery of St Patrick's Cathedral but previously known as Crosspoddle St because it used to cross the Poddle at this point. Take a left onto Patrick St and across the street you will see the imposing **St Patrick's Cathedral 19** (p96). Also visible are the attractive red-brick apartments built by Lord Iveagh in the 19th century to house the company's workers. They have recently been restored to their former beauty. As you enter the grounds of St Patrick's, you will notice that the level drops about 2m – this was the original elevation of medieval Dublin.

Just beyond the bend is **Marsh's Library 20** (p95) on the left. St Patrick's is inextricably linked with author, poet and satirist Jonathan Swift (see p95 and p98). The **Deanery 21** where Swift once lived is on your right, even though the present building is a more recent replacement.

Marsh's Library (p95)

On your way, you'll pass a medieval stone horse trough.

Continue along St Patrick's Close to Upper Kevin St. On your left along Kevin St is a **police station 22** that was once the Episcopal Palace of St Sepulchre, seat of the Archbishops of Dublin from the end of the 12th century to the early 19th century. The Dublin Metropolitan Police took over the building in the 1830s.

Turn left onto Bride St and then walk north past some **low-income housing 23** that are more examples of Lord Iveagh's constructive philanthropy. When you reach Golden Lane (on your right), the northeastern corner is taken up by a newer block of elegant public housing, though the links with the past are maintained through the beautifully sculpted roundels that depict scenes from **Gulliver's Travels 24**. To the east is Stephen St: at **No 67 25** (now the offices of Dunnes Stores), John Boyd Dunlop founded the world's first pneumatic tyre factory in 1889.

Turn left from Stephen St onto Great Ship St and walk around to Little Ship St. Steps on the left at the end lead to **7 Hoey's Ct 26**, birthplace of Jonathan Swift (1687); you'll probably have to settle for staring up the small street as the gates are usually closed. At the end of Little Ship St is Werburgh St and the eponymous **church 27** dedicated to the daughter of a Saxon king. Opposite is **Leo Burdock's 28** (p149), Dublin's most famous fish and chip shop. They're no longer wrapped in old newspaper, but it's still the place for the best fresh cod and chips.

From the church, take the next right onto Castle St, until the 20th century the main westward route out of the city. Here you come to the enormous expanse of Dublin Castle (p82). The striking powder-blue tower on the right is **Bermingham Tower 29**, built in the 13th century and used to detain state prisoners. It was badly damaged by a gunpowder blast in 1775 and rebuilt in an astonishing Strawberry Gothic style. Opposite the Bermingham Tower, the Old Barracks have been restored; the **Clock Tower 30** now houses the Chester Beatty Library (p81), one of Dublin's most fascinating collections of rare books and manuscripts.

PINTLY PERAMBULATION

OK, so you've done the city's history, architecture and notable names. Now it's time for a little hedonism. But first, here's a teaser: how do you walk the streets of Dublin without passing a pub? Easy. Go into each and every one. We don't recommend it, because you wouldn't get very far. Instead, try this walk, which has plenty of pit stops along the way as well as the odd sight.

Start this walk sitting down in the drawing room of the **Shelbourne Hotel** 1 (p200), which serves the classiest cup of tea in town. You should plan to be here some time in the late afternoon, preferably around 4pm.

When you're done treating yourself like a member of the 18th-century gentry, leave the Shelbourne and turn right towards Grafton St. With a stomach lined with tea and scones, it's time to go liquid – with a late-afternoon cocktail. Turn left at the intersection with Grafton St and pop into the **Fitzwilliam Hotel** 2 (see the boxed text on p199), which serves the best mixed drinks in some pretty cool surroundings. Leave the hotel and turn left and walk down Grafton St, perhaps stopping along the way to listen to a busker or two. About halfway down the street, take a left onto Johnson's Ct to Clarendon St. As it's probably dinner-time by now, why not grab some moving sushi from the conveyer belt at **Aya** 3 (p132) and wash it down with a jug of sake?

Walk back down Clarendon St and turn right onto Coppinger Row. Facing you is **Grogan's Castle Lounge** 4 (p159), a long-time favourite of the city's art brigade who love its homey, welcoming atmosphere and its great pint of Guinness. Leave Grogan's and take a left onto Castle Market. If it's before 6pm, amble through **George's St Arcade** 5 (p182) with its array of

Walk Facts

Start Shelbourne Hotel, St Stephen's Green
End Rí Rá nightclub, Dame Ct
Distance 3.8km
Duration There's booze involved, so how long is a piece of string?

Walking Tours – Thematic Walks

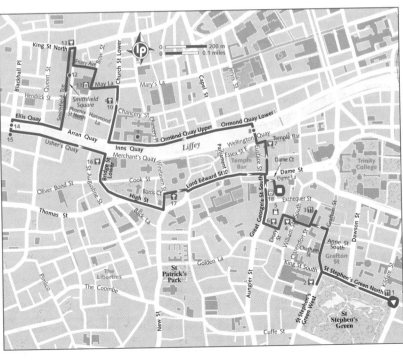

trendy stalls and shops. Otherwise, take a left onto Drury St and then right along Fade St. About halfway down on the right is the entrance to the **Market Bar** 6 (p160), a brand-new spot in what was formerly a sausage factory. Turn right onto South Great George's St. Cross the Dame St intersection into Temple Bar. At the bottom of Temple Lane, on your right, is the **Temple Bar** 7 (p158), aka Flannery's, one of the district's most popular pubs. Resist – if you can – the temptation to ensconce yourself here for the evening and walk left along Temple Bar proper and take a right on Eustace St.

Facing you is the city's second-newest bridge, the **Millennium Bridge** 8. Cross to the other side of the Liffey and take a left along the pleasant waterside boardwalk up to Capel St Bridge. Walk down the quays along Upper Ormond and Inns quays, passing the **Four Courts** 9 (p110) and then take a right up Church St. Take a left past **St Michan's Church** 10 (p112) onto May Lane and then right on Bow St past the **Old Jameson Distillery** 11 (p110) Take a left onto Friary Ave until you reach **Smithfield Sq** 12. At the northern end of the square, is the **Cobblestone** 13 (p163), a beautiful old bar where you can listen in on some of the best traditional music to be heard in the city. By the time you're done with the smoky atmosphere, you'll probably need a bit of fresh air. Cross the length of Smithfield Sq back towards the Liffey. Turn right along Ellis Quay and cross over the city's newest structure, the **James Joyce Bridge** 14 (see the boxed text on p49), built by Spanish architect Santiago Calatrava and so named because the 'dark, gaunt house' directly facing it at **15 Usher's Quay** 15 is the setting of Joyce's short story 'The Dead' from *Dubliners*.

Walk east along Usher's Quay and take the first right onto Bridge St. Near the corner is Dublin's oldest pub, the **Brazen Head** 16 (p161), where Leopold Bloom, from *Ulysses*, figures you'll get 'a decent enough do' – meaning food – but by this stage it'll probably be too late. Walk up Bridge St and around **Christ Church Cathedral** 17 (p91) until you get to Lord Edward St, which then becomes Dame St. Walk to the intersection with South Great George's St and turn right and then left again, down the small lane onto Dame Ct. About halfway up on your left is the last stop on your walk, **Rí Rá** 18 (p172), where you can dance the rest of the night away and hopefully sweat out some of the booze.

NEIGHBOURHOOD WALKS

We all agree that Dublin's healthy heart beats loudest on the south side, particularly on and around Grafton St and Temple Bar. It's where visitors spend the majority of their time and have most of their fun. Yet it's a shame not to venture north of the Liffey or south of St Stephen's Green, for here you can find some of the city's most interesting and beautiful sections.

TAKE A WALK ON THE NORTH SIDE

While most visitors spend the lion's share of their time south of the Liffey, it is on the neglected north side that you will find a more traditional Dublin.

Start your walk in slightly dilapidated **Mountjoy Sq** 1, once one of Dublin's most beautiful and prestigious addresses. By the beginning of the 20th century most of the posh residents had fled to the south side, but not before subdividing their properties into one-room apartments for rent. Once elegant and genteel, they became squalid tenements ignored by their landlords except on rent day. The buildings have long since been cleared out, but their sorry state lasted until recently, when a long-overdue programme of urban renovation began.

Take a left at the northwestern corner of the square and walk down Gardiner Pl, turning right onto North Temple St. Up ahead on Hardwicke Pl is the fine, but now deconsecrated, **St George's Church** 2 (p106) designed by Francis Johnston (who lived close by in a now-demolished house at 64 Eccles St). The church bells came from Johnston's own back garden bell tower, but the only noise coming from the building these days is the thumping sound of hardcore dance music, as the church is now a nightclub, Temple Theatre (p173). Take a left onto Hardwicke St and left again onto North Frederick St. On your right, the **Abbey Presbyterian Church** 3, built in 1864, is often referred to as Findlater's Church after the grocery magnate who financed the building's construction.

The northern slice of Parnell Sq is the **Garden of Remembrance** 4 (p103), opened in 1966 to commemorate the 50th anniversary of the 1916 Easter Rising. Outside the garden is a small **monument** 5 to the victims of a Loyalist paramilitary terrorist bomb campaign in Dublin on 17 May 1974.

On the northern side of the square, facing the park is the **Hugh Lane Municipal Gallery of Modern Art** 6 (p103), next to the Dublin Writers Museum (p103), covered in the Literary Dublin walking tour. The southern part of Parnell

Walk Facts

Start Mountjoy Sq
End St Michan's Church, Church St
Distance 2.5km
Duration 2 hours

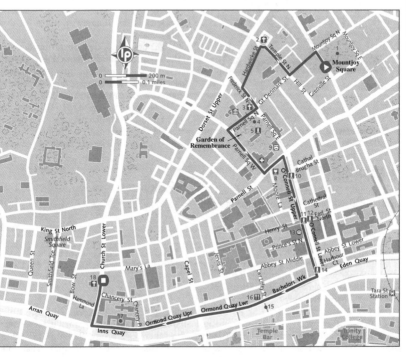

Sq is occupied by the **Rotunda Hospital 7** (p106), built in 1757. As you walk along the southern side of the square look for **Patrick Conways 8** (p164), a pub that opened in 1745. In the southeastern corner of the square is the **Gate Theatre 9** (p174) in part of the old Rotunda complex.

O'Connell St, Dublin's major boulevard, begins at this corner of the square and sweeps south to O'Connell Bridge and the Liffey. Unfortunately, the street has had a hard time of it this century. One side was burnt out in the 1916 Easter Rising, the other during the Civil War, and whatever remained was ripped out by short-sighted property developers in the 1960s and 1970s.

Despite this, O'Connell St has numerous points of interest, including a varied collection of statues down the centre (see p105), the first of which is a grandiose **statue of Charles Stewart Parnell 10**. Continue down O'Connell St, passing the 120m-high **Spire 11** (p106). There's a notable **statue of James Joyce 12** at the O'Connell St end of pedestrianised Earl St. His bemused look perhaps reflects the irony that a writer whose masterpiece was banned in his own country throughout his life should be so honoured. However, we'd like to think that it's more a reaction to the nickname with which ordinary Dubliners refer to the statue: the 'prick with the stick'.

Ha'penny Bridge (p49)

On the other side of O'Connell St, the **General Post Office 13** (p103) towers over the street. Its role as the starting point for the 1916 Easter Rising makes this an important site in Ireland's recent history. At the river end of the street the **statue of Daniel O'Connell 14** looks squarely up the street that bears his name.

At the bottom of the street, turn left and walk along the handsome new boardwalk. On your right, after passing the **Ha'Penny Bridge 15**, rest your bones, grab a coffee and peruse a book in the upstairs café (p152) of the **Winding Stair Bookshop 16** (p192), one of the loveliest in the whole city.

Continue west along the Ormond Quay, past James Gandon's imposing **Four Courts 17** (p110) and then take a left onto Church St to admire the grisly vaults of **St Michan's Church 18** (p112).

WATERSIDE WANDER

Dublin's Grand Canal is one of the most beautiful parts of the city and a favourite walk for Dubliners looking to get away from the office at lunchtime. There are a number of good pubs along the way, should you need liquid refreshment.

Begin at the **Portobello 1**, a popular watering hole that was built to service the solid (and liquid) hungers of workers building the canal. Directly across the street is **Portobello College 2**, built in 1807 as Portobello House, one of the five original hostels that lined the canal between Dublin and the River Shannon. In the 20th century it served as a nursing home and, since the mid-1980s, as a technical college. From 1950 until his death, however, it was the residence of Jack B Yeats (1871–1957), who though not quite as famous

Walk Facts

Start Portobello Pub, South Richmond St
End City Quay
Distance 5km
Duration 2–2½ hours
Transport Bus 16, 16A, 19, 19A, 65 & 83 from Trinity College & South Great George's St

I'll Meet You in...

There's a famous story that tells of a meeting along the canal between Patrick Kavanagh and the hell-raising writer Brendan Behan. They chatted for a while, then Kavanagh suggested they go for a drink. He suggested a pub, to which Behan said 'no'. He was barred from that particular establishment, he explained, 'how about somewhere else?' Kavanagh asked Behan to recommend a spot, but when Behan did, Kavanagh demurely explained that *he* was barred from *that* pub. They shook hands and each went on their merry way.

as his Nobel-prize winning brother William, is still considered one of the greatest artists the country has ever produced (see p38). Turn left at the Grand Canal and begin your stroll along the towpath, passing several old locks that are still in operation. About 300m past Leeson St Bridge is a **statue 3** of the poet Patrick Kavanagh relaxing on the bench. This was, in fact, the poet's favourite spot to sit in the city (see p99). Not only was it a pleasant place to sit, Kavanagh insisted, but it was somewhere that he couldn't be barred from (see the boxed text above).

Kavanagh may have been a publican's nightmare, but you don't have to be. When you get to Baggot St Bridge take a right onto Baggot St and stop off for a drink at **Searson's 4** (☎ 660 0330; 42 Upper Baggot St) before returning to the canal and continuing eastward, diverting left at Mount St Crescent for **St Stephen's Church 5** (p89), a Greek Revival structure known as the 'Pepper-canister' on account of its curious shape. Back on the towpath, turn right at Northumberland Rd and left onto Haddington Rd for the **National Print Museum 6** (p100), housed in an old barracks. Turn left at Upper Grand Canal St and divert right to Barrow St, where you can climb the steps of the DART Station to see an ornate Victorian gas ring. Retrace your steps, then turn right at Grand Canal Quay for the **Waterways Visitor Centre 7** (p100), where you can find out everything you could possibly want to know (and

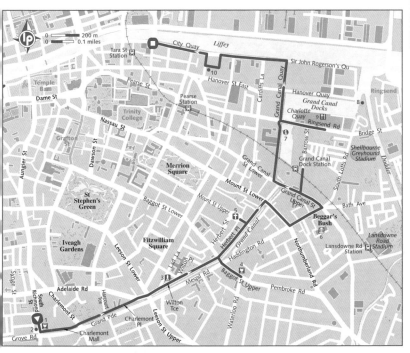

plenty more besides) on the construction of the country's canals and waterways. It sounds like a water-boffin's perfect day out, but it's actually quite interesting. A brand-new building, known as the **U2 Tower** 8 (see p49), is about to go up right at the point where the Grand Canal meets the Liffey. The band's new studios will be on the top three floors. (The Grand Canal Dock, on which sits the Waterways Visitor Centre, p100, was where the band shot the video for *Gloria*, way back in 1981).

Before heading back to the city, stop for something to eat in **Ocean** 9 (p148), a beautiful, glassed-in restaurant on the Grand Canal Dock. Back on Grand Canal Quay, walk north to the newly done-up Sir John Rogerson's Quay. Turn left and if you turn left again at Windmill Lane you can take a look at the **Windmill Lane Studios** 10, where U2 recorded all of their early records up to *The Unforgettable Fire*. Back on Rogerson's Quay, walk west (left) along the quays and back into the city.

Eating

Eating

Dublin's cheeks are a lot rosier since the food revolution of the 1990s, and good grub is now the rule rather than the exception here. Everywhere from greasy-spoon necessities to Michelin-starred indulgences have cranked up the quality, and new challengers are appearing every week. It may not have been the lure of food that brought you to Dublin, but it may well be one of the reasons you come back.

Dubs are into food these days; it's a favourite topic of conversation and in certain social circles you're not so much what you eat as *where* you eat. Some restaurants are developing the kind of kudos formerly reserved for nightclubs, and if a place impresses on opening night, it'll probably be reservation-only come the weekend. The city is awash with all kinds of hip restaurants with fabulous decor, stylish menus and staff who might seem more at home parading down a catwalk. But decor, beauty and plenty of press do not necessarily a good restaurant make. Substance is more important than style to your average Dublin diner, and you can rely on at least half of the population to point out that the Emperor is, in fact, stark bollock naked. What's on the plate is utmost; if it doesn't please local tastes, the restaurant will probably close down. This is the new Dublin, no longer the gastronomic minefield it was for travellers just a decade ago.

However – and this is a 24-carat however – food is very expensive in Dublin and you'll rarely get what you'd consider value for money (unless you're earning sterling or yen). Go to a smart restaurant, order three courses a la carte and wash them down with a decent European red, and two of you will be lucky to get change out of €150. On the other hand, choose well and you get a memorable meal for half that. In these pages, we've given you an even spread of the city's eateries, from the choicest cheap to choosiest chic – scan them well before you go out.

A Value Judgement

Nobody – at least nobody spending their own hard-earned money – would say that Dublin restaurants are renowned for offering good value. That's not just to say that restaurants here are stonkingly expensive, which many are, but lots don't offer the full package and the service is often the greatest let down. There doesn't seem to be much effort made to integrate floor staff into the overall scheme of the restaurant, and waiting staff can often subsequently seem detached, ill-informed and uninterested. Things have improved quite a bit, particularly with the influx of young continental Europeans who often have a better understanding of what makes good service in the food industry, but Dublin still lags behind in Europe.

You can't really do anything about the service during your trip but you *can* get better value by availing of the increasing number of special menus on offer. Many top-end restaurants are now offering set menus for lunch and dinner. While being corralled down certain culinary avenues may not be ideal, you can save an arm and a leg on what the same meal would have cost had you gone a la carte. Another trend that might suit you is the early-bird menu. It's mostly available at mid-range places, where you can have two or three courses for as little as half-price as long you're out before 7pm or so.

Opening Hours & Meal Times

Dubliners follow a fairly rigid fuelling schedule; they like to eat their evening meal early, generally between 7pm and 9.30pm, while lunch goes down between 1pm and 2pm. Cafés are open 8.30am to 6.30pm Monday to Saturday and 10am to 6pm Sunday. Most restaurants are open Monday to Saturday for lunch between noon and 3pm and dinner from 5.30pm and 10.30pm, although many mid-range restaurants stay open throughout the day. Top-end joints are more likely to close for Saturday lunch. Throughout these listings you can presume every place is open daily, unless otherwise specified. While we've noted where places stray from the standard, if you're going out of your way it's always safest to telephone ahead.

Booking Tables

Reserving a table has become just about compulsory for many of the city's best restaurants from Thursday to Saturday, and for the hippest ones all week. Thankfully, very few places have adopted the exceedingly annoying system of multiple sittings that is used in many of London's top restaurants. However, the most popular places – if you can get a reservation at them at all – often give you very small window through which to clamber through before the more important diners arrive.

Tipping

It's customary to tip around 10% of your bill, but if the service has been exceptional the size of the gratuity should be limited only by your generosity and/or level of inebriation. If it's been lousy don't be afraid to leave nothing at all.

Café Culture & Best Coffees

Although not as bad as in London, there is a proliferation of café chains taking over Dublin's streets. You won't have to look far for the likes of O'Briens, Rhubarb, Bar Expresso, Café Sol, Insomnia, Brown Bag, Gerard's and West Coast Coffee Company, which all cater mainly to office workers and are mostly much of a mediocre muchness. However, the following places do stand out:

Bar Italia (Map pp269-71; ☎ 679 5128; The Bookend, Essex Quay; mains €10-15; ☺ closed 6pm & Sun) Daily pasta specials, frantic and friendly Italian staff, and arguably the best espresso in Dublin are the highlights of this tiny, glass-fronted café at the edge of Temple Bar (right where you get the bus to Kilmainham). The coffee is by Palombim. There's also an outlet in the Epicurean Food Hall (p152).

Bewley's Oriental Cafés (Map pp272-3; www.bewleys.com; 78 Grafton St; all-day breakfasts €6, mains around €12) Bewley's is a Dublin institution, combining the style of English breakfast rooms with cosy hideaway cafés; the other branches are at 11-12 Westmoreland St (Map pp269–71) and 40 Mary St (Map pp264–5). Dimly lit and burgundy-furnished, they are the perfect antidote to a rainy day and will leave you with long, lingering memories of Ireland. And this will be quite an achievement really, because the bain-marie food and coffee are rubbish. They've been renovated in recent years – and the Grafton St branch has been turned into a supposedly fancy restaurant – but they all still do what Bewley's does best – a cup a tea, a bun and the *Irish Times* crossword.

La Boulangerie (Map pp266-8; ☎ 476 3812; 10 Upper Camden St; pastries €2-5; ☺ closed Sun) This endearing little spot has great coffee, but the real treats are the delicious French pastries.

Brown's Bar (Map pp272-3; ☎ 679 5666; Brown Thomas, Grafton St) Not as cool as it used to be, thank God; this is in Dublin's finest department store and is the best place to stop for a mid-shop revival.

Butler's Chocolate Café (Map pp272-3; ☎ 671 0591; 24 Wicklow St) Heavenly hedonistic, the coffee might not be the *very* best in town, but the combination of a delicious handmade chocolate and damn good coffee is hard to beat. Actually, sod the coffee and double up with its famous hot chocolate for an unforgettable treat.

Coffee Society (Map pp269-71; ☎ 878 7984; 2 Lower Liffey St) It looks most uninviting from the outside and only has paper cups, so it's a good job that this place has some of the best coffee-to-go in the city. There are various branches around town.

Milk Bar (Map pp266-8; ☎ 487 8450; 18 Montague St; ☺ closed Sat & Sun) Don't go to Iveagh Gardens (p85) without visiting this groovy little sandwich bar, which serves some of the best coffee in Dublin. The blend is a little mild, but if its standard offerings don't hit the mark these are the most benevolent baristas in Dublin and are happy to tweak their coffee – a little cooler, warmer, stronger, milkier, sweeter – until you get your fix exactly how you like it.

Munchies (Map pp272-3; ☎ 679 7296; 1-3 South William St; sandwiches €5; ☺ closed Sun) Now with two branches in the city centre – the other's on Lord Edward St (Map pp269–71) – Munchies has delicious sandwiches and baps, but only so-so coffee. This branch has a glass façade offering a great view onto this groovy little street, and if you're the millionth customer you get a smile from the girls behind the counter.

Queen of Tarts (Map pp269-71; ☎ 670 7499; Cork Hill; breakfast €6-9; ☺ lunch until 1/2pm only Sat & Sun) Diet dodgers rejoice for this doughty little café is to cakes what Willie Wonka was to chocolate, and you'll think you're in a dream when you see the displays of tarts, meringues, crumbles, cookies and brownies, never mind taste them. There are also great brekkies, such as potato and chive cake with mushroom and egg, the coffee's splendid and the service sweet. A treasure.

Bear in mind that snappy service is more the exception than the rule in Dublin – it's just not that kind of place. Most top-end places attend to all the details and then tack an automatic service charge of at least 10% to your bill. However, you're not legally obliged to pay this charge, so if you weren't happy with the service, let them sing for it. Otherwise you shouldn't expect much, even at mid-range places, where you might have to go looking for waiting staff (with your eyes at least) to order and not see them at all after your meal has been delivered. Keep a sense of humour about you, and be content with warm and competent service. In more basic places, you can just assume there's only counter service – or sit for a minute or two innocently twiddling your thumbs while the person glowers at you from *behind* the counter. No service, no tip, easy.

It's a tough call whether or not to reward substandard service. If we carry on tipping, restaurateurs will carry on neglecting service, but by not tipping we may be punishing innocent poor sods who are just trying to eke out a living. It's up to you, but here's a general tip for the Dublin restaurant industry: lift your game.

Self-Catering

Dubliners' new taste for food extends to cooking and market shopping, and a number of artisan street markets have opened up in recent years. If you're keen to self-cater – or just to take advantage of a sunny afternoon and an empty park – the most famous and most authentic market is on Moore St, where the colour of the produce is matched by the language of the dentally challenged spruikers. The more discerning shopper should head south of the river where there are a few terrific delis, cheesemongers and bakeries (see p182).

SOUTH OF THE LIFFEY

Most visitors to Dublin choose to dine on the south side where there is an abundance of eating options that will be sure to satisfy all palates. The range in taste is matched by the range in price: from good and groovy cheap eats to world-class cuisine.

Around Grafton Street

Vegetarian, international, pubs, pizzerias, cafés, great coffee, pioneering fast food and fine dining – as you'd expect from the heart of the capital, around Grafton St has it all.

AVOCA Map pp272–3   *Café*
☎ 677 4215; 11-13 Suffolk St; mains around €10;
😊 breakfast & lunch, closed Sun
Above Avoca Handweavers, this light-filled café serves terrific wholesome Irish cuisine with an organic bent, such as bangers and mash or a range of salads, along with glorious

---

desserts and reliable coffee. It's always filled with gorgeous young mothers and their exceedingly cute offspring.

AYA Map pp272–3   *Japanese*
☎ 677 1544; Clarendon St; mains average €15;
😊 closed Sun
Attached to the swanky Brown Thomas department store, this relative newcomer and absolute cracker has a revolving sushi bar where you can watch the chef making up the courses and passing them along to you, or you can order a la carte from the great menu with everything from prawn and vegetable tempura to beef *tataki* (thin slices of delicate spiced rare fillet). The furniture is wooden minimalist, but book early enough and you might get one of the cosy padded banquettes. There's also a Japanese mini-mart next door should you need *wasabi* for your picnic.

CAFÉ MAO Map pp272–3   *Asian*
☎ 670 4899; 2-3 Chatham Row; mains around €11;
😊 closed Sun
There's a mad mix of Oriental dishes at this hugely popular lunch-time spot, where Far Eastern flavours are combined with local ingredients. All the dishes – which include nasi goreng and *bulkoko* – are cooked fresh so may take a minute or two longer than you had in mind – but hey, you're on holiday and it's a cordial little place to hang out.

> ## Top Five Grafton Street Eats
>
> - Dunne & Crescenzi (opposite)
> - Aya (this page)
> - La Stampa (opposite)
> - Avoca (above)
> - Jacob's Ladder (opposite)

LE CAVE Map pp272–3 *French/Wine Bar*
☎ 679 4409; 28 South Anne St; ☺ until 2am, closed lunch Sun

It looks like a mobster's pool hall from the outside but if you wind yourself down the stairs you'll find a pleasantly chic Parisian-style wine bar with crimson walls, tiny tables and an exuberant crowd. The light French cooking is decent, although it's the groovy ambience and wine-list that really set this place apart.

DUNNE & CRESCENZI Map pp272–3 *Italian*
☎ 677 3815; 4 South Frederick St; mains around €12; ☺ closed Sun

Italian wines by the glass, suave service, excellent coffee, and a simple and ever-satisfying deli menu make D&C a must. It's so busy that you can't get a look-in on weekends, but mid-week this a sensational place to nibble on a panini, get picky with antipasto or choosy with cheese and chill out for an afternoon of luxury.

GOTHAM CAFÉ Map pp272–3 *Italian*
☎ 679 5266; 8 South Anne St; mains €8-13; ☺ closed Sun

Vibrant and youthful, Gotham is decorated with framed Rolling Stones album covers and is fully deserving of its reputation for delicious doughy discs (yeah, pizzas) named after districts of the Big Apple (yeah, New York). Swing past early and put your name down at busy times.

JACOB'S LADDER
Map pp266–8 *Modern Irish*
☎ 670 3865; 4-5 Nassau St; mains €25-32; ☺ closed Sun & Mon

Looking over the playing fields of Trinity College – which counts as a view in Dublin – this fashionably formal restaurant is spread over two floors and is renowned for its exquisite and innovative Irish cuisine (which flirts with modern European influences). The food is a winner, with entrees like grilled goat's cheese and mains such as mackerel and potato terrine guaranteed to impress.

KILKENNY KITCHEN Map pp266–8 *Café*
☎ 677 7066; 1st floor, 6 Nassau St; lunch from €8; ☺ closed Sun

Opposite Trinity and upstairs from the Kilkenny Shop, this big self-service cafeteria has a jolly good buffet featuring home-made soups, casseroles, salads, and lots of breads and pastries. Queues can be discouragingly long for lunch, but at other times snag a window table for views over the famous college.

RAJDOOT TANDOORI Map pp272–3 *Indian*
☎ 679 4274; 26-28 Clarendon St; mains around €19

Visitors to India may remember Rajdoot as a popular brand of Indian motorcycle; in Dublin, the name is synonymous with outstanding Indian cuisine. The menu is predominantly from the northwest of India, so takes its inspiration from the meaty *mughlai* cuisine, particularly anything that comes out of the tandoor, although there are also plenty of excellent vegetarian options.

SHANAHAN'S ON THE GREEN
Map pp266–8 *American*
☎ 407 0939; 119 West St Stephen's Green; steaks €36-45; ☺ closed Sat lunch & Sun

Possibly the best steak in Ireland can be found at this pioneering Dublin restaurant set over three floors of a lovely Georgian residence. The 'Oval Office' contains memorabilia from various US presidents but don't let that put you off the grub. The most tender Irish Angus beef steak, creamy mashed potatoes, a boost of seasonal greens and, as the locals say, you're laughing.

LA STAMPA Map pp272–3 *Modern European*
☎ 677 8611; 35 Dawson St; mains €25-55; ☺ closed Sun

A classic on Dublin's restaurant scene, La Stampa has a gorgeous *belle époque* setting in a 19th-century house draped in richly coloured fabrics and decorated with modern artworks. The crowd is singularly well heeled

---

Vegetarian Dublin

Dublin can be difficult dining for vegetarians, although things are improving and there are a number of dedicated restaurants. The Irish adore their meat – flesh of some description is the centrepiece of virtually every Irish meal and most Irish people won't feel like they've eaten unless their incisors have been challenged. Solidly vegetarian places include Cornucopia (p148), Fresh (p148), Govinda (p148), Juice (p136), Nude (p150) and Blazing Salads (p148); if you're dining in a mixed group you'll find choice and flavour at Café Irie (p148), the Irish Film Centre (p135), Lemon (p149), Yamamori (p137), Rajdoot Tandoori (above), 101 Talbot (p150), Chameleon (p134) and Jacob's Ladder (this page).

La Stampa (p133)

(or at least out to give that impression) and the food superb. You can have caviar for entree, grilled lobster for main and chips on the side. Darling, when you're paying these prices you can have chips on your head if you so desire.

TIGER BECS Map pp272–3 *Thai*
☎ 677 8677; 36 Dawson St; mains €9-25;
🕑 closed Sun

Below oriental superpub, SamSara (p157), this long and cavernous restaurant serves top-notch Thai nosh (would it be going too far to suggest a top night?) to Dublin's beautiful young things. The crispy aromatic duck entree is delicious and a meal in itself. You're probably paying a little too much for the sense of style, but nevertheless this loud, buzzing place has oodles of atmosphere and is a great place to launch yourself into a night on the razzle.

Temple Bar

Temple Bar is a microcosm of Dublin's dining scene; there are some great eateries to suit every pocket but choose casually and you may pay the price.

AR VICOLETTO Map pp269–71 *Italian*
☎ 670 8662; 5 Crow St; mains €12-25

When it's good, this cosy little osteria is very, very good, with excellent Italian dishes washed down with splendid Italian reds and enjoyed in a convivial atmosphere. But it's a little inconsistent and sometimes the standard menu of pasta, meaty mains and seafood misses, and at these times it doesn't seem like good value at all, although the warm Gorgonzola salad never disappoints.

BAD ASS CAFÉ Map pp269–71 *Pizzeria*
☎ 671 2596; 9-11 Crown Alley; 🕑 until midnight;
mains €12-15

Sinéad O'Connor used to work as a waitress at this charismatic, warehouse-style pizzeria that's been here since long before Temple Bar was a twinkle in a developer's eye. It's still cheerfully plying its trade in a convivial atmosphere and has pulleys to whip orders to the kitchen at busy times. While always popular with kids, it's been proscribed as uncool by Dublin's fashion police in recent years. Tough titty to them who are missing out on decent, well-priced and amply portioned pizza, pasta and burgers.

CHAMELEON Map pp269–71 *Indonesian*
☎ 671 0362; 1 Lower Fownes St; mains €14-20;
🕑 dinner only, closed Mon

Friendly, cute and full of character, Chameleon is draped in exotic fabrics and serves up perky renditions of Indonesian classics, such as satay, *gado gado* and nasi goreng but if you can't decide you can always plump for the *rijsttaffel*, a selection of several dishes with rice. The top floor has low seating on cushions, which is perfect for intimate group get-togethers.

DISH Map pp269–71 *Modern European*
☎ 671 1248; 2 Crow St; mains €15-20;
🕑 until 11.30pm

One of the original übertrendy restaurants in Temple Bar, Dish moved away from the centre to grow up a little and has never looked or tasted better. It's self-confident without being smug, the service is thoughtful and efficient, and the menu is full of new twists on old

Top Five Temple Bar Eats
- Odessa (opposite)
- Café Irie (p148)
- Mermaid Café (opposite)
- Il Baccaro (opposite)
- El Bahia (opposite)

avourites, such as steamed sea bass with clams, oven dried tomatoes, black olives and fresh herbs. Bravo.

EDEN Map pp269–71 *Modern European*
☎ 670 5372; Meeting House Sq; mains €15-23; ☒ closed Sun

Although no longer quite the restaurant *du jour*, starkly modern Eden still has a rock-solid reputation for its fabulous food, which includes the likes of blackened salmon, pork brochette with a peanut sauce and other fusion surprises. There's also an excellent – and only moderately marked-up – wine list, while the terrace is much coveted in summer.

EL BAHIA Map pp272–3 *Moroccan*
☎ 677 0213; 1st floor, 37 Wicklow St; mains €10-18; ☒ closed Sun

Dark and sultry, Ireland's only Moroccan restaurant looks a little like how we imagine a desert harem might be. Or maybe we just got carried away with the Moroccan sounds and smells. There are some rather fetching geometric designs on the ceilings and walls, and the gimme-gimme food includes the likes of tasty *tajines* (stews), couscous and *bastile* (pastry stuffed with chicken), while the sweet and spicy Moroccan coffee is an unusual treat.

ELEPHANT & CASTLE
Map pp269–71 *American*
☎ 679 3121; 18 Temple Bar; mains €10-22; ☒ closed Sun

Long famous for its spicy chicken wings and omelettes, the E&C had a change of management in recent years and, although maintaining its popularity for the time being, is struggling to maintain the standards of its tried and tested American-style menu that includes burgers and salads. Sadly, this Dublin institution might not make the next edition.

IL BACCARO Map pp269–71 *Italian*
☎ 671 4597; Meeting House Sq; mains €9.50-20.50

Tucked away in the atmospheric Diceman's Corner (so-called after a local mime artist), this trattoria is a wonderfully rustic piece of the old boot popular with Dublin's Italian community who come here to make merry and wave their hands around a lot. The food is exuberantly authentic, ranging from bruschetta, home-made pasta, Italian sausage, cannelini beans and the like. The Italian wines are *bellissimo*.

Top Five Irish Cuisine
- Chapter One (p151)
- Avoca (p132)
- Jacob's Ladder (p133)
- Roly's Bistro (p148)
- Trocadero (p137)

IRISH FILM CENTRE Map pp269–71 *Café/Bar*
☎ 677 6788; 6 Eustace St; mains €6-10

The light café fare – with vegetarian and Middle-Eastern menus – is good if nothing special, but this is the coolest, most relaxing place in the city for a beer and bite and a movie (see p175). The coffee and hot chocolate are decent too.

MERMAID CAFÉ Map pp269–71 *Seafood*
☎ 670 8236; 22 Dame St; mains €20-30; ☒ closed Sun

One of Dublin's best, the Mermaid dishes up terrific seafood, such as crab cakes with piquant mayonnaise and monkfish wrapped in prosciutto and rosemary (hop on the phone and make a booking now!), in bright and airy surrounds and a casual and friendly atmosphere.

MONTY'S OF KATHMANDU
Map pp269–71 *Nepalese*
☎ 670 4911; 28 Eustace St; mains €14-18; ☒ closed lunch Sun

The only Nepalese joint in town is also one of Dublin's favourite new ethnic eateries. The varied menu of Nepalese and subcontinent staples – including lamb done every which way – can be a little bland so request some chilli if you like things spicy. The atmosphere can be a bit hushed but the service is warm.

NICO'S Map pp269–71 *Italian*
☎ 677 3062; 53 Dame St; mains €10-18; ☒ closed Sun

You know those seemingly run-of-the-mill places in your hometown where it seems everyone who works in the food industry likes to go when they knock off? Well, this old-fashioned and long-serving trattoria is Dublin's version. The traditional Italian food is consistently good, service sort of charming, the decor simple and homey, while the prices are reasonable and the piano tinkles softly.

ODESSA Map pp272–3 *Mediterranean*
☎ 670 7634; 13 Dame St; mains €10-20

A stylish, fashionable place where comfort and design get equal billing, Odessa's simple dishes are decidedly delicious, and include the likes of Eggs Benedict for brekkie, burgers for lunch and tender fillets of steak for dinner. It's popular for cocktails all week, while Sunday brunch is a firm favourite with the city's hip young things.

TANTE ZOÉ'S Map pp269–71   Cajun/Creole
☎ 679 4407; 1 Crow St; mains average €18;
⏰ closed Sun

Every night's a mardi gras for the senses in this lively and gregarious spot where the menu consists of gumbo, jambalaya, bayou steaks, and lots of Cajun-blackened this and Creole-infused that. It has long been popular with discerning groups hellbent on letting the good times roll.

TEA ROOMS AT THE CLARENCE
Map pp269–71   Modern Irish
☎ 670 7766; The Clarence, ♿ -8 Wellington Quay; three courses €52.50; ⏰ closed lunch Sat

Designed to resemble a church, the Clarence's Tea Rooms are spacious with a soaring ceiling and double-height windows flooding the room with natural light. Appropriately, the innovative food commands respect, and includes the likes of warm white asparagus with morel dressing, and pan-fried seabass with lobster tortellini. The clientele is unfailingly fashionable.

SoDa
This strip's more about funky food than fine dining, and you'll find many pioneering eateries including Dublin's best chipper, creperie, juice bars and ethnic eats.

Top Five SoDa Eats
- Lemon (p149)
- La Maison des Gourmets (opposite)
- Yamamori (opposite)
- Pig & Heifer (opposite)
- Cedar Tree (this page)

CAFÉ METRO Map pp272–3   Café
☎ 679 4515; 43 South William St; mains around €7;
⏰ closed Sun

Mellow music, excellent coffee, exceptionally friendly staff and frills-free café fare (like salads and toasties) keep Metro's customers loyal. It's particularly sociable in summer when outside tables are the perfect spot for 10 minutes with the paper or an hour with your buddies.

CEDAR TREE Map pp272–3   Lebanese
☎ 677 2121; 11a St Andrew's St; mains €12-20;
⏰ until midnight

The best of a handful of Lebanese restaurants in town, this is a low-key and relaxed basement to while a night away in the company of delicious meze (falafel, spicy sausage, dips, meatballs, kofta and several bottles of red wine. Service is warm and considerate.

CHILI CLUB Map pp272–3   Thai
☎ 677 3721; 1 Anne's Lane; mains €17-22;
⏰ closed Sun

Cosy, comfy and a million miles from the hubbub of modern Dublin – well, a block – this is one of the longest-serving Thai restaurants in town, and has built its reputation on unfailingly good – and unremittingly hot – curries, satays and soupy broths at reasonable prices.

GOOD WORLD RESTAURANT
Map pp272–3   Chinese
☎ 677 5373; 18 South Great George's St; mains €10-20; ⏰ until 3am

For the best Chinese grub in SoDa...you'll have to learn Cantonese, because the bilingual menu here is broken down into the fairly bland versions for the Irish palate and the more exciting dishes for the Chinese community who congregate here. But even the dishes in English are good, and the dim sum outstanding.

GUY STUART Map pp272–3   Food Stall
George's St Arcade, Drury St; sandwiches around €4;
⏰ closed Sun

'Slow-food' exponents Jenny Guy and Lara Stuart opened this food stall in the George's St Arcade a few years ago to immediate success. The emphasis is on fresh Mediterranean produce, to be savoured slowly and with relish either in a sandwich or in their range of delicious soups. There are also great daily specials and coffee.

JUICE Map pp272–3   Vegetarian
☎ 475 7856; Castle House, 73 South Great George's St; smoothies €5, mains around €11; ⏰ late Fri-Sat, closed Sun

This trendy and self-conscious vegetarian restaurant offers up terrific Pacific Rim–style cuisine as well as tasty stir-fries, soups, wraps, soya desserts, organic wines and, of course, delicious fresh juices and smoothies. We just wish the staff had smiled a little more when we were there.

A MAISON DES GOURMETS

Map pp272–3 *French*

☎ 672 7258; 15 Castle Market; mains average €10;
✿ breakfast, lunch & afternoon tea, closed Sun

If it's Saturday you can forget about trying to get a seat at this gorgeous little salon (above a wonderful gourmet bakery/patisserie), which will be filled with shoppers and queues of harrumphing Francophile regulars. The menu is small but select, and includes deliciously light and refined tartines (open sandwiches with the likes of pesto and aubergine), plates of charcuterie (cured meats), versions of the same for breakfast, and wine by the half- and full bottle. The only downside is sometimes the service is ridiculously slow.

PAD THAI Map pp260-1 *Thai*

☎ 475 5551; 30 South Richmond St; mains €12-17;
✿ closed Sat & Sun lunch

If you fancy hanging with the local hipsters, scoot down to this colourful and spacious joint, where the menu is a lively mix of spicy soups, Thai salads, noodles, and oodles more meat and veggie mains.

PIG & HEIFER Map pp266–8 *Café*

☎ 478 3182; 2 Charlotte Way; lunch €5-6; ✿ closed at night & Sun

This simple, modern café does a splendid line in cholesterol-building cooked breakfasts and generously proportioned New York–style deli sandwiches. There are dozens of different breads and bagels to choose from, the cheeses are from the owner's farm, and there's plenty of horseradish, sauerkraut, pickle and mustard to dollop on your pastrami.

TROCADERO Map pp272–3 *Traditional Irish*

☎ 677 5545; 3 St Andrew's St; mains around €14;
✿ until midnight, closed Sun

Seedy on the outside and impressively Art Deco within, the Troc has long been a favourite with thespians, hacks, musos and TV execs. There are no culinary dashes, just big portions of honest-to-goodness dishes of steak, lamb and fish, and that's the way the regulars like it.

YAMAMORI Map pp272–3 *Japanese*

☎ 475 5001; 71-72 South Great Georges St; entrees €6-7.50, noodles €12-14; ✿ closed lunch Sun

Hip, inexpensive and generally fabulous, Yamamori never disappoints with its bubbly service and vivacious cooking that swoops from succulent sushi and sashimi to whopping great

plates of noodles and plenty more besides. It's a great spot for a sociable group – that includes vegetarians – although you'll have to book on the weekend to be one of the happy campers.

Georgian Dublin

Forget about lunch-times here because every place from sandwich bars to silver servers will be packed with the office crowds. On the other hand, cafés are lovely and relaxed outside lunch hours, while the restaurants are generally not too busy at night.

Top Five Georgian Dublin Eats

- L'Ecrivain (p138)
- Restaurant Patrick Guilbaud (p138)
- Thornton's (p147)
- Bang Café (below)
- Papaya (p138)

BANG CAFÉ Map pp266–8 *Danish*

☎ 676 0898; 11 Merrion Row; mains around €22;
✿ closed Sun

Owned by the handsome Stoke twins, Bang brings a touch of Danish to Dublin in appropriately stylish and hip surrounds – and is therefore predictably buzzing with trendy 30-somethings. But the modern European grub is innovative, meaty, particularly strong on seafood and damn good value for the price tag. Reservations are a must, even for lunch.

BROWNES Map pp272–3 *Brasserie*

☎ 638 3939; 22 St Stephen's Green; mains average €25

Certainly one of the most beautiful places to refuel, this well-bred *belle époque* charmer has a lovely dining room with French chandeliers and Italian-style friezes. There was a spell when this place was ironically hip, although it's usually just a rather stuffy moneyed set in attendance these days. That said, the brasserie fare – including the likes of monkfish wrapped in pancetta – is splendid and this is still a great place for an evening of understated elegance.

DIEP LE SHAKER Map pp266–8 *Asian*

☎ 661 1829; 55 Pembroke Lane; mains €18-30;
✿ closed Sat lunch & Sun

This modern, light-filled space is tucked down an alley off prestigious Pembroke St, and is popular with the local business crowd, establishment movers and shakers, and people generally consumed by their own self-importance. It's the ugly side of the Celtic Tiger. The predominantly Thai grub is inventive and excellent, but you get the impression you're paying for the company and it ain't worth it.

DOBBINS WINE BAR Map pp266–8   French
☎ 676 4679; 15 Stephen's Lane; mains €17-27; ☺ closed Sat lunch & Sun

This old stalwart, opposite a row of council houses, was where the privileged came for lunch before the Celtic Tiger brought privilege to half the city. Its traditional French fare, homey setting and old-fashioned hospitality have served it well over the last quarter of a century, and it's still a favourite with politicians, journalists and spin doctors (often at the same table).

L'ECRIVAIN Map pp266–8   French
☎ 661 1919; 112 Lower Baggot St; mains €38-45; ☺ closed Sat lunch & Sun

Many a Dublin foodie's favourite, L'Ecrivain got a hard-earned Michelin star in 2003. It blends sophisticated French cooking with the best Irish ingredients in an intimate room decorated with portraits of famous Irish writers. The menu's constantly on the go but always delivers a cavalcade of delicious treats, and this is *the* place to sample local specialities, such as Irish salmon and Dublin Bay prawns.

ELY Map pp266–8   Wine Bar
☎ 676 8986; 22 Ely Pl; mains around €15; ☺ until 2am Thu-Sat, closed Sun

Wines from around Europe are what this solidly sophisticated little joint does best – the wine list runs to 10 pages – but there's also some very decent rustic cooking to be savoured, announced on a refreshingly straight-talking menu and leaning towards organic produce. Whether you're dining light on salmon pate or tucking into a surf 'n' turf kebab, don't look past the handmade choccies for dessert.

FADÓ Map pp272–3   Modern Irish
☎ 676 7200; Mansion House, Dawson St; mains around €25; ☺ closed Sun

Most definitely not for solo diners, Fadó ('once upon a time') occupies a huge single, *belle époque* dining room next door to the Lord Mayor's pad on Dawson St. The atmosphere is as good or as buzzy as the crowd and the time of week, although the contemporary Irish food (with inevitable international twists) is consistently superb. The service can be a little all over the place but it's always charming.

FITZER'S Map pp272–3   Modern European
☎ 677 1155; 51 Dawson St; mains €15-24; ☺ closed Su

Fitzer's was the first to bring casually upmarket international dining to Dublin – and was slated as pretentious for its trouble – and is still doing a splendid job of delivering good fusion cuisine (predominantly Mediterranean) in this elegant and airy space. There's another terrific branch in the National Gallery (Map pp266–8) nearby.

PAPAYA Map pp266–8   Thai
☎ 676 0044; 8 Ely Pl; mains €15-18; ☺ closed lunch Sat-Sun

In the heart of Georgian Dublin, this cute little place is in an attractively vaulted basement with well-spaced tables and velour-upholstered chairs. Only one of the friendly waiters is Thai but all know their way around the extensive menu that's unmistakably Mekong-based, with terrific starters such as satay chicken on a skewer and crispy duck for main.

Restaurant Patrick Guilbaud

RESTAURANT PATRICK GUILBAUD
Map pp266–8   French
☎ 676 4192; The Merrion Hotel, 21 Upper Merrion St; mains €32-48; ☺ closed Mon & Sun

With two Michelin stars in its crown, this is the most prestigious restaurant in the country and *the* venue for a special occasion. The service is

(Continued on page 147)

aurant Patrick Guil-
(p138) **2** Juice (p136)
ding Stair Bookshop &
p152)

1 Palace Bar (p158) 2 Porter House Brewing Company (p158) 3 Half pint – lady's drink (p154) 4 Gravity Bar, Guinness Storehouse (p94)

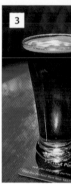

Voodoo Lounge (p164)
ernational Bar (p156)
1 Jameson Distillery
0)

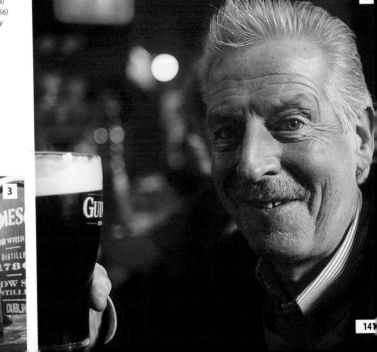

1 Football at Phoenix Pa[rk] (p111) 2 Hurley and sliot[ar] (p179) 3 Traditional Irish music (p170)

1 *Brown Thomas wind* (p184) 2 *Moore St mar* (p190) 3 *Meeting Hous Square Market, Temple* (p186)

1 Castletown House (p.)
2 Howth (p222) 3 Ancie
glacial lake at Glendal
(p216)

Continued from page 138)

ormal, the setting elegant, the wine list awe-
ome and the fare proudly French. While the
ood is innovative – expect the likes of lobster
avioli and roast quail coated in hazelnuts – it's
arely too fiddly, just beautifully cooked and
uperbly presented.

THORNTON'S Map pp272–3   *International*
☎ 478 7015; Fitzwilliam Hotel; three-course set
unch/dinner €40/65; ✓ closed Sun & Mon

Kevin Thornton is the top dog in Dublin's
kitchen and this is arguably the finest restau-
ant in Ireland. The exquisite and innovative
nternational cuisine tips its hat to France,
out has a strong Irish lilt. The restaurant is on
he 1st floor of the Fitzwilliam Hotel (p199)
and looks out over St Stephen's Green (p89).
Menus change regularly but the signature is
gamey meats. Book before you board.

UNICORN Map pp266–8   *Italian*
☎ 676 2182; 12b Merrion Ct, Merrion Row; mains
€38-45; ✓ closed Sun

Saturday lunch here is a tradition for Dublin's
media types, socialites, politicos and their
cronies who guffaw and clink glasses in
conspiratorial rapture. At lunch many opt
for the extensive antipasto bar, while the
bistro-style evening menu features Italian
classics done well and priced to fit in with the
fashionable surrounds.

Kilmainham & the Liberties

Heading west of Dublin's centre, eating
options are limited, as the area resists
the revamps and remains a working-class
stronghold.

THE GALLIC KITCHEN
Map pp262–3   *French/Café*
☎ 454 4912; 49 Francis St; meals around €6; ✓ until
7pm, closed Sun

Our food is so fucking good you won't believe
t.' advises the sign on the wall of this little bakery shop front. Standing at a bench, devour-
ng a goat's cheese brioche, salmon roulade,
smoked haddock quiche and chocolate pecan
tart, we – wait for it – tend to agree.

Beyond the Grand Canal
If you fancy a change of pace, head on into
the inner southern suburbs, such as Ranelagh, Ballsbridge and Rathmines, where
you will be rewarded with some great eating options.

DIEP NOODLE BAR Map pp260–1   *Asian*
☎ 497 6550; Ranelagh Rd, Ranelagh; mains average €13

Thai and Vietnamese noodle dishes are the
speciality of this 2003 smash hit, which represents a very useful addition to Ranelagh's
burgeoning culinary reputation, although
not nearly as good – and certainly not as
funky – as the locals make out. Dishes such
as seafood rice noodles and red snapper ver-
micellia *are* great and bursting with flavour,
but noodles needn't cost so much and the
formally 'trendy' atmosphere and lack of a
single Asian face just don't seem right for a
noodle joint.

> ## Top Five Quick Eats
>
> - Lemon (p149)
> - Bad Ass Café (p134)
> - The Gallic Kitchen (this page)
> - Gruel (p149)
> - Soup Dragon (p152)

LOBSTER POT RESTAURANT
Map pp260–1   *French/Seafood*
☎ 668 0025; 9 Ballsbridge Tce; mains €20-50;
✓ closed Sat lunch & Sun

Seafood's the speciality at this old-fashioned and low-key choice, decorated with
nautical paraphernalia and the occasional
plastic lobster. The food is traditional French –
moules marinière, fish *provençale* and seafood
chowder – and bookings are *de rigueur*. Some
of the tables are a bit close together, which is
a problem in a city where everyone is talking
about one another.

MASH Map pp260–1   *International*
☎ 497 9463; Castlewood Ave, Rathmines; mains
average €12; ✓ closed Sun

This tiny and eclectic place is run by Bobby
and Jerome, possibly the friendliest hosts in
the capital. It is well regarded for its tasty,
home-made dishes and cosy atmosphere,
and the small menu features daily specials,
like Thai chicken curry, roast red snapper,
organic steaks or the popular range of Mash
potato cakes, all made with TLC and served
with a smile.

Top Five Ethnic Eats

- Monty's of Kathmandu (p135)
- Cedar Tree (p136)
- Kelly & Ping (p151)
- Il Baccaro (p135)
- Aya (p132)

OCEAN Map pp260–1 *Seafood*
☎ 668 8862; Charlotte Quay Dock, Ringsend; mains €12-18

Once the docks are redeveloped, Ocean will have one of the best views in town (hence the floor to ceiling windows). The problem is it's already charging for the view while it, and the seafood, aren't quite there yet. Standards include oysters, crab salad and a langoustine cocktail, but portions are small and the convoluted cooking unreliable. That said, there's a nice terrace should the sun stick its head out.

ROLY'S BISTRO
Map pp260–1 *Traditional Irish*
☎ 668 2611; 7 Ballsbridge Tce, Ballsbridge; mains €20-25

A local favourite, Roly's does basic (leek and potato soup) and adventurous (pork stuffed with rhubarb and apple) with equal aplomb. There's a terrific atmosphere, good value and *always* a need to book. Its selection of freshly baked speciality breads is reason enough to mosey on down.

TRIBECA Map pp260–1 *American Brasserie*
☎ 497 1474; 65a Ranelagh Rd, Ranelagh; mains €8-15; ☺ closed Sun

The chicken wings and other soul food – like salmon burgers and goat's cheese omelettes – upon which the old Elephant & Castle (p135) made its name can now be afound in all their secret, spicy glory at this New York-style brasserie, which is so popular that punters have been known to queue outside in the rain. The food, decor and service are all perfectly pitched – smart, straightforward and sassy – while the room is too small for a reputation this big.

Cheap Eats
BLAZING SALADS
Map pp272–3 *Vegetarian*
☎ 671 9552; 42 Drury St; mains €3-7; ☺ closed Sun
Great name, no seating, this terrific vegetarian deli specialises in cheap and hearty salads,

sandwiches and smoothies that will help pu the romp back in your stomp. There are also o ganic breads, including some for special diet

BUSYFEET & COCO CAFÉ
Map pp272–3 *Caf*
☎ 671 9514; 41 South William St; lunch €5-8; ☺ closed Sun

Marvellous winter-warming *chai* (tea) is on of the main draws of this cosy café, where bi windows let you look out on to Dublin's hip pest street. The cosy vibe extends to the fare with lots of fried breakfasts or danishes and th like for breakfast, splendid open sandwiche for lunch and good coffee all day.

CAFÉ IRIE Map pp269–71 *Caf*
☎ 672 5090; 11 Upper Fownes St; lunch €5; ☺ 9am-8.30pm

Not at all Jamaican, as the name and colour would suggest, although every sentence a this brilliant little student place is followe by 'man' (in the traditional Dublin way, no the pseudo hippy crap) and if the very cut waiters were any more laidback they woul be horizontal. The basic café fare range from cornflakes to fry-ups for breakfast, whil lunch is all about wraps, paninis and sand wiches, with fillings like creamy basil pest and chicken.

CORNUCOPIA Map pp272–3 *Vegetaria*
☎ 677 7583; 19 Wicklow St; mains around €6; ☺ closed Sun

As far as you can get from traditional stodg Irish food, the 'Cup of Plenty' is a little hippy chic with headscarved girls serving hot dishe such as cafeteria-style casseroles to an ap preciative and laidback clientele. There ar also hot vegetarian breakfasts if muesli an yoghurt doesn't grab you.

FRESH Map pp272–3 *Vegetaria*
☎ 671 9552; top floor, Powerscourt Townhouse shopping centre; lunch from €5-9; ☺ closed Sun
This long-standing vegetarian preference serve up a variety of filling salads and hot daily spe cials. Many dishes are dairy and gluten-fre without compromising on taste.

GOVINDA'S Map pp266–8 *Vegetaria*
☎ 475 0309; 4 Aungier St; mains €5-9; ☺ closed Sun
You can smell the patchouli oil from 50m a this authentic beans-and-pulses vegetaria

Eating – Cheap Eats

place, which is run by happy Hare Krishnas and has daily specials ranging from wholesome salads to Indian-style hot meals.

GRUEL Map pp269–71   *Sandwich Bar*

☎ 670 7119; 68a Dame St; lunch €5-7; ☽ closed Sun

The best sandwich joint in the city centre, Gruel's soup kitchen decor perfectly matches the gourmet greasy spoon fare being dished up. The daily 'roast-in-a-roll' is a mighty mountain of meat doused in your preferred sauce, while the 'deli roll' is a changing veggie version. The queues out the door are testament to this place's popularity. There's not much room to eat so consider heading across the road to Castle Gardens, in front of the Chester Beatty Library (p81).

HAVANA Map pp266–8   *Tapas*

☎ 476 0046; 3 Camden Market, Grantham St; tapas €5-7; ☽ late Fri & Sat, closed Sun

Bursting with energy, this Cuban–Spanish joint is one of the reasons for SoDa's new reputation for cool. Wines, beers and cocktails lubricate the mixed and mingling crowd who munch endlessly on tasty titbits from tortilla to chorizo, while shakin' it a little to 'big salsa sounds' on Friday and Saturday night after 10pm.

LEMON Map pp272–3   *Creperie*

☎ 672 9044; 66 South William St; crepes from €3.50; ☽ closed Sun

Not much bigger than a postage stamp, Dublin's original, oft-imitated and unparalleled creperie occupies a cool corner of the city and is a superb place for a quick bite during the day or early evening. It's run by a young and friendly crew that take pride in their delicious sweet and savoury crepes (such as one smothered in Grand Marnier or a delicious vegetarian 'power-crepe' with spinach), while good coffee is a bonus.

LEO BURDOCK'S

Map pp266–8   *Fish & Chipper*

☎ 454 0306; 2 Werburgh St; fish & chips €5-8; ☽ until 11pm, closed Sun

Don't be surprised to see queues snaking out of this place, Dublin's best chipper, where even celebs like Tom Cruise and Bruce Springsteen have to get in line. In the shadow of Christ Church Cathedral (p91) since 1913, Burdock's is famous for its batter (the recipe is kept secret), fresh fish and thick chips. Standards have

Worth the Trip

Ayumi Ya (☎ 283 176; Newpark Centre, Newpark Ave, Blackrock; dinner average €35; ☽ closed Sun lunch; Ⓟ) For the best Japanese food, Dubs head to the smug, southern suburb of Blackrock to this small dining room and the carnival of flavours, combinations and textures on offer. Service is gentle and attentive, while the *norimaki* (rolls) and deep-fried dishes like tofu and pork with bean sprouts and vegetables are the culinary standouts. Its sister restaurant, Aya (p132), is in the city centre.

The Bar & Brasserie (☎ 844 7501; Dublin Airport; mains €15-20; Airport Express Coach; Ⓟ) Worth an early trip, this summer 2003 creation will leave a great lasting impression of Dublin and its food. Although it's aiming for business travellers, this is a great little restaurant with very friendly and efficient black-clad staff, long white cushioned benches, maroon walls and terrific brasserie fare ranging from light and refined entrees to meaty mains and a wonderful platter of Irish cheeses. The only downside are the airport musak and the absence of a farewell Guinness (available at another bar nearby).

Caviston's (☎ 280 9120; 59 Glasthule Rd, Sandycove; mains €10-20; ☽ noon-6pm; DART to Sandycove; Ⓟ) Dublin's finest seafood restaurant has only 10 tables and a lovely casual bistro feel. The three daily lunch sittings (noon-1.30pm, 1.30-3pm, 3-5pm) are always packed with slavering punters drawn by wonderful fresh fish which, cooked simply, speaks for itself. What does swordfish with a béarnaise sauce garnished with cress say to you? Bookings are essential. The next door deli sells the raw materials and gourmet items.

Johnnie Fox's (☎ 295 5647; Glencullen, County Wicklow; mains average €23; bus 44B from Hawkins St; Ⓟ) Technically it's not even in the capital yet no visit to Dublin is complete without a trip to Ireland's highest pub, about 45 minutes from the city centre. Although it can feel kitschy, touristy and overdone, Fox's is great craic (traditional fun) and it's actually an authentic old pub full of bric-a-brac, gnarled benches, sawdust floors and crackling open fires. There's terrific, if slightly overpriced, seafood while views of rolling countryside and Irish music (the 'howya boys and girls' variety) are other rewards for the trek.

slipped a little since it has become a tourist Mecca but it's still a worthy pit stop, particularly after a few pints. It is takeaway or no way; you can eat at the park down the road in front of St Patrick's Cathedral (p96).

LISTONS Map pp266–8 *Deli*
☎ 405 4779; 25 Camden St; lunch €3-8; ◷ closed Sun
The lunch-time queues streaming out the door of this place are testament to its reputation as Dublin's best deli. Its sandwiches with fresh and delicious fillings, roasted vegetable quiches, rosemary potato cakes and sublime salads will have you coming back again and again – the only problem is there's too much choice! On fine days, take your gourmet picnic to the nearby Iveagh Gardens (p85).

Pubs & Sustenance

If you're a traditionalist and think food's main function is for soaking up the booze (like generations of Dubs before you), waste no time and eat at the pub. You'll get solid steak and chips – and strangely moreish plastic-coated, toasted cheese sandwiches – at the Stag's Head (p160), great burgers and fish at Eamonn Doran's Imbibing Emporium (p171) and perky pasta at the ever-fashionable the Bailey (p156). Davy Byrne's (p156) has been associated with food since Leopold Bloom dropped in for a Gorgonzola sandwich and a burgundy in *Ulysses*. A century later, excellent oysters, salmon and other seafood make up the fare. Dublin's oldest pub, The Brazen Head (p161), does a mean carvery and summer alfresco, and the new Ba Mizu (p159) has bragging rights for its beef and Guinness stew.

NECTAR Map pp260–1 *Café*
☎ 491 0934; 53 Ranelagh Rd, Ranelagh; mains €5-11
In the centre of this still-genteel (for now) village, this modern little juice bar has a tempting selection of hot wraps, healthy daily specials, and flavoursome smoothies and juices. It's a good spot for vegetarians, as is the city branch at 7-9 Exchequer St (Map pp272–3) in SoDa.

NUDE Map pp272–3 *Vegetarian/Fast Food*
☎ 675 5577; 21 Suffolk St; mains €5-6; ◷ closed Sun
This fabulous and environmentally friendly take on Dublin fast food looks like the juice bar at the end of the universe. The massive kitchen is fronted by a space-age counter, while the communal benches are very human

and sociable. Just checking out the huge pre packaged display makes your vitamin coun surge, with lots of juices, salads and cold dishes, while the hot menu mainly feature hunky and healthy Asian-filled wraps

SIMON'S PLACE Map pp272–3 *Caf*
☎ 679 7821; George's St Arcade; ◷ closed 5pm & Sur
Hogging a prime corner spot off the ver groovy George's St Arcade (p182), Simon' Place is a bustling café that serves up big chunky sandwiches, nutritious, rich soups and decent pastries. The coffee is only satisfactory but the cute European staff are more than alright. Avoid downstairs which is dark and dingy.

STEPS OF ROME Map pp272–3 *Italian*
☎ 670 5630; Unit 1 Chatham Ct, Chatham St; pizza €8-10; ◷ until midnight, closed Sun
A contender for best pizza – and friendlies service – in Dublin, the Steps is a tiny, one room concern just off Grafton St, perfect for a quick bite in or on the run (there's also good coffee). It's hugely popular with young slacker and older bachelors, and has recently opened another, bigger branch just off Trinity St (Map pp272–3). When in Dublin, do as the Dublin ers do: the terrific potato and rosemary pizza of course!

NORTH OF THE LIFFEY
Like just about every facet of Dublin life cafés and restaurants north of the Liffey tend to be more down-to-earth than their southern counterparts. While there are fewer options, there are some great café and ethnic eats.

Around O'Connell Street
O'Connell St is lined with fast-food factories, although there are a couple of cracking restaurants close by. We suggest keeping an eye on the area around Parnell Sq which is bound to gain more multicultura eats in the near future.

101 TALBOT
Map pp264–5 *Modern European*
☎ 874 5011; 100-102 Talbot St; mains from €6.50; ◷ closed Sun & Mon
It's an old favourite but the service is fresh and friendly, and the food some of the best this side of the Liffey. The menu melds Mediter

anean and Middle-Eastern influences in a no-nonsense way much loved by thespians and Abbey Theatre regulars.

ALILANG Map pp264–5 *Korean*

☎ **874 6766; 102 Parnell St; mains €6-15; until late**

This Korean restaurant, on ethnically diverse Parnell St, is introducing multiculturalism to Dublin all on its lonesome, with elements of Chinese, Japanese and Thai all appearing in its vast pan-Asian menu. Tasty dishes such as *padun* (a seafood pancake), cod and tofu hotpot, or barbecued meats brought to your table DIY-style, with gas burner, skillet and spicy marinade, make the food a talking piece. The bright and shiny decor may not be conducive to romantic first dates, nor would the dull wine list.

CHAPTER ONE Map pp264–5 *Modern Irish*

☎ **873 2266; Dublin Writers Museum, 18-19 Parnell Sq; mains €24-30; closed Sat lunch & Sun**

One of the best restaurants on the north side, this venerable old trooper sets its ambitions no further than modern Irish cuisine, which it realises brilliantly. Menus change regularly – seared scallops and fennel give you some idea – but the dishes are always top-notch, the service first class and the atmosphere reassuringly reserved. There are excellent pre-theatre menus if you're thinking about heading to the Gate next door.

Top Five North of the Liffey Eats

- Chapter One (above)
- 101 Talbot (opposite)
- Kelly & Ping (this page)
- Cobalt Café & Gallery (p152)
- Soup Dragon (p152)

Smithfield & Phoenix Park

You'll find some of the city's best eating dotted around this precinct, from rediscovered market cafés to slick new designer restaurants.

HALO Map pp269–71 *French-Oriental*

☎ **878 2999; Morrison Hotel, Ormond Quay; mains around €28; closed Sun**

Housed in this superslick hotel, the visually stunning Halo has soaring ceilings, a wall of mirrors and striking artwork, but don't let it distract you from the superb Ireland-meets-continental Europe fusion fare that includes the likes of spiced monkfish and warm lobster salad. The aromas from the kitchen mingle with the smell of money from the clientele. The food at Halo is divine, glowing – yes, yes all those things.

KELLY & PING Map pp262–3 *Asian*

☎ **817 3840; Smithfield Village; mains €17-19.50; closed lunch Sun**

East meets West, they get married and live happily ever after under their adopted name Kelly & Ping. This restaurant in itself makes for a worthwhile visit to the rejuvenating Smithfield area. It's a slick, modern restaurant with decoration provided by the odd Bhudda here and the occasional bonsai there, but the highlights are the bright and cheery service, and the superb fusion cooking that comes up with the likes of tempura of goat's cheese for entree and Thai marinated sirloin for main.

PADDY'S PLACE Map pp269–71 *Café*

☎ **873 5130; Dublin Fruit Market, St Michan's St; lunch €5.50; closed Sat & Sun**

The food at Paddy's Place is as staunchly Irish as the name suggests, and this is where you should come for traditional fired breakfasts, as well as rustic versions of Dublin and Irish specialities like coddle and Irish stew.

PANEM Map pp269–71 *Café*

☎ **872 8510; 21 Lower Ormond Quay; mains €7-10; closes 5pm & Sun**

Pasta, focaccia and salads are the standard fare at this diminutive quay-side café, but the specialities are wickedly sweet and savoury pastries, which are all made on site. The croissants and brioche – filled with Belgian chocolate, almond cream or hazelnut amaretti – are the perfect snack for a holiday stroll along the Liffey Boardwalk. Lunch-times are chaotic.

RISTORANTE ROMANO

Map pp269–71 *Italian*

☎ **872 6868; 12 Capel St; mains €7-14; closed Sun**

The pink interior in this eccentric little Italian joint is a little loud, but the delicious homemade pasta and crisp pizza from a wood-burning oven deserve all the attention (and they won't cause a racket in your wallet).

EPICUREAN FOOD HALL

Map pp269–71   *Internationa*
Lower Liffey St; 😊 **closed Sun**
This is essentially just a food court but some of Dublin's best eateries have outlets here, and it's a worthy day-time stop off for a snack, a coffee, lunch or specialist supplies. It's perfec if you're not sure what you fancy or if there' discord among your number, because once you get here you can choose between bagels Italian, French, Mexican, Japanese, Indian and Lebanese to name just a few.

SOUP DRAGON Map pp269–71   *Soup Ba*
☎ 872 3277; 168 Capel St; soups €5-10; 😊 closed Sun
There's even more than the wonderful dozer or so soups (including vegetable gumbo) a this increasingly popular and buzzy takeaway joint, which also does smoothies, breads and all-day brekkies, such as generous bowls o yogurt, fruit and muesli or poached egg in a bagel.

WINDING STAIR BOOKSHOP & CAFÉ

Map pp269–71   *Café*
☎ 873 3292; 40 Lower Ormond Quay; lunch €5-10;
😊 closed 6pm & Sun
Upstairs from the beautifully dusty old book shop of the same name (p192), this grea café is spread over two floors with views ove the lovely Ha'Penny Bridge. Murals, wooder benches, gingham tablecloths and a relaxed nicotine-stained crowd lend this place an art fully dishevelled air, while the kitchen serves up a solid line in soups, salads, sandwiches and crepes.

Epicurean Food Hall

Cheap Eats
COBALT CAFÉ & GALLERY

Map pp264–5   *Café*
☎ 873 0313; 16 North Great George's St; mains €5-7;
😊 closed Sun
This splendid little café is our favourite on the north side. On the ground floor of an elegant Georgian building, it is bright and airy with a big fireplace to warm you up in the cold weather. The honest-to-goodness food is mostly generously stuffed sandwiches.

Drinking

Drinking

The chances are that you came to Dublin for the pub life, and finding out there was decent food and engaging culture has come as a bit of a surprise, even an unwelcome distraction. Since Irish life is so tied up with pub culture, sampling its finest hostelries is an absolute must if you're interested in seeing what fuels this unique and vibrant culture.

Despite the changes wrought on Dublin life over the last decade, the new-found wealth, its race towards modernisation, and its flirtations with fads and fashions, the pub is still the hub of the city's social life. It is a meeting point for friends and strangers alike, the place where Dubliners are at their friendly and convivial best (and, it must be said, sometimes their drunken and belligerent worst!).

You'll be disappointed if you come to Dublin expecting a cosy world of wooden bars being propped up by flat-capped gentlemen staring into their pints, who can't wait to tell you a few stories and sing you an auld song. That's not the Dublin of the 21st century and nowhere is the city's transformation of the last decade more obvious than in its drinking dens. While the Irish pub was being exported around the world, like the McDonald's of the 1990s, Dublin seemed hell-bent on emulating the kind of bland, superbars that you can find anywhere else around the world. Such was the rush to modernise and cash in on the tourist renaissance that for a while there it looked like Dublin might soon be the only place on the planet *not* to have a traditional Irish bar.

Thankfully, commonsense prevailed. The uberbars are on the wane and some truly great modern bars have opened in recent years to reassure the nostalgic among us that Dublin's reputation as pub capital of the world is in safe hands.

There are more than 700 pubs across the city (an average of one per 1119 population), so there's bound to be one to suit your every mood. Many are packed to the rafters most nights, particularly around touristy Temple Bar, which sometimes feels like Ibiza in the rain. There are many busy, sociable and traditional bars on either side of Grafton St. South William St in SoDa is the new corridor of cool, although Dawson St, which it replaced, is still putting up a fight. Georgian Dublin has a good mix of pubs, most of which fill up with office workers after hours (although that's not as unattractive a proposition as it might sound elsewhere). There are many unreconstructed boozers north of the Liffey, although O'Connell St and its environs are not particularly pleasant or safe places to hang at night, and you should keep your wits about you when out and about.

But we won't leave this section on that note. From centuries-old taverns to slick DJ bars, there's plenty to please in Dublin these days whether you're supping Guinness, quaffing wine or sipping cocktails. While some still bemoan the loss of the traditional and the proliferation of slick designer bars, we've accepted the development now and like to think that it leaves more room for us in our favourite snugs.

In Terms of Irish Drink

When drinking stout, beer or ale, the usual measure is a 'pint'. Half a pint is called a 'glass' and these are generally drunk by women. While this sounds sexist, it's because most men, even if they're in a hurry and don't have time for a full pint, will buy a half-measure and pour in into a pint glass (rather than be seen drinking a glass which, as we said, are generally drunk by women).

If you come to Ireland via Britain and drink spirits (or 'shorts' as they're called here), watch out: the English measure is measly 23ml, while in Dublin you get a whopping 35ml, over 50% more.

Hours & Licensing Laws

Opening hours were extended in 2000 but pulled back a little in 2003 following concerns about teenage drinking and alcohol abuse in general (see p9). Last orders are now at

11.30pm from Monday to Thursday, 12.30am on Friday and Saturday, and 11pm on Sunday, with half an hour supping-up time each night. However, many central pubs avail of late licenses that allow them to serve up until around 1.30am. As part of the new 2003 licensing laws, happy hours have been banned and pubs have been instructed to get much tougher on underage drinkers (so if you look young, bring ID).

The Traditional Irish Pub

Simply put, the pub is the heart of Dublin's social existence. It's the great leveller where status and rank hold no sway, where generation gaps are bridged, inhibitions lowered, tongues loosened, schemes hatched, songs sung, stories told and gossip embroidered. It's a unique institution: a theatre and a cosy room, a centre stage and a hideaway, a debating chamber and a place for silent contemplation. It's whatever you want it to be, and that's the secret of the great Irish pub.

Talk – whether it is frivolous, earnest or incoherent – is the essential ingredient. Once tongues are loosened and the cogs of thought oiled, your conversation can go anywhere and you should follow it to its natural conclusion. An old Irish adage suggests you should never talk about sport, religion or politics with unfamiliar company. But just be mindful and you needn't restrict yourself too much. While it's a myth to say you can walk into any Dublin pub and be befriended, you probably won't be drinking on your own for long – unless that's what you want of course. There are few more spiritual experiences than a solitary pint in a Dublin pub in the mid-afternoon.

> ### Dublin's Landmark Pubs
>
> **Oldest** Brazen Head (p161)
> **Smallest** Dawson Lounge (p156)
> **Longest** Long Hall (p159)
> **Highest** Johnnie Fox's (p149)

Pub Etiquette

The rounds system – the simple custom where someone buys you a drink and you buy one back – is the bedrock of Irish pub culture. It's summed up in the Irish saying, 'it's impossible for two men to go to a pub for one drink'. Nothing will hasten your fall from social grace here like the failure to uphold this pub law. The Irish are extremely generous and one thing they can't abide is tight-fistedness.

Another golden rule about the system is that the next round starts when the first person has finished (preferably just about to finish) their drink. It doesn't matter if you're only halfway through your pint, if it's your round get them in.

Your greatest challenge will probably be trying to keep up with your fellow drinkers, who may keep buying you drinks in every round even when you've still got a clatter of unfinished pints in front of you and you're sliding face first down the bar.

You should be aware that banter is the fibre of sociability. 'Slagging', or teasing, is the city's favourite pastime. If you can give as good as you get, they'll love you. Remember to pack a wad of self-deprecation, for they'll warm to you much quicker if you don't take yourself too seriously.

Irish Drinks

They've been brewing beer in Ireland possibly since the Bronze Age and definitely since the arrival of Christianity. The beer for which they're most famous though, stout, was in fact first brewed in Britain and became known as porter because of its popularity among London market porters.

Irish whiskey shares equal billing as the national drink, and the Irish version is distinguished from Scotch whisky because it is distilled three times and is spelt with an 'e'. Probably the biggest difference, though, is that the Scottish malt barley is dried over peat fires, which gives the drink its smoky flavour, whereas Irish malt is dried in smokeless kilns.

SOUTH OF THE LIFFEY

Just like everything else in Dublin, the south side has the lion's share of great boozers, and has seen the most dramatic changes over the last decade.

Around Grafton Street

Amid the designer shops and trendy eateries of the Grafton St area, a few top-notch Victorian pubs combine elegance and traditional style to pull in the punters from far and near.

THE BAILEY Map pp272–3
☎ 670 4939; 2 Duke St

Perpetually popular with arty types and frustrated office workers, the Bailey has wall light boxes and comfortable seating perfect for an evening schmooze, or outside gas braziers that allow you to sit on the pavement and observe the street life by day. It has tasty but pricey continental lunches.

THE BANK Map pp269–71
☎ 677 0677; College Green, Dame St

This architecturally dazzling new bar occupies the site of a former Victorian bank and has opulent decoration, including a stained-glass ceiling, hand-carved plasterwork and mosaic-tiled floors to occupy your time while you wait for your pint of Guinness to settle. The atmosphere is conversational, and the bar staff are excellent.

BRUXELLES Map pp272–3
☎ 677 5362; 7-8 Harry St

Although it has largely shed its heavy metal and alternative skin, Bruxelles is still a raucous, fun place to hang out and there are different music areas. It's comparatively trendy on the ground floor, while downstairs is a great, loud and dingy rock bar with live music each weekend. Dress in black and don't shave.

CAFÉ-EN-SEINE Map pp272–3
☎ 677 4369; 40 Dawson St

Dublin's 'in' bar when it opened in 1995, Café-en-Seine lost its place and was then overhauled into one of the most spectacular bars in the drinking world. Decorated in an opulent, wildly extravagant 19th-century style, which includes glass panelling and real 12m-high trees! The highlight, though, is propping up the beautiful wood and marble bar and checking out the beautiful people.

DAVY BYRNE'S Map pp272–3
☎ 677 5217; 21 Duke Street

Where Leopold Bloom popped in for a Gorgonzola sandwich and a glass of burgundy, Davy Byrne's is famous for its literary connections and is one of a host of venerable boozers flanking Grafton Street. It's not much to look at inside, but the craic (traditional fun) is usually good and it's particularly popular with 'blow-ins' (people from elsewhere in Ireland).

DAWSON LOUNGE Map pp272–3
☎ 677 5909; 25 Dawson St

This is *the* smallest bar in Dublin, through a tiny doorway, down a narrow flight of steps and into two tiny rooms that always seem to be filled with a couple of bedraggled drunks who look like they're hiding.

THE DUKE Map pp272–3
☎ 679 9553; 9 Duke St

The Duke is a fairly bland-looking bar (thanks to a bad refurbishment), but the crowd is less pretentious and more relaxed than in any of the other bars along this strip.

INTERNATIONAL BAR Map pp272–3
☎ 677 9250; 23 Wicklow St

Our favourite spot for an afternoon pint, this is a tiny pub with a huge personality. It has a long bar, stained-glass windows, red velour seating, great pints and a convivial atmosphere. Some of Ireland's most celebrated comedians stuttered through their first set in the Comedy Cellar, which is, of course, upstairs.

KEHOE'S Map pp272–3
☎ 677 8312; 9 South Anne St

This is one of the most atmospheric pubs in the city centre and a favourite with all kinds of Dubliners. It has a beautiful Victorian bar, a wonderful snug, and plenty of other little nooks and crannies. Upstairs, drinks are served in what was once the publican's living room – and looks it!

MCDAID'S Map pp272–3
☎ 679 4395; 3 Harry St

One of Dublin's best-known literary pubs, this classic boozer was Brendan Behan's 'local' and still oozes character. The pints are perfect, and best appreciated during the day when it's not full of our type. Thankfully, there's no music, just conversation and raucous laughter.

NEARY'S Map pp272–3
☎ 677 8596; 1 Chatham St

One of a string of off-Grafton St, classic Victorian boozers once patronised by Dublin's legless literati, Neary's is a perfect stop-off day or night. It combines great service, a bohemian atmosphere and attractively worn furnishings, and is popular with actors from the nearby Gaiety Theatre (p167).

O'NEILL'S Map pp272–3
☎ 679 3671; 2 Suffolk St

This rambling old pub near Trinity College has plenty of nooks and crannies, as well as punters to fill them. The odd combination of students and stockbrokers lends the place a chaotic atmosphere. There are also hefty portions of decent pub grub.

SAMSARA Map pp272–3
☎ 671 7723; 35-36 Dawson St

This huge Middle-Eastern–themed drinking emporium is packed at weekends with gorgeous young things and thingies air-kissing and comparing their designer ware. It's ridiculously long and narrow and has impossibly uncomfortable seats, but think of the eye candy and try to ignore the overwhelming vibe of 'me, me, me!'.

THING MOTE Map pp272–3
☎ 677 8030; 15 Suffolk St

Just off Grafton St, this grungy little bar is very popular with students. At night it is almost too popular, but on dark winter afternoons it's a terrific meeting place or *thing mote*, as the Anglo-Saxons used say.

Temple Bar

While Temple Bar is a magnet for tourists these days, the refurbishment of the area has sadly left its cobbled streets virtually devoid of old-style, traditional pubs. Dublin earned a reputation as the stag and hen party capital of the world in recent years, and most of the activity was around here. Although most pubs have banned these big groups, the same atmosphere often prevails. It's a great place for a drink midweek but its strictly for tourists on the weekend.

AULD DUBLINER Map pp269–71
☎ 677 0527; 17 Anglesea St

Predominantly patronised by tourists, 'the auld foreigner' as the locals have dubbed it,

has a carefully manicured 'olde worlde' charm that has been preserved – or refined – after a couple of renovations. It's a reliable place for a sing-song and a laugh, as long as you don't mind taking 15 minutes to get to and from the 'jax' (loo).

BOB'S Map pp269–71
☎ 677 5482; 35 East Essex St

This used to be known as Bad Bob's, but after a 2000 renovation the owners went on the straight and narrow, which in this case meant chasing the new money. It's a typical Dublin superpub, with three floors, bland modern decor, young groups and shirty security staff.

BROGAN'S Map pp269–71
☎ 679 9570; 75 Dame St

Only a couple of doors down from the Olympia Theatre (p169), this is a wonderful old-style bar where conversation – not loud music – is king. The beer is also pretty good.

DAME TAVERN Map pp272–3
☎ 679 3426; 18 Dame Ct

Directly opposite the Stag's Head (p160), this is a hard-drinking bar, where the only non-alcoholic entertainment is the sport-spewing TV and the weekend bands that go through the catalogue of '70s and '80s rock anthems with comfortable ease.

Auld Dubliner

Drinking – Temple Bar

FARRINGTONS Map pp269–71
☎ 671 5135; 27-29 East Essex St
If you're looking for a famous pub called the Norseman, you're a few years to late. What was a truly magnificent old Dublin pub was completely renovated in 2000 and transformed into yet another modern bar. It's still sociable and friendly enough, but we can't forgive them. The pints are more expensive upstairs.

FRONT LOUNGE Map pp269–71
☎ 670 4112; 33-34 Parliament St
The unofficially gay 'Flounge' is a sophisticated and friendly bar that is bright and airy during the week and positively mobbed on weekends. It's by no means exclusive, but its clientele is predominantly gay and preposterously handsome.

JOHN MULLIGAN'S Map pp266–8
☎ 677 5582; 8 Poolbeg St
This brilliant old boozer was established in 1782 and has barely changed over the years. In fact, the last time it was renovated was when Christy Brown and his rowdy clan ran amok here in the film My Left Foot. It has one of the finest pints of Guinness in Dublin and a colourful crew of regulars. It's just off Fleet St, outside the eastern boundary of Temple Bar.

MESSRS MAGUIRE Map pp269–71
☎ 670 5777; 1-2 Burgh Quay
This uberbar and microbrewery is spread across three levels connected by a truly imperious staircase, and is a disconcerting mix of old and new, young and old, intimate and brash. Its own beers are worth contemplating, but not on the weekend when the place is absolutely jammers.

OCTAGON BAR Map pp269–71
☎ 670 9000; the Clarence, 6-8 Wellington Quay
Temple Bar's trendiest watering hole is where you'll find many of Dublin's celebrities (including mates of the owner's, U2) and their hangers-on, swaggering and sipping cocktails in front of stylish wood panelling and amid perpetual daylight. Drinks are expensive, but if such things concern you, don't even try getting past the bouncers.

OLIVER ST JOHN GOGARTY
Map pp269–71
☎ 671 1822; 58-59 Fleet St
The traditional music sessions at this pub at the junction of Fleet and Anglesea Sts are extremely popular with tourists, who don't really mind that the craic is a little contrived, the music less than authentic and the prices astronomical. The kitchen serves up dishes that most Irish cooks have consigned to the culinary dustbin.

PALACE BAR Map pp269–71
☎ 677 9290; 21 Fleet St
With its mirrors and wooden niches, this is one of Dublin's great Victorian pubs and used to be the unofficial head office of the *Irish Times* newspaper. Throughout the 1990s, it steadfastly refused to accommodate the cubs of the Celtic Tiger and has always had a reputation as a place where yuppie bullshit is barred. While the Temple Bar vibe is encroaching on it a little, the staff's razor sharp sarcasm can still bring uppity patrons down the required peg or two.

Lazing on a Sunny Afternoon

Good weather needn't spoil your drinking in Dublin these days, as there are plenty of terraces and beer gardens to lap up the rays while downing the pints. Bruxelles (p156), Café-en-Seine (p156), the Bailey (p156) and Ocean (p148) have good terraces, while there's outdoor imbibing at the International Bar (p156), the Stag's Head (p160) and Grogan's (opposite). For a beer garden, try to squeeze into the Temple Bar (below) or the Brazen Head (p161), or alternatively get your drinks at the Pav (Pavilion Bar; Map pp266–8; ☎ 608 1279; College Park, Trinity College; ☺ noon-11pm Mon-Sat) and stretch out on the cricket oval.

PORTER HOUSE BREWING COMPANY Map pp269–71
☎ 679 8847; 16-18 Parliament St
The second biggest brewery in Dublin, the Porter House is a big handsome pub on the fringe of Temple Bar that produces some of the best brews in the city, including its Plain Porter, perhaps Dublin's best stout. Although it inevitably gets crowded, this pub is for the discerning drinker and has lots of its own delicious brews, as well as unfamiliar imported beers.

TEMPLE BAR Map pp269–71
☎ 677 3807; 48 Temple Bar
The most photographed pub façade in Dublin, perhaps the world, the Temple Bar is smack bang in the middle of the tourist precinct and is usually choc-a-bloc with visitors. It's good craic, though, and presses all the right buttons

with traditional musicians, a buzzy atmosphere and even a beer garden. It's also one of the most expensive pubs in Dublin.

THOMAS READ'S Map pp269–71
☎ 670 7220; 1 Parliament St
The clientele at this spacious, airy bar spread across two levels seems to favour a selection of wine and coffee over beer. During the day, it's a great place to relax and read a newspaper. For a more traditional setting, its annexe, The Oak, is still a great place for a pint.

TURK'S HEAD Map pp269–71
☎ 679 9701; 27-30 Parliament St
This superpub is decorated in two completely different styles – one really gaudy, the other a recreation of LA circa 1930 – and is one of the oddest and most interesting in Temple Bar. It pulsates nightly to a young, pumped-up crowd of mainly tourists out to boogie to chart hits. Be mindful of hidden steps all over the place.

SoDa
Dublin's coolest area is naturally where you'll find many of its coolest pubs. There is plenty of choice around here from the trendiness of South William St to the alternative vibe of Camden St and the Victorian gems in between.

BA MIZU Map pp272–3
☎ 674 6712; Powerscourt Townhouse Shopping Centre, South William St
Tucked away beside the grand entrance to Powerscourt Townhouse is the latest feather in South William St's well-plumed cap o' cool. Head downstairs to an intimate lobby dominated by a central square bar and surrounded by cosy nooks perfect for ice-breaking first dates.

BLEEDING HORSE Map pp266–8
☎ 475 2705; 24 Upper Camden St
A warm and welcoming multistorey tavern, the Bleeding Horse has stood here in some form for more than two centuries. This modern but tasteful incarnation has lots of interconnected rooms, heavy beams and a lively, flirtatious crowd.

DAKOTA Map pp272–3
☎ 672 7696; 8 South William St
Surprisingly chilled out for a superpub, Dakota is distinguished by dimmed lights, funky tunes, crafty cocktails and a slick modern layout.

Unfortunately, we found the weekend bouncers to be goons, the beer patchy and the bar staff so frosty that if you stuck your tongue out at them it might stick.

THE GEORGE Map pp272–3
☎ 478 2983; 89 South Great George's St
You can't miss the purple exterior of the George, Dublin's original and best gay venue. This huge place is busy virtually every night, and it's standing-room only if you're lucky for the legendary bingo on Sunday night (see the box text on p172).

THE GLOBE Map pp272–3
☎ 671 1220; 11 South Great George's St
One of the few 'cool' pubs in town that is all-embracing and doesn't give a fig what you look like, the Globe is loud, lively and immensely popular. Everyone looks good in its discreet light and against its plain brick walls (rather than on its wooden floors). It's also a popular coffee haunt by day and later in the night it doubles as a chill-out room for the excellent Rí Rá (p172).

GROGAN'S CASTLE LOUNGE
Map pp272–3
☎ 677 9320; 15 South William St
This place is known simply as Grogan's (after the original owner), and it is a city-centre institution. It has long been a favourite haunt of Dublin's writers and painters, as well as others from the Bohemian, alternative set, most of whom seem to be waiting for the 'inevitable' moment when they are finally recognised as geniuses. A peculiar quirk of the pub is that drinks are marginally cheaper in the area with a stone floor than in the carpeted lounge, even though they are served by exactly the same bar!

HOGAN'S Map pp272–3
☎ 677 5904; 35 South Great George's St
Once an old-style, traditional bar, Hogan's is now a gigantic boozer spread across two floors. A popular hang-out for young professionals, it gets very full at weekends with folks eager to take advantage of its late licence and rev up for a night on the razzle.

LONG HALL Map pp272–3
☎ 475 1590; 51 South Great George's St
Luxuriating in full Victorian splendour, this is one of the city's most beautiful and best-loved pubs. Check out the ornate carvings in

the woodwork behind the bar and the elegant chandeliers. The bartenders are experts at their craft, an increasingly rare attribute in Dublin these days.

MARKET BAR Map pp272–3
☎ 613 9094; 14a Fade St

If you can ignore the fleshed-out suits asking for two pints of 'heino' in a nasal DART accent (see p13), this brand-new bar is an airy alternative to the city's increasingly bland selection of superbars. It is an architectural beauty: a giant redbrick and iron girder room that was once a Victorian sausage factory. Unlike virtually every other new pub in town, there's no music.

OLD STAND Map pp272–3
☎ 677 7220; 37 Exchequer St

Refreshingly unreconstructed, this is one of the oldest pubs in Dublin and seems to be just sauntering along at the same pace it was 10 years ago, as if the whole Celtic Tiger thing never happened. It's named after the old stand at Lansdowne Rd Stadium, and is a favourite with sports fans and reporters.

PETER'S PUB Map pp272–3
☎ 677 8588; 1 Johnston Pl

A pub for a chat and a convivial catch up, this humble and friendly place is more like Peter's Living Room, and is one of the few remaining drinking dens in this area that hasn't changed personality in recent years or gone chasing new money.

SOSUME Map pp272–3
☎ 478 1590; 64 South Great George's St

This is a huge bar where you could easily get lost on your way back from the toilet. It's generally packed with 20-somethings who look like they want to party but are feeling a little too self-conscious to really let their hair down. This could be anywhere in the world.

STAG'S HEAD Map pp272–3
☎ 679 3701; 1 Dame Ct

Built in 1770, remodelled in 1895 and unbeatable in 2004, the Stag's Head is the best pub in Dublin (and, therefore, possibly the world). While you're waiting for your steak and chips, you may find yourself philosophising in the ecclesiastical atmosphere, as James Joyce did. It's probable that some of the fitters that worked on this pub would have also worked on churches in the area, so the stained-wood-and-polished-brass similarities are no accident.

No 'mean Cavan man' jokes in here, because all the staff hail from that much-maligned county.

WHELAN'S Map pp266–8
☎ 475 8555; www.whelanslive.com; 26 Wexford St

This is one of the premier venues for live music in Dublin, of the singer-songwriter kind at least (see p170). The attached bar is old-fashioned and good-natured, although there's one particularly stony-faced regular that you shouldn't even bother greeting – you'll know the one.

Georgian Dublin

Away from the city centre there are a number of fine pubs worthy of the trek. Many fill up with office workers straight after (or just before) clocking-off time and then get quieter as the night progresses.

DOHENY & NESBITT'S Map pp266–8
☎ 676 2945; 5 Lower Baggot St

A standout even in a city of wonderful pubs, Nesbitt's is equipped with antique snugs and is a favourite place for high-powered gossip among politicians and journalists; Leinster House (p85) is only a short stroll away.

GINGER MAN Map pp266–8
☎ 676 6388; 40 Fenian St

Although we've been refused entry due to our 'inappropriate' attire (trainers), we've enjoyed the leather-heeled and conservatively convivial atmosphere of this pub on many occasions. It's very popular, so it can get very crowded.

HARTIGAN'S Map pp266–8
☎ 676 2280; 100 Lower Leeson St

This is about as spartan a bar as you'll find in the city, and is the daytime home to some serious drinkers, who appreciate the quiet, no-frills surroundings. In the evening it's popular with students from the medical faculty of University College Dublin (UCD).

HORSESHOE BAR Map pp266–8
☎ 676 6471; Le Méridien Shelbourne, St Stephen's Green

An old joke in Dublin is that the major political decisions of the day aren't made in the Dáil but in the Shelbourne's Horseshoe Bar, where politicians of every hue rub shoulders with journalists and businessfolk in a fairly relaxed atmosphere – the perfect ambience for Irish politicking!

JAMES TONER'S Map pp266–8
☎ 676 3090; 139 Lower Baggot St

Toner's, with its stone floors and antique snugs, has changed little over the years and is the closest thing you'll get to a country pub in the heart of the city. The shelves and drawers are reminders that it once doubled as a grocery shop. The writer Oliver St John Gogarty once brought WB Yeats here, after the upper-class poet – who only lived around the corner – decided he wanted to visit a pub. After a silent sherry in the noisy bar, Yeats turned to his friend and said, 'I have seen the pub, now please take me home'. These days, it's a good-natured business crowd making the racket.

LINCOLN INN Map pp266–8
☎ 676 2978; 19 Lincoln Pl

What is it about medical students and dingy bars? If UCD students love Hartigan's (opposite), then their Trinity equivalents flock to this pokey little hole at the back of the college. Perhaps doctors-to-be like slumming it before they hit pay dirt? Don't be put off by the complete lack of decor: this is a wonderful little place with an ambience created entirely by its clientele.

ODEON Map pp266–8
☎ 478 2088; Old Harcourt St Station, 57 Harcourt St

This former train station is light, airy, and jam-packed with Art Deco elegance and *joie de vivre*. The comfy sofas are too scarce but this is the kind of place to be parading rather than sitting down, or standing along it's impossibly long bar. Sunday afternoons are all about indulgence and taking it nice and easy with Bloody Marys, the newspapers and comfort foods.

O'DONOGHUE'S Map pp266–8
☎ 661 4303; 15 Merrion Row

This is the most renowned traditional music bar in all Dublin, where the world-famous folk group the Dubliners refined their raspish brand of trad in the 1960s. On summer evenings a young, international crowd spills out into the courtyard beside the pub. It's also a famous rugby pub and the Dublin HQ for many Irish and visiting fans. The craic is mighty on rugby weekends.

Kilmainham & the Liberties

Like what's happening in the rejuvenated Smithfield across the river, some of the pubs in Dublin's oldest area are now being rediscovered by new crowds jaded with the superpub phenomenon.

BRAZEN HEAD Map pp262–3
☎ 679 5186; 20 Lower Bridge St West

This is reputedly Dublin's oldest pub, and thirsty patrons have been coming here since 1198 when it set up as a Norman tavern. Though its history is uncertain, the sunken level of the entrance courtyard clearly indicates how much street levels have altered since its construction. It's a bit away from the city centre, and the clientele is made up of foreign-language students, tourists and some grizzly auld locals. Robert Emmet (see p64) was believed to have been a regular visitor, while in *Ulysses*, James Joyce reckoned 'you get a decent enough do in the Brazen Head'.

THE CLOCK Map pp262–3
☎ 677 5563; 110 Thomas St

This bar has been a favourite haunt of students (and teachers) of the nearby National College of Art & Design for decades, and they mix easily with the more conservative (and older) locals. A traditional pub with great pints and no airs or graces.

FALLON'S Map pp262–3
☎ 454 2801; 129 The Coombe

Just west of the city centre in the heart of medieval Dublin, this is a fabulously old-

161

fashioned bar that has been serving a great pint of Guinness to a most discerning clientele since the end of the 17th century. Prize fighter Dan Donnelly, the only boxer ever to be knighted, was head bartender here in 1818. It's a genuine Irish bar with local Dubs.

THOMAS HOUSE Map pp262–3
☎ 671 6987; 86 Thomas St
Once a dingy 'old man's pub', Thomas House, down the road from the National College of Art & Design, was given a cheap lick of paint and, hey presto, the city's arty alternative crowd can't get in its doors quick enough. This place is a genuine dive, thankfully, and a great antidote to the increasing number of characterless superpubs springing up over town. It rocks most nights with quality name and no-name-yet DJs.

Beyond the Grand Canal
These are two very different reasons to go beyond the Grand Canal: for a glimpse of Dublin new and old.

ICE BAR Map pp260–1
☎ 665 4000; Four Seasons Hotel, Simmonscourt Rd
Not to be confused with the Dice Bar (p163) in a taxi; practise your elocution because both bars are worlds apart in every sense. This is the newest, hottest place for young, single 20-somethings with infinite disposable incomes to see and be seen. Flash your convertible beemer car keys at the door for speedy access. The all-white chichi interior with central chrome and marble bar is softened by some lovely, specially commissioned wall hangings by Irish artists. Vodka-based cocktails are the house speciality.

RANELAGH HOUSE Map pp260–1
☎ 496 6711; 60 Ranelagh Rd, Ranelagh
This is a very ordinary pub, which makes it one of a dying breed and something to behold. Pop down here for a few scoops some weekday evening, see how ordinary locals socialise without fuss and then get a bag of great chips from Luigi's across the road for the walk home. Now you're a local.

NORTH OF THE LIFFEY
Slower to benefit from the Celtic Tiger's facelift, a number of the north side's traditional bars have been rediscovered by Dubs looking for the authentic drinking experience, but there are also an increasing number of hip and stylish new bars springing up north of the Liffey, particularly around the Smithfield area.

Around O'Connell Street
The city's main thoroughfare is not the place to be hanging around with a skinful of booze after dark, so if you want to sample these pubs, we suggest you do so during

Bertie's Boozers
While he's leading the drive to stamp out alcohol abuse in Ireland, the Taoiseach Bertie Ahern is also a dab hand at opening pubs, with 13 to his name at the last count. When he's not too busy indulging in opening-night freebies, he can often be found at his local, Fagan's, in his native Drumcondra.

daylight or at least stay alert at night.

FLOWING TIDE Map pp264–5
☎ 874 0842; 9 Lower Abbey St
This beautiful and atmospheric old pub is directly opposite the Abbey and is predictably very popular with theatre goers – it can get swamped around 11pm when the curtain comes down. They blend in with some no-bullshit locals that give the place a vital edge, and make it a great place for a drink and a natter.

JOXER DALY'S Map pp264–5
☎ 860 1299; 103-104 Lower Dorset St
This Victorian-style pub is conveniently close to Harvey's (p205) and Marian (p206) guesthouses. A word of warning, however; if you're in this area late at night, you should be particularly vigilant because the streets around here have been plagued by crime and a certain amount of violence due to heroin abuse.

LIFE Map pp264–5
☎ 878 1032; Irish Life Mall, Lower Abbey St
This stylish bar near Busáras and Connolly Station may have lost some of the 'cool' appeal it had when it opened, but it's still a good place to spend a weekend night.

THE OVAL Map pp269–71
☎ 872 1259; 78 Middle Abbey St
This is great little pub, where young and

old come together in conversation and rich, creamy pints go down a treat. It's much bigger than it looks from the outside, spreading over three floors.

PRAVDA Map pp269–71
☎ 874 0076; 35 Lower Liffey St
As unIrish as you could probably get, this huge, multilevel Russian-themed bar was all the rage when it opened a few years ago. It has got a party atmosphere and is a great pick-up joint for young tourists, but you can forget about conversation at night (because the music is so loud) and the bouncers are especially dim-witted.

SACKVILLE LOUNGE Map pp264–5
☎ 874 5222; Sackville Pl
This tiny 19th-century one-room, wood-panelled bar lies just off O'Connell St and is popular with actors from the nearby Abbey and Peacock theatres, as well as a disproportionate number of elderly drinkers. It's a good pub for a solitary pint.

SEAN O'CASEY'S Map pp264–5
☎ 874 8675; 105 Marlborough St
The antithesis of the Dublin superpub, this is the kind of place where the male drinkers (and there seems to be *only* male drinkers) look up and grunt when you walk through the door. It's a Kerry pub, and so decked out in the county's Gaelic Athletic Association (GAA) colours. It's particularly lively when Kerry are playing in Croke Park.

Smithfield & Phoenix Park
It's the dynamic between the mainly old and relative new, mostly gritty and occasionally superslick drinking dens around Smithfield that make this area so engaging these days.

THE COBBLESTONE Map pp264–5
☎ 872 1799; 77 North King St
This pub, in the heart of Smithfield, has a great atmosphere in the cosy upstairs bar where there are superb nightly music sessions from traditional (especially Thursday) and up-and-coming folk acts.

DICE BAR Map pp262–3
☎ 674 6710; 79 Queen St
Co-owned by Huey from the Fun Lovin' Criminals, the Dice Bar looks like something you might find on New York's Lower East Side. Its dodgy locale, black and red painted interior, dripping candles and stressed seating, combined with rocking DJs most nights, make it a magnet for Dublin's beautiful beatnik crowds. It has Guinness and local microbrews.

FORUM BAR Map pp264–5
☎ 878 7084; 144 Parnell St
A great addition to the scene, this bar is the first run by and catering (though not exclusively) to Dublin's thriving black community. The decor is fairly minimalist, the cocktails mean and the doormen surprisingly friendly. It heaves on weekend nights with young scenesters and bar staff jiggling to funky rhythm and blues and hip-hop.

GLIMMER MAN Map pp264–5
☎ 677 9781; 14-15 Stoneybatter; bus 38, 39 & 39A from Middle Abbey St or Essex Quay
It's slightly out of the way, to the west of Smithfield, but this is a terrific bar. In warm weather, the beer garden out the back is a great place to enjoy a pint.

GUBU Map pp269–71
☎ 874 0710; 7-8 Capel St
This bar was relatively quiet when it opened a few years back, so it changed tack in 2001 and advertised itself as Dublin's newest gay and lesbian bar. Hey presto! Nicknamed 'gaybu', it is stylish and groovy with velvet curtains, a carefully lit ambience and a juke box bulging with disco hits. The bar now cheekily describes itself as 'straight friendly'.

HUGHES' BAR Map pp262–3
☎ 872 6540; 19 Chancery St
By day, this pub is popular with barristers, solicitors and their clients from down the street in the Four Courts (p110), all of whom probably need a pint – for different reasons! By night, however, once the last wigs have gone, this is where you'll hear some of the best traditional music in the city. The owner's son is an extraordinary fiddle player.

MORRISON HOTEL BAR Map pp269–71
☎ 878 2999; Upper Ormond Quay
This is the north side's version of the Octagon Bar (p158), only far more difficult to get into if you don't look the part. If you haven't spent a fortune on your outfit (or managed to fake it), forget it. You wouldn't have enjoyed the luxurious John-Rocha–designed dark, oak and

cream interior, the views over the Liffey, the suave and sophisticated clientele. Nah, you didn't miss much.

NEALON'S Map pp269–71
☎ 872 3247; Capel St

The warm and cosy decor of this traditional pub is matched by the exceptionally friendly staff. It's a bit of old Dublin on a street getting ready to take off, so catch it while you can. There's live jazz on Sunday.

PATRICK CONWAYS Map pp264–5
☎ 873 2687; 70 Parnell St

This gem of a pub has been lining up drinks since 1745 and joyous fathers – including Colm Meaney's character in *The Snapper* – have been skulling celebratory pints at its bar since the day the Rotunda Maternity Hospital opened across the road in 1757. It now has a live music venue upstairs, the 'Boom Boom Room', with jazz and folk on Thursday and Friday.

SLATTERY'S Map pp269–71
☎ 872 7971; 129 Capel St

The original home of punk rock – and a firm favourite with many expats – Slattery's has been done up in recent years and is coming back to life like this whole street. The Wednesday night pub quiz is good fun.

VOODOO LOUNGE Map pp262–3
☎ 873 6013; 37 Arran Quay

Run by the same crew as Dice Bar (p164), the Voodoo Lounge is a long, dark bar with decadent, Gothic Louisiana-style decor, great service, a friendly atmosphere and loooo-uuud music just the way the fun-lovin' crowd likes it.

ZANZIBAR Map pp269–71
☎ 878 7212; 36 Lower Ormond Quay

This enormous bar actually seems to pride itself on keeping you waiting before allowing you in. The African theme is wild, although it

African Guinness

If black mannequins in the windows of greener-than-green department store Penney's (p191) didn't convince you of Dublin's new multiculturalism, consider that Guinness are planning to brew the stronger and sweeter 'African' Guinness in Ireland due to the increase in the number of Africans residing here. It has never before been brewed outside Nigeria.

can get on your nerves after a bit, just like the attitude of the staff and the cattle mart subtlety of some of the drunken patrons.

Beyond the Royal Canal

It is just beyond the north side's canal that you can find some of the best traditional pubs in Dublin, and these are highly recommended.

THE GRAVEDIGGERS (AKA KAVANAGH'S)
1 Prospect Sq, Glasnevin; bus 13 from O'Connell St

This pub, backing on to Glasnevin Cemetery (p115), is where you can drink one of the best pints of Guinness in town, served in an atmosphere that appears not to have changed in 150 years. Here you'll find an older Dublin, unhurried and not so concerned with modernity. What you won't find, however, is a phone – far too contemporary for this wonderful spot.

RYAN'S Map pp262–3
☎ 677 6097; 28 Parkgate St; bus 23, 25 & 26 from city centre

Near Phoenix Park, this is one of only a handful of city pubs that has retained its Victorian decor virtually intact, complete with ornate bar and snugs. An institution among Dublin's public houses, this is truly worth the trip.

Entertainment

Entertainment

It is redundant to say that Dublin is a great drinking town. The vast majority of visitors, if they're not here on business, come to see the sights and get to know the pubs; even the business crowd will do so when their work is done. Hard to fathom, but there is nightlife beyond the pub. Or, put more accurately, there is life *around* the pub. In Dublin, you can enjoy a pre- and post-theatre drink in the knowledge that the bit in between can make for a memorable evening. You can sit in the comfort of a glassed box, betting slip in one hand, glass of wine in the other, watching dog No 6 make a late dash for the line and enjoy the whole experience so much that it'll surprise you. You can put on your glad rags and hum your way through a Beethoven concerto at the National Concert Hall (p167) before that intermezzo G&T. Or, if your tastes are a little less high falutin', you can shake your head and air guitar your way through a rock gig along with 300 other like-minded individuals at one of the city's many music venues. And when everything else has closed its doors for the night, you can go back to the pub or negotiate your way past the bouncers and strut your funky stuff on a packed dance floor. Whatever it is that floats your boat, you're sure to find a version of it in Dublin.

Where to play? The most obvious and most popular area is Temple Bar, which transforms itself nightly into a party district with few rivals in Europe. It is extremely popular with groups of English on a stag or hen weekend – although in 1998 many of Temple Bar's publicans announced that they would no longer cater for these often loud and raucous groups because they alienated the local trade. We think Temple Bar is a victim of its own success. If you're looking for something to do beyond sloppy hedonism, we urge you to consider elsewhere. The south side remains the part of Dublin with the most to offer, but the city's north side is definitely on the rise, with plenty going on to titillate the night owl.

What's On

To make sense of Dublin's entertainment options, a number of resources will come in handy. Listings of virtually every event appear in the following publications – available at all newsagents except for the *Dublin Event Guide*, which is available in hostels, cafés and bars – and websites.

Newspapers

Hot Press (www.hotpress.com; €3.50; see p239) Dublin's premier weekly entertainment magazine lists all gigs and events.

In Dublin (€2.48) A fortnightly publication that lists most of the main events.

Irish Times (€1.45) Thursday's edition has an excellent pull-out section called *The Ticket*, which has reviews and listings of upcoming events.

Evening Herald (€1) Thursday's edition features listings of pop and rock concerts, movies and other popular activities.

Dublin Event Guide (free) A comprehensive weekly listings newspaper.

Online

www.mcd.ie Ireland's biggest promoter has a comprehensive list of upcoming gigs.

www.entertainment.ie A catch-all listings page listing what's on.

www.eventsoftheweek.com An excellent website that does exactly what it says and is updated weekly.

www.dublinpubscene.com An exhaustive list of where to go for night-time fun, including club nights.

BOOKINGS

Theatre, comedy and classical concerts are usually booked directly through the venue, while tickets for touring international bands and big-name local talent are either sold at the venue or through a number of booking agencies. These include **Big Brother Records** (p188), which sells tickets to smaller alternative gigs and DJ sets; **HMV** (p185; 24-hour credit card booking line ☎ 456 9569), which sells tickets to pop and rock gigs; and **Ticketmaster** (☎ 1890 925 100; www.ticketmaster.ie), which sells tickets to every genre of big- and medium-sized show, but be aware that it charges a 12.5% service charge *per ticket*.

MUSIC

CLASSICAL

Classical music is constantly fighting an uphill battle in Dublin, plagued by inadequate funding, poor management and questionable repertoires, all contributing to its limited appeal. It's a sad testament to a vibrant musical city that in 1742 hosted the first performance of Handel's *Messiah:* there really hasn't been much ground broken since then. Count John McCormack, unquestionably one of the great tenors of the 20th century, has been dead for over 75 years, and no-one has emerged that can hold a candle to him.

Irish orchestras have neither the talent nor the funds to match their European counterparts, and the top Irish classical musicians usually do a short stint in a local orchestra before going overseas to join more reputable ensembles. Still, there are a number of companies that perform admirably in such difficult circumstances, and Dublin's classical music scene is often enhanced by visiting performers and orchestras.

Dublin has a number of venues that host classical concerts and opera. Bookings can be made at the venues or through Ticketmaster and HMV (see p167).

BANK OF IRELAND ARTS CENTRE
Map pp269–71

☎ 671 1488; www.bankofireland.ie; Foster Pl; admission free; ☽ 1.15pm

The arts centre hosts a regular Wednesday lunch-time recital, usually featuring a soloist with accompaniment. The performers are excellent. The centre also hosts an irregular evening programme of concerts. Call for details.

GAIETY THEATRE Map pp272–3

☎ 677 1717; www.gaietytheatre.net; South King St

Amid its repertoire of popular plays (see p174) the Gaiety occasionally plays host to the more salubrious sounds of classical music, including performances by Opera Ireland.

HELIX

☎ 700 7000; www.thehelix.ie; Collins Ave, Glasnevin; bus 11, 13A & 19A from city centre

Based in Dublin City University, the stunning new Helix theatre hosts, among other things, an impressive array of international operatic and classical recitals and performances. Check the website for details.

HUGH LANE MUNICIPAL GALLERY OF MODERN ART Map pp264–5

☎ 874 1903; 22 North Parnell Sq

From September to June, the art gallery (p103) hosts up to 30 concerts of contemporary classical music. The concerts are at noon on Sunday.

NATIONAL CONCERT HALL Map pp266–8

☎ 475 1572; www.nch.ie; Earlsfort Tce

Leaden acoustics and a none-too-aesthetic conversion of University College Dublin's old lecture hall are the main criticisms levelled at Ireland's premier orchestral venue, but the cream of the classical crop perform here throughout the year as part of a rich and various programme of concerts and recitals. There's also a series of excellent lunch-time concerts (€8) from 1.05pm to 2pm on Tuesday, June to September.

ROYAL DUBLIN SOCIETY SHOWGROUND CONCERT HALL
Map pp260–1
☎ 668 0866; Merrion Rd, Ballsbridge; bus 7 from Trinity College
The RDS (p100) hosts a rich line-up of classical music and opera throughout the year.

JAZZ
Sadly, jazz is a marginal art form in Dublin and mostly the preserve of a small clique of loyal listeners; for most others it's nothing more than background music. Hardly surprising then that there's not a lot of choice when it comes to jazz gigs. Despite this, however, the yearly **Dublin Jazz Festival** (☎ 877 9001; www.jazzireland.com) takes place during the first week in July at a number of venues throughout the city, including Whelan's (p170) and Vicar St (opposite). Organised by the Improvised Music Company, which also organises individual events throughout the year, the line-up is usually top class, featuring a mix of home-grown players and international stars from the US, Europe and South America. The week also features talks and workshops by the performers.

AVOCA HANDWEAVERS Map pp272–3
☎ 677 4215; 11-13 Suffolk St; admission free;
☺ noon-4pm
Sunday brunch has some live jazz accompaniment at this gorgeous department store (p184). The restaurant (p132) is upstairs.

GLOBE Map pp272–3
☎ 671 1220; 11 South Great George's St; admission free; ☺ 3-7pm Sun
This trendy café-bar (p159) is one of the only places to hear decent jazz, but only on Sunday afternoons. The atmosphere is usually terrific, and the players are generally pretty good, even though you're unlikely to hear John Coltrane's successor.

JJ SMYTH'S Map pp266–8
☎ 475 2565; 12 Aungier St; admission €5-9;
☺ 8-11.30pm
The best place in Dublin to hear good jazz is at this pub, in a suitably smoky lounge where the stage is almost on top of the punters. The intim-acy of the place, coupled with the generally high standard of musicians performing here, make this a must for any fans of the genre.

POPULAR
It's hard to believe, but until the 1970s Dublin had never produced a bona fide international success. Phil Lynott and Thin Lizzy were the first, but they merely paved the way for four lads from the suburb of Ballymun, who in 1978 began a musical career that would eventually lead them to the kind of mega-stardom whereby the Pope would gratefully accept a gift of the lead singer's trademark wraparound shades. U2 have raised the bar to an almost impossibly high level, but since they became supernovas in the pop firmament the local scene has developed a vitality and confidence never before seen. Dublin has become a stop on the international touring schedule of virtually every rock and pop act in the world, and Dublin fans have handsomely rewarded them for coming here. In August 2003, Robbie Williams played to 135,000 screaming fans in the Phoenix Park and was so taken by the experience that he declared (with no little emotion) that this was the best night of his career. He could have been playing to the crowd, of course, but there's no denying the fact that Dubliners know how to cheer their favourite artists. The fans really let loose, and their ability to raise the energy levels of a gig are renowned to the point that others – including such different performers as Garth Brooks and Guns 'n' Roses – have publicly stated that their favourite place to play outside of their home towns is Dublin.

Big and small, Dublin has venues to suit every taste and crowd requirement. Check the newspapers for upcoming events (see p166). You can buy tickets at the venue itself, but you're probably better off going through an agent (see p167). Prices range dramatically, from as low as €5 for a tiny local act to anywhere up to €140 for the really big international stars.

AMBASSADOR THEATRE Map pp264–5
☎ 1890 925 100; O'Connell St
Once a theatre and then a cinema, the Ambassador is now a live music venue that feeds the punters a regular diet of top-notch acts, mostly of the left-of-centre variety. Alternative rock, hip-hop, electro and live DJ sets (complete with musicians) are usually on the bill.

Festival Frolics

The last decade has seen the growth of the huge music festival with an exhaustive line-up of local and top-class international talent. Sponsored by the drinks industry, these boozy and often brilliant festivals see hundreds of thousands gather for a weekend of music and moshing.

Heineken Green Energy Festival (☎ 284 1747; www.mcd.ie; ✸ May bank holiday weekend) Dublin's first major festival began in spectacular fashion in the mid-1990s and has continued to grow ever since. With a base in Dublin Castle, dozens of venues and pubs across the city go green over four days at the end of May; recent events have brought on top international stars like Beck as headline acts.

Slane Festival (☎ 041-982 4207; Slane, County Meath; ✸ July; special buses from O'Connell St) Forty-six kilometres northwest of Dublin, Slane Castle (Map p210) is home to this yearly festival that has seen the top names in international rock perform to crowds upwards of 80,000 strong. REM, Bruce Springsteen, U2 and Bob Dylan have all performed here.

Witness (Map p210; ☎ 284 1747; www.witnness.com; Fairyhouse Racecourse, County Meath; ✸ mid-July–early Aug; special buses from O'Connell St) This fabulous music festival, sponsored by Guinness, takes place over a summer weekend and manages to pack a few dozen acts into its two-day line-up. The performances are divided across four stages, Main, Rising, Uprising and Dance. The 2003 festival featured over 40 acts including Coldplay, David Gray, Röksopp, Manic Street Preachers and DJ Dave Clarke.

GAIETY THEATRE Map pp272–3
☎ 677 1717; www.gaietytheatre.com; South King St;
✸ 11pm-4am Fri-Sat
This old Victorian theatre is an atmospheric place to come and listen to late-night jazz, rock or blues on weekends; performing bands are generally put on as part of the nightclub entertainment (p171).

ISAAC BUTT Map pp264–5
☎ 855 5884; Store St
Local garage, rock, metal and indie bands sweat it out most nights in this grungy venue opposite Busáras. It's basic, but that's the point: no fancy light shows, just cranked-up guitars and plenty of energy.

OLYMPIA THEATRE Map pp269–71
☎ 677 7744; www.olympia.ie; 72 Dame St
This beautiful Victorian theatre generally puts on light plays, musicals and pantomime (see p174), but Friday night is Midnight @ The Olympia, with everything from country to disco. Occasionally, they put on some top-class gigs: in 2003 Radiohead played their only Irish nights here.

POINT DEPOT Map pp260–1
☎ 836 3633; East Link Bridge, North Wall Quay
This is the premier indoor venue for all rock and pop acts playing in Dublin. Originally constructed as a rail terminus in 1878, it has a capacity of around 6000. The Rolling Stones, Prince and Coldplay are just some of the acts that played here in 2003.

RED BOX Map pp266–8
☎ 478 0166; Harcourt St
Mostly renowned for the high quality of its club nights (see p172), the Red Box also plays host to the occasional live music gig, mostly hip-hop acts and live DJ sets. French dance guru Laurent Garnier brings a whole orchestra with him when he plays here, and hip-hop giants Run DMC and Jurassic 5 have put on some incredible shows.

TEMPLE BAR MUSIC CENTRE
Map pp269–71
☎ 670 0533; Curved St
This venue has a widespread offering of musical acts, with anything from traditional Irish music to drum-and-bass (and all things in between) for a non-image-conscious crowd. One night you might be shaking your glow light to a thumping live set by a top DJ and the next you'll be shifting from foot to foot as an esoteric Finnish band drag their violin bows over their electric guitar strings.

VICAR ST Map pp262–3
☎ 454 5533; www.vicarstreet.com; 58-59 Thomas St
Smaller performances take place at this intimate venue located near Christ Church Cathedral (p91). It has a capacity of 1000 between its table-serviced group seating downstairs and theatre-style balcony. Vicar St offers a varied programme of performers, with a strong emphasis on soul, folk, jazz and ethnic music.

VILLAGE Map pp266-8
☎ 475 8555; www.thevillagevenue.com; 26 Wexford St
Opened in March 2003 by the people who run Whelan's next door, this attractive new mid-sized venue hosts a range of acts from local singer-songwriters to visiting rock bands.

WHELAN'S Map pp266-8
☎ 478 0766; www.whelanslive.com; 26 Wexford St
Irish singer-songwriters know they have arrived if they get a gig here. Its intimate setting with ground and balcony levels make it a good place to hear the soul-searching sounds of the best local talent (Glen Hansard and The Frames are regulars) and up-and-coming international acts. If you're into shoe-gazer rock, this is the place for you.

TRADITIONAL & FOLK
Dublin has always had an ambivalent relationship with traditional music. Many middle-class Dubliners, eager to bask in a more 'cosmopolitan' light, have been largely dismissive of the genre as belonging to less progressive rural types with nicotine-coloured fingers and beer-stained beards. Instead, they packed their CD collections with 'world music' – folk and traditional music from *other* cultures. In the last few years, however, the irony has become all-too apparent and there has been a slow (and often grudging) recognition that one of the richest and most evocative veins of traditional expression is on their very doorstep.

For the most part, you will only hear traditional music in drinking establishments around the city (see the Drinking chapter on p154). Scheduled and improvised 'sessions' are extremely popular with foreign visitors, who relish any opportunity to drink and toe-tap to some extraordinary virtuoso performances.

COMHALTAS CEOLTÓRÍ ÉIREANN
☎ 280 0295; www.comhaltas.com; 32 Belgrave Sq, Monkstown; admission €4-9; ☽ Mon, Wed & Fri; DART Monkstown
Dublin's best venue for enjoying traditional music and dancing, the atmosphere is very informal and everyone is encouraged to join in the dancing, at least until the going gets serious and the real pros take over. The musicians are all fabulous, as are the Friday night *céilidh* (communal dance) dancers, who move with speed and plenty of grace.

CLUBS
Dublin nightclubs, famous in the 1990s for the no-holds-barred party vibe that made the city one of the best places to get wasted and dance until you dropped, have tightened their belts and shored up the madness in the last few years. The scene is in an uncertain transition as club owners are trying to figure out how best to tackle their biggest problem: late-night bars. The law (see boxed text, p167) is such that clubs only run about an hour later than late-night bars, and many punters are happier to keep the €12 in their pockets and stay put, where the music is just as loud and the booze is (marginally) cheaper.

The other big problem these days is variety. When in doubt, play safe. There may be thousands of young people looking for a party on any given night, but most of them aren't all that interested in a night of Brazilian funk or the furious drive of electro-punk; if it isn't house, R'n'B or charty sounds, most of them won't bother. Club owners know this, and today the city's clubs offer a pretty samey list of music: house and techno fans go one place, rhythm and blues and poppy dancers go elsewhere. A new club with a new sound may run for a few weeks, but then the punters start to fall away and the club owner forces the promoter to tow a safer, more popular line.

Yet Dublin manages to hold onto its reputation as a top town for clubbing. This is down to the attitude of fun that prevails. Clubbers want to party, and Dublin has a good selection of DJs who willingly oblige. Some are among the best in the business, true experts at working the crowd into an ecstatic frenzy (see boxed text on p37).

The busiest nights of the week are, invariably, Thursday to Saturday, but something's going on every other night of the week (except Sunday). The listings magazines and papers (see p166) have comprehensive, night-by-night coverage of who and what's playing where and when. Admission to most places is between €5 and €8 Monday to Thursday, rising to up to €15 or even €20 Friday and Saturday. For discounts, look out for the thousands of fliers that are distributed around most of the city centre's pubs.

BREAK FOR THE BORDER Map pp272–3
☎ 478 0300; Lower Stephen St; admission €6-10

This huge, country-and-western–style eatery reverts to a nightclub once the pub closes. It's good fun, if a little cheesy, and is renowned in Dublin as one of the biggest pick-up joints .

DOWN UNDER IN MAJOR TOM'S
Map pp272–3

☎ 478 3266; South King St; admission €8; ☽ Fri & Sat

This huge Aussie-themed basement bar has club nights only at weekends; if you're there before 11pm it's free entry. It's a loud, in-your-face kind of place with a fairly safe selection of chart hits and old favourites. Tourists and locals alike love it.

EAMONN DORAN'S IMBIBING
EMPORIUM Map pp269–71
☎ 679 9773; 3a Crown Alley; admission €5-9

This is a large place with food, drink and mostly indie rock. Live music is generally followed by a DJ who takes dancers through until closing time.

FIREWORKS Map pp266–8
☎ 648 1099; Old Central Fire Station, Tara St; admission €10-12; ☽ 4pm-3am Mon-Sat

This enormous, three-levelled, futuristic pleasure palace in a converted fire station (the sliding poles are gone, we're afraid) has become one of the city's most popular late-night venues for unadulterated hedonism. American pool tables on the ground floor keep the punters happy in the early evening, but weekend nights are an altogether less sedate affair. The soundtrack is utterly predictable (chart hits, old classics and cheesy anthems) but the 1000 or so revellers that pack the place on weekend nights have no complaints.

GAIETY THEATRE Map pp272–3
☎ 677 1717; www.gaietytheatre.com; South King St; ☽ 11pm-4am Fri-Sat

Over 800 punters cram into the theatre (p174) after hours for dancing and plenty of drinking. It's loose, fun and very popular. The music is a mix of Latin and soul.

HUB Map pp269–71
☎ 670 7655; 11 Eustace St; admission €7-15

Formerly the excellent Switch, the deep house at this basement nightclub has made way for more commercial sounds, and we hear that rock is on the menu for the future. Guitar music never really went away.

LILLIE'S BORDELLO Map pp272–3
☎ 679 9204; Adam Ct; admission €8-15

Lillie's is strictly for the well heeled – the favourite nightclub of local and visiting celebrities. As you might expect, the music is mostly safe and commercial, but most eyes are on the doors to the exclusive Library Bar, night-time home of celebs and their mates.

METROPOLITAN Map pp269–71
☎ 875 6988; 11 Eden Quay; admission €5-10; ☽ Thu-Sat

This brand-new venue goes late every night with DJs who rock a mixed bag of sounds, from

---

Top Five Club Nights

- **ART** (PoD, p172; ☽ Sat) Ireland's best techno DJ Billy Scurry shows the crowd why he's the best with his fabulous mixing of modern techno and electro house. Rocky T keeps things a little mellower in the Chocolate Bar. Hardcore dance music may have seen more popular days, but they're not letting go here without a fight.
- **Firehouse Skank** (Parnell Mooney, p172; ☽ Wed) Bass-heavy dub reggae served on a platter by DJ Paul and MC Larry is a favourite with Irish rasta-heads and the city's growing African community. It's deep, dark and absolutely brilliant. Our main concern is what are they going to do when the smoking ban is put into effect in January 2004. Smokeless pot?
- **Frisky Disco** (Rí Rá, p172; ☽ Sat) Hip-hop, R'n'B, soul, funk and a little bit of soulful house are the ingredients of Dublin's most popular Saturday nightclub. The mixed crowd isn't looking to be educated but entertained, and the DJs do so with plenty of gusto, throwing in the odd rock song to really get everybody going.
- **Prophesy** (Spirit, p172; ☽ Sat) This is the city's sweatiest and most full-on house and techno night, fuelled by illegal substances, water and the simply enormous sound of the house system, artfully manipulated by Hugh Scully and Noel Phelan.
- **Turn it Loose** (Traffic, p173; ☽ Thu) DJ Arveene (p37), Razor and techno supremo Johnny Moy (p37) knock out the hardcore sounds of punk-funk. Believe us, this is where the new sounds are at.

the excellent Mojo Club on Friday nights, where the northern soul crowd come to show off their moves, to Thursday night's Electricity, where the beats go fast and electric. Each month it holds Helter Shelter, a rocking club of purely alternative music.

PARNELL MOONEY Map pp264–5
☎ 873 1544; 71 Parnell St; admission €7
This late-night bar at the top of O'Connell St is only worth going to on a Wednesday, when it hosts the fabulous Firehouse Skank (see boxed text on p171), Dublin's only hard reggae and dub night.

Top Five Gay Nights

- **Bingo Night** (The George, p159; ☼ Sun) The highlight of the week is Shirley Temple Bar calling the numbers with double entendre dripping in his voice ('Legs eleven. Oo-er'). Sounds drab? It's absolutely brilliant fun and one of the best-frequented gay nights around. Invariably, it's followed by a superloud house party.

- **Fridge Lite** (Eamonn Doran's Imbibing Imporium, p171; ☼ Tue) Well-cut male strippers, a camouflage dungeon and camp house classics make this one of the most sexually explosive nights on the Dublin scene.

- **HAM** (PoD, this page; ☼ Fri) Dublin's most enduring gay night is Homo Action Movies, a high-energy progressive house party conducted by one of Ireland's best DJs, Shay Hannon, plus guests.

- **Hilton Edwards** (Spy, this page; ☼ Sun) Named after the gay co-founder of the Gate Theatre, this weekly club requests only that you're gay and reasonably well dressed. It's cool, chic and, invariably, also frequented by straights.

- **SEX** (Hub, p171; ☼ Tue) Uplifting house and anthems from the '80s and '90s, mixed superbly by DJ Revvlon, keep the dancers on their toes. Off the floor, performance art gives this night a slightly more artistic vibe.

PoD Map pp266–8
Place of Dance; ☎ 478 0025; www.pod.ie; 35 Harcourt St; admission €5-20
Dublin's most renowned nightclub, this futuristic, metal-Gothic cathedral of dance attracts a large weekend crowd of twenty-somethings. To get past the notoriously difficult bouncers you'll really need to look the part. Admission

is €5 cheaper if you get there before 11.30pm on Saturdays.

RED BOX Map pp266–8
☎ 478 0225; www.pod.ie; 35 Harcourt St; admission €9-20
Upstairs from the PoD, this is actually the coolest dance club in town. The floor is enormous and the crowds readily fill it up. Look out for the big-name international DJs who play here regularly.

RENARD'S Map pp272–3
☎ 677 5876; South Frederick St; admission €8-12
Snooty Renard's offers little in terms of interesting music (mostly pop hits and old classics), but it's a top spot for a little social credibility. Problem is that most of the celebs are safely ensconced in the upstairs lounge, while the ordinary plebs have to make do with the main room. Frankly, the main floor is far better than the stuffy, slightly depressing celebrity lounge.

RÍ RÁ Map pp272–3
☎ 677 4835; www.rira.com; Dame Ct; admission €5-11
Rí Rá is one of the friendlier clubs in the city centre and is full almost every night with a diverse crowd who come for the house-free, mostly funky music downstairs or more laid-back lounge tunes and movies upstairs. Refreshingly, the bouncers here are friendly, funny and very fair. Thursday's Funk Off is a veritable institution and Monday's '80s club Strictly Handbag – the local version of London's School Disco – is now in its ninth year.

SPIRIT Map pp269–71
☎ 877 9999; www.spiritdublin.com; 57 Middle Abbey St; admission €5-20; ☼ Thu-Sat
Dublin's newest dance club provides a whole night's multi-experience for hardcore clubbers under one roof. Spanning three floors, visiting and local DJs play pretty commercial house on one floor, soul and funk in the middle (complete with soundproofed cinema) and downstairs – wait for it – a classical cellist plays in the nonsmoking chill-out area, complete with on-site masseuses, tarot readers and body painters.

SPY Map pp272–3
☎ 679 0014; 59 South William St; admission €10
In a beautiful Georgian building in the Powerscourt Townhouse Shopping Centre, Spy

attracts the city's fine young things in search of a good time. But there's a distinction: Wax, the easy access club in the small vaulted basement, is strictly for dancing and drinking while upstairs an exclusive door policy ensures that only minor celebrities and the rich and beautiful gain access.

SUGAR CLUB Map pp266–8
☎ 678 7188; www.thesugarclub.com; 8 Lower Leeson St; admission €8-10; ☼ Tue-Sun
When a nightclub has table service and a cocktail bar, it means that its clientele don't like hassle and are willing to drop big money for small drinks. Indeed, most of the patrons at the Sugar Club are aged between 25 and 40, and they come here to enjoy the top-quality music (jazz, soul, funk and cabaret) in an elegant atmosphere. There is also plenty of live music.

TEMPLE THEATRE Map pp264–5
☎ 874 5088; St George's Church, Hardwicke Pl; admission €20; ☼ Fri & Sat
The sound of church bells has been replaced by the reverberations of loud house music at this stunning north-side club, formerly a church. Big-name international DJs often play here. Amazingly admission is free before 10.30pm on Saturday.

TRAFFIC Map pp269–71
☎ 873 4800; 54 Middle Abbey St; admission free
This supertrendy new bar becomes a club after 10pm, where the sound of electro, techno and house keep the floor on the move. The constantly rotating list of DJs are all terrific; look out for DJ Arveene, whose hardcore eclectic style has made him one of the best in town (see the boxed text on p37).

THEATRE

Dublin's theatre scene is pretty small but very busy. There's plenty going on any given night, even if the established theatres won't really challenge their audiences with anything new or particularly innovative. If you want different, you'll have to settle for smaller venues and spaces, including converted pub rooms. Theatre bookings can usually be made by quoting a credit-card number over the phone; you can collect your tickets just before the performance. Expect to pay anything between €12 and €20 for most shows, with some costing as much as €25. Most plays begin between 8pm and 8.30pm.

ABBEY THEATRE Map pp264–5
☎ 878 7222; www.abbeytheatre.ie; 26 Lower Abbey St; admission €25
Ireland's national theatre, founded by WB Yeats among others, is just north of the Liffey in an ugly box-like structure that few people like. Its radical heyday, when controversial plays were greeted with scandalous uproar (see p33), have long passed and today it puts on safe, new Irish works as well as revivals of classic Irish plays by writers such as WB Yeats, JM Synge, Sean O'Casey, Brendan Behan and Samuel Beckett. Monday performances are cheaper. Work by up-and-coming writers and more experimental theatre are staged in the adjoining **Peacock Theatre** (☎ 878 7222; admission €12-16).

ANDREW'S LANE THEATRE Map pp272–3
☎ 679 5720; 9-17 St Andrew's Lane; admission €10-14
Apart from the occasional new Irish play, this well-established commercial theatre puts on mainly guaranteed hits, usually extremely well-produced plays of the 'get-them-laughing' variety.

Who Wants Beckett's Coat?
The last great shadow cast by an Irish dramatist was that of Samuel Beckett (1906–89), who moved from Dublin to Paris before he wrote a single word. Thereafter, only Brian Friel has really come close to inheriting the mantle of the 'greatest Irish playwright'. Today, Irish theatre is at an exciting but uneasy crossroads: a new generation of talented dramatists has certainly emerged since 1990 – Conor McPherson, Mark O'Rowe, Marie Jones and Marina Carr among them – but their path to theatrical greatness is littered with the high expectations of critics and a media that is uncomfortable with the fact that Irish theatre currently has no outstanding behemoth, and that is chomping at the bit to proclaim the next Beckett, Wilde or Shaw. There are plenty of dramatists about (see p34), but if we had to pick one who has the mark of greatness rather than merely the rubber stamp of commercial success, it would be Eugene O'Neill, whose first play, *Eden*, was one of the best to hit a Dublin stage since Vladimir and Estragon sat around waiting for a guy who never showed up.

Theatre Festivals

Dublin Fringe Festival (☎ 1850 374 643; www .fringefest.com; admission up to €15) Initially a festival for those shows too out there or insignificant to be considered for the main festival, this is now a three-week extravaganza with more than 100 events and over 700 performances. The established critics may keep their ink for the bigger do, but we strongly recommend the Fringe for its daring and diversity.

Dublin Theatre Festival (☎ 677 8439; www.eirc omtheatrefestival.com; admission €12-35) For two weeks in October, most of the city's theatres participate in this festival, originally founded in 1957 and today a glittering parade of quality productions and elaborate shows.

CIVIC THEATRE

☎ 462 7477; www.civictheatre.ie; The Square, Tallaght; adult/child admission €17/12; bus 49, 49A, 50, 54A, 56A, 65 & 65B from city centre

This purpose-built 350-seat theatre is inconveniently located in the southern suburb of Tallaght, but its state-of-the-art facilities are top-notch and include an art gallery. The plays it puts on are all uniformly good, an interesting mix of Irish and European works.

DRAÍOCHT THEATRE

☎ 885 2622; www.draiocht.ie; Blanchardstown Shopping Centre; adult/child admission €17/12; bus 38, 38A, 39, 39X, 236 & 239 from Middle Abbey St

This multipurpose arts centre (named after the Irish word for 'magic') is one of the most interesting venues in the city. Two separate theatres run all kinds of work, from reinterpretations of classic plays to brand-new work by cutting-edge writers and performers.

FOCUS THEATRE Map pp266–8

☎ 676 3071; 6 Pembroke Pl; adult/child & student €19/15

This small theatre puts on some interesting interpretations of classic plays as well as heavy-going contemporary work. It's challenging, quality theatre at its best.

GAIETY THEATRE Map pp272–3

☎ 677 1717; www.gaietytheatre.net; South King St; adult/child & student €35/20 plus booking fee

The Gaiety's programme of plays is strictly of the fun-for-all-the-family type: West End hits, musicals, Christmas pantos and classic Irish plays keep the more serious-minded away,

but it leaves more room for those looking simply to be entertained.

GATE THEATRE Map pp264–5

☎ 874 4045; www.gate-theatre.ie; 1 Cavendish Row, East Parnell Sq; admission from €23

The city's most elegant theatre, housed in a late-18th-century building, features a generally outstanding repertory of top-class American and European plays. Orson Welles' first professional performance was here, and James Mason played here early in his career. Even today it is the only theatre in town where you might see established international movie stars work on their credibility with a theatre run.

OLYMPIA THEATRE Map pp269–71

☎ 677 7744; www.olympia.ie; 72 Dame St; admission from €21

You won't find serious critics near the place, but the much-loved Olympia, a Victorian beauty that began its life as a music hall, attracts the crowds for its programme of variety shows, musicals and the odd comedian.

PAVILION THEATRE

☎ 231 2929; www.paviliontheatre.ie; Pavilion Complex, Dun Laoghaire; adult €10-20, child €8-15; bus 7, 7A, 8 & 46 from Trinity College, DART to Dun Laoghaire

Like the Draíocht (this page) and Civic (this page) Theatres, this new space in the seaside suburb of Dun Laoghaire offers a dynamic programme of theatre and performance art.

PROJECT ARTS CENTRE Map pp269–71

☎ 1850 260 027; www.project.ie; 39 East Essex St; adult/child €14/11

This is the city's most interesting venue for challenging new work – be it drama, dance, live art or film. Three separate spaces, none with a restricting presidium arch, allow for maximum versatility. You never know what to expect when you go here, which makes it all that more fun: we've seen some awful rubbish here, but we've also been very pleasantly surprised.

TIVOLI THEATRE Map pp262–3

☎ 454 4472; 135-136 Francis St; adult/child & student €20/18

This commercial theatre offers a little bit of everything, from a good play with terrific actors to absolute nonsense with questionable comedic value.

Smaller Theatres & Workshops

Ark (p80) This children's centre has a 150-seat venue that stages shows for kids aged between three and 13.

Bewley's Café Theatre (p131; ☙ 1.10pm) This marvellous space puts on interesting, experimental work by new Irish playwrights at lunch-time; a nice touch is the bowl of soup you get with your admission ticket. It also runs a limited series of evening plays (€12-15).

Crypt Arts Centre (Dublin Castle, p82) The beautiful church crypt in Dublin Castle has a space used by adventurous young Irish companies for experimental work.

International Bar (p156; ☙ 6-8.30pm) Early evening plays in the upstairs space by nonestablished actors offer up some worthwhile stuff; they're on early because they have to clear the room for the established comedy shows (p176).

Lambert Puppet Theatre (☎ 280 0974; 5 Clifton Lane, Monkstown; admission €9; bus 7, 7A & 8 from Trinity College, DART to Monkstown/Salthill) Puppet performances are staged at this theatre every Saturday and daily at Christmas and Easter.

Samuel Beckett Centre (Map p78; ☎ 608 2266; Trinity College; admission €5-22) Used mainly by drama students, the theatre also features the occasional show by established troupes. It's all pretty cerebral stuff.

CINEMAS

Ireland boasts the highest attendances of young cinemagoers in all of Europe. Forty years ago, O'Connell St and the surrounding streets were literally awash with cinemas, but now most of them have long since disappeared. This has left the film-hungry Dubliners with queuing up in the foyer of a suburban multiplex, where they are fed a diet of first-run blockbusters and the odd independent movie. Of the four cinemas left in the city centre, however, two offer a more challenging list of foreign releases and art-house films.

It is best to book cinema tickets in advance by credit card, as otherwise you will need to be prepared to queue for up to half an hour for tickets to night-time screenings. This is especially true for Sunday-evening screenings of popular first-run films: out on the piss Friday and Saturday nights, most Dubliners have neither the energy nor the cash for more of the same, so it's a trip to the cinema at the end of the weekend. Admission prices are generally €6 for afternoon shows, rising to €7.50 after 5pm. If you have a student card, you pay only €5 for all shows.

Movies in the Square

Every Saturday night throughout the summer (from June to August), Temple Bar's Meeting House Sq hosts free screenings of films beginning at 8pm. The movies on offer are usually classics and are often preceded by an Irish short. For tickets, contact **Temple Bar Properties** (Map pp269-71; ☎ 677 2255; 18 Eustace St).

IRISH FILM CENTRE Map pp269-71
☎ 679 5744; 6 Eustace St

The Irish Film Centre (IFC) has a couple of screens and shows classics and new art-house films, although we question some of their selections: weird and controversial can be a little tedious if the film is crap. The complex also has a bar (p135), a café and a bookshop. Weekly (€1.30) or annual (€14, concession €10) membership is required for some uncertified films that can only be screened as part of a 'club' – the only way to get around the censor's red pen. It's a good cinema, but sometimes it can be a little pretentious.

SAVOY Map pp264-5
☎ 01874 6000; Upper O'Connell St

The Savoy is a four-screen, first-run cinema, and has late-night shows on the weekend. Savoy Cinema 1 is the largest one in the country and the best place to view the really spectacular blockbuster movie. The screen is enormous.

SCREEN Map pp266–8
☎ 671 4988; 2 Townsend St

If you like art-house movies or foreign films that wouldn't get a run in a multiplex, this is your best bet. Devoid of the self-awareness that afflicts the IFC, this place puts the emphasis on well-made films rather than experimental ones.

UGC MULTIPLEX Map pp264–5
☎ 872 8400; Parnell Centre, Parnell St

This 16-screen cinema replaced many smaller cinemas and shows only commercial releases. The seats are comfy, the concession stand is huge, but what's with the bad soft drinks?

The Dublin International Film Festival

If you're around in late spring (early to mid-April), most of Dublin's cinemas participate in the Dublin International Film Festival (☎ 679 1616; www.dubliniff.com), a two-weekly showcase for new films by Irish and international directors, and a good opportunity to see classic movies that would hardly get a run in cinemas. A major criticism of the festival, however, is that many of the films included in the schedule would have earned a cinema release regardless, making it more difficult for small-budget films to find a slot.

COMEDY

The Irish are a pretty funny bunch. Off-the-cuff, in the pub, their real speciality is deflationary, iconoclastic humour as used within that other great art form, storytelling. It's all about pacing and not taking yourself too seriously. Like anywhere else, comedy in Dublin can be hit-and-miss, but a few names have risen out of the mire of mother-in-law jokes and earned that elusive tag of great comic. Ardal O'Hanlon, who made stupidity lovable and brilliant as Dougal on *Father Ted*, began his career with two others as the founder of the Comedy Cellar, upstairs in the International Bar (p176). Tommy Tiernan and Deirdre O'Kane are others who have made a name for themselves, while up-and-comers like Kevin Gildea and Des Bishop are worth looking out for. For details of upcoming gigs, you can go online at www.irishwizard.com.

BANKER'S Map pp272–3
☎ 679 3697; 16 Trinity St; admission €5; ⏰ 9-11pm

A new Friday-night improv club is in the basement of this bar near Trinity College. It has yet to establish itself as a success, but it's a good spot to watch wet-behind-the-ears wannabe comics go through their (often terrified) paces. And who said schadenfreude wasn't fun?

GUBU Map pp269–71
☎ 874 0710; 7-8 Capel St; admission free; ⏰ 9.30-11pm

The name's an acronym of the declaration made by former Taoiseach Charlie Haughey when he learned that a wanted murderer had sought refuge in the Attorney General's house in 1980: Grotesque, Unbelievable, Bizarre and Unprecedented. Thankfully, the Thursday-night open-mic comedy club at this trendy gay bar (p163) is nothing of the kind. Lots of double-entendres and smutty references keep everyone smiling.

HA'PENNY BRIDGE INN Map pp269–71
☎ 677 0616; 42 Wellington Quay; admission free; ⏰ 9-11pm

From Tuesday to Thursday you can hear some fairly funny comedians (as well as some truly awful ones) do their stuff in the upstairs room of this Temple Bar pub. Tuesday night's Battle of the Axe, an improvisation night that features a lot of 'crowd participation' (read 'trading insults'), is the best of them.

INTERNATIONAL BAR Map pp272–3
☎ 677 9250; 23 Wicklow St; admission €7.50; ⏰ 9-11pm

The upstairs room above this pub (p176) hosts three comedy nights a week. Monday night is Comedy Improv, the best of the lot as the audience throws up subjects for the established comedians to work with. Wednesday night is Comedy Cellar, Ardal O'Hanlon's original creation, where blossoming talent is given the chance to find out if their material is up to scratch, and Thursday night is the International Comedy Club, hosted by Des Bishop, which generally has a line-up of good comedians.

LAUGHTER LOUNGE Map pp269–71
☎ 1800 266 339; www.laughterlounge.com; Eden Quay

This comedy theatre, which has long been a great venue for good comedy, is currently being redeveloped and is scheduled to re-open in September 2004. In the meantime, the club is constantly moving to a variety of temporary venues. Check the website for its most recent address.

BUSKERS

Street performers abound in Dublin, from mime artists (for those who don't think mime is crime) to evangelical Christians screaming the Good Word to passers-by eager to avoid them. The general quality of the acts is pretty good as an unforgiving theory of natural selection has seen the gifted wheat separated from the out-of-tune chaff. Grafton St and Temple Bar are the main areas for buskers; keep an eye out for the excellent solo musician who doubles up as a sharp-witted comedian (he often performs at the St Stephen's Green end of Grafton St on Saturdays) and, further down the street, a trio of guitar players that include one kid (he can't be more than 17) who is so good on the electric guitar that if you close your eyes you'd swear you were listening to Hendrix. Finally, the sidewalk opposite the main entrance to Trinity College is popular with artists, who can be seen on Saturdays adding lines and colour to their pavement re-creations of Renaissance masterpieces.

SPORTS

Sit in a pub while a match is on and watch the punters foam at the mouth as they yell at the players on the screen, 'They should pay *me* for watching *you*!' Dubliners love giving out, but mostly they just love their sport. Football (soccer), rugby and Gaelic football are the big three, but horse racing is also a big deal, as are the dogs (greyhounds, that is).

FOOTBALL

Dublin is football mad, though there are more fans of British teams – Manchester United, Liverpool, Arsenal and Glasgow Celtic are the big names – than there are of the plenty of local teams in Dublin. It wasn't always the case, but the arrival of televised British football in the late 1960s made the National League seem a little small-fry. Which it is. The national side, made up of Irish players playing nowhere near the National League (most of them play in Britain) is another story, and when the boys in green play an international, **Lansdowne Rd Stadium** (Map pp260–1; 4 Lansdowne Rd, Ballsbridge; DART to Lansdowne Rd) is usually jam-packed. Ireland only play about a half dozen matches a year at Lansdowne Rd, generally a mixture of friendlies and competitive games. Tickets range from €25 to €45, but you've

Local Football Teams

Local die-hards will insist that 'real' football is played on bumpy pitches by 'honest' semi-pros who aren't wandering about the pitch thinking about their image rights. You can find out for yourself between April and November by going to see one of the Dublin clubs in action (they all play in the Premier Division):

Bohemians FC (Map pp260-1; ☎ 868 0923; www.bohemians.ie; Dalymount Park, Phibsboro; adult/child €12/5; bus 10, 19 & 19A from city centre) Known as the Gypsies, this is the north side's pride and joy, and one of only two totally professional teams playing in the league.

Shamrock Rovers FC (☎ 460 4105; www.shamrockrovers.ie) The Hoops' tale is a cautionary one: once the dominant club in Irish soccer, not only have they not won the league in years but they don't even have a permanent home ground, as they await the construction of a purpose-built stadium in the southern suburb of Tallaght.

Shelbourne FC (Map pp260-1; ☎ 837 5536; www.shelbournefc.ie; Tolka Park, Richmond Rd, Drumcondra; adult/child €15/6; bus 3, 11, 11A, 13, 16 & 16A from city centre) This is the most successful Dublin club in recent times; in November 2003 they pipped their rivals Bohemians for the league title (once again).

got the same chances of getting a ticket for a competitive qualifier (for either the World Cup or the European Championships) as Ireland have of actually winning either of the competitions: slim and none. Tickets for friendly internationals are much easier to come by, unless the opponents are one of the world's big teams, like Brazil, Italy or France. For any footy-related info, get in touch with the **Football Association of Ireland** (FAI; ☎ 676 6864; www.fai.ie).

GAELIC FOOTBALL & HURLING

Dublin is a major force in Ireland's most popular game, Gaelic football. But the Blues haven't won an All-Ireland since 1995, and their great provincial rivals, Kildare and Meath, have more often than not stopped them in their tracks. At a national level, their nemesis is Kerry, the greatest of all football teams and Dublin's fiercest rivals during the 1970s, when the two would regularly slug it out for the Sam Maguire Cup.

The football season runs from February to the third Sunday in September and is divided into two separate competitions. The National Football League (NFL), which runs until mid-April, sees the Dubs slug it out for the league title at **Parnell Park** (Clantarkey Rd, Donnycarney; adult/child €8/5; bus 20A, 20B, 27, 27A, 42, 42B, 43 & 103 from Lower Abbey St/Beresford Pl). The league, however, is a poor relation of the All-Ireland Championship, which begins in late April and climaxes in the All-Ireland final at the end of September. The championship is ostensibly

a knockout competition, but in recent years a complicated system of repechage has been introduced up to the quarter-finals stage so that county teams off to a slow start don't see their interest in the competition end abruptly after one match (and so ensure that the gate receipts keep flowing in). Dublin play all of their championship matches at the newly remodelled **Croke Park** (p115), Ireland's largest stadium and the venue for both semi-finals and the final, irrespective of whether the Dubs are involved.

The hurling season runs parallel to the football season, and like football, is divided into two competitions, the National Hurling League (NHL) and the All-Ireland Championship. Dubliners have long dismissed hurling as stick-fighting, but it's probably because they've never been very good at it. Nevertheless, Croke Park is the venue for the latter stages of the All-Ireland Championship, where the sport's traditional powerhouses – Kilkenny (the current champions), Cork, Tipperary and Galway – are usually in the mix for hurling's Holy Grail, the Liam McCarthy Cup, which is played for on the first Sunday in September.

While tickets for the NFL are easy to come by (you can just buy one at the grounds), they're tougher to get for the championship, particularly past the quarter-final stage. Dublin's hurling team usually get pounded long before then, but the football team is generally expected to get to at least the semi-finals. For the early rounds, tickets cost adult/child €15/12, but once the championship reaches the quarter-finals adults and children pay the same: stand prices range from €25 to €50 for the final itself and terrace prices range from €15 to €45. The stand is more comfortable and usually has better views, but if the Dubs are playing and you want to get right into the partisan thick of things, go for the Hill 16 terrace.

The Fast & the Furious

Gaelic games are fast, furious and not for the faint-hearted. Challenges are fierce, and contact between players is extremely aggressive. Both games are played by two teams of 15 players whose aim is to get the ball between what resembles a rugby score: two long vertical posts joined by a horizontal bar, below which is an actual goal, protected by a goal-keeper. Goals are worth three points, whereas a ball placed over the bar between the posts is worth one point. Scores are shown thus: 1-12 means one goal and 12 points, giving a total of 15 points.

Gaelic football is played with a round, soccer-size ball, and players are allowed to kick it or hand-pass it, like Aussie Rules. Hurling, which is considered by far the more beautiful game, is played with a flat ashen stick or bat known as a hurley or *camán*. The ball, called a *slíothar* (small, leather ball), is hit or carried on the hurley; hand-passing is also allowed. Both games are played over 70 action-fuelled minutes.

Both sports are county-based games. The dream of every club player is to represent his county, with the hope of perhaps playing in an All-Ireland final, the climax of a knockout championship that is played first at a provincial and then inter-provincial level.

HORSE & GREYHOUND RACING

Dubliners love the gee-gees, but most of all, they love betting on them. The flat racing season runs from March to November, while the National Hunt season – when horses jump over things – runs from October to April, but there are limited events during the summer. Greyhound racing is very much a minority interest in Dublin, but it's a devoted minority that flock to see them chase the electric hare. It's a great night out, even if you couldn't care less about who wins.

CURRAGH RACECOURSE Map p210
☎ 045-441 205; www.curragh.ie; County Kildare; admission €20-50; special bus from Busáras (p230)
The home of Irish racing hosts five classic flat races between May and September: the 1000

Guineas, 2000 Guineas, Oaks, St Leger and Irish Derby.

FAIRYHOUSE RACECOURSE Map p210
☎ 825 6167; www.fairyhouse.com; Ratoath, County Meath; admission €15-30; special bus from Busáras (p230)
The National Hunt season has its yearly climax with the Grand National, held here on Easter Monday. The course is 25km north of Dublin.

HAROLD'S CROSS PARK Map pp260–1
☎ 497 1081; 151 Harold's Cross Rd; admission €7; ☺ from 8pm Mon, Tue & Fri; bus 16 from city centre
This greyhound track is close to the city centre and offers a great night out for a fraction of what it would cost to go to the horses.

LEOPARDSTOWN RACECOURSE
Map p210
☎ 289 3607; www.leopardstown.com; Foxrock; admission €15-30; special bus from Eden Quay
Specialising in both flat and jump races, Leopardstown's big event is the prestigious Hennessey Gold Cup in February.

PUNCHESTOWN Map p210
☎ 045-897 704; www.punchestown.com; Naas, County Kildare
Although it specialises mostly in flat racing, Punchestown is home to the extremely popular Steeplechase Festival in April. The course is 40km southwest of the city.

SHELBOURNE GREYHOUND STADIUM Map pp260–1
☎ 668 3502; Shelbourne Park, South Lotts Rd; admission €7; ☺ 7-10.30pm Wed, Thu & Sat; bus 3, 7, 7A, 8, 45 & 84 Trinity College
All the comforts, including a restaurant in the covered stand overlooking the track, make going to the dogs one of the best nights out around. Table service – including betting – means that you don't even have to get out of your seat.

RUGBY

There's a hell of a lot of rugby played in and around Dublin these days. Traditionally the sole preserve of Dublin's more affluent south-side neighbourhoods, the game was dismissed by the rest of the city as a mucky pastime for posh thugs. In recent years their suspicions have given way to a growing interest, thanks to rugby's slicker image worldwide and the successes of the Irish national side and the local provincial side, Leinster. Rugby's governing body in Ireland is the **Irish Rugby Football Union** (IRFU; Map pp260–1; ☎ 660 0779; www.irishrugby.ie; 62 Lansdowne Rd), which controls the game from the grassroots up.

At the top of the pile is the national team, which plays in the Six Nations championship against Scotland, Wales, France, Italy and the old enemy England (the current world champions). Ireland plays three home internationals a year, all between February and April at Lansdowne Rd Stadium (see p177). Tickets – which range from €7 for school kids to €75 for a seat in the main covered stand – are like gold; they're generally divided between corporate buyers and the network of small clubs throughout the country, of which you need to be a member if you want a ticket. You can try getting them through the IRFU (which also has a limited online purchasing service), but chances are you'll draw a blank.

You'll have a much better chance to see top-class rugby at an interprovincial level. Leinster, a team selected from a pool of players playing for a dozen or so local club teams, play in two overlapping competitions: the Heineken European Cup (played against provincial teams in the countries that participate in the Six Nations championship) and the Celtic League (played against teams from Scotland and Wales). The Celtic League runs from September to January and the European Cup from December to May. Leinster play their home matches in the European Cup at Lansdowne Rd Stadium (adult/child/family €30/15/70) and their home games in the less-prestigious **Celtic League** (Map pp260–1; ☎ 283 8254; www.leinsterrugby.ie; Donnybrook Rd; adult/child/family €20/12/50). Tickets for both competitions are available at Elvery's outlets in Suffolk St (Map pp272–3; ☎ 679 4142) and Dawson St (Map pp272–3; ☎ 679 1141); at the **Spar** (Map pp260–1; ☎ 269 3261; 54-56 Donnybrook Rd) opposite the rugby ground; or online.

HEALTH & FITNESS

Most health clubs in the city are private, requiring year-long membership commitments, or six months at the very least. The better-equipped hotels usually have their own gyms, but they're open to guests only. The sports centres listed below are open to the public.

LUCE SPORTS CENTRE Map p78

☎ 608 1812; Trinity College; admission €7;
🕙 8am-9pm Mon-Fri Jun-Sep

Trinity's huge sports complex has plenty of facilities, including a large gym and squash courts.

MARKIEVICZ LEISURE CENTRE

Map pp266–8

☎ 672 9121; Townsend St; adult/child €5.80/2.60;
🕙 7am-9.45pm Mon-Thu, 7am-8.45pm Fri, 9am-6pm Sat, 10am-4pm Sun

This excellent fitness centre has a swimming pool, a workout room (with plenty of gym

machines) and a sauna. You can swim for as long as you please, but children are only allowed at off-peak times (10am-5.30pm Mon-Sat).

MESPIL SWIMMING POOL

Map pp266–8

☎ 668 4626; Mespil Estate, Sussex St; adult/child €5.80-14/2.60; 🕙 6.45-9.45am, 11.45am-1.45pm & 4.45-8pm Mon-Fri, 10am-1pm & 2-4pm Sat & Sun

The Mespil has a crowd-free 20m pool, sauna and Jacuzzi. Children are only allowed at weekends.

Shopping

Shopping

Shopping has become a big deal in Dublin in recent years. With heavier wallets and fuller purses, Dubliners have turned shopping into a major social activity to which they devote plenty of time, effort and money. A typical weekend afternoon is a case in point: you can barely walk down Grafton St without clattering into bag-carrying consumers looking for that silk scarf that will tie the new outfit together or that extra component for the speaker system that redefines the concept of stereo sound. Retailers have never had it so good, and have gone to great lengths to make the most of the hedonistic retail therapy that came with the Celtic Tiger boom.

New outlets have opened everywhere, from the exclusive bijou boutique where you can buy one-off creations to the American-style mall that sells everything, including the kitchen sink. As half of the city's population is under 25, there is an overabundance of mid-range fashion outlets, selling mostly mid-priced, mass-produced clobber to a youth market obsessed with aping their British neighbours.

The other big seller in Dublin is tourist souvenirs, but most of it is mass-produced junk foisted on the unsuspecting visitor, from factory-made hawthorn sticks to pretty much

Dublin Shopping Centres

Most of the city's shopping centres cater to specific markets, from the high-end boutique shopper to the bargain bulk buyer who doesn't want to spend a lot of money. Following is a list of Dublin's shopping centres; for stand-out individual shops within these centres, see the reviews listings under the relevant neighbourhood.

George's St Arcade (Map pp272-3; btwn South Great George's St & Drury St) Sheltered within a beautiful Victorian Gothic complex, this marvellous arcade caters primarily to the younger, trendy shopper, with second-hand clothing, records, beads, piercings, tattoos and other bits of exotica on offer. There are a couple of good food stalls here, a fabulous jeweller and a lovely bookshop as well.

ILAC Centre (Map pp264-5; ☎ 704 1460; Henry St) Dublin's first shopping centre seems sadly dilapidated compared to the new kids on the block, but its mix of affordable trendy shops, department stores and bargain retail outlets have kept it one of the city's busiest centres.

Irish Life Centre (Map pp264-5; ☎ 704 1451; entrances on Lower Abbey St & Talbot St) The least visited of all Dublin's shopping centres, and for good reason. Worn out and thin with good shops, this mall just off O'Connell St is in dire need of an overhaul. We wouldn't bother if we were you.

Jervis Centre (Map pp269-71; ☎ 878 1323; Jervis St) A modern shopping centre that features a pretty big selection of High St retail outlets, with shops selling everything from electronic goods to the latest in youth fashion.

Powerscourt Townhouse Shopping Centre (Map pp272-3; ☎ 679 4144; 59 South William St) Sophistication and elegance are the bywords of the city's classiest shopping centre, housed in a huge, converted Georgian town house originally built between 1741 and 1744. High-end fashion, exquisite handicrafts and other top-end sundries share this marvellous space with a number of cafés and restaurants. See also the Neighbourhoods chapter (p83).

Royal Hibernian Way Centre (Map pp272-3; ☎ 679 5919; Dawson St) This walk-through arcade has a number of clothing shops, a trendy bar and several accessories outlets, from jewellery to mobile phones.

St Stephen's Green Shopping Centre (Map pp272-3; ☎ 478 0888; St Stephen's Green) This mock-Victorian arcade on the northeastern corner of St Stephen's Green has a diverse mixture of international chain stores and individual shops. The centre's largest outlet is the very Irish Dunne's Stores; three floors of clothing, home appliances and, in the basement, an excellent supermarket.

Westbury Mall (Map pp272-3; ☎ 679 1589; Clarendon St) Less centre and more arcade, the Westbury Mall is home to a number of very exclusive boutiques that cater to the more discerning (read 'wealthier') shopper. It's right next to the Westbury Hotel (p196).

anything with a shamrock on it. However, a number of shops sell good-quality merchandise; big favourites are the ubiquitous Aran sweater and other woollen goodies, and handcrafted pieces of jewellery with Celtic influences.

In keeping with its proud tradition of being a literary city, Dublin is a terrific place to buy books. Aside from the larger chain retailers, the city has a number of excellent specialist bookshops.

Opening Hours

Most of the city's shops open 9.30am to 6pm Monday to Saturday. Thursday has late-night shopping, and many shops stay open until 8pm. In recent years the lifting of the ban on Sunday trading has seen a large number of shops open for business on this day too, but only from noon to 6pm. Shopping centres keep the same hours. Remember that Dublin is not really an early-rising city, at least not in the retail trade: although a shop may advertise its opening as 9.30am, sleepy-headed staff mightn't pull up the shutters until near 10am (closing times, however, are rigidly adhered to!).

Duty Free

Value-added tax (VAT) is a sales tax of 20% that applies to most goods and services in Dublin, excluding books and children's footwear. EU residents cannot claim a VAT refund, but if you're a non-EU resident and buy something from a store displaying a Cashback sticker, you'll be given a Cashback voucher with your purchase so that you can reclaim the VAT. This voucher can be refunded in US, Canadian or Australian dollars, British pounds sterling or euros at Dublin airport. Alternatively, you can have the voucher stamped at the ferry port and mail it back for a refund.

If you reclaim more than €255 on any of your vouchers, you'll need to get the voucher stamped at the customs booth in the arrivals hall at Dublin airport before you can get your refund from the Cashback desk.

If you leave the EU from terminal three or terminal four of London's Heathrow airport, you must get British customs to stamp your vouchers and then leave them at the Tax Free Shopping Desk. In some circumstances refunds can be posted to you or credited to your credit card.

SOUTH OF THE LIFFEY
Around Grafton Street

Pedestrianised Grafton St is *the* shopping street, Dublin's own Oxford St, and judging from the number of British-owned chain stores here, they're doing a good job of mimicking their London counterpart. Here – and on the surrounding streets – you'll find the city's most reputable outlets, from fancy clothes shops to rare-book sellers and pretty much everything in-between. Prices in the area tend to be higher than elsewhere, but the quality of the goods is generally excellent. Many of the trendier outlets are not on Grafton St itself but on the maze of streets around it, mostly because Grafton St remains the preserve of long-established retailers and the larger chains with more monetary muscle. Johnson Ct, which runs west off the middle of Grafton St, has a number of jewellers.

ALIAS TOM Map pp272–3 *Men's Fashion*
☎ 671 7200; Duke House, Duke Lane
Men's suits by most top international designers (Prada, Armani, Hugo Boss etc) as well as the odd big-name Irish cloth-cutter (John Rocha) pack the racks in the basement; the ground floor is given over to men's shirts and accessories, from sunglasses to luggage.

APPLEBY'S Map pp272–3 *Jewellery*
☎ 679 9572; 5-6 Johnson's Ct
This little shop is renowned for the high quality of its jewellery, which is a mix of Celtic-design work and more classic pieces.

ASPECTO Map pp272–3 *Mixed Fashion*
☎ 671 9302; 6 South Anne St
This supertrendy shop just off Grafton St sells the latest in designer gear. On the ground floor it has shoes and on the 2nd floor clothing.

AVOCA HANDWEAVERS
Map pp272–3 *Department Store*
☎ 677 4215; 11-13 Suffolk St
If only all department stores were as beautiful as this one. This marvellously eclectic store sells a wide array of contemporary Irish designs in every medium, from hand-knits to painted ceramics. It's one of the best places in the city to find an original present. The childrenswear section on the 2nd floor is highly recommended.

BROWN THOMAS
Map pp272–3 *Department Store*
☎ 605 6666; 92 Grafton St
Every top international label is represented here in Dublin's most exclusive department store, but we recommend that you look out for the Irish designers, including Lainey Keogh, Paul Costelloe and Louise Kennedy. Spread across three floors, it is elegant and suitably snooty.

BT2 Map pp272–3 *Mixed Fashion*
☎ 605 6666; 28 Grafton St
Brown Thomas' annexe targets a more youthful, trendy shopper looking for less exclusive brands, such as DKNY, Polo by Ralph Lauren, Tommy Hilfiger and Calvin Klein.

CATHACH BOOKS Map pp272–3 *Bookshop*
☎ 671 8676; www.rarebooks.ie; 10 Duke St
Our favourite bookshop in the city stocks a rich and remarkable collection of Irish-interest books, with a particular emphasis on 20th century literature, including some rare first editions by the big guns: Joyce, Yeats, Beckett and Wilde.

THE DUBLIN BOOKSHOP
Map pp272–3 *Bookshop*
☎ 677 5568; 36 Grafton St
Stocking mostly bestsellers and recent releases this bookshop has a pretty good Irish-interest section. It has recently been given a makeover in an effort to compete with its larger rivals.

EASON'S – HANNA'S BOOKSHOP
Map pp272–3 *Bookshop*
☎ 677 1255; 27-29 Nassau St
This excellent bookshop directly opposite the Nassau St entrance to Trinity College specialises in academic tomes, but there's a good collection of other books, as well as an enormous stationery shop.

GREAT OUTDOORS
Map pp272–3 *Camping & Outdoor*
☎ 679 4293; 20 Chatham St
The best of Dublin's camping equipment shops, with an enormous selection of all kinds of gear for all kinds of activities, from gentle hill-walking and surfing to hardcore mountaineering.

GREENE'S BOOKSHOP
Map pp266–8 *Bookshop*
☎ 873 3149; 16 Clare St
A Dublin institution, this dusty old bookshop, packed with new and second-hand books, seems to have no rhyme or reason to its order

---

A Dying Breed

Smokers are in despair: January 2004 saw their habit banned almost everywhere, leaving them (literally) out in the cold. However, Grafton St is home to two beautiful shops that cater almost exclusively to their needs:

JJ Fox Ltd (Map pp269-71; ☎ 677 0533; 119 Grafton St) Hand-crafted pipes and an (un)healthy selection of quality cigars appeal to the smoker, but the shop has its eye on nonsmokers too, with an array of watches, clocks and silk ties. It's a classic gentleman's shop.

Kapp & Peterson (Map pp269-71; ☎ 671 4652; 117 Grafton St) Pipe lovers will salivate at the extraordinary pipe collection here, most of which require seasoning before they give off that perfect smoke. You can also buy watches and Swiss Army knives. Literary fans may recognise the shop from Beckett's *Waiting for Godot:* it is the shop where Pozzo bought the pipe he smokes throughout the first scene.

but the helpful staff never fail to locate what you're looking for, a minor miracle considering the sheer numbers of books on the shelves.

HMV Map pp272–3 *Music*
☎ 679 5334; 65 Grafton St
The most extensive collection of CDs, videos, DVDs and video games in the city, spread across three floors. Every genre of music is catered to, and downstairs has a small selection of vinyl, mostly dance and hip-hop.

HODGES FIGGIS Map pp272–3 *Bookshop*
☎ 677 4754; 57 Dawson St
Dublin's largest bookshop is spread across three floors and stocks titles for every taste and need. The ground floor has a huge selection of Irish-interest titles.

HOUSE OF IRELAND
Map pp272–3 *Irish Crafts*
☎ 671 4543; 38 Nassau St
Cut crystal, porcelain presents and woolly things made all over the country fill the shelves at this top-end craft shop with an excellent reputation for quality, even if most of the stock is a tad on the traditional side.

KILKENNY CENTRE
Map pp266–8 *Fashion/Irish Crafts*
☎ 677 7066; 6 Nassau St
A Dublin institution, this wonderful shop has a wide stock of goods 'made in Ireland', from glassware, pottery and jewellery to men and women's fashion; look out for the shop's own label, whose creations are the brainchild of talented Irish designer Gráinne Walsh.

KNOBS & KNOCKERS
Map pp272–3 *Oddities*
☎ 671 0288; 19 Nassau St
This shop sells exactly what it says on the tin. Highly recommended as a great souvenir of your Dublin visit are replica Georgian doorknockers, but there are plenty of other souvenir door adornments to look at.

LOUIS COPELAND
Map pp272–3 *Men's Fashion*
☎ 872 1600; 18-19 Wicklow St
Dublin's answer to the famed tailors of London's Saville Row, this shop makes fabulous suits to measure, but also stocks plenty of ready-to-wear suits by a host of international designers.

Clothing sizes
Measurements approximate only, try before you buy

Women's Clothing

Aust/UK	8	10	12	14	16	18
Europe	36	38	40	42	44	46
Japan	5	7	9	11	13	15
USA	6	8	10	12	14	16

Women's Shoes

Aust/USA	5	6	7	8	9	10
Europe	35	36	37	38	39	40
France only	35	36	38	39	40	42
Japan	22	23	24	25	26	27
UK	3½	4½	5½	6½	7½	8½

Men's Clothing

Aust	92	96	100	104	108	112
Europe	46	48	50	52	54	56
Japan	S		M	M		L
UK/USA	35	36	37	38	39	40

Men's Shirts (Collar Sizes)

Aust/Japan	38	39	40	41	42	43
Europe	38	39	40	41	42	43
UK/USA	15	15½	16	16½	17	17½

Men's Shoes

Aust/UK	7	8	9	10	11	12
Europe	41	42	43	44½	46	47
Japan	26	27	27½	28	29	30
USA	7½	8½	9½	10½	11½	12½

MARKS & SPENCER
Map pp272–3 *Department Store*
☎ 679 7855; 15-20 Grafton St
Good-quality clothing and virtually everything else that the body and house might need – all at affordable prices – make this British chain store one of the most popular in Dublin.

SHERIDAN'S CHEESEMONGERS
Map pp272–3 *Food*
☎ 679 3143; 11 South Anne St
Ireland isn't especially known for the rich variety of its cheeses, but it should be. Cheeses of every tang and flavour weigh down the shelves of this marvellous store. It also sells wild smoked salmon, which can be shipped to you.

SUSAN HUNTER
Map pp272–3 *Women's Fashion*
☎ 679 1271; 13 Westbury Mall
Expensive lingerie at this small boutique includes a range of delicates made by La Perla – Dublin's only retailer to stock the brand.

SWEATER SHOP Map pp272–3 *Knitwear*
☎ 671 3270; 9 Wicklow St

Traditional designs of the highest quality are the stock and trade of this well-established shop near Grafton St.

THOMAS PINK Map pp272–3 *Men's Fashion*
☎ 670 3720; 29 Dawson St

English visitors may be familiar with the high-quality shirts made by Thomas Pink, but it might come as a surprise that the brains behind the business are two Irish brothers named Mullan. Shirts in every conceivable cloth, cut perfectly to the smallest detail, make this the best place in the city to find that perfect complement for a suit.

TOWER CRAFT DESIGN CENTRE
Map pp266–8 *Irish Crafts*
☎ 677 5655; Pearse St

Housed in a 19th-century warehouse that was Dublin's first iron-structured building, this design centre has studios for local craftspeople. They produce jewellery in both contemporary and Celtic-inspired designs, Irish pewter, ceramics, silk and other fabrics, pottery, rugs, wall hangings, cards, leather bags and various other handcrafted items. It's immediately opposite the Waterways Visitors Centre, off Lower Grand Canal St.

WATERSTONE'S Map pp272–3 *Bookshop*
☎ 679 1415; 7 Dawson St

This well-stocked English chain is the only serious rival to Hodges Figgis (p185) as the city's most extensive bookshop – and it's directly across the street from it, so if one bookshop is out of the title you're looking for, the other one is sure to have it.

WEIR & SON'S Map pp272–3 *Jewellery*
☎ 677 9678; 96 Grafton St

Dublin's most famous jeweller has a top-notch collection of fancy watches, superbly crafted crystal and elegant gold- and silverware for the more discerning customer.

Temple Bar

Dublin's most visited neighbourhood has a pretty diverse mix of shops. Apart from the usual tourist tack you might expect to find in any tourist trap, Temple Bar's stores traditionally specialised in second-hand clothing and the weird and (sometimes) wonderful, where you can get everything from a Celtic-design wall hanging to a handcrafted bong. In recent years, however, the western end of the quarter has been developed and a number of new shops have opened up; mostly of the high-end luxury design kind, with prices to boot. Saturday is market day here (see the boxed text below).

BOOKS UPSTAIRS Map pp269–71 *Bookshop*
☎ 679 6687; 36 College Green

Facing the main entrance to Trinity College, this two-storey bookshop has a large selection of Irish literature and a fairly comprehensive section of gay literature. So where do they put Oscar Wilde?

CELTIC GIFTS
Map pp269–71 *Alternative Fashion*
☎ 679 7087; 2 Crown Alley

Incense, tie-dye shirts, Celtic-style jewellery, wall hangings, bongs and pipes…you can guess the clientele at this knick-knack store, one of Temple Bar's most popular. It has a range of second-hand clothing too.

Weekend Markets

Temple Bar is home to three excellent markets, all of which take place on Saturday between 9am and 6pm:

Cow's Lane Market (Map pp269-71) This fabulous clothing-and-accessories market is an excellent showcase for Ireland's up-and-coming designers. There are plans to extend the market as far down as the Liffey, but for now it runs the length of Cow's Lane. From November to April the market is moved indoors.

Meeting House Square Market (Map pp269-71) An open-air food market with a multitude of stalls selling top organic produce from around the country; you can also buy diverse snacks, such as sushi, waffles, tapas, oysters and handmade cheeses. Get there early for best pickings and to avoid the huge crowds.

Temple Bar Square Market (Map pp269-71) Second-hand books at really cheap prices are the attraction here, and while the selection isn't that great (we noticed a lot of bad bestsellers), if you look hard enough you are sure to find something worthwhile.

Museum Shops

Most museums have a basic gift shop, but you'll find a few in Dublin that offer more than the usual baubles and trinkets. We recommend the following:

Chester Beatty Library (p81; Dublin Castle) A wonderful little gift shop, with postcards, books, posters and other memorabilia of this extraordinary museum.

Dublin Writers Museum (p103; 18 North Parnell Sq) An excellent bookshop with a great selection of Irish books.

Irish Museum of Modern Art (p96; Military Rd) A comprehensive selection of coffee-table books on Irish contemporary art.

National Gallery (p86; Merrion Sq) Books covering the whole history of Irish and European art.

Trinity Library Shop (Map pp266-8; East Pavilion, Library Colonnades, Trinity College) The big sellers are the titles on the Book of Kells, but you can also get all kinds of other mementos and curios.

CLADDAGH RECORDS Map pp269–71 *Music*
☎ 677 0262; 2 Cecilia St

An excellent collection of good-quality traditional and folk music is the mainstay at this record shop. A profoundly knowledgeable staff should be able to locate that elusive recording.

CONDOM POWER Map pp269–71 *Adult Shop*
☎ 677 8963; 57 Dame St

Multicoloured, multiflavoured condoms, sex toys and a host of other adult accessories line the shelves of this basement shop, along with the usual selection of magazines, videos and DVDs. We must warn you that Dublin is probably Europe's most expensive city for adult entertainment.

DESIGNYARD Map pp269–71 *Crafts*
☎ 677 8453; 12 East Essex St

To call this modern warehouse space a craft shop is a misnomer, as it is more like a commercial gallery that showcases beautiful contemporary work by Irish and European jewellers, potters and craftspeople.

EAGER BEAVER
Map pp269–71 *Second-hand Clothing*
☎ 677 3342; 17 Crown Alley

Need a black suit for a wedding, a cricket jumper or a Victorian shirt, but don't want to spend a fortune? This is your place; spread across two floors, it's a clothing hunter's paradise.

FLIP Map pp269–71 *Second-hand Clothing*
☎ 671 4299; 4 Upper Fownes St

Flip specialises in vintage US clothing. The prices are higher than in other second-hand stores, but that's because the clothing is genuine.

INISH Map pp269–71 *Boutique*
☎ 679 0665; 11 Lord Edward St

Celtic-style jewellery, linen scarves and other traditional trinkets that won't cost a fortune are the feature of this small boutique on the edge of Temple Bar.

SMOCK Map pp269–71 *Women's Fashion*
☎ 613 9000; Smock Alley Ct, West Essex St

This tiny designer shop sells quirky (and very exclusive) international womenswear from investment labels Easton Pearson, Veronique Branquinho and AF Vandevorft, as well as a small range of interesting jewellery.

SOURCE @ URBANA
Map pp269–71 *Gift Shop*
☎ 670 3083; 43 Temple Bar

Undoubtedly Dublin's wackiest shop, this extraordinary place is *the* place to go to find that gift you'd never thought you'd buy. It's all very cool, very contemporary and a lot of fun: why not add a miniature slinky to your luggage or put aside some excess weight money to get the Coca-Cola fridge through customs?

URBAN OUTFITTERS
Map pp269–71 *Fashion*
☎ 670 6202; 4 Cecilia St

With a blaring techno soundtrack, the only Irish branch of this American chain sells ridiculously cool clothes to discerning young buyers. Besides clothing, the shop stocks all kinds of interesting gadgets, accessories and furniture. On the 2nd floor you'll find a hypertrendy record shop (hence the techno).

Shopping – Temple Bar

WHICHCRAFT GALLERY

Map pp269–71　　　　　　　　　　*Artisan Crafts*
☎ 474 1011; www.whichcraft.com; Cow's Lane

This wonderful Irish craft shop features some of the best examples of contemporary design in a variety of mediums, including glass, metal, ceramic and wood. The website has examples from various price categories.

SoDa

The grid of streets south of Dame St offer a diverse mix of shops, from Fair-Trade to fancy, and two extraordinary shopping centres, each with its own marvellous identity. To the west, on and around South Great George's St, second-hand shops and bargain outlets surround the Victorian structure of the George's St Arcade, once a regular market, now a wonderful collection of pokey little shops and stalls. To the east, closer to Grafton St, the shops get posher and more exclusive. Here, elegant boutiques are gathered around the exquisite Powerscourt Townhouse Shopping Centre, Dublin's most elegant shopping mall.

ASIA MARKET Map pp272–3　　*Supermarket*
☎ 677 9764; 18 Drury St

Behind an unassuming shop front and foyer is the city's most extensive Asian supermarket, packed with virtually every ingredient neces- sary for that authentic Asian meal. Naturally enough, most of the clientele are Asian.

BARRY DOYLE DESIGN JEWELLERS

Map pp272–3　　　　　　　　　　　　*Jewellery*
☎ 671 2838; 30 George's St Arcade

Goldsmith Barry Doyle's upstairs shop is one of the best of its kind in Dublin. The handmade jewellery – using white gold, silver, and some truly gorgeous precious and semi-precious stones – is exceptional in its beauty and simplicity. Most of the pieces have Afro-Celtic influences.

BIG BROTHER RECORDS

Map pp272–3　　　　　　　　　　　　　　*Music*
☎ 672 9355; www.bigbrotherrecords.com; 16 Fade St

In the basement of Road Records (opposite), vinyl junkies and indie fans will get a kick out of Big Brother's selection, a good mix of hip-hop, deep house, jazzy beats and drum-and-bass, as well as jazz and soul.

BLUE ERIU Map pp272–3　　*Cosmetics/Beauty*
☎ 672 5776; 7 South William St

Less of a cosmetics shop and more a beauty experience with a Celtic twist, this supertrendy retreat serves up the best (or so we're told) fa- cial in town; the products used are strictly from the top shelf, including Kiehls, Chantecaille and Shu Uemura.

CAMERA EXCHANGE

Map pp272–3   *Photography*

☎ 478 4125; 63 South Great George's St

This is one of the best photographic equipment shops in town and a reputable developer of prints. The staff is friendly and knowledgeable, and will usually assist in answering any camera-related query, even if the equipment is not bought here.

COSTUME Map pp272–3 *Women's Fashion*

☎ 679 4188; 10 Castle Market

Costume is considered a genuine pacesetter by Dublin's fashionistas; it has exclusive contracts with some of Europe's most innovative designers, such as Tempereley and Sabina di Lorenzo. Local designers represented here are Helen James, whose Japanese-influenced obis are enormously popular, and Leigh Tucker.

CRAFTS COUNCIL GALLERY

Map pp272–3   *Irish Crafts*

☎ 679 7368; Powerscourt Townhouse Shopping Centre

One of several craft shops in the Powerscourt building, this gallery has a fine selection of glassware, pottery and jewellery, although you'll need a flexible credit card.

DANDELION BOOKS

Map pp266–8   *Bookshop*

☎ 478 4759; 72 Aungier St

This dusty old bookshop only has second-hand stock; Irish-interest books and novels are crammed in next to one-time bestsellers, history books and other assorted titles.

DESIGN CENTRE

Map pp272–3   *Women's Fashion*

☎ 679 5718; 2nd floor, Powerscourt Townhouse Shopping Centre

If you are looking for the most elegant creations by Irish designers – from long linen skirts to fabulously ornate hats – then this suitably snooty store is the place to go. The big names in women's fashion – Lainey Keogh, Rita Daly and John Rocha – are all represented here.

HARLEQUIN

Map pp272–3   *Second-hand Clothing*

☎ 671 0202; 13 Castle Market

Leather jackets, coats, jeans, shirts and T-shirts are only part of the selection at this wonderful second-hand shop next door to Costume. There is a small selection of suits upstairs.

Top Five Guaranteed Irish

You want to buy something Irish-made to take home? Here's our quick pick:

- **Avoca Handweavers** (p184) Our favourite department store in the city has a myriad of home-made gift ideas.
- **Barry Doyle Design Jewellers** (opposite) Exquisite handcrafted jewellery with a unique contemporary design.
- **Cathach Books** (p184) For that priceless first edition or that beautiful, leather-bound copy of Joyce's *Dubliners*.
- **Louis Copeland** (p185) Dublin's very own top tailor and his made-to-measure suits.
- **Costume** (this page) Elegance, originality and sophistication – and that's just the Irish designers represented at this fabulous shop.

JENNY VANDER

Map pp272–3   *Vintage Clothing*

☎ 677 0406; 50 Drury St

The clothes at Jenny Vander's may have been worn before, but there's nothing second-hand about them. These are vintage outfits, mostly from the middle of the 20th century, and every one of them a beautiful creation. Blouses, hats, shoes and costume jewellery from the same era are also available.

KAVANAGH'S

Map pp266–8   *Confectionary*

☎ 475 2733; 10 Aungier St

This ordinary-looking newsagent is a local institution. Opened in 1925, it is one of the few places left in the whole city where you can still buy sweets – all kinds of sweets, from milk teeth to fizzy cola bottles – by the weight. It's a real Dublin treat.

PLATFORM EILE

Map pp272–3   *Women's Fashion*

☎ 667 7380; 50 South William St

Through an arched laneway, this interesting shop specialises in women's dresses, mostly by up-and-coming Irish designers such as Deirdre Fitzgerald, whose woollen creations are simply beautiful. The shop also stocks a fabulous range of Irish-made accessories.

ROAD RECORDS Map pp272–3 *Music*

☎ 671 7340; 16 Fade St

This small record shop just south of the George's St Arcade has all the latest indie sounds, both local and international. It's also a good place to get tickets for local gigs.

SABOTAGE Map pp272–3 *Fashion*
☎ 670 4789; 14 Exchequer St
Strictly trendy, this popular shop has everything you'll need to look the part, from head to toe. A second branch, for women only, is a couple of doors down on the corner with Drury St.

STOKES BOOKS Map pp272–3 *Bookshop*
☎ 671 3584; 19 George's St Arcade
This small bookshop specialises in Irish historical books both old and new; other titles, covering a range of subjects, include a number of beautiful, old, leather-bound editions.

SUB-CITY Map pp272–3 *Bookshop*
☎ 677 1902; 2 Exchequer St
An excellent bookshop for the grown-up kid, Sub-City has the latest in sci-fi books and comics.

TULLE Map pp272–3 *Women's Fashion*
☎ 679 9115; 29 George's St Arcade
European designers with attitude – Matthew Williamson, Holly and Othtude – are stocked in this small outlet for young women.

WALTON'S Map pp272–3 *Music*
☎ 475 0661; 69-70 South Great George's St
This is the place to go if you're looking for your very own *bodhrán* (goat-skin drum) or indeed any other musical instrument associated with Irish traditional music. It also has an excellent selection of sheet music and recorded music.

WILD CHILD
Map pp272–3 *Second-hand Clothing*
☎ 475 5099; 61 South Great George's St
Original Adidas trainers and tracksuit tops, loud wide-collared shirts and fitted leather jackets…anyone who grooved through the 1970s will feel a hint of nostalgia in this terrific shop; the accompanying soundtrack is superb, thanks to the owner, who is a part-time DJ.

Georgian Dublin
Outside of St Stephen's Green Shopping Centre, there's little else in the way of shops to stop you on your way.

DONEGAL SHOP Map pp272–3 *Knitwear*
☎ 475 4621; St Stephen's Green Shopping Centre
Hand-woven Magee tweed from Donegal deserves its excellent reputation and is probably the best stuff sold at this shop, which also includes machine-made Aran sweaters and a range of knitted hats, bobbins and all.

Kilmainham & the Liberties
The oldest and most traditional of city centre neighbourhoods has little to offer in the way of shopping opportunities, except for one massive exception: Francis St, which is full of antique shops.

JOHNSTON ANTIQUES
Map pp262–3 *Antiques*
☎ 473 2384; 69-70 Francis St
Johnston Antiques is a great place for jewellery, fashion antiques and other curios.

NORTH OF THE LIFFEY
Around O'Connell Street
North of the Liffey, most of the shopping is done along Henry St, which runs off O'Connell St, to the west, and North Earl St, which runs east. Henry St – and Upper Liffey St, which runs off it – offer your standard selection of High St shops: a couple of department stores and a bunch of individual fashion outlets whose wares

Moore Street Melting Pot
Dublin's most distinctive traditional market – and the spiritual home of fictional Molly Malone – runs the length of Moore St, off Henry St. For many Dubliners, it is about as authentic a Dublin street as you could ever find. Unable to compete with the increasing number of supermarkets, the market lost much of its vigour in the last couple of decades, but the last few years has seen its authenticity preserved by the arrival of a new, dynamic force: ethnicity. African and Asian immigrants, eager to get a foothold in the local retail market, have more or less taken over all of the fixed shops along Moore St, much to the delight of the traditional traders, who welcome the renewed interest in their street. The African-owned shops seem obsessed with hair care, while the Asian retailers sell an abundance of far-grown foodstuffs.

are replicas of the latest gear seen on MTV. North Earl St is a bargain-hunter's paradise: everything is dirt-cheap but the quality is pretty poor. O'Connell St has only a small number of shops, but is where you'll find the city's most famous department store, Clery's & Co.

ANN SUMMERS
Map pp264–5   *Adult Shop/Lingerie*
☎ 878 1385; 30-31 O'Connell St
There was holy uproar when this shop opened, but its success suggests that it meets a demand not previously taken care of in Dublin. Compared to its basement peers throughout the city, this is a pretty tame version of an adult shop, and the lingerie (which is very up front and centre) is generally of a high quality even if a lot of it leaves little to the imagination.

ARNOTT'S Map pp269–71   *Department Store*
☎ 805 0400; 12 Henry St
Occupying a huge block with entrances on Henry, Liffey and Abbey Sts, this is probably Dublin's best department store. It stocks virtually everything you could possibly want to buy, from garden furniture to high fashion, and everything is relatively affordable.

CLARK'S Map pp264–5   *Footwear*
☎ 872 1841; 25 Henry St
This well-known shoe store stocks not only its own brand but others too; it also has an excellent selection of Birkenstocks. The branch on O'Connell St (Map pp264–5; ☎ 872 7665; 43 O'Connell St) stocks women's shoes only.

CLERY'S & CO
Map pp264–5   *Department Store*
☎ 878 6000; O'Connell St
This elegant department store is Ireland's most famous retailer, a real Dublin classic. Recently restored to its graceful best, it has sought to shed its conservative reputation by filling its shelves with funkier labels to attract younger buyers.

DUBLIN WOOLLEN COMPANY
Map pp269–71   *Knitwear*
☎ 677 5014; 41 Lower Ormond Quay
Near the Ha'penny Bridge, this is one of the major wool outlets in Dublin. It has a large collection of sweaters, cardigans, scarves, rugs, shawls and other woollen goods, and runs a tax-free shopping scheme.

EASON'S Map pp264–5   *Bookshop*
☎ 873 3811; 40 Lower O'Connell St
Near the GPO, Eason's has a wide range of books and one of the biggest selections of magazines in Ireland.

JAPAN Map pp264–5   *Women's Fashion*
☎ 872 3193; 16 Henry St
Tight-fitting T-shirts, pencil skirts and other flesh-outlining cuts for trendy young women.

MARKS & SPENCER
Map pp264–5   *Department Store*
☎ 872 8833; 24-29 Mary St
A branch of the popular British department store; see p185 for details.

Out-of-the-Way Markets
If you're meandering in the southern suburbs, two weekend markets are worth keeping in mind.

Blackberry Fair (Map pp260–1; Lower Rathmines Rd; ⏰ 10am-6pm Sat & Sun) You'll have to root through a lot of rubbish to find a gem in this charmingly run-down weekend market that has furniture, records and a few clothes stalls. It's cheap, though.

Blackrock Market (Main St, Blackrock; ⏰ 11am-5.30pm Sat, 9am-5.30pm Sun) The long-running Blackrock Market in an old merchant house and yard in this seaside village has all manner of stalls selling everything from New Age crystals to futons.

PENNEY'S Map pp264–5   *Department Store*
☎ 888 0500; 47 Mary St
Ireland's cheapest department store is a northside favourite, a place to find all kinds of everything without paying a fortune for it. The stuff here isn't guaranteed to last, but at prices like these, why quibble over quality?

SCHUH Map pp269–71   *Footwear*
☎ 873 0621; 10 O'Connell St
Two floors of footwear, from trainers to formal shoes, and pretty much everything in-between. The labels represented here are of the High St variety, so don't expect Manolo or Gucci.

WALTON'S Map pp264–5   *Music*
☎ 874 7805; 2 North Frederick St
This is the main branch of the well-known Walton's music store (p190).

WINDING STAIR BOOKSHOP & CAFÉ

Map pp269–71   *Bookshop*

☎ 873 3292; 40 Lower Ormond Quay

This extraordinary bookshop is our favourite in the city, a browser's heaven that puts the premium on spreading the love of the written word rather than on shifting units. It stocks mostly second-hand books, but there is a pretty interesting selection of new books too. There is also an excellent café upstairs (see p152).

Smithfield & Phoenix Park

West of Capel St, there's little to hold your interest save the newish Jervis Centre (see the boxed text on p182). Capel St itself has plenty of shops, but they mostly sell cheap furniture and camping surplus supply.

THE MODEL SHOP

Map pp264–5   *Miniatures*

☎ 872 8134; 13 Capel St

Model enthusiasts can find a host of Dublin vehicles here, from old delivery vans bearing Irish household names to early 20th-century fire engines. The collection of lead European soldiers down through the ages is superbly crafted.

TOP SHOP Map pp269–71   *Mixed Fashion*

☎ 878 0477; Jervis Centre

This is the main Dublin branch of the extremely popular London fashion outlet, which specialises in replicating catwalk styles and selling them at affordable prices.

WATERSTONE'S Map pp269–71   *Bookshop*

☎ 878 1311; Jervis Centre

This is a branch of the well-known British bookshop (see p186).

Sleeping

Sleeping

Where you sleep is one of the more important decisions you'll make while you're in Dublin, as it will play a part in dictating the kind of time you'll have. Short-term visitors will undoubtedly want to stay close to the action, in the heart of the city centre. You'll pay more for the privilege, but besides the obvious advantage of central location, you will avoid the potential nightmare of transport to and from the suburbs. Public transport is slow, and, more importantly, virtually non-existent after midnight. That leaves you relying on taxis, which can be a nightmare to grab. Yet some of the city's most distinctive properties are in the suburbs immediately south of the city, which will have you relying on some form of motorised transport if you can't handle a 20-minute walk.

Dublin has its fair share of large, swanky hotels, many of which have opened their doors (usually with the help of a uniformed bellhop) only in the last 10 years. Most of these are affiliated to the world's most celebrated hotel chains, and while they offer substantial luxury, there's usually a whiff of corporate homogeneity in the carefully ventilated air. The city's traditional hotels, in an effort not to be muscled out by these new superhotels, have gone to great lengths to make improvements to their look and services; the best of these have done so without losing their local identity.

These days, hotel connoisseurs the world over have discovered the more intimate but equally luxurious boutique hotel, where the personal touch is maintained through less rooms, each of which is given lavish attention. Dublin's town houses and guesthouses – usually beautiful Georgian homes converted into lodgings – are this city's version of the boutique hotel, and there are some truly outstanding ones to choose from.

Top Five Boutique Hotels

Take a traditional town house, add a modern twist and you get Dublin's version of a boutique hotel. Sound easy? Well it ain't that simple. Many try, some succeed, but only a few do it to as near perfection as possible. Our top tips are:

- **Number 31** (p200) Designed by Ireland's most famous modern architect, this place is simply unique.
- **Browne's Townhouse** (p198) A Georgian restoration piece that is just a cut above the rest.
- **Pembroke Townhouse** (p202) This modern interpretation of the Georgian aesthetic beautifully combines comfort and luxury.
- **Schoolhouse Hotel** (p202) Bedding down in a converted Victorian schoolhouse…if only the students had such luxury.
- **Townhouse** (p206) A literary fantasy becomes one of the most interesting and out-there lodgings in town.

Dublin's B&Bs, basically town houses without the trimmings, have always been a favourite with visitors from all over, but they too have felt the pressure from above and many have undergone substantial refurbishments in an effort to cater to the increasingly discerning needs of the modern visitor. Fresh linen, hot water throughout the day, and a choice of Irish or continental breakfast are par for the course these days.

Finally, in a city that has undergone a dramatic tourist revolution, budget options are few and far between, and if you want to stay anywhere close to the city centre, you'll have to settle for a hostel. Thankfully, most of these maintain a pretty high standard of hygiene and comfort. Many offer various sleeping arrangements, ranging from a bed in a large dorm to a four-bed room or a double. There are plenty to choose from, but they tend to fill up very quickly and stay full.

Checkout at most establishments is noon, but some of the smaller guesthouses and B&Bs require that you check out a little earlier, usually around 11am.

For more information on accommodation see p233.

Price Ranges

Accommodation prices vary according to season, peaking during the summer months (April to September) and during holidays – particularly the week around St Patrick's Day (17 March), Easter and Christmas. At other times prices are generally lower, but not always substantially so. For budget accommodation (usually a hostel), you can expect to pay up to €29 per person per night. For a mid-range hotel, B&B or guesthouse, expect to fork out between €30 and €75 per person per night. At the top of the scale are the luxury hotels where you won't get much change out of €150 per person per night. You can try to bargain, but it won't make any real difference: if you don't want the room at the quoted price there are plenty of others who do.

While cheap sleeps are a thing of the past, the glut of new hotels has made the market a pretty competitive one, and the bigger hotels slug it out by offering a panoply of special offers, rack rates and other deals. Generally speaking, corporate hotels are cheaper at weekends than mid-week, as their main focus is attracting the business customer. In smaller establishments, no such arrangements exist, but you can usually get a rate for stays of more than two nights.

Bookings

Finding a bed is pretty tough in any price range, especially between April and September. If you can make a reservation, it will make life easier. The alternative is to go to one of the Dublin Tourism offices (see p243) and ask the staff to book you a room. For €4 (€7 for self-service accommodation) plus a 10% deposit on the cost of the first night, they'll find you somewhere to stay, and will do so efficiently and with a smile. Sometimes this may require a great deal of phoning around, so it can be money well spent. If you're travelling with a big group of friends, you might have problems checking into a hotel in Temple Bar, as some of these have been put off large groups by the loud and messy stag and hen parties that have plagued the area. For details of online booking services, see p243.

Long-Term Rentals

Finding long-term accommodation in Dublin is difficult for Dubliners, never mind visitors from abroad. Fáilte Ireland's **Ireland's Reservation Service** (☎ 1800 668 668; www.gulliver.ie) specialises in reserving accommodation. However, while it can find places for up to six months or even a year, it charges a non-refundable deposit of 10% of the total price.

There are several lettings agencies in Dublin. **Abbott & Matthews Letting & Management** (Map pp269-71; ☎ 679 2434; www.abbottmatthews.com; 40 Dame St) specialises in long and short-term leases of apartments and houses, furnished or unfurnished. One-bedroom apartments rent for between €760 and €1200 per month. **Home Locators** (Map pp272-3; ☎ 679 5233; www.homelocators.ie; 35 Dawson St) has a wide selection of properties on its books. It charges a €10 registration fee and then helps you locate suitable accommodation.

A few British newspapers, notably the *Daily Telegraph*, carry advertisements for long-term rentals in Dublin.

Self-Catering Accommodation

The self-catering option is becoming increasingly popular with many travellers, especially families with small children. Considering the relatively high price of the city's hotels, it often makes sound financial sense, as well as offering the possibility of a home away from home. In the city centre, all self-catering options consist of one- or two-bedroom apartments, which usually also include a sitting room, bathroom and a separate kitchen.

Gogarty's Temple Bar Apartments (Map pp269-71; ☎ 671 1822; www.olivergogartys.com; 18-21 Anglesea St; 4-bed apartment €160-180) Run by the same folk who own the hostel (p203) in Temple Bar, these fully fitted apartments include bedrooms with bathroom, dining room, lounge and a balcony. Cots can be provided upon request.

Molesworth Court Suites (Map pp272-3; ☎ 676 4799; www.molesworthcourt.ie; 35 Schoolhouse Lane; apartments €160-350) One- to three-bedroom suites in prime location just off Kildare St, near Dáil Éireann. Designed and furnished in a thoroughly contemporary fashion, it offers all mod-cons.

SOUTH OF THE LIFFEY

The vast majority of visitors to the city try to base themselves on Dublin's south side. Who can blame them? Not only is the south side the true 'centre' of the city, but it has most of the amenities of interest to the tourist, from nightlife to shopping. Accommodations are varied and plentiful, but so is the demand, which has reduced budget options to dorms in a hostel.

Around Grafton Street

Grafton St itself only has one hotel, and there isn't a lot to choose from in the immediate area around it. The choice may not be great, but the quality is top notch.

GRAFTON CAPITAL HOTEL

Map pp272–3   *Hotel*
☎ 475 0888; www.capital-hotels.com; Lower Stephen's St; r from €100; Ⓟ

Hardly recognisable as such today, but this centrally located hotel just off Grafton St is actually a couple of converted Georgian town houses. Its 75 modern, air-con rooms are designed along the lines of function before form, which makes them perfect for the weekend visitor who wants to bed down somewhere central and still keep some credit-card space for a good night out.

MERCER HOTEL Map pp272–3   *Hotel*
☎ 478 2179; www.mercerhotel.ie; Lower Mercer St; s/d €105/170; Ⓟ

Not a stone's throw from Grafton St, the Mercer looks fairly ordinary from the outside, but the largish air-con rooms are light and airy, with antique furniture that give them an elegant, classical look. Outside of the high season, the room prices are slashed to about half.

LA STAMPA HOTEL Map pp272–3   *Hotel*
☎ 677 4444; www.lastampa.ie; 35 Dawson St; s/d from €100/135; Ⓟ

La Stampa is a wonderful, atmospheric little hotel on trendy Dawson St. The theme is contemporary Asian, and its 24 white, air-con rooms are adorned with Oriental rattan furniture and exotic velvet throws. First and foremost a restaurant (see p133), the rooms are a recent addition, and there at the top of two flights of steep stairs. The climbing disadvantage aside, this new spot is excellent value for its superb location.

WESTBURY HOTEL Map pp272–3   *Hotel*
☎ 679 1122; www.jurysdoyle.com; Grafton St; s/d/ste from €330/370/750; Ⓟ

Overlooking Grafton St in perhaps the city's best location, this is easily one of Dublin's most luxurious and sophisticated hotels. Hardly surprising then that it is a favourite with visiting celebrities, who naturally opt for a suite – where they can watch TV from the Jacuzzi before retiring to a four-poster bed.

Temple Bar

For many visitors to Dublin, Temple Bar is the perfect spot to base themselves. Right on top of the action, as it were, and in the heart of where it is all at. Inevitably, hoteliers know this and take full advantage. With very few exceptions, you'll get less for your money here than almost anywhere else in the city. On the plus side, budget travellers can choose from a selection of hostels.

ASTON HOTEL Map pp269–71   *Hotel*
☎ 677 9300; www.aston-hotel.com; 7-9 Aston Quay; s/d €70/135

This hotel makes big use of pine furniture and primary colours, which give the public spaces and rooms a fairly light, modern air. Like so many of Temple Bar's lodgings, it's a little on the bland side, but what it lacks in character it more than makes up for in location. Parking is by arrangement with a local car park.

CLARENCE HOTEL Map pp269–71   *Hotel*
☎ 407 0800; www.theclarence.ie; 6-8 Wellington Quay; r €300-320, ste €615-2100; Ⓟ

There's no questioning the appeal of this celebrity-rich hotel, beautifully positioned over the Liffey. The mere fact that it's owned by Bono and the Edge of U2 has made it one of the most popular destinations for visiting rock and movie stars, who invariably opt for the penthouse suite – we're guessing that the rooftop hot tub has seen its fair share of fun – and its stunning views over the city. The other half generally opt for a standard room, which though elegantly decorated and adorned with artwork by Bono's buddy Guggi (formerly of Irish cult band the Virgin Prunes), tend to be on the smallish side. It's one of the hottest beds in town for sure, but we suspect that what you're really paying for is the hype.

ELIZA LODGE Map pp269–71   *Guesthouse*
☎ 671 8044; www.dublinlodge.com;
23-24 Wellington Quay; s/d/ste €76/177/228
It's priced like a hotel, looks like a hotel, but
it's still a guesthouse. Its 18 bedrooms are
fabulous; the owners have taken great care
to maximise space and comfort. The doubles
and suites have wraparound windows with
180° views of the Liffey and the Millennium
Bridge below.

IRISH LANDMARK TRUST
Map pp269–71   *Self-Catering*
☎ 670 4733; www.irishlandmark.com;
25 Eustace St; 1/3 nights from €275/695
This fabulous heritage house, originally built in
1720, has been gloriously restored to the highest standard by the Irish Landmark Trust charity. You have this unique house all to yourself,
which sleeps up to seven in its double, twin
and triple bedrooms for one or any number
of nights. Furnished with tasteful antiques,
authentic furniture and fittings (including a
grand piano in the drawing room), this kind
of period rental accommodation is rare and
something really unique. You do not need to
be a member of the Trust to rent it.

MORGAN HOTEL
Map pp269–71   *Boutique Hotel*
☎ 679 3939; www.themorgan.com;
10 Fleet St; s/d/ste from €126/215/490
The relatively new Morgan is a boutique hotel
on the edge of Temple Bar. Its all-cream, con-
temporary-designed rooms are on the small
side, with furnishings that look a bit tired for

the price, but on the plus side, come equipped
with satellite TV, video, stereo and minibar. The
duplex Morgan Suite is the latest in designer
cool, with a gilded silver leaf mirror by Carl
Booth and a Pascal Morgue double bed.
Aromatherapy treatments and massages are
extra, as is breakfast (€17.70).

PARAMOUNT HOTEL Map pp269–71   *Hotel*
☎ 417 9900; www.paramounthotel.ie;
Parliament St & Essex Gate; s/d €140/200; P
Behind the Victorian facade is a genuine recreation of a 1930s-style hotel, complete with
stained-wood floors, deep-red leather couches
and heavy velvet drapes. The 70 rooms are
decorated along similar lines, with plenty of
dark wood and subtle colours. Downstairs is
the Turk's Head (p159), one of the area's most
popular bars. Highly recommended.

WESTIN DUBLIN Map pp269–71   *Hotel*
☎ 645 1000; www.westin.com;
Westmoreland St; r from €340; P
The Westin began life as an Allied Irish Bank,
and while much of the old building was gutted
to make way for this fabulous new hotel, the
old bank vaults have been converted into the
basement Mint Bar. The air-con rooms, many
of which overlook a beautiful atrium, are decorated in elegant mahogany and soft colours
that are reminiscent of the USA's finest hotels.
You sleep on the 10 layers of the Westin's own
trademark Heavenly Bed, which is damn comfortable indeed. The hotel's most elegant room
is the former banking hall, complete with gold
leaf plasterwork on the ceiling, now used for
banquets. Breakfast will set you back €25.

SoDa

West of Grafton St and around South Great George's St is an area very much in development. Yet it's an area that's perfect: close to Grafton St, Stephen's Green and Temple Bar. There are a number of good choices here, offering a mix of plain guesthouses to deluxe hotels and one of the city's most popular hostels.

BROOKS HOTEL Map pp272–3   *Hotel*
☎ 670 4000; www.sinnotthotels.com;
59-62 Drury St; s/d from €190/245; **P**

Located a one-minute walk west of Grafton St, Brooks Hotel is a small, plush place where the emphasis is on familial, friendly service. Decor is nouveau classic with high-veneer panelled walls, decorative bookcases and old-fashioned sofas, while bedrooms have air-con, are extremely comfortable and fitted out in subtly coloured furnishings. The clincher for us though are the king- and superking-size beds in all rooms, complete with…a pillow menu. Go figure.

CAMDEN COURT HOTEL
Map pp266–8   *Hotel*
☎ 475 9666; www.camdencourthotel.com;
Lower Camden St; s/d from €140/240; **P**

About 500m from St Stephen's Green, this enormous hotel is a favourite with business travellers, who care little for the standardised, air-conditioned rooms (which are big and bland), but make full use of the hotel's amenities, which include a 16m swimming pool, health club

(with Jacuzzi, sauna and steam room) and a fully equipped gym.

CENTRAL HOTEL Map pp272–3   *Hotel*
☎ 679 7302; www.centralhotel.ie;
1-5 Exchequer St; s/d €95/150; **P**

The rooms at this appositely named hotel are a modern version of Edwardian luxury: heavy velvet curtains and custom-made Irish furnishings (including beds with draped backboards) fit a little too snugly into the space afforded them, but they lend a touch of class. Note that street-facing rooms can get a little noisy. The Library Bar, with its leather armchairs and roaring fireplaces, is also one of the best spots to relax in with a drink or a cup of tea. Rooms are cheaper midweek.

GRAFTON GUESTHOUSE
Map pp272–3   *Guesthouse*
☎ 679 2041; graftonguesthouse@eircom.net;
26-27 South Great George's St; s/d from €65/120

In a Gothic-style building just off Dame St over the George's St Arcade, this friendly guesthouse has 16 bright rooms, with private bathroom, if you don't mind the slightly faded chintzy decor.

Georgian Dublin

Dublin's most desirable real estate lies roughly in the area from St Stephen's Green south to the Grand Canal. Dublin's Georgian elegance is most obvious here, and it is central enough to be considered at the heart of the city. Not surprisingly, most of Dublin's best and luxurious hotels are in the area. You'll pay upwards of €100 for even a basic room, although there are some excellent choices to make your expense worthwhile.

BROWNE'S TOWNHOUSE
Map pp272–3   *Boutique Hotel*
☎ 638 3939; www.brownesdublin.com; 22-23 St Stephen's Green; s/d €185/255, ste €400-500

This exquisite Georgian home is one of the city's best boutique hotels, a slice of country house in the middle of the city. The elegant country theme is pursued throughout; each of the rooms has a rustic, four-poster bed and stylish antique furniture. The fabulous Thomas Leighton Suite is top of the lot, and successfully recreates the kind of style and plush comfort enjoyed by the 18th-century's rich and powerful – plus central heating, electricity and proper piping. Below is the excellent Browne's Brasserie (p137).

BUSWELL'S HOTEL Map pp266–8 *Hotel*
☎ 676 4013, 661 3888; www.quinnhotels.com; 23-27 Molesworth St; s/d €146/220; P

In business since 1882, this elegant hotel – made up of five Georgian town houses – is a Dublin institution. Like the Shelbourne (p200), it has a long association with politicians, who wander across the road from Dáil Éireann to wet their beaks at the hotel bar. The 69 bedrooms have all been given the once-over, but the owners have thankfully resisted the temptation to contemporise the furnishings and have left its Georgian charm more or less intact. A fully equipped workout room was added in 2003.

CLARION STEPHEN'S HALL HOTEL & SUITES Map pp266–8 *Serviced Apartments*
☎ 638 1111; www.premgroup.ie; 14-17 Lower Leeson St; s/d €199/250; P

Near the southeastern corner of St Stephen's Green, this excellent hotel incorporates 37 self-contained, air-con suites consisting of a bedroom, living room, bathroom and fully equipped kitchenette. Each suite also comes with a fax machine, modem point and CD player. Its primary clientele are business people. Breakfast is not included.

CONRAD DUBLIN Map pp266–8 *Hotel*
☎ 602 8900; www.conradhotels.com; Earlsfort Tce; r €240; P

Dublin's first truly international business hotel has not rested on its laurels. Services are being constantly refined – the latest addition is a state-of-the-art fitness centre – and the air-con, king-size bedrooms are equipped to suit every business need. The front-facing rooms overlook the National Concert Hall, one of the city's most beautiful Georgian buildings. The hotel offers a dizzying array of special rates – room prices are often slashed by half – for both business and leisure travellers.

DAVENPORT HOTEL Map pp266–8 *Hotel*
☎ 607 3500; www.ocallaghanhotels.com; Merrion Sq; r from €150; P

Located in Merrion Hall, built in 1863 for the religious Plymouth Brethren, this fine and elegant hotel has 115 rooms tailored to suit the needs of the business visitor (voicemail, ISDN line, and European and American sockets are standard), but is also a good option for the leisure traveller. The rooms have air-con, are large and comfortable, and all feature orthopaedic beds. There's a well-equipped gym downstairs.

FITZWILLIAM HOTEL Map pp272–3 *Hotel*
☎ 478 7000; www.fitzwilliam-hotel.com; St Stephen's Green; r from €165; P

This ultramodern hotel is all about contemporary chic (the interior was designed by Sir Terence Conran's CD partnership group), which supposedly seeks to calm and relax the guests. Soothing colour schemes (lots of off-white), sleek modern furniture and slightly disconcerting modern bathrooms with an 18th-century look may win designer awards, but it left us a little cold. There's no denying the luxury however, or its popularity with its chi-chi clientele. The top floor is home to one of the city's best restaurants, Thornton's (p147).

Top Five Hotel Bars

You don't have to be a high-paying guest to enjoy the luxury of a fancy hotel bar. The best places in town to be seen with a cocktail in hand are:

- **The Shelbourne** (p200) Afternoon tea at this sumptuous hotel is a Dublin institution, while the Horseshoe Bar (p160) is a long-time favourite with politicos.
- **Clarence Hotel** (p196) No-one cares that the service in the Octagon Bar (p158) is appalling, so long as they stand a chance of spotting owner Bono and his gang of celebrity pals.
- **Fitzwilliam Hotel** (above) Elegant, cool and sophisticated, the Fitzwilliam is a favourite watering hole with Dublin's young style brigade.
- **Central Hotel** (opposite) The 2nd-floor Library Bar is one of the most beautiful rooms in town, a genuine Victorian Edwardian drawing room.
- **Westbury Hotel** (p196) Ignored by most, it is probably the reason why visiting celebs feel comfortable relaxing in this large and beautiful bar.

GEORGIAN HOUSE

Map pp266–8   *Boutique Hotel*
☎ 661 8832; hotel@georgianhouse.ie;
18-22 Lower Baggot St; s/d €140/150; P

This fine 200-year-old Georgian building has 47 thoroughly modern rooms, courtesy of a major restoration that has made this one of the best boutique hotels in the area, successfully combining the intimacy of a guesthouse with the luxury of a high-end hotel. Breakfast (€15) is not included.

HARRINGTON HALL

Map pp266–8   *Guesthouse*
☎ 475 3497; www.harringtonhall.com;
69-70 Harcourt St; s/d €/120/170; P

Formerly the home of a Lord Mayor of Dublin, this fine Georgian home has recently been transformed into a smart guesthouse whose rooms stand out for their understated elegance. The traditional Georgian style has been retained, particularly in the ornamental ceilings and sturdy fireplaces of the 1st- and 2nd-floor rooms.

LONGFIELD'S Map pp266–8 *Boutique Hotel*
☎ 676 1367; www.longfields.ie;
9-10 Lower Fitzwilliam St; s/d from €120/190

This 26-room hotel between Merrion and Fitzwilliam Sqs is a little slice of Georgian heaven. The feel is more of a private home than a commercial property, as each room is carefully decorated with period antiques, beautiful fabrics and elegant fittings. The rooms on the lower floors are bigger than the ones above, and some have four-poster or half-tester beds.

LE MÉRIDIEN SHELBOURNE

Map pp266–8   *Hotel*
☎ 676 6471; www.shelbourne.ie;
27 St Stephen's Green; s/d from €305/325; P

Founded in 1824, the famous Shelbourne (aficionados *never* refer to it by its new, clumsier name) remains one of Dublin's best addresses and still retains its enduring old-world grandeur. Rooms are spacious and very comfortable with every modern facility. The Irish Constitution was first drafted here in 1922, and to this day politicians and hacks can be spotted telling lies and swigging malt in its Horseshoe Bar (p160). For the more salubrious, the leisure centre and swimming pool provide a healthy alternative. Afternoon cream teas in the drawing room, overlooking St Stephen's Green, are one of the highlights of a visit to the city.

MERRION Map pp266–8 *Hotel*
☎ 603 0600; www.merrionhotel.com; Upper Merrion St; s/d €300/325, ste €670-2400; P

Arthur Wellesley, the Duke of Wellington, once famously declared that just because one is born in a stable doesn't make one a horse (see p85). Wellesley's 'stable' is one of three magnificent Georgian town houses that in 1997 was converted into this superb five-star hotel that ranks among the city's very best. Crisp Frette linen, Irish fabrics and specially commissioned Kenneth Turner amenities create a marvellous blend of modern convenience and 18th-century opulence. The Tethra Spa is a little slice of imperial Rome – updated to suit modern tastes. Ask for a room in the old house rather than the newer Garden Wing at the back.

NUMBER 31 Map pp266–8 *Boutique Hotel*
☎ 676 5011; www.number31.ie; 31 Leeson Cl; s/d/tr from €100/120/165

Number 31 could be a set from the zeitgeist film *The Ice Storm*. The coach house and former home of modernist architect Sam Stephenson (see p47) still feels like a real 1960s home intact, with its sunken sitting room, leather sofas, mirrored bar, Perspex lamps and ceiling

Sunken lounge, Number 31

to floor windows. A hidden oasis of calm, a five-minute walk from St Stephen's Green, this is one of our favourite places to stay in Dublin. Its 21 bedrooms are split between the retro coach house with its fancy rooms and the more gracious Georgian house, through the garden, where rooms are individually furnished with tasteful French antiques and big comfortable beds. Gourmet breakfasts with kippers, home-made breads and granola are served in the conservatory.

O'NEILL'S TOWNHOUSE
Map pp266–8   *Pub*
☎ 671 4074; www.oneillsdublin.com;
36-37 Pearse St; dm/d €35/100
There's only one thing better than living above a pub. Living in one. The pub in question – where you'll have to settle for the first option – is O'Neill's, a Victorian beauty that is a long-time favourite with the students of Trinity College next door. The eight rooms above the pub are no doubt snug and decorated without too much imagination, but they're warm and cosy; most importantly, the owners are friendly and very helpful. It's central and very convenient.

STAUNTON'S ON THE GREEN
Map pp266–8   *Guesthouse*
☎ 478 2300; stauntononthegreen@eircom.net;
83 St Stephen's Green; s/d/tr €96/152/210
Enviably located right on St Stephen's Green, Staunton's is an upmarket guesthouse with handsome Georgian-style rooms, including floor-to-ceiling windows with views over the Green to the front and a private garden at the back; the latter is a real plus, especially in good weather, as it affords a little bit of pastoral serenity smack in the middle of the city.

STEPHEN'S GREEN HOTEL
Map pp266–8   *Hotel*
☎ 607 3600; www.ocallaghanhotels.com;
St Stephen's Green; s/d €250/300; P
Past the strikingly impressive glass-fronted lobby of this relatively new hotel are 75 thoroughly modern hotel rooms that make full use of the visual impact of primary colours, most notably red and blue. This is a business hotel *par excellence*; everything here is what you'd expect from a top international hotel (including a gym and a business centre), but what you won't find elsewhere is the marvellous view of St Stephen's Green below.

Kilmainham & the Liberties
Accommodation is a little thin on the ground west of Christchurch, as the Liberties remain a traditional working-class enclave that have so far resisted the tug of gentrification.

JURY'S INN CHRISTCHURCH
Map pp266–8   *Hotel*
☎ 454 0000; www.jurysdoyle.com; Christ Church Pl;
r from €96; P
This hotel has 182 anodyne rooms, each of which accommodates up to three adults or two adults and two children. It's a long-standing favourite with Irish business travellers and families, who care little for the standardised style but pay attention to position – the front-facing rooms have sensational views of Christ Church Cathedral (p91) – and price. There's also a covered car park (€10 per day).

Beyond the Grand Canal
Some of the most beautiful hotels and guesthouses in the city lie south of the Grand Canal in the elegant residential neighbourhoods of Ballsbridge and Donnybrook. These are the best examples of Dublin's take on the boutique hotel.

ARIEL HOUSE Map pp260–1   *B&B*
☎ 668 5512; www.ariel-house.net; 52 Lansdowne Rd; s/d €105/130; bus 5, 7, 7A, 8, 18 & 45 from Trinity College; P
With 28 rooms, all with own bathroom, this is hardly your average B&B, but not many B&Bs are listed Victorian homes that have been given top rating by Fáilte Ireland either. Recently restored to its 19th-century elegance, every room is individually decorated with period furniture, which lends the place an air of genuine luxury. Ariel House beats almost any hotel.

BERKELEY COURT Map pp260–1   *Hotel*
☎ 660 1711; www.jurysdoyle.com; Lansdowne Rd;
s/d from €313/333; bus 5, 7, 7A, 8, 18 & 45 from Trinity College; P
This upmarket hotel, southeast of the city centre, in the leafy suburb of Ballsbridge, caters mainly to business travellers. Its decor is firmly traditional while kitted out to the highest standard, and rooms offer every modern amenity. Check the website for special offers, because at the time of writing, rooms were selling for less than half the quoted rate.

BURLINGTON Map pp260–1   *Hotel*
☎ 660 5222; www.jurysdoyle.com; Upper Leeson St; s/d €223/249; bus 5, 7, 7A, 8, 18 & 45 from Trinity College; **P**

With 506 rooms, the Burlington ranks as Ireland's largest hotel, but prides itself on its familial welcome. A traditional place, it's popular with tour groups and Americans. Like its sister hotel, the Berkeley Court, it's well worth checking the website for significant discounts.

HIBERNIAN HOTEL Map pp266–8   *Hotel*
☎ 668 7666; www.hibernianhotel.com; Eastmoreland Pl; r €222-277.50; bus 5, 7, 7A, 8, 18 & 45 from Trinity College

The Hibernian is a charming, homey but luxurious little hotel in a quiet cul-de-sac off Baggot St in Ballsbridge. Dating from 1890, the Victorian building used to be the nurse's home attached to nearby Baggot St hospital. Rooms towards the back seem to be more spacious, but all are cosily furnished in a traditional way, and have cable TV, dataports and lovely bathrooms.

MERRION HALL
Map pp260–1   *Boutique Hotel*
☎ 668 1426; www.halpinsprivatehotels.com; 54 Merrion Rd, Ballsbridge; s/d €99/129, ste €199-249; bus 5, 7, 7A, 8, 18 & 45 from Trinity College; **P**

This ivy-clad Edwardian house, directly across the street from the Royal Dublin Showground, has 12 superbly appointed rooms, each decorated with restored period furniture. The suites have four-poster beds and whirlpool baths. A nice touch in all the rooms are the aromatherapeutic toiletries, a far cry from the usual savonettes. It's close to a DART station.

MESPIL HOTEL Map pp266–8   *Hotel*
☎ 667 1222; www.leehotels.ie; Mespil Rd; r from €135; bus 5, 7, 7A, 8, 18 & 45 from Trinity College; **P**

Nicely located on the banks of the Grand Canal, this large, rather plain hotel has bigger-than-average, comfortable rooms at a very reasonable rate. Ask for one of the bright rooms at the front and on the top floor where, because of the hotel's origin as a government office block, windows are massive and offer great views of the canal and city centre. There are plenty of disabled-access rooms. The hotel offers special discounted rates in winter and it's a 10-minute walk from St Stephen's Green, along Baggot St.

PEMBROKE TOWNHOUSE
Map pp266–8   *Boutique Hotel*
☎ 660 0277; www.pembroketownhouse.ie; 90 Pembroke Rd; s/d €131/196; bus 5, 7, 7A, 8, 18 & 45 from Trinity College; **P**

This superluxurious town house is a wonderful example of what happens when traditional and modern combine to great effect. A classical Georgian house has been transformed into a modern boutique hotel, with each room carefully appointed to reflect the best of contemporary design and style, right down to the modern art on the walls and the lift to the upper floors. The breakfast here really is exceptional.

SCHOOLHOUSE HOTEL
Map pp266–8   *Boutique Hotel*
☎ 667 5014; www.schoolhousehotel.com; 2-8 Northumberland Rd; s/d €159/199; bus 5, 7, 7A, 8, 18 & 45 from Trinity College; **P**

A Victorian schoolhouse dating from 1861, this beautiful building has been successfully converted into an exquisite boutique hotel that is (ahem) ahead of its class. The 31 rooms, each named after a famous Irish writer, are simply top notch and combine an old-world elegance with more modern requirements, such as ISDN lines and satellite TV. The bathrooms come with power showers, gorgeous bathrobes and luxury toiletries.

WATERLOO HOUSE
Map pp260–1   *Guesthouse*
☎ 660 1888; www.waterloohouse.ie; 8-10 Waterloo Rd; s/d €82/164; bus 5, 7, 7A, 8, 18 & 45 from Trinity College; **P**

A short walk from St Stephen's Green, off Baggot St, this lovely guesthouse is spread over two ivy-clad Georgian houses. Rooms are tastefully decorated with high-quality furnishings in authentic, Farrow & Ball Georgian colours, and all have cable TV and kettles. Home-cooked breakfast is served in the conservatory or garden on sunny days.

Cheap Sleeps
Besides hostels and the universities, there's no such thing as cheap accommodation on Dublin's south side. Campus accommodation is only available out of term, between June and September. The listed hostels are all above standard; their quality and location make them very, very popular.

ASHFIELD HOUSE Map pp269–71 *Hostel*
☎ 679 7734; ashfield@indigo.ie;
19-20 D'Olier St; dm/d/f from €15/46/80
A stone's throw from Temple Bar and O'Connell Bridge, this relatively new hostel has only one 14-bed dorm, with bathroom, but its 25 other rooms include four-bed family rooms as well as doubles. It feels more like a small hotel, without the price tag. Maximum stay is six nights.

AVALON HOUSE Map pp266–8 *Hostel*
☎ 475 0001; www.avalon-house.ie;
55 Aungier St; dm/s/d €17-30/34/64
This large hostel is housed in a listed building, formerly a Victorian medical school. Pine floors, high ceilings and large, open fireplaces set the ambience, which is elegant yet informal. Some of the cleverly designed rooms have mezzanine levels, which are great for families. It's one of the most popular hostels in the city, so book well in advance.

BARNACLES TEMPLE BAR HOUSE
Map pp269–71 *Hostel*
☎ 671 6277; www.barnacles.ie;
1 Cecilia St; dm/d from €17/38.50
Bright and spacious, in the heart of Temple Bar, this hostel is immaculately clean, has nicely laid-out dorms and doubles with private bathrooms and that rare beast – in-room storage. Because of its location, rooms are quieter at the back. Top facilities, comfy lounge (with an open fire), and linen and towels provided. Probably the best hostel south of the river. The hostel has a discount deal with a nearby covered car park.

BREWERY HOSTEL Map pp262–3 *Hostel*
☎ 453 8600; breweryh@indigo.ie; 22-23 Thomas St;
dm/d €24/60; bus 68, 68A, 69A & 78A from Dame St; Ⓟ
A small, family-run hostel, right at the doorstep of Guinness Brewery. It has five bedrooms and seven dorms with wooden bunks, all with bathroom. There's a little patio to the rear with a barbecue area.

DUBLIN CITY UNIVERSITY (DCU) *Campus Residence*
☎ 704 5736; campus.residences@dcu.ie; Larkfield Apartments, Campus Residences, Dublin City University, Glasnevin; r per person €25-35; bus 11, 11A, 11B, 13, 13A, 19, 19A, 36 & 36A from Trinity College/Eden Quay; ☽ mid-Jun–mid-Sep
Only 15 minutes by bus or car from the city centre, these rooms at DCU's Glasnevin campus are airy and spacious, with plenty of amenities at hand, including a kitchen and common rooms.

GOGARTY'S TEMPLE BAR HOSTEL
Map pp269–71 *Hostel*
☎ 671 1822; www.olivergogartys.com;
18-21 Anglesea St; dm from €21, d with/without bathroom €40/35; Ⓟ
Next door to the popular Left Bank bar and Vault nightclub, this place isn't really one for a quiet sleep; most of the guests are here to party, and the hostel's location and attitude completely encourages them. When everything eventually closes, you collapse (preferably drunk) into functional dorm rooms with bathrooms, solid wooden bunks and clean linen.

Worth the Trip
Kingswood Country House (☎ 459 2428; www .kingswoodcountryhouse.com; Naas Rd, Clondalkin, Dublin 22; s/d €90/125; bus 69 & 69X from Dame St; Ⓟ) You don't have to travel miles outside of Dublin to stay in a genuine country house hotel. Just off the busy (and ugly) Naas Rd is this gorgeous 280-year-old property – once the home of Irish tenor Joseph Locke (he of the movie *Hear My Song*) – tucked away in its own walled gardens. The seven rooms all have private bathrooms and are decorated in traditional country house fashion: thick duvet covers, plenty of warm lighting, flower-print wallpaper and low, intimate ceilings. If you have your own transport and fancy a bit of peace and quiet, this place is highly recommended. By the time you read this it will be linked to the city via Line A of the LUAS.

HARRINGTON HOUSE HOSTEL
Map pp260–1 *Hostel*
☎ 475 4008; www.hubandhouse.ie; 21 Harrington St; s/d; bus 16A from Dublin Airport/Dame St; dm/d from €25/80; Ⓟ
Plenty of pine and colourful materials set the tone at this friendly hostel, which has a mix of private rooms and small four-bed dorms. It's on leafy Harrington St, one of the city centre's most elegant streets, about 600m southwest of St Stephen's Green.

KINLAY HOUSE Map pp269–71 *Hostel*
☎ 679 6644; www.kinlayhouse.ie;
2-12 Lord Edward St; dm/d from €16/30
An institution among the city's hostels, this former boarding house for boys has massive,

mixed 24-bed dorms as well as smaller rooms. Its bustling location next to Christ Church Cathedral and Dublin Castle is a bonus, but some rooms suffer from traffic noise. There are cooking facilities and a café; and breakfast is included. Not for the faint-hearted.

MERCER COURT CAMPUS ACCOMMODATION

Map pp272–3 *Campus Residence*
☎ 478 0328; www.mercercourt.ie; Lower Mercer St; s/d €52.50/82; ⌚ 26 Jun-26 Sep
Owned and run by the Royal College of Surgeons, this is the most luxurious student-accommodation option in the city: cheaper than Trinity but just as central, close to Grafton St and St Stephen's Green. The rooms are modern and up to hotel standard.

TRINITY COLLEGE

Map pp266–8 *Campus Residence*
☎ 608 1177; reservations@tcd.ie; Accommodations Office, Trinity College; r per person €39-61.50; ⌚ 14 Jun-27 Sep; Ⓟ
The closest thing to living like a student at this stunningly beautiful university is crashing in their rooms when they're on holidays. The location is second-to-none, and the rooms are large and extremely comfortable. Rooms and two-bed apartments in the newer block have their own bathrooms; the others in the older (and more beautiful) blocks have to share, though there are private sinks. Breakfast is included.

NORTH OF THE LIFFEY

Except for a couple of grand hotels that date from a time when O'Connell St and Parnell Sq were the epicentre of Dublin life, for many years most of the accommodation on the city's north side paled in comparison to their southerly neighbours. Not anymore. As the south side becomes more and more congested, hoteliers of every taste have taken to rebuilding the north side's battered image, and today you will find a large selection of excellent guesthouses and hotels in areas that until recently were deemed less than salubrious. Even Gardiner St, for years full of dilapidated B&Bs, has gone to great lengths to meet the more exacting needs of the modern traveller. Improvements notwithstanding, you will still get more for your money on the north side.

Around O'Connell Street

Dublin's most important thoroughfare has been through some tough decades, but things are looking up. The fancy hotels of yesteryear don't seem as out of place anymore, as the refurbishment of the street and its environs continues to gather momentum. In addition to the cleaned-up old classics, a number of excellent new hotels have made the area an interesting spot to bed down in again.

Further around O'Connell St you come to B&B land. Virtually every building on Gardiner St, which runs north from Connolly Station to the top of Mountjoy Sq, is a B&B. Until not so long ago, most of these were old and dusty, and some were downright fleapits. No more. A new attitude prevails, which puts the needs and demands of the modern visitor first. Although the whole area is being rejuvenated, we still advise you to exercise some caution, especially at night, around Upper Gardiner St and the area immediately around Connolly Station and Busáras, the central bus station.

ACADEMY HOTEL Map pp264–5 *Hotel*
☎ 878 0666; www.academy-hotel.com; Findalater Pl; s/d €99/134
This popular new hotel, just off Upper O'Connell St near Parnell Sq, has 98 modern rooms with all the basic amenities, including bathroom. It's a cheery place, with bright, light colours, even if the decor is a little too pastel and bland for our tastes. Guests get a parking discount (per day €14) at the nearby car park.

ANCHOR GUESTHOUSE

Map pp264–5 *Guesthouse*
☎ 878 613; www.anchorguesthouse.com; 49 Lower Gardiner St; s/d from €56/72
The Anchor has elegant, very comfortable rooms all with private bathroom. This lovely Georgian guesthouse with delicious wholesome breakfasts comes highly recommended by readers.

CASTLE HOTEL Map pp264–5 *Hotel*
☎ 874 6949; fax 872 7674; Great Denmark St; s/d/tr from €45/99/130
Established in 1809, the Castle Hotel claims to be Dublin's oldest and has been in the hands of only three families. Furnishings are likewise traditional and a tad antiquated throughout its

50 rooms, many of which are generous in size and retain their lovely Georgian cornicing and proportions. There's a fabulous *palazzo*-style grand staircase and the house, though rough around the edges, still feels like an authentic 19th-century home. Its owner, Fionn MacCumhaill, will happily regale you with local history from the bar.

CELTIC LODGE Map pp264–5   *Guesthouse*
☎ 677 9955; 81-82 Talbot St; s/d €65/70

This cheap and cheerful guesthouse situated above a pub has 29 simply furnished rooms. Because of the pub's live music below, you might want to ask for a room at the back if you'd rather not join in the sing-song from your bed.

CHARLES STEWART
Map pp264–5   *Guesthouse*
☎ 878 0350; www.charlesstewart.ie; 5-6 Parnell Sq; s/d/tr €65.50/89/120; **P**

Just north of O'Connell St, Oliver St John Gogarty's birthplace has been converted into the Charles Stewart, a large and functional guesthouse with 76 clean and spacious rooms. The ceilings are very high, but the bathrooms are small. Rooms in the new extension to the rear are huge and very quiet.

CLARION HOTEL Map pp264–5   *Hotel*
☎ 433 8800; www.clarionhotelifsc.com; Custom House Quay; r €235, ste €350-500; **P**

This swanky hotel in the heart of the Irish Financial Services Centre opened in 2001, and has earned nothing but praise for its elegance and sophistication. Almost exclusively geared to the business set, its rooms are quite beautiful, with contemporary light oak furnishings and a blue and taupe colour scheme that is supposed to relax the mind after a long day of meetings. We prefer to relax with a swim in the Sanovitae health club downstairs.

CLIFDEN GUESTHOUSE
Map pp264–5   *Guesthouse*
☎ 874 6364; www.clifdenhouse.com; 32 Gardiner Pl; s/d from €45/80; **P**

A great place to stay in the area, the Clifden is a very nicely refurbished Georgian house with 14 tastefully decorated rooms. They all come with bathroom, are immaculately clean and extremely comfortable. A nice touch is the free parking, even after you've checked out!

GRESHAM HOTEL Map pp264–5   *Hotel*
☎ 874 6881; www.gresham-hotels.com; Upper O'Connell St; s/d from €190/255, penthouse €900; **P**

The Gresham, a landmark hotel and one of Dublin's oldest and, until now, most traditional, underwent a significant facelift in 2002, shedding its cosy granny's parlour look to reveal a brighter, smarter, more modern look. The hotel's apparent clientele – elderly groups on shopping breaks to the capital and well-heeled Americans – has remained loyal. Rooms have air-con, are spacious and well serviced, though the decor is a little fussy.

HARVEY'S GUESTHOUSE
Map pp264–5   *Guesthouse*
☎ 874 8384; www.harveysguesthouse.com; 11 Upper Gardiner St; s/d €70/140

Spread across two attached houses, this superfriendly, nonsmoking guesthouse just north of Mountjoy Sq gets plenty of kudos for its all-round congenial atmosphere. The refurbished rooms have beautiful wooden French sleigh beds and brand-new bathrooms.

HOTEL SAINT GEORGE
Map pp264–5   *Hotel*
☎ 874 5611; hotels@indigo.ie; 7 East Parnell Sq; s/d €75/130; **P**

In a restored Georgian building, this hotel oozes elegance and class. The 36 rooms, all with bathroom, are surprisingly large, with simple but graceful furniture and large, comfortable beds. It's a little slice of Parisian style in Dublin.

LYNDON HOUSE Map pp264–5   *B&B*
☎ 878 6950; fax 878 7420; 26 Gardiner Pl; s/d €40/80

There are seven simple rooms with private bathroom and two small standard rooms in this modestly furnished but very friendly Georgian house. For its price range its one of the best B&Bs on the street.

LYNHAM'S HOTEL Map pp264–5   *Hotel*
☎ 888 0886; www.lynams-hotel.com; 63-64 O'Connell St; s/d/tr from €70/130/165

Bang in the middle of O'Connell St, beside the General Post Office (p103), this smart, friendly little hotel is a gem. All 42 rooms are nicely furnished with country pine furniture and tasteful fabrics. Room No 41 is a lovely triple with an additional camp bed, handy for groups who want to share. Ask for discounts midweek.

MARIAN GUESTHOUSE

Map pp264–5 *Guesthouse*
☎ 874 4129; 21 Upper Gardiner St; s/d €35/64
This tiny guesthouse has only six basic rooms, which ensures that the friendly staff is always on hand to cater to your needs. The breakfast is excellent.

OLD DUBLINER Map pp264–5 *Guesthouse*
☎ 855 5666; dublinerbb@aol.com; 62 Amiens St; s/d from €70/100; P
This long-established guesthouse, right opposite Connolly train station, has 14 elegant and very comfortable rooms, all with private bathroom. Ask for discounts midweek.

Top Five Hotel Views

- **Clarence Hotel** (p196) Dublin from a rooftop hot tub? You'll need to book the penthouse suite.
- **Eliza Lodge** (p197) Wraparound windows with an unparalleled view of the Liffey.
- **Staunton's on the Green** (p201) The best views of Dublin's most elegant Georgian square, St Stephen's Green.
- **Chief O'Neill's Hotel** (p206) The upper floors have an uncluttered view of the whole city, warts and all.
- **Jury's Inn Christ Church** (p201) Anodyne rooms for sure, but you won't get a better view of Christ Church Cathedral.

ROYAL DUBLIN HOTEL

Map pp264–5 *Hotel*
☎ 873 3666; www.royaldublin.com;
40 Upper O'Connell St; r from €120; P
O'Connell St's 'other' fancy hotel is directly across the street from the Gresham (p205), and a lot less impressive from the outside. Once inside, however, it's a different story. This is a truly luxurious hotel, from the elegant foyer right up to the rooms, which feature soft fabrics, light colours and light oak furnishings.

TOWNHOUSE Map pp264–5 *Boutique Hotel*
☎ 878 8808; www.townhouseofdublin.com;
47-48 Lower Gardiner St; s/d/tr €75/125/138
One of the north side's most exquisite little hotels, this place is simply fabulous. Each of the rooms is decorated differently: some in a contemporary style, such as No 328, called 'A Japanese Miscellany', with light wood floors and furniture. Others are more flamboyantly Victorian, such as the highly memorable 'Rip Van Winkle' honeymoon suite (No 208), which has a four-poster bed draped in red velvet – and a working fireplace. It shares a dining room with the Globetrotters Tourist Hotel (p207) next door. There is also a small Japanese garden.

WALTON'S HOTEL Map pp264–5 *Hotel*
☎ 878 3131; waltonshotel@eircom.net;
2-5 North Frederick St; s/d from €55/109; bus 36 & 36A from O'Connell St; P
Just north of Parnell Sq, this relatively new hotel is run by the Walton family, whose legendary musical instrument shop is next door. There are 43 simply furnished rooms with TV and modern decor. Children under 12 stay for free. It's a very friendly place in the centre of town.

Smithfield & Phoenix Park

Despite the untrammeled optimism of the late 1990s, the Smithfield area has been slow to really get going, a situation largely due to the slowdown of the economy. It remains a mostly traditional neighbourhood, with the exception of the main square, where you'll find the one lodging option.

CHIEF O'NEILL'S HOTEL

Map pp264–5 *Hotel*
☎ 817 3838; www.chiefoneills.com;
Smithfield Village; d/ste €250/375; P
This thoroughly modern hotel is a master class in contemporary design and its bold statement of intent is evident throughout. Some will argue that the bedrooms are devoid of warmth, but we love the sharp, decisive lines, the overabundance of glasswork and the all-round futuristic look that makes the rooms seem like the captain's quarters on the *Enterprise*. The bathrooms are a little impractical, sacrificing function over form, but we do like the large, separate shower rooms. The penthouse suites have their own balconies from which there are some great views of the city.

MORRISON HOTEL Map pp269–71 *Hotel*
☎ 887 2400; www.morrisonhotel.ie; Lower Ormond Quay; r from €270-570, penthouse €1490; P
Since opening its doors in 1999, the eternally hip Morrison has been vying with

he Clarence (p196) across the river in the tyle stakes for Dublin's coveted title of the Trendiest Hotel in Town. Hong Kong–Irish Fashion designer John Rocha helped create the Morrison's sophisticated, earthy look using his signature velvet throws, dark wood and contemporary white furnishings. The Loosely Oriental-style rooms are bright, if a little compact, and feature CD players, aircon and modem facilities, as well as Egyptian cotton linen and pieces of Rocha's own line of crystal.

ORMOND QUAY HOTEL
Map pp269–71 *Hotel*
☎ 872 1811; www.ormondquayhotel.com; 7-11 Upper Ormond Quay; s/d €120/200
Beside the river, this hotel has a plaque outside noting its role in the sirens episode of *Ulysses*. The 60 rooms have a bright, cheery decor and simple but elegant furniture. This hotel is openly gay-friendly.

Beyond the Royal Canal
About 30 minutes' walk (3km, five minutes by bus) east of Upper O'Connell St (along Dorset St), on the road to the airport, is the leafy suburb of Drumcondra, a popular area for B&Bs. Most of the houses here are late-Victorian or Edwardian, and are generally extremely well kept and comfortable. As they're on the airport road, they tend to be full virtually throughout the year, so advance booking is definitely recommended.

GRIFFITH HOUSE
B&B
☎ 837 5030; www.griffithhouse.com; 125 Griffith Ave; s/d €40/70; bus 36 & 36A from O'Connell St; P
This elegant house on a beautiful, tree-lined avenue has four bedrooms, three of them with private bathroom, and is nonsmoking. Each room is tastefully appointed, with large, comfortable beds and nice furniture.

ST ANDREW'S GUESTHOUSE
Guesthouse
☎ 837 4684; fax 857 0446; 1-3 Lambay Rd; s/d from €45/65; bus 11A & 11B from Trinity College; P
This place has 16 comfortable rooms, with elegant period-style beds and their own bathroom. It's located off the Drumcondra Rd, down Griffith Ave and the third turn to the left. The buses stop on the adjacent Home Farm Rd.

TINODE HOUSE
B&B
☎ 837 2277; www.tinodehouse.com; 170 Upper Drumcondra Rd; s/d €55/75; bus 11A, 11B, 36 & 36A from O'Connell St; P
This comfortable Edwardian town house has four elegant bedrooms, all with bathrooms. A familial welcome and excellent breakfast are part of the package.

Cheap Sleeps
ABBEY COURT HOSTEL
Map pp269–71 *Hostel*
☎ 878 0700; www.abbey-court.com; 29 Bachelor's Walk; dm/d €21/88
Spread over two buildings, this large, well-run hostel has 33 clean dorms with good storage. Its excellent facilities include a dining hall, conservatory and barbecue area. Doubles with bathroom are in the newer building where a light breakfast is provided in the adjacent café, Juice. Not surprisingly, this is a popular option for travellers. Reservations are advised.

GLOBETROTTERS TOURIST HOSTEL
Map pp264–5 *Hostel*
☎ 878 8088; gtrotter@indigo.ie; 46-48 Lower Gardiner St; dm/d €19/50
This is a really friendly place with 94 beds in a variety of dorms, all with bathrooms and under-bed storage. The funky decor is due to the fact that it shares the same artistic ethos (and a dining room) as the Townhouse (p206) next door. There's a little patio garden to the rear for the elusive sunny day.

ISAACS HOSTEL Map pp264–5 *Hostel*
☎ 855 6215; www.isaacs.ie; 2-5 Frenchman's Lane; dm/d from €11.50/52.50
Located just around the corner from its sister hostel, Jacob's Inn (below), in a 200-year-old wine vault, this busy, grungy hostel has loads of character and is probably the cheapest bed in town. Summer barbecues and live music in the foyer – courtesy of musicians playing later in the Isaac Butt pub (p169) next door – are an added feature. A recent major facelift has resulted in a new hang-out area, Internet facilities and a disabled access room.

JACOB'S INN Map pp264–5 *Hostel*
☎ 855 5660; www.isaacs.ie; 21-28 Talbot Pl; dm/d from €16.50/65
Just behind Busáras, this clean, modern hostel offers spacious accommodation with private

bathroom and outstanding facilities, including some disabled access rooms, a bureau de change, bike storage and a self-catering kitchen.

MARLBOROUGH HOSTEL

Map pp264–5   *Hostel*
☎ 874 7629; www.marlboroughhostel.com;
81-82 Marlborough St; dm/d from €14/52

Next to the Pro-Cathedral (p107), this well-located hostel has 76 beds and adequate facilities. High Georgian ceilings make up for small rooms. The slightly jaded showers,

in the basement, are a bit of a trek from th dorms.

MOUNT ECCLES COURT

Map pp264–5   *Hoste*
☎ 873 0826; info@eccleshostel.com;
42 North Great George's St; dm/d €25/84

In a renovated Georgian town house on on of the north side's most beautiful streets, thi pristine place with dorms and doubles, a with own bathroom, is a great choice. Facili ties include a full kitchen, two lounges and bureau de change.

Excursions

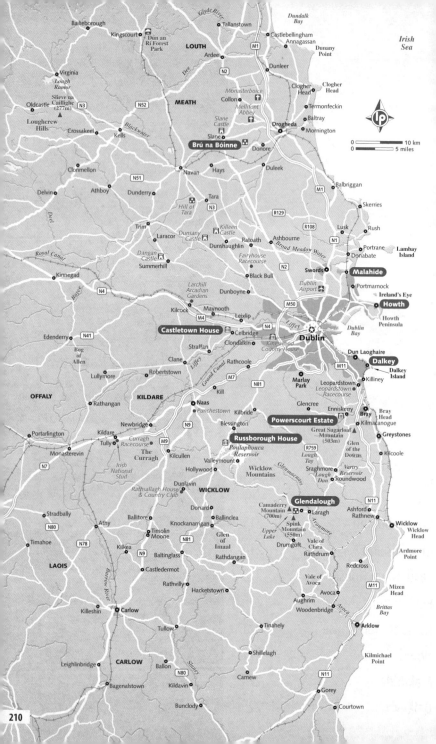

Excursions

When the good weather comes, most Dubliners can't wait to get out of the city. Whether it's a trip to the beach, a drive to the countryside or an exploration of Ireland's past, come the summer weekend the roads, buses and trains are generally full of day-trippers looking to kick back and relax. Ireland is a pretty small place, so virtually everywhere is within weekend reach, but you don't have to travel to Kerry or Donegal to get the best of what Ireland has to offer. Within a couple of hours' drive from Dublin there are plenty of opportunities to get a taste of life outside the capital and do something worthwhile or pleasurable in the process.

If lounging by the sea is your thing, you can just hop on a bus or a DART train and within half an hour grey concrete gives way to seaside villages with cosy harbours and sandy beaches. If you want to dig a little into the country's remote and recent past, Dublin's neighbouring counties – Wicklow to the south, Kildare to the west and Meath to the north – have ruins, prehistoric sites and stately country piles that rank among the country's most important historical attractions. And if you just fancy a rugged walk or gentle gambol in the Irish countryside, then there are plenty of spots to indulge, from the taxing hikes around the mountains surrounding Glendalough in County Wicklow to the gorse-bracketed paths of Howth Head immediately north of Dublin Bay.

If you're on a short visit to Dublin, then obviously timing is all-important. Sure, there's plenty to keep you amused, entertained and interested within the confines of the city centre, but Dublin's environs are as much a part of the Dublin experience as a weekend in Temple Bar; to most Dubliners, in fact, even more so. All of the sights listed in this chapter are worthwhile destinations in their own right and deserving of any effort you make to get to them, but what makes them doubly attractive for the short-term visitor is that they're all a short distance from the city and travel to and from them is generally hassle-free.

COASTAL BREAKS

You'd never think it walking around the city centre, but Dublin is a stone's throw from a number of lovely seaside towns, most of which have been incorporated into the greater city but have still managed to retain that quiet village feel. The traditional fishing village of Howth (p222)– that bulbous headland on the northern edge of Dublin Bay – is now one of Dublin's most prestigious addresses, primarily because the residents are jealously protective of the unspoilt headland dotted with fancy houses rising above the beautiful harbour where many of them keep their pleasure boats. Further north along the coast is the ever-elegant village of Malahide (p224), fronted by a long, sandy coastal basin and an impressive marina full of shops, restaurants and – naturally – expensive boats.

To the south of Dublin Bay is Dalkey (p225), a compact village that is virtually attached to the southern suburbs. You can rent boats at the small harbour and explore the southern reaches of the bay, and after you've hit dry land there are a couple of great restaurants that alone make the journey worthwhile.

Visiting all three is pretty easy. All are connected to the city centre via the DART, which cuts travel time to no more than 45 minutes in any direction. The obvious itinerary is to visit Howth and Malahide in one day, but each is worth devoting a little more time to. If golf is your thing, Howth's wonderful golf courses will take up the better part of half a day, leaving you the rest of the day to explore the port and have a seafood dinner in one of the harbour's restaurants. If you don't feel like spoiling a good walk, then an amble across the top of Howth Head to the lighthouse is a thoroughly enjoyable experience, especially in good weather.

As Dalkey lies on the opposite end of Dublin Bay, it is really a trip unto itself, but there's plenty to keep you amused for at least half a day. Besides renting a boat and exploring the nearby waters and offshore island, there are some lovely walks in the hills above the town and further south in Killiney (see the boxed text Detour: South to Killiney on p225), which is also home to a fabulous beach that is popular with swimmers.

THE DISTANT PAST

Dublin is old, but it ain't that old. If you really want to get stuck into Ireland's past, you need to get out of the city, but you don't have to go far. The obvious destination for fans of all things prehistoric is magnificent **Brú na Bóinne** (opposite), an extensive Neolithic graveyard northeast of Dublin in County Meath. This is, without question, one of the most important prehistoric sites in Europe, a testament to the genius and imagination of the pre-Celts. A fabulous interpretative centre explains the history and use of the passage tombs in a thoroughly satisfying way, but the tours of the two graves themselves (Newgrange and Knowth; a third, Dowth, is under excavation) is the real treat.

To the south of Dublin, and skipping forward a couple of thousand years, is the ancient monastic settlement of **Glendalough** (p216), once a contemplative paradise for Ireland's first monks and now one of the country's most important set of early-Christian ruins. Although undoubtedly fascinating in themselves, it is their setting that makes this place so special, around two glacial lakes at the foot of a secluded valley in the middle of the Wicklow Mountains. There are plenty of walking opportunities here, including a couple of mountain hikes.

Although Brú na Bóinne and Glendalough are only 40km and 25km respectively from Dublin, they are not easily accessible by public transportation. A private bus company runs buses to and from Glendalough twice a day from the city centre, but Brú na Bóinne is a little harder to get to if you don't have a car. The latter is best visited by organised coach tour, the price of which includes transport and all admission fees. And aside from leaving the hassle of getting there in someone else's hands, there's the bonus of a guide, who has all the facts and will answer any questions you may have about the site. There are also organised tours to Glendalough, although the main advantage to joining one is that you can kill a few birds with one stone and get in a visit to Russborough House (p221) as well as a quickie tour of northern Wicklow. Organised tour options are listed below each entry.

STATELY HOMES

The 17th-century Protestant Ascendancy were responsible for the creation of Georgian Dublin, a single-minded commitment to make their city one of the most beautiful in Europe. Accordingly, they built themselves beautiful town houses on and around the fashionable squares on both sides of the Liffey.

But it is in their country retreats, away from the hustle and bustle of city life, that the full extent of their architectural ambitions and enormous wealth are fully revealed, and here we have included the three finest houses of all. Each is a breathtakingly magnificent and stunning example of what vainglorious power and oodles of money can produce.

In County Wicklow, to the south, are two examples of Georgian top dog Richard Cassels' finest work: the wonderful **Powerscourt Estate** (p220), built for the Power family and embellished by one of the most beautiful gardens in Europe; and **Russborough House** (p221), home to an extraordinary art collection built up over the years by Sir Alfred Beit that despite a number of robberies remains one of the most important private collections in the world.

West of Dublin, County Kildare is home to not just the most important private stud farms in Ireland, but to the grandest Georgian pile of the lot, **Castletown House** (p218).

Powerscourt Estate (p220)

The first complete example of the Palladian style that was all the rage between 1720 and 1820, Castletown is simply huge, without a doubt reflecting owner William Conolly's vast wealth (he was, in his day, Ireland's richest man). Not far from the house are a relatively undiscovered delight, the Larchill Arcadian Gardens (see the boxed text on p219). Here, amid the wonderfully wild garden layout, are a number of follies, proof of the owners' oddities and eccentricities.

The actual houses at Russborough and Castletown are open to visitors, but Powerscourt House is not; since a massive fire gutted the insides in 1974 a process of restoration has been ongoing which will eventually restore each room to its original splendour. However, a visit is still more than worthwhile as the estate itself, with its gardens the main draw, is a marvellous place to while away an afternoon. The nearby waterfall is the tallest in Britain and Ireland, and the surrounding countryside is perfect for a good walk.

All three houses are within an hour and a half or so from Dublin's city centre and are served by public bus. Organised tours to Glendalough also take in a visit to Powerscourt.

BRÚ NA BÓINNE

A thousand years older than Stonehenge, the extensive Neolithic necropolis known as Brú na Bóinne (the Boyne Palace) is, quite simply, one of the most extraordinary sites in Europe, a powerful and evocative testament to the mind-boggling achievements of prehistoric humans.

This necropolis was built to house VIP corpses. They were the largest artificial structures in Ireland until the construction of the Anglo-Norman castles four thousand years later. The area consists of many different sites, the three principal ones being Newgrange, Knowth and Dowth.

Over the centuries these tombs decayed, were covered by grass and trees and were plundered by everybody from Vikings to Victorian treasure hunters, whose carved initials can be seen on the great stones of Newgrange. The countryside around them is littered with countless other ancient mounds (or tumuli) and standing stones.

The entire complex, including the three main passage tombs (of which only Newgrange and Knowth are accessible) can only be visited as part of a tour run by the **Brú na Bóinne Visitor Centre**, south of the River Boyne and 2km west of Donore. This high-quality interpretative centre provoked enormous controversy when it opened in 1997, largely because it was deemed an unwelcome and artificial interference in a unique natural setting. Whatever the case may be, the centre has turned out to be a fairly remarkable place, with an extraordinary series of interactive exhibits on the passage tombs and prehistoric Ireland in general.

You should allow plenty of time to visit this marvellous centre. If you're only planning on taking the guided tour of the interpretative centre, give yourself about an hour. If you plan a visit to Newgrange or Knowth, allow at least two hours. If however, you want to visit all three in one go, you should plan at least half a day. In summer, particularly at the weekend, and during school holidays, the place gets very crowded and you will not be guaranteed a visit to either of the passage tombs. Call ahead to book a tour and avoid disappointment. In summer, the best time to visit is midweek and/or early in the morning.

From the surface **Newgrange** is a somewhat disappointing flattened, grass-covered mound about 80m in diameter and 13m high. Underneath lies the finest Stone Age passage tomb in Ireland and one of the most remarkable prehistoric sites in Europe. It dates from around 3200 BC, predating the great pyramids of Egypt by some six centuries. The purpose for which it was constructed remains uncertain. It may have been a burial place for kings or

Transport

Distance from Dublin 40km

Direction Northeast

Bus Bus Éireann (return €12.70, 1½hr, one daily) to the interpretative centre.

Car Take M1 north to Drogheda and then N51 west to Brú na Bóinne.

a centre for ritual – although the alignment with the sun at the time of the winter solstice also suggests that it was designed to act as a calendar.

Over the centuries, Newgrange, like Dowth and Knowth, deteriorated and was even quarried at one stage. There was a standing stone on the summit until the 17th century. The site was extensively restored in 1962 and again in 1975.

A superbly carved kerbstone with double and triple spirals guards the tomb's main entrance. The front facade has been reconstructed so that tourists don't have to clamber in over it. Above the entrance is a slit or roof box, which lets light in. Another beautifully decorated kerbstone stands at the exact opposite side of the mound. Some experts say that a ring of standing stones encircled the mound, forming a Great Circle about 100m in diameter, but only 12 of these stones remain – with traces of some others below ground level.

Holding the whole structure together are the 97 boulders of the kerb ring, designed to stop the mound from collapsing outwards. Eleven of these are decorated with motifs similar to those on the main entrance stone, although only three have extensive carvings.

Newgrange & Irish Mythology

Although it is commonly accepted that the name Newgrange derives from 'new granary' (the tomb served as a repository for wheat and grain at one stage), locals and Celtophiles insist that the name is a corruption of the Irish for 'Gráinne's Cave'. The reference is to the Celtic myth taught to every Irish schoolchild: that of *The Pursuit of Diarmuid and Gráinne*, a story that tells of the illicit love between the wife of Fionn MacCumhaill (or Finn MacCool), leader of the Fianna, and one of his most trusted lieutenants. When Diarmuid was fatally wounded, his body was brought to Newgrange by the god Aengus in a vain attempt to save him, and the despairing Gráinne followed him into the cave, where she remained long after he died. This suspiciously Arthurian legend (for Diarmuid and Gráinne read Lancelot and Guinevere) is undoubtedly untrue, but it's still a pretty good story. Newgrange also plays another role in Celtic mythology, serving as the site where the hero Cúchulainn was conceived.

The white quartzite was originally obtained from Wicklow, 80km to the south, and there is also some granite from the Mourne Mountains in Northern Ireland. Over 200,000 tonnes of earth and stone also went into the mound.

You can walk down the narrow 19m passage, lined with 43 stone uprights, some of them engraved, which leads into the tomb chamber, about one-third of the way into the colossal mound. The chamber has three recesses, and in these are large basin stones that held cremated human bones. Along with the remains would have been funeral offerings of beads and pendants, but these were stolen long before the archaeologists arrived.

Above, the massive stones support a 6m-high corbel-vaulted roof. A complex drainage system means that not a drop of water has penetrated the interior in 40 centuries.

At 8.20am during the winter solstice (19 to 23 December), the rising sun's rays shine through the slit above the entrance, creep slowly down the long passage and illuminate the tomb chamber for 17 minutes. There is little doubt that witnessing this is one of the country's most memorable, even mystical, experiences. However, places to experience this annual event are booked up for at least 15 years, and the waiting list is now closed. For the legions of daily visitors there is a simulated winter sunrise for every group taken into the mound.

The burial mound of **Knowth** (Cnóbha), northwest of Newgrange, was built around the same time and seems set to surpass its better-known neighbour, both in the extent and the importance of the discoveries made here. It has the greatest collection of passage-tomb art ever uncovered in Western Europe. Under excavation since 1962, it recently opened to the public at last.

Modern excavations at Knowth soon cleared a 34m passage to the central chamber, much longer than the one at Newgrange. In 1968 a second 40m passage was unearthed on the opposite side of the mound. Although the chambers are separate, they're close enough for archaeologists to hear each other at work. Also in the mound are the remains of six early-Christian souterrains (underground chambers) built into the side. Some 300 carved slabs and 17 satellite graves surround the main mound.

Human activity at Knowth continued for thousands of years after its construction, explaining the site's complexity. The Beaker folk, so called because they buried their dead with drinking vessels, occupied the site in the Bronze Age (circa 1800 BC), as did the Celts in the Iron Age around 500 BC. Bronze and iron remnants from these periods have been discovered. Around AD 800 to AD 900 it was turned into a rath (earthen ring fort), a stronghold of the very powerful Uí Néill (O'Neill) clan. In 965, it was the seat of Cormac MacMaelmithic, later Ireland's high king for nine years. The Normans built a motte and bailey here in the 12th century. In about 1400 the site was finally abandoned. Further excavations are likely to continue at least for the next decade, and one of the thrills of Knowth is being allowed to watch them at work.

The circular mound at **Dowth** (Dubhadh, meaning 'dark') is similar in size to Newgrange – about 63m in diameter – but is slightly taller at 14m high. It has suffered badly at the hands of everyone from road builders and treasure hunters to amateur archaeologists, who scooped out the centre of the tumulus in the 19th century. For a time, Dowth even had a teahouse ignobly perched on its summit. Relatively untouched by modern archaeologists, Dowth shows what Newgrange and Knowth looked like for most of their history. Because it's unsafe, Dowth is closed to visitors, though the mound can be viewed from the road. Excavations began in 1998 and will continue for years to come.

There are two entrance passages leading to separate chambers (both sealed), and a 24m early-Christian souterrain at either end that connect up with the western passage. This 8m-long passage leads into a small cruciform chamber, in which a recess acts as an entrance to an additional series of small compartments, a feature unique to Dowth. To the southwest is the entrance to a shorter passage and smaller chamber.

North of the tumulus are the ruins of Dowth Castle and Dowth House.

If you're looking for something for the kids to do, the 135-hectare **Newgrange Farm**, about 400m down the hill to the west of Newgrange tomb, is your best bet for entertainment. The truly hands-on, family-run farm allows visitors to feed the ducks and lambs and tour the exotic bird aviaries. Charming Farmer Bill keeps things interesting and demonstrations of threshing, sheepdog work and shoeing a horse are absorbing. Sunday at 3pm is a very special time when the 'sheep derby' is run. Finding jockeys small enough wasn't easy, so teddy bears are tied to the animals' backs. Visiting children are made owners of a sheep for the race.

Sights & Information

Brú na Bóinne Visitor Centre (☎ 041-988 0300; www.heritageireland.ie; Donore; adult/child & student/senior €2.50/1.20/1.90 incl guided tour; ⏰ 9am-7pm Jun–mid-Sept, 9am-6.30pm mid-Sep–end Sep & May, 9.30am-5.30pm Oct & Mar-Apr, 9.30am-5pm Nov-Feb)

Knowth (Knowth & Brú na Bóinne Visitor Centre adult/child & student/senior €3.80/1.50/2.50; Knowth, centre & Newgrange €8.80/4.10/6.30; ⏰ same hours as visitor centre but only May-Oct)

Newgrange (Newgrange & Brú na Bóinne Visitor Centre adult/child & student/senior €5/2.50/3.80; Newgrange, centre & Knowth €8.80/4.10/6.30; ⏰ same hours as visitor centre)

Newgrange Farm (☎ 041-982 4119; Newgrange, off N51 btwn Drogheda & Slane; adult/family €5/14; ⏰ 10am-5.30pm Mon-Fri, 2-5.30pm Sun Easter-Sep, also 2-5.30pm Sat Jul & Aug)

Eating

Boyle's Licensed Tea Rooms (☎ 041-982 4195; Main St, Slane) About 2km west of Knowth, this is a wonderful tea shop and café with a 1940s ambience at the back of an equally beautiful shopfront. The menu – written in 12 languages – is strictly of the tea-and-scones type (around €3).

Sleeping

Glebe House (☎ 041-983 6101; off N51, Dowth; r per person €45) This old country house near the Dowth burial mound has gorgeous rooms with open, log-burning fireplaces.

Mattock House (☎ 041-982 4592; off N51, Newgrange; s/d €35/50) A classic Irish farmhouse with large, comfortable rooms and a breakfast that struggles to fit on the plate.

Tours

Two good organised tours run throughout the year from Dublin.

Bus Éireann (☎ 836 6111; www.buseireann.ie; adult €24.20-30, child €12.10-19.50, student €20-28; ⏰ depart 9.30am, return 5.45pm Thu-Sat Apr, Mon-Thu & Sat-Sun May-Sep, depart 10am & return 4.15pm Thu-Sat Oct-Dec)

Mary Gibbons (☎ 283 9973; tour & admission fees €35; ⏰ depart from Northside Star Hotel, Amiens St 9am, Buswells Hotel, Molesworth St 10am, Dublin Tourism Centre, Suffolk St 10.15am, Royal Dublin Hotel, O'Connell St 10.30am, Mon-Wed & Fri) This is highly recommended.

GLENDALOUGH

Glendalough (Gleann dá Loch, 'Valley of the Two Lakes') is a magical place – an ancient monastic settlement tucked beside two dark lakes and overshadowed by the sheer walls of a deep valley. It's one of the most picturesque settings in Ireland and the site of one of the most significant ancient monastic settlements in the country. Inevitably, Glendalough's success made it a key target of Viking raiders, who sacked the monastery at least four times between 775 and 1071. The final blow came in 1398, when English forces from Dublin almost completely destroyed it. Efforts were made to rebuild and some life lingered on here as late as the 17th century, when, under renewed repression, the monastery finally died.

Huge popularity is the price of such beauty. Visit early or late in the day – or out of season – to avoid the big crowds. Remember that a visit here is all about walking, so wear comfortable shoes.

At the valley entrance, before the Glendalough Hotel, is the **Glendalough Visitor Centre**,
which has a high-quality 20-minute audiovisual presentation on the Irish monasteries as well as a model which should help you fix where everything is in relation to everything else.

The original site of St Kevin's settlement, Teampall na Skellig, is at the base of the cliffs towering over the southern side of the Upper Lake and accessible only by boat; unfortunately, there's no boat service to the site and you'll have to settle for looking at it across the lake. The terraced shelf has the reconstructed ruins of a church and early graveyard. Rough wattle huts once stood on the raised ground nearby. Scattered around are some early grave slabs and simple stone crosses.

Just east of the lake and 10m above its waters is the 2m-deep artificial cave called St Kevin's Bed, said to be where Kevin lived. The earliest human habitation of the cave was long before St Kevin's era – there's evidence that people lived in the valley for thousands of years before the monks arrived. In the green area just south of the car park is a large circular wall thought to be the remains of an early-Christian *caher* (stone fort).

Transport

Distance from Dublin 25km

Direction South

Bus St Kevin's Bus (☎ 281 8119) Departs 11.30am & 6pm Mon-Sat, 11.30am & 7pm Sun from outside the Royal College of Surgeons, St Stephen's Green West, return 7.15am & 4.15pm Mon-Fri, 9.45am & 4.15pm Sat & Sun (single/return €9/15, 1½hr).

Car N11 south to Kilmacanogue, then R755 west through Roundwood, Annamoe and Laragh.

St Kevin & Glendalough

In AD 498 a priest named Kevin arrived in the valley and set up home in what had been a Bronze Age tomb on the southern side of the Upper Lake. For seven years he slept on stones, wore animal skins, ate sparingly and had only birds and animals as companions. Word soon spread of Kevin's natural lifestyle, and he began attracting disciples unaware of the irony that they were flocking to hang out with a hermit who wanted to live as far from other people as possible.

Kevin's preferred isolationism notwithstanding, a settlement quickly grew and by the 9th century Glendalough rivalled Clonmacnoise as the island's premier monastic city. Thousands of students studied and lived in a thriving community that was spread over a considerable area.

Follow the lakeshore path southwest of the car park until you find the considerable remains of Reefert Church above the tiny Poulanass River. This is a small, rather plain, 11th-century, Romanesque nave-and-chancel church with some re-assembled arches and walls. Traditionally, Reefert (meaning King's Burial Place) was the burial site of the chiefs of the local O'Toole family. The surrounding graveyard contains a number of rough stone crosses and slabs, most made of shiny mica schist.

Climb the steps at the back of the churchyard and follow the path to the west and you'll find, at the top of a rise overlooking the lake, the scant remains of St Kevin's Cell, a small beehive hut.

While the Upper Lake has the best scenery, the most fascinating buildings lie in the lower part of the valley east of the Lower Lake.

Walks Around Glendalough

The easiest and most popular walk is the gentle hour-long walk along the northern shore of the Upper Lake to the lead and zinc mine workings, which date from 1800. The better route is along the lakeshore rather than on the road, which runs 30m from the shore. Continue on up the head of the valley if you wish.

Alternatively, you can go up Spink Mountain (550m), the steep ridge with vertical cliffs running along the southern flanks of the Upper Lake. You can go part of the way and turn back, or complete a circuit of the Upper Lake by following the top of the cliff, eventually coming down by the mine workings and going back along the northern shore. The circuit is about 5km long.

The third option is the 7.5km hike up and down Camaderry Mountain (700m), hidden behind the hills that flank the northern side of the valley. The walk starts on the road just 50m back towards Glendalough from the entrance to the Upper Lake car park. Head straight up the steep hill to the north and you come out on open mountains with sweeping views in all directions. You can then continue up Camaderry to the northwest or just follow the ridge west looking over the Upper Lake.

Just round the bend from the Glendalough Hotel is the stone arch of the monastery gatehouse, the only surviving example of a monastic entranceway in the country. Just inside the entrance is a large slab with an incised cross.

Beyond that lies a graveyard, which is still in use. The 10th-century round tower is 33m tall and 16m in circumference at the base. The upper storeys and conical roof were reconstructed in 1876. Near the tower, to the southeast, is the Cathedral of St Peter and St Paul, with a 10th-century nave. The chancel and sacristy date from the 12th century.

At the centre of the graveyard to the south of the round tower is the Priest's House. This odd building dates from 1170 but has been heavily reconstructed. It may have been the location of shrines of St Kevin. Later, during the 18th century, it became a burial site for local priests – hence the name. The 10th-century St Mary's Church, 140m southwest of the round tower, probably originally stood outside the walls of the monastery and belonged to local nuns. It has a lovely western doorway. A little to the east are the scant remains of St Kieran's Church, the smallest at Glendalough.

Glendalough's trademark is St Kevin's Church or Kitchen at the southern edge of the enclosure. With its miniature round-tower–like belfry, protruding sacristy and steep stone roof, it's a masterpiece. How it came to be known as a kitchen is a mystery as there's no indication that it was anything other than a church. The oldest parts of the building date from the 11th century – the structure has been remodelled since but it's still a classic early Irish church.

At the junction with Green Rd as you cross the river just south of these two churches is the Deer Stone in the middle of a group of rocks. Legend claims that, when St Kevin needed milk for two orphaned babies, a doe stood here waiting to be milked. The stone is actually a *bullaun*, used as a grinding stone for medicines or food. Many are thought to be prehistoric and they were widely regarded as having supernatural properties: women who bathed their faces with water from the hollow were supposed to keep their looks forever. The early churchmen brought them into their monasteries, perhaps hoping to inherit some of the stones' powers.

The road east leads to St Saviour's Church, with its detailed Romanesque carvings. To the west a nice woodland trail leads up the valley past the Lower Lake to the Upper Lake.

Sights & Information

Glendalough Visitor Centre (☎ 0404-45325, 0404-45352; adult/student & child/senior €2.70/1.25/2; ☼ 9am-5.15pm Jun-Aug, 9.30am-5.15pm Sep–mid-Oct & mid-Mar–May, 9.30am-4.15pm mid-Oct–mid-Mar)

Eating

Glendalough Hotel (☎ 0404-45135; Glendalough; lunch €19) The hotel's enormous restaurant serves a very good three-course lunch of the chicken and chips variety.

Lynham's of Laragh (☎ 0404-45345; Laragh; ☼ noon-7pm; mains €12-16) Large portions of the standard hotel restaurant fare, from chicken and chips to fish in batter.

Wicklow Heather Restaurant (☎ 0404-45157; Main St, Laragh; mains €12-15) This restaurant is the best place for a good lunch; we recommend you try the excellent fresh fish.

Sleeping

Glendale (☎ 0404-45410; www.glendale-glendalough
.com; Laragh East; s/d €40/60; **P**) An immaculately tidy
B&B with large, comfortable rooms.

Glendalough Hotel (☎ 0404-45135; www.glendalough
hotel.com; Glendalough; s/d €97/150; **P**) 44 luxurious
bedrooms right next to the ruins.

Valeview (☎ 0404-45292; lisa.mc@oceanfree.net;
Laragh; s/d €30/50; **P**) Beautifully maintained,
nonsmoking rooms and great views of the valley.

Tours

A hassle-free way of visiting Glendalough
and stopping off at other sights in the area
is by organised coach tour from Dublin.
These are very well organised and usually
a lot of fun. You can opt for a full-day or
half-day tour.

Aran Tours (☎ 280 1899; www.wildcoachtours.com;
adult/child €28/25; ☽ depart 9.30am & return 5.30pm)
The 'Wild Wicklow Tour' never fails to generate rave
reviews for atmosphere and all-round fun. It also includes
a short Dublin city tour and a visit to Avoca and the
Sally Gap. It has a number of different pick-up points
throughout Dublin – check the point nearest to you when
booking.

Bus Éireann (☎ 836 6111; www.buseireann.ie; adult/
child €30/19.50 Apr-Oct, €25/16.25 Nov-Mar; ☽ depart
10.30am, return 5.45pm Apr-Oct, depart 10.30am, return
4.30pm Wed & Sun only Nov-Mar) Solid and dependable
tour if not spectacular.

Irish Rover Tours (☎ 836 4684, 1800 226 242; www
.tirnanogtours.com; 57 Lower Gardiner St, Dublin 1;
adult/child €28/22; ☽ depart 9am from Gardiner St &
9.30am from Dublin Tourism Centre Tue, Thu, Fri, Sat
& Sun) Daily full-day tours of Wicklow, which include
Glendalough, the Sally Gap, Lough Tay, Laragh, Rathdrum
and Avoca.

Mary Gibbons Tours (☎ 283 9973; per person €35;
☽ depart 10.15am & return 4.30pm) This is a wonderful
and insightful full-day tour of Glendalough and Powerscourt Estate run by expert guides with an in-depth
knowledge of their subject matter. We highly recommend
this tour.

CASTLETOWN HOUSE

In a country full of elegant Palladian mansions, it is no mean feat to be considered the
grandest of the lot, but Castletown House simply has no peers. It is Ireland's largest and
most imposing Georgian estate, a testament to the vast wealth enjoyed by the Anglo-Irish
gentry during the 18th century.

The house was built between the years 1722 and 1732 for William Conolly (1662–1729),
speaker of the Irish House of Commons, and at the time Ireland's richest man. Born into
relatively humble circumstances in Bally-
shannon, County Donegal, Conolly made
his fortune through land transactions in
the uncertain aftermath of the Battle of
the Boyne (1690).

The original design of the house was
by the Italian architect Alessandro Galilei
(1691–1737), who in 1718 designed the facade of the main block so as to resemble a
16th-century Italian *palazzo* (palace). Construction began in 1722 but Galilei didn't
bother hanging around to supervise, having left Ireland in 1719. Instead, the project
was entrusted to Sir Edward Lovett Pearce
(1699–1733), who returned from his grand tour of Italy in 1724 (where he had become
friends with Galilei).

Inspired by the work of Andrea Palladio, which he had studied during his visit to
Italy, Pearce enlarged the original design of the house and added the colonnades and the
terminating pavilions. The interior is as opulent as the exterior suggests, especially the
Long Gallery, replete with family portraits and exquisite stucco work by the Francini
brothers. Pearce's connection with Conolly was a fortuitous one, as he was commissioned
in 1728 to design the House of Commons in Dublin. That building, now the Bank of
Ireland (p75) at College Green, is one of the most elegant examples of the Georgian style
in Dublin.

Transport

Distance from Dublin 21km

Direction West

Bus Dublin Bus 67 & 67A (single €1.60, about 1hr,
hourly) depart from D'Olier St for Celbridge and stop
at the gates of Castletown House.

Car Take N4 to Celbridge.

As always seems the way with these grand projects, Conolly didn't live to see the completion of his wonder-palace. His widow continued to live at the unfinished house after his death in 1729, instigating many of the improvements made to the house after the main structure was completed in 1732. Her main architectural contribution was the curious 42.6m Obelisk, known locally as the Conolly Folly. Designed to her specifications by Richard Cassels, and visible from both ends of the Long Gallery, it is 3.2km north of the house.

The house remained in the family's hands until 1965, when it was purchased by Desmond Guinness. He spent vast amounts of money in order to restore the house to its original splendour, an investment that was continued from 1979 by the Castletown Foundation. In 1994 the Castletown House was transferred to state care and today it is managed by Dúchas.

Immediately to the east of the grounds of Castletown House, and on private property that never belonged to the house, you will find the even more curious, conical **Wonderful Barn**. Standing at 21m high, this extraordinary five-storey structure, which is wrapped by a 94-step winding staircase, was commissioned by Lady Conolly in 1743 to give employment to local tenants whose crops were ruined by the severe frosts of the winters of 1741 and 1742. The building was ostensibly a granary, but it was also used as a shooting tower – doves were considered a delicacy in Georgian times. Flanking the main building are two smaller towers, which were also used to store grain.

Detour: Larchill Arcadian Gardens

Green thumbs and shrubbery fanatics will not want to miss a detour to the **Larchill Arcadian Gardens** (Map p210; ☎ 628 7354; Kilcock, County Kildare; adult/student & child €7/5; ☼ noon-6pm Tue-Sun May-Aug, Sat & Sun only Sep, by appointment rest of year), 12km northwest of Castletown House in Kilcock. Painstakingly restored to their original splendour between 1994 and 1999, these 26-hectare gardens are unique in Ireland and England as they are the only surviving example of the *ferme ornée* style that followed the stiff formality of the Italianate garden and predated the more modern landscaped garden. The term literally means 'ornamental farm', and the style, originally created by Marie Antoinette at Versailles, was intended to create a pastoral paradise, complete with ornamental buildings, statuary, water features and walkways. The French queen added a dairy to her gardens and was known to dress up as a milkmaid to really get in the mood.

Larchill is embellished by 10 classical and Gothic buildings or follies. The most noteworthy are the Shelled Tower in the walled garden, a lake island castle known as Gibraltar and a curious foxes' earth, designed by a very superstitious and very penitent Mr Watson, who was convinced he would be reincarnated as a fox and wanted a convenient escape route from the hounds of hell. A handy, 1km circular walk along a beech-lined avenue is the best way to explore these fabulous gardens, which in 2002 won the prestigious Europa Nostra Award for conservation, the only Irish project ever to do so. The **Barn Tearooms** (afternoon tea €5), aside from serving delicious scones and a great cup of tea, has an interesting diorama display on the gardens and their restoration.

Sights & Information

Castletown House (Map p210; ☎ 628 8252; Celbridge; adult/student & child €3.80/1.50; ☼ 10am-6pm Mon-Fri & 1-6pm Sat & Sun May-Sep, 10am-5pm Mon-Fri & 1-5pm Sun Oct, 1-5pm Sun Nov)

Wonderful Barn (☎ 624 5448; Leixlip; ☼ closed to public)

Eating

Michelangelo Restaurant (☎ 627 1809; Main St, Celbridge; mains €12-17; ☼ 6pm-midnight Tue-Sat, 12.30-2.30pm Sun) A cosy Italian restaurant near the gates of Castletown

House that serves up the usual fare of pastas, pizzas and meat dishes.

Sleeping

Ardenode Hotel (☎ 045-864 198; www.ardenodehotel .com; Ballymore Eustace; s/d €75/130; **P**) A beautiful country hotel with superelegant rooms; some have four-poster beds.

Kildare Hotel & Golf Club (☎ 601 7200; www.kclub.ie; Straffan; r from €290; **P**) Better known for the superb golf course that will host the 2007 Ryder Cup, the estate is home to a palatial Palladian villa that is one of the best hotels in Ireland. It is 6km southwest of Celbridge just off the R403.

POWERSCOURT ESTATE

About 500m south of the charming village of Enniskerry is the entrance to the 64 sq km **Powerscourt Estate**, Wicklow's grandest country pile. This is one of the most popular day trips from Dublin, and the village – built in 1760 by Richard Wingfield, Earl of Powerscourt, so that his labourers would have somewhere to live – is a terrific spot to while away an afternoon.

Powerscourt Estate came into being in 1300, with the construction of a Norman castle for the Le Poer (later anglicised as Power) family. The castle was passed into the hands of a number of Anglo–Irish nobles before finally being given to Richard Wingfield, the newly appointed Marshall of Ireland, in 1603. It was to remain in the family's hands for the next 350 years. In 1731 the German-born architect Richard Cassels (aka Castle) was commissioned to build a Palladian-style mansion around the guts of the old castle. He completed his work in 1743, but an extra storey was added in 1787 and other alterations were made during the 19th century. The Wingfields left the house in the 1950s, after which it underwent extensive restorations, but the day before it was due to open to the public in 1974 a fire gutted the whole building. Today it is owned by the Slazenger family, but except for a small exhibition room and a cafeteria, the house remains off limits to the public while the painstaking process of restoration continues.

Visitors need not despair, however, as the 20-hectare formal gardens are more than splendid enough to keep you occupied. Originally laid out in the 1740s, they were redesigned in the 19th century by one Daniel Robertson, whose horticultural genius was matched by his propensity for booze (see the boxed text below). Perhaps this influenced his largely informal style, which resulted in a magnificent blend of landscaped gardens, sweeping terraces, statuary, ornamental lakes, secret hollows, rambling walks and walled enclosures replete with over 200 types of trees and shrubs, all beneath the stunning natural backdrop of the Great Sugarloaf Mountain to the east. Tickets come with a map laying out 40-minute and hour-long tours of the gardens. Don't miss the exquisite Japanese Gardens or the Pepperpot Tower, modelled on a three-inch actual pepperpot owned by Lady Wingfield. Our own favourite, however, is the animal cemetery, final resting place of the Wingfield pets and even some of their favourite milking cows. Some of the epitaphs are astonishingly personal.

A 7km walk to a separate part of the estate takes you to the 130m **Powerscourt Waterfall**. It's the highest in Britain and Ireland, and is most impressive after heavy rain. You can also get to the falls by road following the signs from the estate. A nature trail has been laid out around the base of the waterfall, taking you past giant redwoods, ancient oaks, beech, birch and rowan trees. There are plenty of birds in the vicinity, including the chaffinch, cuckoo, chiffchaff, raven and willow warbler.

Transport

Distance from Dublin 18km

Direction South

Bus Dublin Bus 44 (€1.65, 1¼hr, every 20min) from Hawkins St.

Car South on Ranelagh Rd (R117), right onto Milltown Rd, left onto Dundrum Rd and on through Kilternan and Enniskerry; alternatively, south to Bray along N11 and west for 3km on R117.

Train DART to Bray (€1.70) & Bus 185 to Enniskerry (€1.35, 20min, hourly) from station.

The Boozy Gardener

Daniel Robertson was not your typical gardener. He supervised the construction of the gardens from a wheelbarrow, in which he would lay prostrate, armed only with a bottle of sherry. To his underlings he would bark orders that, as the day passed, grew more and more incoherent as much as his bottle became lighter. Work usually went on until 5pm, when the tanked-up Robertson would call an end to the day's work on account of bad light. A perfectly reasonable suggestion, you may think, but considering that the summer day doesn't end until at least 10pm…

Sights & Information

Powerscourt Estate (Map p210; ☎ 204 6000; www.powerscourt.ie; Enniskerry; house & gardens adult/child €8.50/5.10, house only €2.50/1.60, gardens only €6/3.50; ☯ 9.30am-5.30pm Feb-Oct, 9.30am-4.30pm Nov-Jan)

Powerscourt Waterfall (☎ 204 6000; Powerscourt Estate, Enniskerry; adult/child €4/3; ☯ 9.30am-7pm, to dusk Oct-Jan)

Eating

Buttercups (☎ 286 9669; Main St, Enniskerry; dishes €4.50) Small deli and bread shop serving delicious takeaway food.

Johnnie Fox's (☎ 295 5647; Glencullen; mains €12-17) Superb seafood and nightly traditional music sessions. A local legend.

Poppies Country Cooking (☎ 282 8869; The Square, Enniskerry; lunch €14) Solid lunches and great cakes in a rustic atmosphere.

Powerscourt Terrace Café (☎ 204 6070; Powerscourt House; dishes €8-12) A cut above the usual tourist-attraction café; this place serves lovely food overlooking the terraced gardens.

Wingfield's Bistro (☎ 204 2854; Church Hill, Enniskerry; mains €15-22) Top-notch eatery serving traditional Irish cuisine.

Sleeping

Corner House (☎ 286 0149; Main St, Enniskerry; s/d €38/58; ℗) A 200-year-old place in Enniskerry with three huge rooms with shower only.

Knockree Hostel (☎ 286 4036, bookings 830 4555; www.irelandyha.org; Knockree, Enniskerry; dm €11, Oct-May €9) Spartan hostel with splendid views over Glencree. Book through An Óige office in Dublin.

Powerscourt Arms (☎ 282 8903; fax 286 4909; Main St, Enniskerry; s/d €50/90 with breakfast; ℗) What this modern hotel lacks in traditional charm it more than makes up for in comfort.

Summerhill House Hotel (☎ 286 7928; www.summerhillhousehotel.com; off the N11, Enniskerry; s/d €90/140; ℗) Enniskerry's best hotel is a fabulous country mansion set amid its own grounds.

Tours

The tours by Aran Tours and Mary Gibbons Tours include visits to Powerscourt; see Tours (p218) under Glendalough.

RUSSBOROUGH HOUSE

Five kilometres southwest of Blessington is one of Ireland's finest stately homes, a magnificent Palladian villa built for Joseph Leeson (1705–83), later the 1st earl of Milltown and later still Lord Russborough.

Built between 1741 and 1751, it was designed by Richard Cassels, at the height of his fame and ability (although he did not live to see it completed), with the help of another Irish architect, Francis Bindon.

The house was taken by Irish forces during the 1798 Rising and then by government forces, who only left in 1801 after a furious Lord Russborough challenged the commander of the British forces, Lord Tyrawley, to a duel 'with blunderbusses and slugs in a sawpit'.

The house remained in Leeson family hands until 1931. In 1952 it was sold to Sir Alfred Beit, the eponymous nephew of the co-founder of the de Beers diamond mining company. Uncle Alfred was an obsessive art collector, and when he died his impressive haul – which includes works by Velázquez, Vermeer, Goya and Rubens – was passed on to his nephew, who brought it to Russborough House. Thus began the sorry saga of the Beit collection.

The house has been the victim of three major robberies, beginning in 1976 when 16 paintings were stolen for the Irish Republican Army (IRA); all were eventually recovered. Ten years later, despite increased security, notorious Dublin gangster Martin Cahill masterminded another robbery, but this time the clients were Loyalist paramilitaries. Some paintings were recovered, though several were irreparably damaged – a good thief does not a gentle curator make. Twice bitten but thrice shy, Beit decided to give the most valuable paintings to the National Gallery in 1988. In return, the National Gallery often lends paintings to the collection as temporary exhibits.

Transport

Distance from Dublin 35km

Direction Southwest

Bus Dublin Bus 65 (€3, 1½ hr, 10 daily) from Eden Quay.

Car N81 southwest to Blessington.

But the story doesn't end there. In June 2001 a pair of thieves drove a jeep through the front doors and walked out with two paintings worth nearly €4 million, including a Gainsborough that had already been stolen – and recovered – twice before. Thankfully, all of the paintings were recovered and the house – which is often criticised as being unsuitable as a gallery for works of such importance – has once more tightened its security measures.

The admission price includes a 45-minute tour of the house and all the important paintings. You can take an additional 30-minute tour of the bedrooms upstairs containing more silver and furniture.

Sights & Information

Russborough House (Map p210; ☎ 045-865239, Blessington; adult/child/student €6/3/4.50, 30-min tour adult/child €3.50/free; ☾ 10am-5pm Apr-Sep, 10.30am-5.30pm Sun & bank holidays Oct, closed rest of year, tours 2.15pm Mon-Sat, hourly on Sun)

Eating

Old Schoolhouse (☎ 045-891420; Old Kilbride Rd, Blessington; lunch mains €8-10, dinner mains €13-18; ☾ closed Mon) This good Italian restaurant just off Main St has a fairly standard lunch menu of salads and pizzas and a more interesting dinner menu.

Sleeping

Downshire House Hotel (☎ 045-865199; www.down shirehouse.com; Main St, Blessington; s/d €84.50/150) Blessington's most prominent landmark is this family-run hotel, which has 25 simply furnished, tidy rooms.

Haylands House (☎ 045-865183; haylands@eircom.net; Dublin Rd, Blessington; s/d €40/60) Highly recommended B&B with a warm welcome and lovely rooms.

Rathsallagh House & Country Club (Map p210; ☎ 045-403112; www.rathsallagh.com; Dunlavin, off the N81; s/d €175/250, 5-course meal €60) This fabulous country manor, converted from Queen Anne stables in 1798, has splendidly appointed rooms.

HOWTH

The bulbous Howth Peninsula forms the northern end of Dublin Bay. En route you pass Clontarf, site of the pivotal clash between Celtic and Viking forces at the Battle of Clontarf in 1014. Further along is North Bull Island, a wildlife sanctuary where many migratory birds pause in winter.

Howth is a popular excursion from Dublin and has developed as a residential suburb. It is a pretty little town built on steep streets running down to the waterfront. Although the harbour's role as a shipping port has long gone, Howth is now a major fishing centre and yachting harbour.

Most of the town backs onto the extensive grounds of Howth Castle, originally built in 1564 but much changed over the years, most recently in 1910 when Sir Edwin Lutyens gave it a modernist makeover. Today the castle is divided into four separate – very posh and private – residences. The original estate was acquired in 1177 by the Norman noble Sir

Transport

Distance from Dublin 9km

Direction Northeast

Bus Dublin Bus 31, 31A & 31B (€1.80, 45 min, every 30min) from Lower Abbey St.

Car Northeast along Clontarf Rd, along northern bay shoreline.

Train DART (€1.80; 20min, every 20min) to Howth.

Howth & History

Howth (which rhymes with 'both') was named by the Vikings and comes from the Danish word *hoved* (head). Fast-forward 2000 years to 1807, when the harbour was built, primarily to service packet boats coming in from England. By 1813, however, the harbour had begun to silt up, and 20 years later it was pretty much abandoned in favour of Dun Laoghaire. On the West Pier is the footprint of King George IV, who landed here in 1821 and literally staggered off the boat as he was pissed out of his head.

In 1914 Howth hit the headlines again when Robert Erskine Childers' yacht, the *Asgard*, brought ashore a shipment of 900 rifles to arm nationalists, only for the guns to be seized by the British. The yacht is now on display at Kilmainham Gaol in the city centre.

Almeric Tristram, who changed his surname to St Lawrence after winning a battle at the behest (or so he believed) of his favourite saint. The family has owned the land ever since, though the unbroken chain of male succession came to an end in 1909. Also on the grounds are the ruins of the 16th-century Corr Castle and an ancient dolmen (a Neolithic grave memorial built of vertical stones and topped by a table stone) known as Aideen's Grave. Legend has it that Aideen died of a broken heart after her husband was killed at the battle of Gavra near Tara in AD 184, but the legend is rubbish because the dolmen is at least 300 years older than that.

The **castle gardens** are worth visiting, however, as they're noted for their rhododendrons, which bloom in May and June, for their azaleas and for a long, 10m-high beech hedge planted in 1710.

Also within the grounds are the ruins of **St Mary's Abbey**, originally founded in 1042 by the Viking King Sitric, who also founded the original church on the site of Christ Church Cathedral. The abbey was amalgamated with the monastery on Ireland's Eye (see the boxed text above) in 1235. Some parts of the ruins date from that time, but most are from the 15th and 16th centuries. The tomb of Christopher St Lawrence (Lord Howth) in the southeastern corner dates from around 1470.

A more recent addition is the rather ramshackle **National Transport Museum**, which has a range of exhibits including double-decker buses, a bakery van, fire engines and trams – most notably a Hill of Howth electric that operated from 1901 to 1959. To reach the museum go through the castle gates and turn right just before the castle.

The allure of history and public transportation aside, most visitors set foot in the demesne armed with golf clubs, as here you'll find **Deer Park Golf Course**, a public facility attached to a hotel. An 18-hole course, two nine-hole courses and a Par-3 course, all with splendid views of Dublin Bay and the surrounding countryside, are the big draw.

Howth is essentially a very large hill surrounded by cliffs, and the summit (171m) has excellent views across Dublin Bay right down to Wicklow. From the summit you can walk to the top of the Ben of Howth, which has a cairn said to mark a 2000-year-old Celtic royal grave. The 1814 Baily Lighthouse at the southeastern corner is on the site of an old stone fort and can be reached by a dramatic cliff-top walk. There was an earlier hill-top beacon here in 1670.

Detour: Ireland's Eye

A short distance offshore from Howth is Ireland's Eye, a rocky sea-bird sanctuary with the ruins of a 6th-century monastery. There's a Martello tower at the northwestern end of the island, where boats from Howth's East Pier land, while the eastern end plummets into the sea in a spectacularly sheer rock face. As well as the sea birds overhead, you can see young birds on the ground during the nesting season. Seals can also be spotted around the island. Take the trip by boat with **Doyle & Sons** (☎ 831 4200; return €8; weekend afternoons May-Aug).

Howth

Sights & Information

Castle Gardens (admission free; ⊙ 24hr)

Deer Park Golf Course (☎ 832 2624; Howth Castle; 18-holes Mon-Fri/Sat & Sun €16/23.50, club rental €7; ⊙ 8am-dusk Mon-Fri, 6.30am-dusk Sat & Sun)

National Transport Museum (☎ 832 0427; Howth Castle; adult/student & child €2.50/1.25; ⊙ 10am-5pm Mon-Fri & 2-5pm Sat & Sun Easter-Aug, 2-5pm Sat & Sun rest of year)

St Mary's Abbey (Abbey St, Howth Castle; admission free; ⊙ see caretaker or read instructions on gate)

Eating

Aqua (☎ 832 0690; West Pier; mains €24-32) Interesting variations on traditional seafood dishes in a minimalist setting. Carnivores also well served.

Abbey Tavern (☎ 839 0307; Abbey St; mains around €24, 3-course dinner €30) Better-than-average pub grub, with the emphasis on seafood and meat at this 16th-century tavern.

King Sitric (☎ 832 5235; East Pier; mains €25-55, 5-course dinner €49) Howth's best restaurant has rightfully been praised for its exquisite seafood. Top-notch wine list too.

Sleeping

Deer Park Hotel (☎ 832 2624; sales@deerpark.iol.ie; Howth Castle; r from €100; P) The headland's top hotel has large rooms with all the comforts.

Highfield (☎ 832 3936; Thormanby Rd; s/d €40/65; P) A fine Victorian house with three rooms decorated with a mix of antiques and modern comforts.

Inisradharc (☎ 832 2306; Balkill Rd; s/d from €54/70; P) A modernist 1950s house with three rooms, all with private bathroom and views of Ireland's Eye.

King Sitric (☎ 832 5235; East Pier; s/d €121/198) Eight beautifully decorated rooms above Howth's most famous restaurant.

MALAHIDE

Once a small village with its own harbour a long way from the urban jungle of Dublin, the only thing protecting Malahide (Mullach Ide) from the northwards expansion of Dublin's suburbs is Malahide Demesne, 101 well-tended hectares of parkland dominated by a castle once owned by the powerful Talbot family. The handsome village remains relatively intact, but the once quiet marina has been massively developed and is now a bustling centre with a pleasant promenade and plenty of restaurants and shops.

Despite the vicissitudes of Irish history, the Talbot family managed to keep Malahide Castle under its control from 1185 to 1976, apart from when Cromwell was in power (1649–60). It's now owned by Dublin County Council. The castle is the usual hotchpotch of additions and renovations. The oldest part is a three-storey, 12th-century tower house. The facade is flanked by circular towers, tacked on in 1765.

The castle is packed with furniture and paintings. Highlights include a 16th-century oak room with decorative carvings and the medieval Great Hall with family portraits, a minstrel's gallery and a painting of the Battle of the Boyne. Puck, the Talbot family ghost, is said to have last appeared in 1975.

The country's biggest collection of toy trains is the **Fry Model Railway**, a 240-sq-metre model that authentically displays much of Ireland's rail and public transport system, including the DART line and Irish Sea ferry services, in O-gauge (32mm track width). A separate room features model trains and other memorabilia. Unfortunately the operators suffer from the overseriousness of some grown men with complicated toys. Rather than let you simply look and admire, they herd you into the control room in groups for demonstrations.

The **parkland** around the castle is a good place for a picnic.

If you fancy a bit of Dublin from the sea, **Sea Safaris** runs speedboats from the marina as far south as Dalkey and back.

Transport

Distance from Dublin 13km

Direction North

Bus Dublin Bus 42 (€1.50, 45min, every 30min) from Lower Abbey St.

Car North along Malahide Rd.

Train DART (€2.40, 35min, every 20min) to Malahide.

Sights & Information

ry Model Railway (☎ 846 3779; Malahide Castle; adult/child/student/family €6/3.50/5/16.50, incl castle 10/5.50/8/28; 🕑 10am-1pm & 2-5pm Mon-Sat, 2-6pm un Apr-Sep, 2-5pm Sat, Sun & holidays only rest of year

Malahide Castle (☎ 846 2184; Malahide; adult/child/ student/family €6/3.50/5/16.50; 🕑 10am-5pm Mon-Sat, 11am-6pm Sun Apr-Oct, 11am-5pm Sat & Sun Nov-Mar)

Malahide Castle Parkland (admission free; 🕑 10am-pm Apr-Oct, 10am-5pm Nov-Mar)

Sea Safaris (☎ 806 1626; www.seasafari.ie; Malahide Marina; €25 per hr)

Eating

Beanos (☎ 806 1880; 1-3 The Green; mains €15-22) There are excellent pizzas (€9), a huge selection of burgers (€6-10) and a range of main courses at this popular new eatery.

Bon Appétit (☎ 845 0314; 9 St James' Tce; mains €23-33) The village's best restaurant features a superb menu of fish, meat and vegetarian options.

Cruzzo Bar & Restaurant (☎ 845 0599; The Marina; dishes €12-21) An American-style Italian restaurant that serves up solid but unspectacular dishes.

Le Restaurant 12A (☎ 806 1928; 12A New St; dishes €13-22) A limited menu of French-inspired dishes presented in an elegant setting.

Siam Thai Restaurant (☎ 845 4698; Gas Lane, The Marina; dishes €12-16) Thai classics for local palates means that you can vary the spiciness and be assured no MSG is used.

Sleeping

Grand Hotel (☎ 845 0000; www.thegrand.ie; Main St; s/d €210/260; Ⓟ) A 19th-century hotel that is a Dublin classic, with beautifully furnished rooms and a tradition of excellent service. There's a swimming pool too.

DALKEY

In medieval times Dalkey (Deilginis) was Dublin's most important port town, a far cry from the dormitory town it is today, but there are still some revealing vestiges of its important past. There were eight castles in the area, but only the remains of three still exist. Facing each other on the appositely named Castle St are the 15th-century Archibold's Castle and Goat Castle. The latter, along with the adjoining St Begnet's Church, have been converted into the **Dalkey Castle & Heritage Centre**, where models, displays and exhibitions form a pretty interesting history of Dalkey and an insight into the area during medieval times.

Overlooking Bullock Harbour are the remains of Bulloch Castle, built by the monks of St Mary's Abbey in Dublin around 1150.

A few hundred metres offshore is Dalkey Island, home to **St Begnet's Holy Well**, the most important of Dalkey's so-called holy wells. This one is reputed to cure rheumatism, making the island a popular destination for tourists and the faithful alike. It is easily accessible by boat from Coliemore Harbour; you can't book one so just show up. The waters around the island are popular with scuba divers; qualified divers can rent gear in Dun Laoghaire, further north, from **Ocean Divers**.

Transport

Distance from Dublin 8km

Direction South

Bus Dublin Bus 8 (€1.60, 1hr, every 25min) from Burgh Quay to Dalkey.

Car N11 south to Dalkey.

Train DART south to Dalkey (€1.60, 20min, every 10-20min).

Detour: South to Killiney

About 1km south of Dalkey is the super-affluent seaside suburb of Killiney, home to some of Ireland's wealthiest people and a handful of celebrities, including Bono, Enya and filmmaker Neil Jordan. The attraction is self-evident, from the long, curving sandy beach of Killiney Bay (which 19th-century residents felt resembled Naples' Sorrento Bay, hence the Italian names of all the local roads) to the gorse-covered hills behind it, which make for a great walk. Alas, for most of us Killiney will always remain a place to visit: on the rare occasion that a house comes on the market, it would take a cool €5 million to get your hands on it.

To the south there are good views from the small park at Sorrento Point and from Killiney Hill. Dalkey Quarry is a popular site for rock climbers, and originally provided most o the granite for the gigantic piers at Dun Laoghaire Harbour. A number of rocky swimming pools are found along the Dalkey coast.

Sights & Information

Dalkey Castle & Heritage Centre (☎ 285 8366; Castle St; adult/child/student €4/2.50/3.50; ☺ 9.30am-5pm Mon-Fri May-Oct, 11am-5pm Sat & Sun all year)

Ocean Divers (☎ 280 1083; www.oceandivers.ie; West Pier; half-day dive, full equipment & boat €50)

St Begnet's Holy Well (admission free; boat from Coliemore Harbour €25 per hr)

Eating

Nosh (☎ 284 0666; 111 Coliemore Rd; lunch €10, dinner €20) A newish restaurant with an exceptional menu at lunch and dinner featuring a wide range of international dishes.

Queen's (☎ 285 4569; 12 Castle St; lunch €8-10) A Dalkey institution offering a great pub lunch of meat and fish dishes

Ragazzi (☎ 284 7280; 109 Coliemore Rd; pizza €8-10) Possibly the best Italian bistro in County Dublin is renowned for its thin-base pizzas and marvellously chaotic atmosphere.

Directory

DIRECTORY

TRANSPORT
AIR

There are direct flights to Dublin from all major European centres (including a dizzying array of options from the UK) and from Boston, Baltimore, Chicago, New York and Los Angeles in the USA. Flights from further afield (Australasia or Africa) are usually routed through London. From the UK, one-way fares with a low-fare airline such as Ryanair or CityJet can be as low as €10 (plus tax), but more often than not they are between €50 and €100. Low-fare airlines are the cheapest way of getting to Dublin from mainland Europe – with discount deals offering flights from cities such as Paris for €29 – but they need to be booked weeks in advance and cannot be changed. From the USA the Irish national airline Aer Lingus offers a constantly changing menu of fares, but you should expect to pay between €200 and €300 for a one-way fare from New York.

Airlines

No airline has a walk-in office in Dublin, but most have walk-up counters at Dublin airport. Those that don't have their ticketing handled by other airlines. The website of the **Fáilte Ireland** (Irish Tourist Board; www.ireland.travel.ie) has information on getting to Dublin from a number of countries.

Airlines that serve Dublin include:

Aer Arann (☎ 814 5240; www.aerarann.com)

Aer Lingus (departures & arrivals ☎ 886 6705, reservations ☎ 886 8888; www.aerlingus.com)

Aeroflot (☎ 844 6166; www.aeroflot.org)

Air Canada (☎ 679 3958, 1800 709 900; www.aircanada.ca)

Air France/CityJet (☎ 844 5633; www.airfrance.co.uk, www.cityjet.com)

Alitalia (☎ 844 6035; www.alitalia.co.uk)

Austrian Airlines (☎ 1800 509 142; www.aua.com)

British Airways (☎ 1890 626 747; www.british airways.com)

British Midland (☎ 407 3036; www.flybmi.com)

Delta Air Lines (☎ 1800 768 080; www.delta-air.com)

EuroManx (☎ 677 9606; www.euromanx.com)

Finnair (☎ 844 6565; www.finnair.co.uk)

Iberia (☎ 407 3017; www.iberia.com)

Lufthansa Airlines (☎ 844 5544; www.lufthansa.com)

Qantas Airways (☎ 407 3278; www.qantas.com.au)

Ryanair (www.ryanair.com)

Scandinavian Airlines (SAS; ☎ 844 5440; www.scandinavian.net)

Swiss (☎ 1890 200 515; www.swiss.com)

Warning

The information in this section is particularly vulnerable to change: prices for international travel are volatile, routes are introduced and cancelled, schedules change, special deals come and go, and rules and visa requirements are amended. In addition, the travel industry is highly competitive and there are many lurks and perks.

Get opinions, quotes and advice from as many airlines and travel agents as possible before you part with your hard-earned cash and double-check you understand how a fare (and any ticket you may buy) works. The details given in this chapter should be regarded as pointers and are not a substitute for your own careful, up-to-date research into the current situation.

Airport

Dublin's only **airport** (Map p274; ☎ 814 1111, www.dublinairport.com) is 13km north of the city centre. Along with pubs, restaurants, shops, ATMs and car-hire desks, airport facilities in the one passenger terminal include:

Aer Rianta Information Desk (Irish Airport Authority; 🕑 6am-11pm)

Bank of Ireland (🕑 10am-4pm Mon-Tue & Thu-Fri, 10.30am-5pm Wed; bureau de change 🕑 5.30am-8pm Mon-Thu, 5.30am-9pm Fri-Sun)

Dublin Airport Pharmacy (☎ 814 4649; 🕑 6.30am-6.30pm Mon-Thu, 9am-10.30pm Fri-Sun)

Dublin Tourism Office (🕑 8am-10pm)

Greencaps Left Luggage and Porterage Office (☎ 814 4633; left luggage per 24 hr €6-8; 🕑 6am-11pm)

International Currency Exchange (🕑 5.30am-midnight)

Nursery (🕑 9am-10pm)

Post Office (🕑 9am-5pm Mon-Fri)

There is no train service to and from the airport. It takes about 45 minutes to get there by bus or taxi. Transport options are as follows:

BUS

Aircoach (☎ 844 7118; www.aircoach.ie; single/return €6/10) Private coach service from the airport to 15 destinations in a loop throughout the city (see the boxed text below).

Airlink Express Coach (☎ 872 0000, 873 4222; www.dublinbus.ie; adult/child €5/2) Bus 747 runs every 10 to 20 minutes from 5.45am to 11.30pm between the airport, central bus station (Busáras; Map pp264-5) and Dublin Bus office on Upper O'Connell St (Map pp264-5); bus 748 runs every 15 to 30 minutes from 6.50am to 22.05pm between the airport and Heuston and Connolly stations (Maps pp262-3 & pp264-5, respectively).

Dublin Bus (☎ 872 0000; www.dublinbus.ie; 59 Upper O'Connell St; adult/child €2/0.75) A number of buses serve the airport from various points in Dublin, including buses 16A (Rathfarnham), 746 (Dun Laoghaire) and 230 (Portmarnock); all cross the city centre on their way to the airport.

Aircoach Stops

Outbound

Gresham Hotel (O'Connell St)

Trinity College

American College (Merrion Square North)

Jury's Hotel (Ballsbridge)

Toyota Centre (Merrion Rd)

Bewley's Hotel (Simmonscourt Rd)

Inbound

Ever Ready Garage (Donnybrook)

Burlington Hotel (Upper Leeson St)

Grand Canal (Upper Leeson St)

Stephen's Hall Hotel (Lower Leeson St)

Lucent House (St Stephen's Green)

Thomas Pink (Dawson St)

McCullough Piggott (Suffolk St)

Eddie Rocket's (O'Connell St)

Royal Dublin Hotel (O'Connell St)

TAXI

There is a taxi rank directly outside the arrivals concourse. A taxi should cost about €20 from the airport to the city centre, including a supplementary charge of €2.50 (not applied going to the airport). Make sure the meter is switched on.

Online Booking Agencies

- www.bestfares.com
- www.cheapflights.com
- www.ebookers.com
- www.expedia.com
- www.flycheap.com
- www.opodo.com
- www.priceline.com
- www.statravel.com
- www.travelocity.com

BICYCLE

Rust-red cycle lanes throughout the city make cycling in Dublin easier than ever, although traffic congestion, motorised maniacs and seemingly permanent roadworks can make the city something of an obstacle course. Bike theft is a major problem, so be sure to park on busier streets, preferably at one of the myriad U-shaped parking bars. Never leave your bike on the street overnight.

Cycle-logical (Map pp269-71; ☎ 872 4635; 3 Bachelor's Walk) A shop for serious enthusiasts, with all the best equipment as well as a good source of information on upcoming cycling events. It does not, however, do repairs.

Square Wheel Cycleworks (Map pp269-71; ☎ 679 0838; Temple Lane South) Does repairs, and will have your bike back to you within a day or so (barring serious damage).

Hire

Bike rental has become increasingly more difficult to find because of crippling insurance costs. Typical rental for a mountain bike is around €25 per day or €100 per week. Raleigh Rent-a-Bike agencies can be found through **Eurotrek** (☎ 456 8847; www.raleigh.ie). Agencies in Dublin include:

C Harding for Bikes (Map pp269-71; ☎ 873 2455; 30 Bachelor's Walk)

Hollingsworth Bikes (☎ 296 0255; 1 Drummartin Rd, Stillorgan, Dublin 14)

Irish Cycling Safaris (☎ 260 0749; UCD)

Joe Daly (☎ 298 1485; Lower Main St, Dundrum)

Little Sport (Map pp260-1; ☎ 833 2405; 3 Marville Ave, Fairview, Dublin 3)

MacDonalds Cycles (Map pp266-8; ☎ 475 2586; 38 Wexford St)

Bicycles on Public Transport

Bikes are only allowed on suburban trains (not the DART), either in the guard's van or in a special compartment at the opposite end of the train from the engine. There's a €4 charge for transporting a bicycle up to 56km.

BOAT

Dublin has two ferry ports. The **Dun Laoghaire ferry terminal** (☎ 280 1905; Dun Laoghaire), 13km southeast of the city centre, serves Holyhead in Wales and is easily accessible via the DART and public bus. The **Dublin Port terminal** (☎ 855 2222; Alexandra Rd), which serves Holyhead, Mostyn and Liverpool, is 3km northeast of the city centre and public transport is linked to ferry departure and arrival times.

Between Dublin and Holyhead, the ferry crossing takes just over three hours and costs around €30/140 (one way, foot passenger/medium-sized car with two passengers). The fast-boat service from Holyhead to Dun Laoghaire takes a little over 1½ hours and costs €39/265. The ferry takes seven hours from Mostyn to Dublin, or 7½ hours from Liverpool, and costs €30/200. Cabins are obligatory on overnight sailings and cost more. The fast-boat service takes four hours and costs up to €60/300.

The ferry companies that run services to and from Dublin are:

Irish Ferries (Map pp266-8; ☎ 1890 313 131; www .irishferries.com; 2-4 Merrion Row, Dublin 2) Ferry and fast-boat services from Holyhead to Dublin.

Isle of Man Steam Packet Company/Sea Cat (☎ 836 4019; www.steam-packet.com; Maritime House, North Wall, Dublin 1) Ferry and fast-boat services from Liverpool to Dublin via Douglas on the Isle of Man.

P&O Irish Sea (☎ 407 3434; www.poirishsea.com; Terminal 3, Dublin Port) Ferry services from Liverpool or Mostyn to Dublin.

Stena Line (☎ 204 7777; www.stenaline.com; Ferry Terminal, Dun Laoghaire) Ferry and fast-boat services from Holyhead to Dun Laoghaire.

To/From the Ferry Terminals

Buses go to the central bus station, Busáras, from the Dublin Port terminal after all ferry arrivals from Holyhead. Buses also run from Busáras to meet ferry departures. For the 9.45am ferry departure from Dublin, buses leave Busáras at 8.30am. For the 9.45pm departure, buses depart Busáras at 8.30pm. For the 1am sailing to Liverpool, the bus departs Busáras at 11.45pm. All buses cost €2.

To travel between Dun Laoghaire ferry terminal and Dublin, take bus No 46A to St Stephen's Green, or bus No 7, 7A or 8 to Burgh Quay, or take the DART to Pearse Station (for south Dublin) or Connolly Station (for north Dublin).

BUS
To/From UK

It's possible to combine bus and ferry tickets from major UK centres to Dublin on the bus network, but with the availability of cheap flights it's hardly worth the hassle. The journey between London and Dublin takes about 12 hours and costs UK£27 one way. For details in London contact **Eurolines** (☎ 0870 514 3219; www.eurolines.com).

Around Dublin

The **Dublin Bus Office** (Map pp264-5; ☎ 872 0000; www.dublinbus.ie; 59 Upper O'Connell St; ☺ 9am-5.30pm Mon-Fri, 9am-2pm Sat) has free single-route timetables of all its services.

Busáras (Map pp264-5; ☎ 836 6111; www .buseireann.ie; Store St) is just north of the river behind Custom House; it has a left-luggage facility costing €2.50 per item.

Buses run from around 6am (some start at 5.30am) to 11.30pm. Fares are calculated according to stages:

1-3 stages €0.80

4-7 stages €1.20

8-13 stages €1.40

14-23 stages €1.60

23+ stages €1.70 (inside Citizone), €2 (outside Citizone)

The city centre (Citizone) is within a 13-stage radius. You must tender exact change when boarding; anything more and you will be given a receipt for reimbursement, only possible at the Dublin Bus main office.

Fare-saver passes include:

Adult (Bus & Rail) Short Hop (€7.70) Valid for unlimited one-day travel on Dublin Bus, DART and suburban rail travel, but not Nitelink or Airlink.

Family Bus & Rail Short Hop (€11.60) Valid for travel for one day for a family of two adults and two children aged under 16 on all bus and rail services except for Nitelink, Airlink, ferry services and tours.

Rambler Pass (one/three/five/seven days €5/9.50/14.50/ 17.50) Valid for unlimited travel on all Dublin Bus and Airlink services, but not Nitelink.

Transfer Ninety Citizone (€2) Valid for two consecutive bus journeys within Citizone, provided second journey begins within 90 minutes of beginning of first.

Nitelink

Nitelink late-night buses run from the College St, Westmoreland St and D'Olier St triangle (Map pp266-8). From Monday to Wednesday, there are usually only two departures, at 12.30am and 2am. From Thursday to Saturday, departures are at 12.30am, then every 20 minutes until 4.30am on the more popular routes and until 3.30am on the less frequented ones. Fares are €4 (€6 to the far suburbs).

Road Safety Rules in Dublin

- Drive on the left, overtake to the right.
- Safety belts must be worn by the driver and all passengers.
- Children aged under 12 aren't allowed to sit on the front seats.
- Motorcyclists and their passengers must wear helmets.
- When entering a roundabout, give way to the right.
- Speed limits are 30mph (48km/h) or as signposted in the city, 60mph (96km/h) on all roads outside city limits and 70mph (112km/h) on motorways.
- The legal alcohol limit is 80mg of alcohol per 100mL of blood or 35mg on the breath (roughly two units of alcohol for a man and one for a woman).

CAR & MOTORCYCLE

Driving

The **Automobile Association of Ireland** (AA; Map pp272-3; ☎ 677 9481, breakdown ☎ 1800 667 788; 23 Suffolk St, Dublin 2) is located in the city centre.

Traffic in Dublin is a nightmare, and parking is an expensive headache. There are no free spots to park anywhere in the city centre during business hours (7am to 7pm Monday to Saturday), but there are plenty of parking meters, 'pay & display' spots (€2.50 per hour) and over a dozen sheltered and supervised car parks (around €4 per hour).

Clamping of illegally parked cars is thoroughly enforced, with a €80 charge for removal. Parking is free after 7pm Monday to Saturday and all day Sunday in all metered spots and on single yellow lines.

Car theft and break-ins are a problem, and the police advise visitors to park in a supervised car park. Cars with foreign number plates are prime targets; never leave your valuables behind. When you're booking accommodation check on parking facilities.

Rental

Car rental in Dublin is expensive, so you're often better off making arrangements in your home country with some sort of package deal. In July and August it's wise to book well ahead. Most cars are manual; automatic cars are available but they're more expensive to hire. Motorbikes and mopeds are not available for rent.

Nova Car Hire (www.rentacar-ireland.com) acts as an agent for Alamo, Budget, European and National and offers greatly discounted rates. Typical weekly high-season rental rates with Nova are around €150 for a small car, €190 for a medium-sized car and €525 for a five-seater people carrier. People aged under 21 aren't allowed to hire a car; for the majority of rental companies you have to be aged at least 23 and have had a valid driving licence for a minimum of one year. Many rental agencies will not rent to people over 70 or 75.

The main rental agencies, which also have offices at the **airport** (⏰ 6am-11pm), are:

Avis Rent-a-Car (Map pp266-8; ☎ 1890 405 060; www.avis.com; 1 East Hanover St)

Budget Rent-a-Car (Map pp260-1; ☎ 837 9611, airport ☎ 844 5150; www.budget.ie; 151 Lower Drumcondra Rd, Dublin 7)

Dan Dooley Car Hire (Map pp266-8; ☎ 677 2723, airport ☎ 844 5156; www.dan-dooley.ie; 42-43 Westland Row, Dublin 2)

Europcar (Map pp266-8; ☎ 614 2800, airport ☎ 844 4179; www.europcar.com; Baggot St Bridge, Dublin 4)

Hertz Rent-a-Car (Map pp260-1; ☎ 660 2255, airport ☎ 844 5466; www.hertz.com; 149 Upper Leeson St, Dublin 2)

Sixt Rent-a-Car (☎ 862 2715, airport ☎ 844 4199; www.irishcarrentals.ie; Old Airport Rd, Santry, Dublin 9)

Thrifty (Map pp262-3; ☎ 454 6600, airport ☎ 840 0800; www.thrifty.ie; 125 Herberton Bridge, South Circular Rd, Dublin 8)

TAXI

All taxi fares begin with a flagfall fare of €2.75, followed by €0.15 per unit (one-ninth of a mile or 30 seconds) thereafter from 8am to 10pm, or €0.20 per unit from 10pm to 8am and bank holidays. In addition there are a number of extra charges – €0.50 for each extra passenger, €0.50 for each piece of luggage and €1.50 for telephone bookings.

Taxis can be hailed on the street and are found at taxi ranks around the city, including O'Connell St (Map pp269-71), College Green in front of Trinity College (Map pp269-71) and St Stephen's Green at the end of Grafton St (Map pp272-3). There are numerous taxi companies that will dispatch taxis by radio. These include:

City Cabs (☎ 872 2688)

National Radio Cabs (☎ 677 2222)

Phone the **Garda Carriage Office** (☎ 475 5888) if you have any complaints about taxis and queries regarding lost property.

Taxi Trauma

Taxi queues are frustratingly long late at night (when the bars and clubs close), making for waits of up to an hour and more. Calling one by phone is often met with a negative response during these busy hours, and you can't book one in advance (unless you're travelling to the airport). Try to avoid the busy period between 2am and 3.30am; otherwise we suggest learning tantric meditation to deal with the interminably long queues.

TRAIN
DART

The **Dublin Area Rapid Transport** (DART; Map p274; ☎ 836 6222) provides quick train access to the coast as far north as Howth (about 30 minutes) and as far south as Bray (about 30 minutes), although upgrades to tracks and stations have limited these routes on weekends (see the boxed text below). Pearse Station is convenient for central Dublin south of the Liffey, and Connolly Station for north of the Liffey. There are services every 10 to 20 minutes, sometimes even more frequently, from around 6.30am to midnight Monday to Saturday. Services are less frequent on Sunday. Dublin to Dun Laoghaire takes about 15 to 20 minutes. A one-way DART ticket from Dublin to Dun Laoghaire or Howth costs €1.70; to Bray it's €2.50.

There are also Suburban Rail services north as far as Dundalk, inland to Mullingar and south past Bray to Arklow.

DART passes include the following:

Adult Weekly Inner Rail Pass (€20) Valid on all DART and suburban train services between Bray to the south and Rush & Lusk to the north.

All Day Ticket (adult/child €6.50/3) One-day unlimited travel on DART and suburban rail services.

Irish Explorer Rail Pass (adult/child €105/53) Five days of travel within 15 days in standard class on all Republic of Ireland rail services, DART and suburban trains.

Three-Day Rolling Pass (train only/train & bus €13/15) Three consecutive days unlimited travel on DART and suburban rail services; bus option includes all Dublin Bus services but not Nitelink or Airlink.

Irish Rail

All rail information, including timetables and ticket and pass sales, is available from the **Rail Travel Centre** (Iarnród Éireann; Map pp264-5, ☎ 836 6222; www.irishrail.ie; 34 Lower Abbey St). The city has two main train stations: Heuston Station (Map pp262-3), on the western side of town near the Liffey, and Connolly Station (Map pp264-5), a short walk northeast of Busáras, behind Custom House. Heuston Station has left-luggage lockers of three sizes, costing €1.50/3/5 for 24 hours. At Connolly Station the facility costs €2.50.

LUAS

LUAS (from the Irish word for 'light'; www .luas.ie) is a light rail system that has been under construction since 1999. At the time of writing, work on three lines was to be completed by Christmas 2003 and it was to be up and running in early 2004. The huge project has been beset by delays and budgetary problems so nothing is entirely certain. What is sure, though, is that traffic has been seriously disrupted throughout the city as construction of the lines proceeds towards uncertain completion.

DART Upgrade

As a result of a massive programme of station and track improvement, there will be no DART service south of Connolly Station Saturday and Sunday until mid-2004, and north of Connolly Station the same days for nine months thereafter. Transport authorities have tripled the number of buses serving these routes to make up for the inevitable hassle, but it is bound to cause plenty of delays and headaches.

During peak times, the trams will depart at five-minute intervals. When open, the LUAS will operate along the following lines:

Line A Tallaght-Abbey St (38 minutes; via St James's Hospital, Heuston Station, IMMA, Smithfield, Four Courts and Jervis Centre)

Line B Sandyford Industrial Estate-St Stephen's Green (22 minutes; via Ranelagh, Charlemont St and Harcourt St)

Line C Extension of Line A from Abbey St to Connolly Station (via Busáras)

PRACTICALITIES

ACCOMMODATION

Sleeping entries in this book are divided geographically into two main sections: north of the Liffey and south of the Liffey. They are further divided into neighbourhoods, and then alphabetically. Budget options (Cheap Sleeps) are included at the end of the two main sections. See p195 for details of price ranges, bookings and long-term rentals.

B&Bs

Bed-and-breakfasts are family homes that take in visitors during the holiday season. Most have between two and four rooms, typically equipped with a bed, tea and coffee-making facilities and, in some cases, a hand basin. Most do not come with a bathroom, nor do they have phones. All B&Bs serve breakfast, which is included in the price. It is usually served between 7am and 9.30am; if you want it earlier, check with the owner. They generally won't provide one after they've stopped serving everyone else. In Dublin, the only central B&Bs are along Gardiner St; all the rest are in the outlying suburbs. Dublin Tourism also refers to them as town houses, but most of these are more like guesthouses.

Guesthouses & Town Houses

These are fancier versions of the B&B, usually converted Georgian or Edwardian houses with up to 10 rooms (some have added annexes and more rooms) that operate as a small hotel. Unlike hotels, they don't have a bar and a restaurant open to nonresidents. Rooms here are generally of a pretty good standard and come with bathroom. A large number of more upmarket houses have taken to calling themselves boutique hotels, and that is precisely what they are. Special care is taken in the decor, whether it be modern minimalist or traditional Georgian, and it is not unusual for rooms to have specially made furniture and/or antiques to give the place a particular atmosphere. Modern touches like direct-dial phones and even modem connections are increasingly common. Service is of a very high standard, as these accommodations pride themselves on their ability to provide a personalised attention not found in larger hotels. In Dublin, there are a number of extraordinary houses that outdo even luxury hotels in their efforts to make a guest comfortable. Breakfasts, which are also included in the price, are of a very high standard, and there's plenty of choice, from the ubiquitous Irish fry to the continental choice of breads, fruits and cereals.

Hostels

In Dublin, hostels provide the only reasonable budget accommodation. Most of them have plenty of character and decent facilities, including TV lounges, bulletin boards, kitchens, laundry, bike-parking facilities and Internet access. Some have en-suite bathrooms, even the dorms. Most city centre hostels now have family rooms and doubles.

With one exception, all of Dublin's hostels are independently run. **An Óige** (Map pp264-5; ☎ 830 4555; www.irelandyha.org; 61 Mountjoy St, Dublin 1; ☺ 9.30am-5.30pm Mon-Fri) is the Irish affiliate of Hostelling International (HI) and has 33 hostels scattered throughout the country. Its Dublin hostel, however, is in a dodgy part of town and simply does not stand up well compared to other hostels in the city. For information on independent hostels, **Independent Holiday Hostels of Ireland** (IHH; Map pp264-5; ☎ 836 4700; www.hostels-ireland.com; 57 Lower Gardiner St, Dublin) is a reliable association.

Hotels

Hotels range from the traditional 20-room hostelry with faded decor to the supermodern international chain hotel with 300 rooms and all the trimmings. Hotels on the lower end of the scale have gone to great lengths to update their look and facilities in an effort to counter the threat of upper-end guesthouses, which in recent years have poached a larger share of hotel customers. Most hotels in Dublin, and all of those listed in the Sleeping chapter, maintain high standards in keeping with their price bracket: a mid-range property, for instance, will have decent-size bedrooms with bathrooms, direct-dial phones, TV and tea and coffee-making facilities. The further up the scale you go, the more luxury you can expect. The top hotels are no different to the ones you'd find in London, Paris or New York. Most of these also have added facilities like a health club and, in some cases, a swimming pool.

BABYSITTING

Many hotels can provide babysitting on request (normally per hour €8 to €12). You could also try agencies that provide professional nannies. It's up to you to negotiate a fee with the nanny but €15 per hour is the average, plus taxi fare if s/he isn't driving. You'll need to sign a form beforehand that the agency will fax to your hotel. Agencies to try include:

Belgrave Agency (☎ 280 9341; 55 Mulgrave St, Dun Laoghaire; per hr €13 plus 21% VAT)

Executive Nannies (Map pp264-5; ☎ 873 1273; 43 Lower Dominick St; per hr €20)

BUSINESS HOURS

Compared to other European capitals, Dublin is relatively late-rising, and you won't see much life on the streets before 9am. For general opening hours for Dublin's various businesses, see the Quick Reference on the inside front cover.

A small number of city-centre cafés are open until midnight – later at weekends – while some restaurants only open for dinner and stay open as long as there are customers to be served. Some city-centre pubs have late licences that entitle them to serve alcohol until 2.30am every night except Sunday, when the 11.30pm closing time is strictly enforced. Pubs are only closed two days a year: Good Friday and Christmas Day.

CHILDREN

Dublin is a very child-friendly city. Hotels will provide cots at no extra charge and most restaurants have highchairs. Overall, restaurants and hotels will go to great lengths to cater for children, although some restaurants lose their interest in kids after 6pm. Children are not allowed in pubs after 7pm. Under-fives travel free on all public transport.

Family tickets to most attractions are available, and many tourist sites have made their exhibitions more child-friendly, creating interactive spaces for kids to play (and learn) in.

Although breast-feeding in Dublin is not a common sight (Ireland has one of the lowest rates of it in the world), you can do so with impunity pretty much everywhere without getting so much as a stare. There are virtually no nappy-changing facilities in Dublin, so you'll have to make do with a public toilet. For more information and inspiration on how to make travelling with children as hassle-free as possible, see the boxed text on p86 and also check out Lonely Planet's *Travel With Children* by Cathy Lanigan.

CLIMATE

Dublin enjoys a milder climate than its northerly position might indicate, largely thanks to the influence of the North Atlantic Drift, or Gulf Stream. The warmest months of the year are July and August, when temperatures range from 15° to 20°C, while the coldest months – January and February – see the thermometer drop to between 4° and 8°C. It never gets too cold (major snowfalls are a rarity) but it never gets too hot either: even in summer you're better off carrying a sweater or a light jacket.

Dublin is one of the drier parts of Ireland, but in a typical year it still rains on 150 days (a total yearly average of 75cm). Summers are a meteorological lottery: it's impossible to predict whether it'll be a wet one or not, making forecasting a favourite subject of amateurs throughout the city ('Well, it rained all of April, so that means we'll have a good June'). Bring an umbrella. What is a certainty, however, is the long summer day: in July and August there are about 18 hours of daylight; it's only truly dark after about 11pm.

For weather forecasts, dial ☎ 1550 123 822.

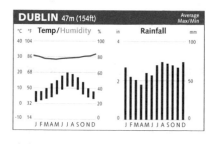

COURSES

Dublin is well known for its English-language schools. For a complete list of these and other courses, get a copy of the yearly *Dublin's Evening*

Classes (Oisín Publications; €4.99), available at most bookshops. Most courses available in the city run for extended periods ranging from four to six weeks to a year and more.

CUSTOMS

Duty-free sales are not available when travelling within the European Union (EU). Goods for personal consumption bought in and exported within the EU incur no additional taxes, if duty has been paid somewhere in the EU. Over certain limits you may have to show that they are for personal use. The amounts that officially constitute personal use are: 800 cigarettes, 400 cigarillos, 200 cigars or 1kg of tobacco; 10L of spirits, 20L of fortified wine, 60L of sparkling wine, 90L of still wine or 110L of beer.

Travellers coming from outside the EU are allowed to import, duty-free: 200 cigarettes, 1L of spirits or 2L of wine, 60mL of perfume and 250mL of toilet water.

It is illegal to bring into Ireland meat (and meat products) and plants and plant products (including seeds). Dogs and cats from anywhere outside Ireland and the UK are subject to strict quarantine laws. The EU Pet Travel Scheme, whereby animals are fitted with a microchip, vaccinated against rabies and blood-tested six months prior to entry, will come into force in the Republic of Ireland mid-2004. In the meantime, animals arriving into Ireland are quarantined for six months unless they first pass through the UK and meet British criteria for entry. Contact the **Department of Agriculture, Food & Rural Development** (☎ 607 2000; www.agriculture.gov.ie) for further details.

When leaving the country, non-EU visitors are allowed take home the equivalent of US$4000 worth of goods per person.

DISABLED TRAVELLERS

In 2003 Dublin hosted the Special Olympics World Games to a resounding success, which brought the needs and entitlements of people with disabilities to the forefront of the national debate. What is clear is that despite the fact that many of the city's hotels, restaurants and sights are increasingly being adapted for people with disabilities, there's still a long way to go, especially as there still exists an attitude that can best be summarised as 'if a problem comes up, we'll find a solution somehow'. Fáilte Ireland's annual accommodation guide, *Be Our Guest*, indicates which places are ac-

cessible by wheelchair. Public transport can be a nightmare, although a limited number of buses are now equipped with electronic elevators for wheelchairs, and nearly all DART stations have ramps and/or elevators.

The **Access Service** (Map pp264–5; ☎ 874 7503; www.comhairle.ie; 44 North Great George's St), which is part of the Social Service Board (Comhairle), provides plenty of helpful information regarding Dublin's accessibility to wheelchairs.

Another useful organisation is the **Irish Wheelchair Association** (☎ 818 6400; Áras Chúchulain, Blackheath Dr, Clontarf, Dublin 3).

DISCOUNT CARDS

Senior citizens are entitled to discounts on public transport and museum fees (with proof of age) and students and under-26s are entitled to a variety of discounts, from admission fees to cinema tickets, so long as they have the appropriate card (International Student Identity Card, International Youth Travel Card or European Youth Card/Euro<26). Other local discount cards worth checking out include:

Aer Lingus Thousand Welcomes Programme (www.aerlingus.com) Offers discounts on accommodation, car rental, restaurants, museum admissions, theatre tickets and other activities. Available only to visitors flying into Dublin with Aer Lingus from the USA. Sign up online.

Heritage Card (☎ 647 3000; www.heritageireland.com; adult/student & child €20/7.50; Education & Visitor Service, 6 Upper Ely Pl, Dublin 2) Entitles you to free access to all Dúchas-managed sights in and around Dublin.

ELECTRICITY

The standard electricity supply in Dublin is 220 volts AC and all sockets fit a three-pin plug. Pin converters are available in all electrical suppliers.

EMBASSIES & CONSULATES

Countries with diplomatic offices in Dublin include:

Australia (Map pp266–8; ☎ 664 5300; www.australianembassy.ie; 2nd floor, Fitzwilton House, Wilton Tce, Dublin 2)

Canada (Map pp266–8; ☎ 417 4100; 4th floor, 65 St Stephen's Green, Dublin 2)

France (☎ 260 1666; 36 Ailesbury Rd, Dublin 4)

Germany (☎ 269 3011; 31 Trimleston Ave, Booterstown, County Dublin)

Italy (Map pp266-8; ☎ 660 1744; 63 Northumberland Rd, Dublin 4)

Netherlands (☎ 269 3444; 160 Merrion Rd, Dublin 4)

New Zealand (Map pp260-1; ☎ 660 4233; 37 Leeson Park, Dublin 6)

UK (Map pp260-1; ☎ 205 3700; www.britishembassy.ie; 29 Merrion Rd, Ballsbridge, Dublin 4)

USA (Map pp260-1; ☎ 668 7122; aedublin@indigo.ie; 42 Elgin Rd, Dublin 4)

EMERGENCIES

For emergency assistance phone ☎ 999 or ☎ 112. This call is free and the operator will connect you with the type of assistance you specify: fire, police (gardai), ambulance, boat or coastal rescue. There are garda stations at Fitzgibbon St (Map pp264-5; ☎ 836 3113), Harcourt Tce (Map pp266-8; ☎ 676 3481), Pearse St (Map pp266-8; ☎ 677 8141) and Store St (Map pp264-5; ☎ 874 2761).

A full list of all emergency numbers can be found in the front pages of the telephone book). Included are:

Alcoholics Anonymous (Map pp260-1; ☎ 453 8998, after hours ☎ 679 5967; 109 South Circular Rd, Dublin 8)

Confidential Line Freefone (☎ 1800 666 111) Garda confidential line to report crime.

Drugs Advisory & Treatment Centre (Map pp266-8; ☎ 677 1122; Trinity Ct, 30-31 Pearse St, Dublin 2)

Rape Crisis Centre (Map pp266-8; ☎ 1800 778 888, 661 4911; 70 Lower Leeson St)

Samaritans (Map pp264-5; ☎ 1850 609 090, 872 7700; 112 Marlborough St) For people who are lonely, depressed or suicidal.

Senior Helpline (☎ 1850 440 444) For senior citizens with any kind of problem.

Women's Emergency Hostel (Map pp264-5; ☎ 873 2279; Haven House, Morning Star Ave, Dublin 7)

GAY & LESBIAN TRAVELLERS

Dublin's gay scene has never been more confident, more relaxed or more fun. Irish attitudes to homosexuality may still bear a conservative, traditional stamp in rural areas, but that's a million miles from the reality in Dublin. For a country with such a traditionally Catholic (hence antigay) reputation, laws that affect gays and lesbians are some of the most progressive and respectfully liberal in Europe – despite the fact that homosexuality was only decriminalised in 1993 (among men, that is,

as lesbianism was never illegal). The age of consent is 17. Dublin may be overwhelmingly Catholic, but the local church maintains a cautious silence on homosexuality, despite the vocal posturing of Rome.

Organisations that deal with gay & lesbian issues include:

National Lesbian and Gay Federation (Map pp269-71; ☎ 671 9076; homepage.tinet.ie/~nlgf; Unit 2 Scarlett Row, Essex St West, Temple Bar, Dublin 2) Ireland's main body for gays and lesbians.

Outhouse (Map pp264-5; ☎ 873 4932; www.out house.ie; 105 Capel St, Dublin 1) A gay, lesbian and transgender community centre.

The best publication in the city is the free, monthly *Gay Community News* (GCN; www .gcn.ie), published by the National Lesbian and Gay Federation, a good resource for information on being out in Dublin. *Free* is a brand-new magazine for gay men featuring good nightlife listings, topical stories and gay-related features. For nightlife info, see the Drinking & Entertainment chapters (p154 and p166, respectively).

Useful online resources for gay and lesbians in Dublin include:

Dublin Pride Festival (www.dublinpride.org) The official website of the Dublin Pride Festival (see also p10).

Gaire (www.gaire.com) An online bulletin board where you can post personals, find places to stay and buy stuff.

Gay Ireland (www.gay-ireland.com) Features, articles, entertainment listings and personal ads, plus a 'hunk of the month' feature.

HOLIDAYS

During the summer, Dublin is swamped by foreign students on English-language courses (see p234), which make for a noisy and enjoyable distraction on public transport (15 vocal Italian kids sporting the same Invicta backpacks are hard to miss), but the real problems occur when you try to get a hotel room without a prior reservation. During the summer, patience and plenty of phone calls will eventually get you somewhere, but forget about it during the St Patrick's Day festivities.

Public Holidays
New Year's Day 1 January
St Patrick's Day 17 March
Easter (Good Friday to Easter Monday inclusive) March/April
May Holiday 1 May

June Holiday 1st Monday in June

August Holiday 1st Monday in August

October Holiday Last Monday in October

Christmas Day 25 December

St Stephen's Day 26 December

St Patrick's Day, St Stephen's Day and May Day holidays are taken on the following Monday should they fall on a weekend.

School Holidays

Mid-term 16–20 February (two days only for primary schools)

Easter 5–16 April

Summer 1 June–31 August (from 1 July for primary schools)

Mid-term 27–31 October

Christmas 24 Dec–6 January

INTERNET ACCESS

If your computer isn't equipped to handle 220 volts AC or a three-point socket, you'll need a universal AC adapter and a plug adapter, which will enable you to plug in anywhere. All hotel rooms have phone lines and you can plug the phone lead into the back of your laptop; although most have direct-dial services, you'll most likely have to dial an outside line access number (usually 9) to get online. Provided you're dialling a local access number you'll be charged the price of a local call (which from a hotel is usually 50% more than usual).

Major Internet service providers (ISPs) such as **AOL** (www.aol.com), **CompuServe** (www.compuserve.com) and **AT&T Business Internet Services** (www.attbusiness.net) have dial-in nodes in Ireland. If you access your email account through a home-based ISP, your best option is to open an account with a local, global ISP provider: the most reliable ones are **Eircom** (☎ 702 0022; www.eircom.ie) or **O2** (☎ 1800 924 924; www.o2.ie).

If you want hassle-free Internet access, your best bet is to rely on Internet cafés, which are everywhere in Dublin. The connections are usually very quick, and you shouldn't pay any more than €5 per hour. The following city-centre Internet cafés offer quick, reliable connections:

Central Cyber Café (Map pp272-3; ☎ 677 8298; 6 Grafton St; ⏰ 9am-9pm)

Global Cyber Café (Map pp269-71; ☎ 878 0295; 8 Lower O'Connell St; ⏰ 8am-11pm)

Internet Exchange (Map pp269-71; ☎ 670 3000; 1 Cecilia St; ⏰ 24hr)

LEGAL MATTERS

If you need legal assistance contact the **Legal Aid Board** (☎ 1890 615 200). It has eight offices spread throughout Dublin; the central operator will direct you to the one most convenient to you.

The possession of small quantities of hash or marijuana (deemed Class C drugs) attracts a fine or warning, but harder drugs are treated more seriously: cocaine, ecstasy and heroin are considered Class A drugs; if you're caught in possession you can count on being arrested and prosecuted. The consumption of alcohol on the street and public drunkenness are both illegal, but the police are usually pretty lenient and at worst will issue a verbal warning and confiscate your booze. The legal drinking age is 18.

You are not legally required to carry any form of identification with you. The legal age for voting is 18, as it is for marriage (or 17 with consent of court). The age of consent for heterosexual and homosexual sex is 17, also the legal age for driving (full drivers licence).

MAPS

Lonely Planet publishes a laminated pocket-size map of Dublin, which is widely available in bookstores around town. The free maps of Dublin are usually quite adequate, at least for the major sites in the city centre. The Dublin Tourism Centre has a basic map of the city centre (€1), which covers the major sights, but it also has fairly detailed maps for hotels and restaurants.

If you would prefer to have an indexed street directory, the **Dublin Street Guide** (€12.70; scale 1:15,000, city centre 1:10,000), published by the Ordnance Survey Ireland (OSI; see p111), is the best. A handy pocket-size version of the same (€5.50; 1:10,000) is also available, but it does not include the outlying suburbs.

The OSI also publishes a **Map of Greater Dublin** (€8; scale 1:20,000), which includes a street index and details of bus routes. The Collins Streetfinder Map (€8; scale 1:15,000) is also pretty good, with easy-to-use laminates that won't get damaged in the (inevitable) rain.

You can buy a limited selection of maps in most bookshops and some newsagents, but the **National Map Centre** (Map pp266-8; ☎ 476 0471; 34 Grafton Hall, Aungier St) has a comprehensive selection of all OSI maps and other geographic sundries.

MEDICAL SERVICES
Dentists

Dental care is a costly business in Dublin. Unless you have a medical card (only available to registered residents), you can expect to pay from €45 for a basic check, about €60 for a cleaning and €80 for a filling. Reliable city-centre dentists include:

Anne's Lane Dental Centre (Map pp272-3; ☎ 671 8581; 2 Anne's Lane; 9am-6pm Mon-Fri, by appointment Sat)

Dame House Dental Surgery (Map pp269-71; ☎ 670 9256; 24-26 Dame St; 9am-6pm)

Gallagher & Associates (Map pp266-8; ☎ 670 3735; 38 Fenian St; 9am-8pm Mon, 8am-8pm Tue-Wed, 9am-5pm Thu-Fri, 9am-4pm every second Sat)

Doctors

If you don't have a medical card you will have to pay for all visits to a doctor. Charges begin at €40 for even a cursory examination. You can request a doctor to call out to your accommodation at any time on the 24-hour private **Doctors on Call** (☎ 453 9333) service line.

The **Eastern Regional Health Authority** (ERHA; Map pp262-3; ☎ 679 0700, 1800 520 520; www.erha.ie; Dr Steeven's Hospital, Dublin 8) has a Choice of Doctor Scheme, which can advise you on a suitable general practitioner (GP) from 9am to 5pm Monday to Friday. The ERHA also provides information services for those with physical and mental disabilities.

Your hotel or embassy can also suggest a doctor, but two good walk-in doctors clinics in town are:

Grafton Medical Practice (Map pp272-3; ☎ 671 2122; 34 Grafton St; 9am-6pm Mon-Fri)

Mercer Medical Centre (Map pp272-3; ☎ 402 2300; Lower Stephen St; 9am-6pm Mon-Thu & 9am-5pm Fri)

Hospitals

EU citizens are encouraged to obtain an E111 form before they leave home which will cover hospital costs should you require hospitalisation. This form, which covers you for a year, is easily obtained from a local health authority or, in the UK, the post office. The main city-centre hospitals are:

Baggot St Hospital (Map pp266-8; ☎ 668 1577; 18 Upper Baggot St)

Mater Misericordiae Hospital (Map pp264-5; ☎ 830 1122; Eccles St off Lower Dorset St)

St James's Hospital (Map pp262-3; ☎ 453 7941; James St)

MONEY
ATMs

Most banks have ATMs, although we've noticed recently that the machines in the city centre quickly run out of smaller denominations (€10 and €20) on Friday night, and the smallest denomination they'll dispense is €50. Some even run out of money altogether, and as the cash deposits aren't replenished until Monday morning, the machine stays out of order until then. We strongly recommend that if you're staying in the city centre, get your money out early Friday: not only will you avoid the problems described above but you won't have to face the enormous queues that form behind every central ATM after about 8pm.

Currency & Exchange Rates

Ireland's currency is the euro (€), which is divided into 100 cents. While the notes are all the same throughout the 12 countries of the EuroZone, the Irish coins feature a harp on the reverse side, but all non-Irish euro coins are also legal tender. For information on Dublin's economy and costs, see p22.

See the Quick Reference on the inside front cover for a list of exchange rates.

Credit Cards

Visa and MasterCard are more widely accepted in Dublin than Amex or Diners Club, which are often not accepted in smaller establishments. You can also use credit cards to withdraw cash, but be sure to obtain a PIN from your bank before you leave. This service usually carries an extra charge, so if you're withdrawing money, take out enough so that you don't have to keep going back.

If a card is lost or stolen, inform the police and the issuing company as soon as possible, otherwise you may have to bear the cost of the thief's purchases. Here are some 24-hour hotlines for cancelling your cards:

Amex ☎ 1800 282 728

Diners Club ☎ 0818 300 026

MasterCard ☎ 1800 557 378

Visa ☎ 1800 558 002

Changing Money

The best exchange rates are obtained at banks. Bureaux de change and other exchange facilities usually open for more hours but the rate and/or commission will be worse. Many post offices have a currency-exchange facility and open on Saturday morning. There's a cluster of banks located around College Green opposite Trinity College and all have exchange facilities. You can change money at the following:

Allied Irish Bank (Map pp269-71; ☎ 679 9222; Westmoreland St; ⏰ 10am-4pm Mon-Wed & Fri, 10am-5pm Thu)

Amex (Map pp272-3; ☎ 605 7709; Dublin Tourism Centre, St Andrew's St; ⏰ 9am-5pm Mon-Sat)

Bank of Ireland (Map pp269-71; ☎ 677 6801; 2 College Green; ⏰ 10am-4pm Mon-Wed & Fri, 10am-5pm Thu)

First Rate (Map pp269-71; ☎ 671 3233; 1 Westmoreland St; ⏰ 8am-9pm Mon-Fri, 9am-9pm Sat, 10am-9pm Sun Jun-Sep, 9am-6pm Oct-May)

Thomas Cook (Map pp269-71; ☎ 677 1721, 677 1307; 118 Grafton St; ⏰ 9am-5.30pm Mon-Tue & Fri-Sat, 10am-5.30pm Wed, 9am-7pm Thu)

Travellers Cheques

Most major brands of travellers cheques are readily accepted in Ireland. We recommend that you carry them in euros, as you can use them in other EuroZone countries and avoid costly exchange rates. Amex and Thomas Cook travellers cheques are widely recognised and branches don't charge commission for cashing their own cheques. Travellers cheques are rarely accepted for everyday transactions so you'll need to cash them beforehand.

Eurocheques can be cashed in Dublin, but special arrangements must be made before you travel if you are thinking of using personal cheques.

NEWSPAPERS & MAGAZINES

Newspapers

Dubliners are avid consumers of the printed word. There are newspapers and magazines to suit virtually every taste and interest. All the main English newspapers are readily available; News Corp, the Rupert Murdoch–owned media group that publishes *The Times* and the *Sun*, has an Irish office that's responsible for an Irish edition of their papers, which basically consists of nothing more than a couple of pages of Irish news and sports inserted into the English version.

DAILY NEWSPAPERS

The main daily local newspapers are:

Evening Herald (€1) Available from just after lunchtime, this evening tabloid is a bit of a scurrilous rag specialising

in shock-horror headlines about government wastage, heartless killers and immigrant scams. Nobody takes it all that seriously and it usually makes for good bus-journey reading on the way home. It is, however, the best newspaper for finding a flat, and its Thursday entertainment listings pages are pretty thorough.

Irish Examiner (€1.45; www.examiner.ie) Formerly the *Cork Examiner*, this paper went national in 2001 but still hasn't shed its rural slant. It's a very good paper nonetheless, with well-written features and news stories. We suspect that it's a little anti-Dublin though, as it tends to ignore the goings-on in the capital whenever it can.

Irish Independent (€1.45; www.independent.ie) Ireland's most widely read broadsheet is great for breaking domestic stories, as its journos usually have the one-up on every other hack for stories of national importance. It has good features on all facets of Irish current affairs, but its foreign coverage is appalling: limited to the back page, the content is usually reliant on stories about Russian women who've given birth to eight children, the break-up of Hollywood marriages and other 'you'll never believe this' titbits.

Irish Times (€1.45; www.ireland.com) The country's oldest and most serious daily newspaper, it is the most liberal broadsheet published in Ireland. In recent years its reputation for excellent journalism has been somewhat tarnished by the fact that it picks up far too many of its stories from its liberal British counterparts (most notably the *Guardian*) and the news wires, with the result that it doesn't break as much news as it used to. Non-Dubliners dismiss it as an Anglocentric newspaper that devotes far too much space to issues that aren't pertinent to the country; it is, however, still an excellent read. The online version of the paper is now a partly pay-and-view service (weekly/monthly/yearly €7/14/79); you can only read the breaking news and front page for free.

Star (€0.60) Ireland's answer to the English *Sun*, this tabloid is pretty much what you'd expect: plenty of celebrity pictures and very little news. It prides itself, however, on its efforts to reveal the sordid underbelly of Irish affairs: politicians on the take and gangsters on the make are a big part of its news cycle. Most of the stories are blatant exaggerations and simplistic takes on what's really going on.

SUNDAY PAPERS

Most Dubliners buy English Sunday papers, as the Irish equivalents just can't match their size and content. Irish newspapers are:

Ireland on Sunday Utterly vacuous content with celebrity exposés and lightweight political analysis.

Sunday Business Post (€1.80) The best financial newspaper in the country, it does exhaustive stories on all matters concerning the Irish economy.

Sunday Independent (€2) A Sunday edition of the daily broadsheet, with similar news content but plenty more lifestyle sections, restaurant reviews and plenty of social gossip.

Sunday Tribune (€1.95) Although its content pales in comparison to its English rivals, this is the best Irish Sunday paper. It offers the best summary of the week's events, has good features and also breaks its fair share of pertinent stories.

Sunday World A fairly low-brow tabloid paper with the usual fare about celebrities and their misdoings, politicians and their backroom deals and oodles of sport. The paper's crime correspondent, Paul Williams, is the country's foremost authority on the criminal underworld; his two books on the subject, *The General* and *Gangland*, are bestsellers.

Star on Sunday The usual tabloid nonsense, with plenty of juice and very little news. If you want a salacious tabloid, buy the Sunday Mirror; at least the sports pages are better.

Magazines

Generic international magazines aside, local publications include:

Dubliner (€2.99) Glossy and gossipy, this monthly magazine takes a soft look at the issues concerning the city's groovy brigades. Its credo is Oscar Wilde's dictum that 'history is gossip, and scandal is gossip made boring by morality'. Such cleverness does not disguise the fact that the mainstay of its content is to tell us where and with whom we need to be seen having dinner and what we should be wearing and discussing while doing it.

Dublin Event Guide (free; www.eventguide.ie) The best weekly listings magazine, it has film, theatre and music reviews, a feature or two and a comprehensive guide to what's on and where.

Hot Press (€3.50; www.hotpress.ie) The first, and once the best, guide to the city's music scene, this fortnightly publication is a bit like the Rolling Stones: once a cutting-edge force that shaped musical minds, today it's stuck in the past and is reluctant to come to terms with modern times. Its reputation and prestige ensures that it is still the most widely read of the city's music mags.

Image (€3.70) Ireland's version of the glossy woman's magazine. Aside from the usual focus on beauty tips and fashion hints, what we really love about this monthly mag is its vain attempt to turn the country's B-list celebs into international superstars. *Cosmo* goes parochial.

Phoenix (€2) A fortnightly magazine that specialises in clever political satire. The problem for non-nationals is that many of the references are strictly insider, so you'll have to know your current affairs to get the jokes.

Social & Personal (€2) Utter nonsense really, but who doesn't get stuck in while waiting in the dentist's ante-room? Lifestyles of the rich and often unknown make up the bulk of the content of this monthly publication; like most mags of its kind, it seeks to confirm that if only we plebs had what they had, then we'd be happy. Yeah right.

For information on gay and lesbian–specific publications, see p236.

PHARMACIES

All pharmacies in Dublin are clearly designated by a green cross. There are branches of the English chain pharmacy Boots spread throughout the city centre. Most pharmacies stay open until 7pm or 8pm, but the following city-centre chemists stay open until 10pm:

City Pharmacy (Map pp269-71; ☎ 670 4523; 14 Dame St)

O'Connell's Late Night Pharmacy (Map pp269-71; ☎ 873 0427; 55-56 O'Connell St)

POST

The Irish postal service, An Post, is reliable, efficient and usually on time. Post boxes in Dublin are usually green and have two slots: one for 'Dublin only', the other for 'All Other Places'. Postal rates (priority) are as follows:

Type	Ireland	Britain	Europe	Other
letter/postcard (25g)	€0.41	€0.50	€0.57	€0.57
letter (up to 100g)	€0.60	€0.85	€1.20	€1.20
package (250g)	€0.92	€1.75	€2	€2
package (1kg)	€4.25	€4.80	€8	€10

Economy 2nd-class rates are slightly cheaper, but delivery is considerably slower.

Mail can be addressed to poste restante at post offices, but is officially held for two weeks only. If you write 'hold for collection' on the envelope it may be kept for a longer period.

All mail to Britain and Europe goes by air so there is no need to use airmail envelopes or stickers.

Post Offices

Post offices in the city centre include:

An Post (Map pp272-3; ☎ 677 7127; South Anne St; ☺ 9am-6pm Mon-Fri)

An Post (Map pp272-3; ☎ 705 8206; St Andrew's St; ☺ 8.30am-5pm Mon-Fri)

General Post Office (GPO; Map pp264-5; ☎ 705 7000; O'Connell St; ☺ 8am-8pm Mon-Sat, 10am-6.30pm Sun & holidays)

Postal Codes

Postal codes in Dublin, presented as 'Dublin + number' are fairly straightforward. Their main feature is that all odd numbers refer to areas north of the Liffey and all even ones to areas south of the Liffey. They fan out numerically from the city centre, so the city centre to the north of the river is Dublin 1 and its southern equivalent is Dublin 2.

RADIO

Radio na Telefís Éireann (RTE) is Ireland's government-sponsored national broadcasting body and runs four radio stations. Licensed, independent broadcasters are gradually filling up the airwaves, replacing the old pirate stations that are being perpetually closed down, though some continue to operate. A scroll through the FM frequency will bring up the following:

Anna Livia (103.2FM) A community radio station that plays mostly alternative music.

Beaumount Hospital Radio (107.6FM) A lite programme of talk and music.

Dublin's Country (106.8FM) Banjos, slide guitars and doleful lyrics about 'momma'.

Dublin South FM (104.9FM) Community radio only on from 4pm to 9pm

FM 104 (104.4FM) Commercial radio playing Top 40 tunes almost exclusively.

Lite FM (102.2FM) Strictly MOR; easy listening.

Lyric FM (96-99FM) State-sponsored classical music radio.

Mater Hospital Radio (107.4FM) Community-based hospital radio.

Newstalk 106 (106FM) Twenty-four-hour news, with headlines every 20 minutes.

98FM (98FM) Commercial music station playing a predictable range of popular tunes.

Premier (92.6FM) Playing mostly hits from '70s and '80s.

Radio na Liffe (106.4FM) Irish-language radio with the best and most wide-ranging music programmes on the airwaves.

Radio Na Gaeltachta (92.6-94.4FM) State-sponsored Irish-language station; culture, music and current affairs.

RTE Radio 1 (88-94FM) Culture, current affairs and music.

RTE Radio 2 (90.2-92.4FM) Commercial radio with some evening alternative shows.

Spin (103.8FM) Youth-orientated programming of talk and music.

Today FM (100-102FM) Biggest independent radio station, with music, current affairs and good alternative shows in the evening.

If you fancy tuning in to Irish radio before you get here, you can try out the following web-streamed radio stations:

RTE Radio www.rte.ie

Today FM www.todayfm.com

SAFETY

Dublin is a safe city by any standards, except maybe those set by the Swiss. The general rule of thumb here is: do what you would at home. Like anywhere, certain parts of the city are pretty dodgy due to the presence of drug addicts and other questionable types; these include, on the north side, north and northeast of Gardiner St and along parts of Dorset St; and, on the south side, west along Thomas St.

TELEPHONE

You shouldn't have any problems making phone calls to anyone, anywhere.

Eircom is the largest telephone service provider in Ireland. The deregulation of the telephone industry has seen the arrival of a number of other providers to Ireland, all of which, however, rent their lines from Eircom. Eircom's main competitor is O2. Peak per-minute charges for international calls from Ireland to selected countries include the following:

Australia €0.85

Canada €0.19

France €0.39

Germany €0.38

Italy €0.48

Netherlands €0.38

New Zealand €0.85

UK €0.15

USA €0.19

Prices are lower in the evening and at the weekend. The above prices are for calls placed from land-line phones to other land-line phones; international calls to mobiles can cost significantly more. Phone calls from hotel rooms cost at least double the standard rate. You can send and receive faxes from post offices (up to €2 per page locally) or most hotels.

Local telephone calls from a public phone in the Republic cost €0.25 for around three minutes (around €0.50 to a mobile), regardless of when you call.

The number for local and national directory enquiries is ☎ 11811. For International it's ☎ 11818.

Pre-paid phonecards by Eircom and private operators are available in newsagencies and post offices and work from all payphones. For cheap international phone calls, try the following phone centres:

Talk Is Cheap (Map pp264-5; ☎ 872 2235; 87 Capel St)

Talk Is Cheap (Map pp264-5; ☎ 874 6013; 55 Moore St)

Talk Shop (Map pp269-71; ☎ 672 7212; www.talkshop.ie; 20 Temple Lane)

Talk Shop (Map pp264-5; ☎ 872 0200; www.talkshop.ie; 5 Upper O'Connell St)

Direct Home Call Codes

Rather than placing reverse-charge calls through the operator in Dublin, you can dial direct to your home-country operator and then reverse the charges or charge the call to a local phone credit card. To use the home-direct service dial the codes shown below, then the area code and, in most cases, the number you want. Your home-country operator will come on the line before the call goes through.

Australia (☎ 1800 550 061 + number)

France (☎ 1800 551 033 + number)

Italy (☎ 1800 550 039 + number)

New Zealand (☎ 1800 550 064 + number)

Spain (☎ 1800 550 034 + number)

UK – BT (☎ 1800 550 044 + number)

USA – AT&T (☎ 1800 550 000 + number)

USA – MCI (☎ 1800 551 001 + number)

USA – Sprint (☎ 1800 552 001 + number)

Mobile Phones

Virtually everyone in Dublin has a mobile phone. Ireland uses GSM 900/1800, which is compatible with the rest of Europe and Australia but not with North American GSM 1900 or the totally different system in Japan (though some specially equipped North American phones do work here). There are three service providers in Ireland. Vodafone (087) is the most popular, followed by O2 (086) and the latest arrival, Meteor (085).

All three service providers are linked with most international GSM providers, which will allow you to 'roam' onto a local service once you arrive in Dublin. This means you can use your mobile phone to make local calls, but will be charged at the highest possible rate.

For around €50 you will get a Ready-to-Go pre-paid phone, your own number and anywhere up to €25 worth of air-time. As you use up your air-time, you simply buy more at newsagencies. The other service providers have variations on this scheme.

Phone Codes

The area code for Dublin is 01. When calling Dublin from abroad, dial your international access code, followed by 353 and 1 (dropping the 0 that precedes it). To make international calls from Dublin, first dial 00, then your country code followed by the local area code and number.

TELEVISION

Ireland has three state-controlled stations and one independent channel, but most TVs in Dublin are connected by cable rather than aerial, which means they also receive, as standard, the main British stations – BBC1, BBC2, Channel 4 and UTV (the regional version of ITV). One advantage that Dublin viewers have over their British neighbours is that thanks to cable, Sky One and Sky News are freely available. Many of the fancier hotels have satellite and/or digital TV, which makes for a long list of channels, including CNN and other international news stations. The main Irish channels are:

RTE 1 Ireland's main station, with a pretty standard mix of programmes, from news, current affairs and sports programmes to variety shows, soap operas and movies.

Network 2 The second state-controlled channel has generally lighter programmes.

TnaG A mostly Irish-language station (most programmes have English subtitles) that also offers a terrific selection of English-language movies and sport (try watching a Spanish league match with an Irish commentary).

TV3 An independent channel with a strictly lightweight programming philosophy; it does show the odd good film though.

TIME

In winter, Dublin (and the rest of Ireland) is on GMT, also known as Universal Time Coordinated (UTC), the same as Britain. In summer, the clock shifts to GMT plus one hour. When it's noon in Dublin in summer, it's 3am in Los Angeles and Vancouver, 7am in New York and Toronto, 1pm in Paris, 8pm in Singapore, and 10pm in Sydney.

TIPPING

In restaurants, it is common to tip around 12% of the bill and up to 15% to 20% for especially good service, unless a service charge has been automatically added to the bill. If so, check to make sure that the staff actually receive it; if they don't, you can refuse to pay it. With other services, from hotel porters to hairdressers, a small gratuity is commonplace, although you're under no obligation to fork out. The same applies to taxi drivers; usually a euro or two is plenty.

TOILETS

Forget about the few public facilities on the street: they're dirty and usually overrun with drug dealers and addicts. All shopping centres have public toilets; if you're nowhere near one, go into any bar or hotel.

TOURIST INFORMATION

The **Dublin Tourism Centre** (Map pp272-3; ☎ 605 7700; www.visitdublin.com; St Andrew's Church, 2 Suffolk St; ⊙ 9am-7pm Mon-Sat, 10.30am-3pm Sun Jul-Aug, 9am-5.30pm Mon-Sat Sep-Jun) is where you'll find everything you need to kick-start your visit. Besides general visitor information on Dublin and Ireland, the centre also has an accommodation booking service, a book and gift shop, an Amex bureau de change, a branch of Ticketmaster (for booking tickets to all major events in the city, including concerts), local and national bus information, rail information, a car-hire desk, tour information and bookings and a café.

The tourism centre has five other branches throughout the city:

Baggot St Bridge (Map pp266-8; foyer of Fáilte Ireland office; ⊙ 9.30am-noon & 12.30-5pm Mon-Fri)

Dublin Airport (⊙ 8am-10pm)

Dun Laoghaire (Ferry Terminal; ⊙ 10am-1pm & 2-6pm Mon-Sat)

14 Upper O'Connell St (Map pp264-5; ⊙ 9am-5pm Mon-Sat)

Tallaght (The Square Shopping Centre; ⊙ 9.30am-noon & 12.30-5pm Mon-Sat)

None of these tourist information offices will provide information over the phone – they are exclusively walk-in services. All telephone bookings and reservations are operated by Gulliver Ireland, a computerised information and reservation service that is available at all walk-in offices or from anywhere in the world. It provides up-to-date information on events, attractions and transport, and can also book accommodation. In Ireland, call ☎ 1800 668 668; from Britain call ☎ 00800 6686 6866; from the rest of the world call ☎ 00 353 669 792083.

For information on the rest of the country, call into the head office of **Fáilte Ireland** (Map pp266-8; ☎ 1850 230 330; www.ireland .travel.com; Wilton Tce, Baggot St Bridge; ⊙ 9am-5.15pm Mon-Fri). Web-based tourist information on Dublin is available at the following sites:

www.dublinks.com A catch-all website with info on things like shopping, parking, hotels, restaurants and other necessary titbits.

www.dublinpeople.com News on the city and links to things to see and places to stay and eat.

www.dublintourist.com An excellent and thorough guide to virtually every aspect of the city, from booking a room to going for a drink.

www.lunch.ie Sponsored by Newstalk 106 and *Dubliner* magazine, this offers you the chance to get to know the city by being taken to lunch in the city by a local stranger and then returning the favour quid pro quo: a new slant on 'there's no such thing as a free lunch'.

www.temple-bar.ie Website dedicated to Dublin's cultural quarter.

www.wow.ie A comprehensive entertainment guide to Ireland, including the capital.

TRAVEL AGENCIES

Amex and Thomas Cook both have offices in the centre of Dublin (see p239). Otherwise, try:

USIT (Map pp269-71; ☎ 602 1600; www.usit.com; 19 Aston Quay; ⊙ 9.30am-6.30pm Mon-Wed & Fri, 9.30am-8pm Thu, 9.30am-6.30pm Sat) Travel agency of the Union of Students in Ireland.

VISAS

UK nationals don't need a passport to visit Dublin, but are advised to carry one (or some other form of photo identification) to prove that they are a UK national. It's also necessary to have a passport or photo ID when changing travellers cheques or hiring a car. EU nationals can enter Ireland with either a passport or a national ID card.

Visitors from outside the EU will need a passport, which should remain valid for at least six months after their intended arrival.

For citizens of EU states and most Western countries, including Australia, Canada, New Zealand and the USA, no visa is required to visit either the Republic or Northern Ireland. Citizens of India, China and many African countries do need a visa for the Republic. Full visa requirements for visiting the Republic are available online at www.gov.ie/iveagh/services/visas.

EU nationals are allowed to stay indefinitely, while other visitors can usually remain for three to six months. To stay longer in the Republic, contact the local garda station or the **Department of Foreign Affairs** (Map pp266-8; ☎ 478 0822; www.gov.ie/iveagh; 80 St Stephen's Green, Dublin 2).

Although you don't need an onward or return ticket to enter Ireland, it could help if there's any doubt that you have sufficient funds to support yourself while in Dublin. For work visas, see below.

WOMEN TRAVELLERS

Women travellers will probably find Dublin a blissfully relaxing experience, with little risk of hassle on the street or anywhere else. Nonetheless, you still need to take elementary safety precautions. Walking alone at night, especially in less salubrious parts of the city, and hitching are probably unwise. Should you have serious problems, be sure to report them to the local tourist authorities.

There's little need to worry about what you wear in Dublin, even if the climate will probably dictate your choice of clothing. Finding contraception is not the problem it once was, although anyone on the pill should bring adequate supplies. For female health issues, including contraceptives and the morning-after pill (€39), contact the **Well Woman Clinic** either on **Lower Liffey St** (Map pp269-71; ☎ 661 0083; 35 Lower Liffey St) or **Pembroke Rd** (Map pp266–8; ☎ 660 9860; 67 Pembroke Rd).

In the unlikely event of a sexual assault, get in touch with the police and the Rape Crisis Centre (see p236).

WORK

Citizens of other EU countries can work legally in Dublin without a visa. Non-EU citizens require a work permit or work visa, although there is plenty of black market labour about, especially in low-paying seasonal jobs in

The City Handbook

From barbers to yoga and art galleries to shoe repair, it's all in **The City Handbook** (www.dublincityhandbook.ie; €12.99), an easy-to-read Dublin directory. The ethos behind the handbook is refreshingly different: its upfront billing to refugee groups, homeless shelters and other like-minded organisations highlights the needs of those the official tourist authorities would prefer to ignore. It is available at all of the bigger bookshops throughout the city.

the tourist industry. Contact you local Irish embassy for more information. Work-related information can be found at:

Department of Enterprise, Trade & Employment (Map pp266-8; ☎ 631 2121; www.entemp.ie; Davitt House, 65A Adelaide Rd, Dublin 2)

Working Ireland (Map pp269-71; ☎ 677 0300; www.workingireland.ie; 26 Eustace St; ✆ noon-6pm Mon-Fri) An excellent new resource is this one-stop, state-funded help centre which for €30 a year, will lay out your CV, set up interviews, help find accommodation, recommend language courses and offer discounts on tours and phone calls.

www.nixers.com An excellent online resource listing jobs in Dublin.

A large number of recruitment agencies in Dublin will locate work for non-nationals, whether they be travelling backpackers or long-term residents in Dublin. These include:

Brightwater Selection (Map pp266-8; ☎ 662 1000; 36 North Merrion Sq, Dublin 2)

Careers Register (Map pp266-8; ☎ 679 8900; 26 Lower Baggot St, Dublin 2)

Global Partnerships (Map pp266-8; ☎ 661 8740; 95 Lower Baggot St, Dublin 2)

Planet Recruitment (Map pp266-8; ☎ 874 9901; 21 Eden Quay, Dublin 1)

Reed Recruitment Agency (Map pp272-3; ☎ 670 4466; www.reed.ie; 47 Dawson St, Dublin 2)

Behind the Scenes

THE LONELY PLANET STORY

The story begins with a classic travel adventure: Tony and Maureen Wheeler's 1972 journey across Europe and Asia to Australia. There was no useful information about the overland trail then, so Tony and Maureen published the first Lonely Planet guidebook to meet a growing need.

From a kitchen table, Lonely Planet has grown to become the largest independent travel publisher in the world, with offices in Melbourne (Australia), Oakland (USA), London (UK) and Paris (France).

Today Lonely Planet guidebooks cover the globe. There is an ever-growing list of books and information in a variety of media. Some things haven't changed. The main aim is still to make it possible for adventurous travellers to get out there – to explore and better understand the world.

At Lonely Planet we believe travellers can make a positive contribution to the countries they visit – if they respect their host communities and spend their money wisely.

THIS BOOK

This 5th edition of *Dublin* was updated by Fionn Davenport and Martin Hughes. The previous 3rd and 4th editions were revised and expanded by Fionn Davenport. The 2nd edition was updated by Tom Smallman and Pat Yale and the 1st edition was written by Tony Wheeler. The guide was commissioned in Lonely Planet's London office, and produced by:

Commissioning Editor Amanda Canning
Assisting Commissioning Editors Fiona Christie, Michala Green & Imogen Franks
Coordinating Editor Fionnuala Twomey
Coordinating Cartographer Simon Tillema
Coordinating Layout Designer Sally Darmody
Assisting Editors Dan Caleo, Melanie Dankel, Anne Mulvaney, Kristin Odijk, Katrina Webb & Simon Williamson
Assisting Layout Designer Dianne Zammit
Cover Designer Annika Roojun
Series Designer Nic Lehman
Series Design Concept Nic Lehman & Andrew Weatherill
Managing Cartographer Mark Griffiths
Managing Editor Darren O'Connell
Layout Manager Adriana Mammarella
Mapping Development Paul Piaia
Project Manager Eoin Dunlevy
Regional Publishing Manager Katrina Browning
Series Publishing Manager Gabrielle Green
Series Development Team Jenny Blake, Anna Bolger, Fiona Christie, Kate Cody, Erin Corrigan, Janine Eberle, Simone Egger, James Ellis, Nadine Fogale, Roz Hopkins, Dave McClymont, Leonie Mugavin, Rachel Peart, Ed Pickard, Michele Posner, Howard Ralley and Dani Valent
Thanks to Kate McDonald, Michelle Lewis, Glenn Beanland, Ryan Evans, Gerard Walker, Piotr Czajkowski, Joelene Kowalski, Martin Heng, Yvonne Bischofberger, Jacqui Saunders, Jennifer Garrett, Carol Chandler, Graham Imeson
Cover photographs by Lonely Planet Images: A man wanders through a labyrinthe at Dublin Castle, Corinne Humphrey (top); Yet another pub in the Temple Bar area of Dublin, Richard Cummins (bottom); The Father Mathew Bridge over the Liffey in Dublin (back).

Internal photographs by Olivier Cirendini/Lonely Planet Images except for the following: p2 (#1, #3), p55 (#2), p142 (#3), p144 (#3), p146 (#2), p177 Doug McKinlay/Lonely Planet Images; p2 (#5), p58 (#1), p146 (#1, #3), p223 Richard Cummins/Lonely Planet Images; p145 (#1) Ann Cecil/Lonely Planet Images; p212 Greg Gawlowski/Lonely Planet Images. All images are the copyright of the photographers unless otherwise indicated. Many of the images in this guide are available for licensing from Lonely Planet Images: www.lonelyplanetimages.com.

ACKNOWLEDGMENTS

Many thanks to the following for the use of their content:

Oda O'Carroll, author of the Dublin chapter in *Ireland 6*, for her contribution to the Sleeping chapter.
Dublin Transit Map : © Iarnród éireann 2004

THANKS

FIONN DAVENPORT

First and foremost, I want to thank my fellow author in this endeavour, Martin Hughes. Working with him on the book was a real pleasure, as was his general enthusiasm and expertise. Secondly, I want to thank Amanda Canning at Lonely Planet for her wisdom in pairing us to do the update and for all her incisive ideas and support throughout. A big thankyou to Fionnuala Twomey, Dan Caleo and Katrina Webb in Melbourne, whose eagle eyes and intelligent suggestions at the editing stage greatly improved the chapters, and to Simon Tillema for the excellent maps.

In Dublin, I want to thank Libby McCormack for all of her patience and support while I worked on the guide; I know it couldn't have been easy to watch me pace and mumble about the apartment at all hours of the day and night in my efforts to write semi-literate copy. Finally, thanks to each and everyone who helped me during my research with suggestions, tips and guidance. Your help is greatly appreciated (financial remuneration is, alas, not really an option).

MARTIN HUGHES

Martin wishes to extend sincere thanks to Kirsti for her patience and his mum and dad for their tolerance. Also special thanks to Alan, Andrea, Thomas, Aisling, Sean, Dave, Jane, Ardal, Melanie, Emily, Buckets, Redmond, AJ, Tommy, Anne, Ciaran, Jim, Ned, Derek, Niall, Amanda, Fionnuala and last, but most *definitely* least, co-author Fionn.

OUR READERS

Many thanks to the travellers who used the last edition and wrote to us with helpful hints, useful advice and interesting anecdotes. Your names follow:

Jadwiga Adamczuk, Gordon Adamson, Carrie and Eran Bachar, Wilbur S Bailey, Loredana Banham, Tracy Bays, Lizzie Belbeck, Richard & Sarah Bennett, Tanny Blackman, Christine Boeckle, John Bourke, Marcella Brown, Nicola Byrne, Juan Pablo Castel, Sala Clarke, Sharon Clerkin, Kathleen Dadey, Sally Darragh, Caroline Davies, Sherla Davies, Kara Davis, Kathy Douglas, Margaret Ellis, Humphrey Evans, Elaine Fallon, Shaun Finch, Arthur Fink, Jerry George, Katherine George, Peter Gould, Lynda Green, Andrea Gryak, Stacy Hague, David Hall, Tanyia Harrison, K G Hellyen, Irene Hennessey, Maureen Holland, Steven Holland, Field Horne, Francis Huddy, Elisabeth Imholz, Patrick James Logue, Sue Johnson, John Kennedy, P S Kennedy, Stephen Kinsella, David Kremer, Michael Krischer, Graham Lenton, Graham & Rosemarie Lenton, Elaine Logan, Rhona Mackay, Tom McCluskey, Ian McGinley, Kev McCready, Laura Melton, Michael Middleton, Paul Mitchell, KS Moore, Paul Murphy, Søren Nørby, Victor Odumenya, Jean O Sullian, Tuija Paukkunen, John Perkins, Jan Peter, Lisa Pickard, Mike Pilcher, Ade Pritchard, Steve Psallidas, Jo Renty, Mary Rice, Melissa Roberts, Jane Robertson, Kristen Ross Outi Saarinen, Tom William Skarre, P Skinner, Sandra Standifer, Matthew Starr, Sanford Sternlicht, Marianne Strusinski, Gannon Sugimura, Mark Sweeting, Marianne Teglengaard, Ursula Thummer-Wolf, Koen Van Treeck, Kenneth Wardrop, Teresa Webb, Michael Whittington, Stephanie Wilson, Howard Wollman, Elad Yom-Tov

SEND US YOUR FEEDBACK

We love to hear from travellers – your comments keep us on our toes and help make our books better. Our well-travelled team reads every word on what you loved or loathed about this book. Although we cannot reply individually to postal submissions, we always guarantee that your feedback goes straight to the appropriate authors, in time for the next edition. Each person who sends us information is thanked in the next edition – and the most useful submissions are rewarded with a free book.

To send us your updates – and find out about LP events, newsletters and travel news – visit our award-winning website: www.lonelyplanet.com.

Note: We may edit, reproduce and incorporate your comments in Lonely Planet products such as guidebooks, websites and digital products, so let us know if you don't want your comments reproduced or your name acknowledged. For a copy of our privacy policy visit www.lonelyplanet.com/privacy.

Notes

Notes

Notes

Index

See also separate indexes for Eating (p256), Drinking (p257), Entertainment (p257), Shopping (p257) and Sleeping (p258).

Index

Index

MAP LEGEND

ROUTES

Freeway	Mall/Steps
Primary Road	Tunnel
Secondary Road	Walking Tour
Tertiary Road	Walking Tour Detour
Lane	Walking Trail
One-Way Street	Walking Path

TRANSPORT

Rail	Rail (Underground)

HYDROGRAPHY

River, Creek	Water

AREA FEATURES

Area of Interest	Cemetery, Christian
Building, Featured	Land
Building, Information	Mall
Building, Other	Park
Building, Transport	Reservation
Campus	Sports

POPULATION

⊙	**CAPITAL (NATIONAL)**	⊙	**CAPITAL (STATE)**
●	**Large City**	●	**Medium City**
●	Small City	●	Town, Village

SYMBOLS

Sights/Activities
- Castle, Fortress
- Christian
- Jewish
- Monument
- Museum, Gallery
- Point of Interest
- Ruin
- Zoo, Bird Sanctuary

Eating
- Eating

Drinking
- Drinking

Entertainment
- Entertainment

Shopping
- Shopping

Sleeping
- Sleeping
- Camping

Transport
- Bus Station
- Taxi Rank

Information
- Bank, ATM
- Embassy/Consulate

- Hospital, Medical
- Information
- Internet Facilities
- Parking Area
- Police Station
- Post Office, GPO
- Telephone

Geographic
- Lookout
- Mountain, Volcano
- Pass, Canyon

Map Section

DUBLIN

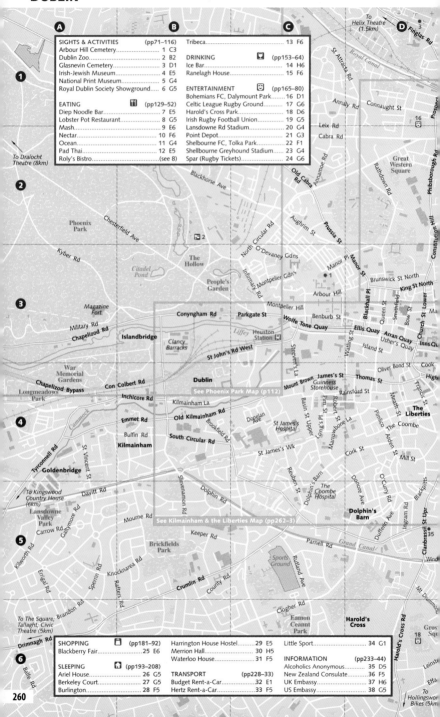

KILMAINHAM & THE LIBERTIES

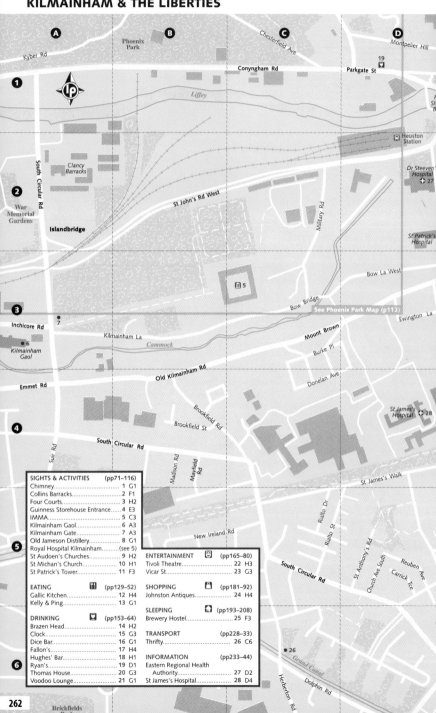

See North of the Liffey
Map (pp264–5)

E

Collins Barracks

● 2

Benburb St

Wolfe Tone Quay

F

Blackhall Pl

Blackhall St

Hendrick St

Queen St

James
Joyce
Bridge

Ellis Quay

16 ▣

21
▣

G

Friary Ave

Smithfield Tce

🖾 1

New Church St

13

Phoenix St North

Bow St

May La

▥ 8

🕈 10

Hammond La

Arran Quay

Usher's Quay

H

Cuckoo La

Mary's La

Church Ave
West

Dublin

Creek La

Chancery St

18 ▣

Inns Quay

Father
Mathew
Bridge

Merchant's Quay

3 ●

St Francis'

1

2

Watling St

Island St

Bonham St

Usher St

St Augustine St

St James's
Guinness Brewery

Oliver Bond St

John's St West

National College
of Art & Design

14 ▣

Bridge St Lower

Bridge St
Upper

Cook St

9
🕈

Borris
Court

Schoolhouse La

High St

James's St

Echlin St

Grand Canal Pl

James's
Ave

Guinness
Storehouse

● 4

Portland St
West

11 ●

Rainsford St

Market St
South

Bellevue

Robert St

Thomas St

15
▣

Hanbury La

St Catherine's
Church

School St

Earl St South

Meath Pl

▣ 25

23
🖾

Vicar St

Catherine St

Swift's Al

Liberty
Market

Meath St

Garden La

Carman's Hall

20 ▣

🖾 22

Lamb Al

Iveagh
Market

Dean Swift Sq

Thomas Davis
St South

St Nicholas
Without

Francis St

John Dillon St

Nicholas St

Back La

**The
Liberties**

Hanover La

▣ 12

3

Basin St Upper

Our Lady's Rd

Loreto Rd

Rosary Rd

Newport St

Long's Pl

Pim St

Forbes La

Marrowbone La

Summer St South

Braithwaite St

Pimlico

John St South

Allingham St

Cork St

Ormond Rd

Brickfield La

Gray St

The Coombe

Brabazon St

Weavers St

Arden St

Brabazon
Row

Newmarket

Chamber St

Oscar
Sq

Brown St South

Mill St

Ward's Hill

Mark's Al West

Ash St

New Row South

Clarence Mangan Rd

St Thomas Rd

Dean St

17 ▣

24 ▥

Patrick St

4

Dolphin's Barn

Cameron St

Maxwell St

Darley's Tce

Fingal St

Harman St

St Teresa's Gdns

Ebenezer Tce

Hamilton St

Donore Ave

Rutledge Tce

Donore Tce

Susan Tce

O'Curry Rd

O'Donovan Rd

Petrie Rd

Gilbert Rd

Long La

Blackpitts

New St

Clanbrassil St Lower

5

The
Coombe
Hospital

**Dolphin's
Barn**

Dufferin Ave

Ingram Rd

Vincent St

Clanbrassil St Upper

See South Central
Dublin Map (pp266–7)

6

See Kilmainham & the Liberties Map (pp262–3)

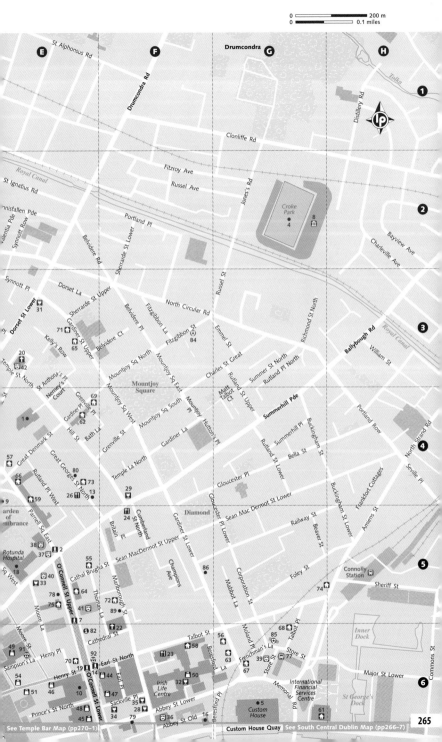

SOUTH CENTRAL DUBLIN

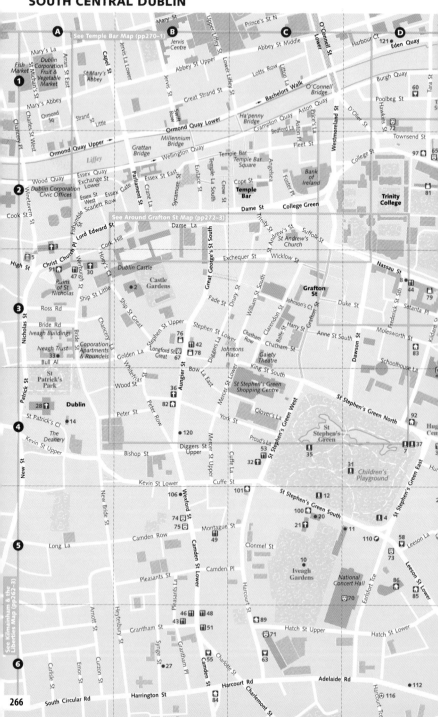

200 m
0.1 mi

E **F** **G** Guild St **H** North Wall

North Wall Quay

Custom House Quay

Liffey

City Quay Sir John Rogerson's Quay

See North of the Liffey Map (pp264–5)

re's Quay
Moss St
City Arts Centre
Gloucester St South

See Trinity College Map (p78)

102 •

Spring Garden La
• 113
Shaw St
Mark St
Mark's La
Pearse St
St Mark's Church

Lombard St East
Magennis Pl
Sandwith St Lower
Creighton St
Windmill La
Hanover St East
Cardiffs Ln

Luce Sports Centre
by and

Pearse Station

Grand Canal Quay

Hanover Quay **2**

Grand Canal Docks

64 • 64
College La
Lincoln Pl
61 •
Dental Hospital
er St S
103 •
Westland Row
St Andrew's Church

Cumberland St South
Boyne La
Boyne St
Macken St

80 • 1 •
Ringsend Rd
34 •
Barrow St **3**

Clare St
Clare La
16 • 15 • 77 •
Merrion Sq West
87 •
57 •
Fenian St
115 •
Hogan Pl
Denzille La
23 •
24 •
109 •

Grand Canal Quay

Grand Canal Dock Station

19 •
Merrion Square
National Maternity Hospital
Grant's Row
Grattan St
Grand Canal St Lower

9 •
52 •
Merrion Sq Upper
Fitzwilliam La
Merrion Sq South
Merrion Sq East
Verschoyle Pl
Stephen's La
Mount St Lower
Grand Canal St Upper **4**

94 •
6 •
Merrion Row
56 • 88 •
59 •
Roe La
111 •
118 • 93 •
Fitzwilliam St Lower
22 •
40 •
Mount St Upper
James's St East
James's Pl East
29 •
Herbert St
Herbert La
Herbert Pl
99 • **5**
Lansdowne Park

45 •
Windsor Pl
Pembroke St Lower
Pembroke La
39 •
Fitzwilliam St Upper
Baggot St Lower

s Pl
Fitzwilliam Sq West
Fitzwilliam Sq North
Fitzwilliam Square
Fitzwilliam Sq East
Hagan's Ct
Lad La
Pembroke Row
Haddington Rd

66 •
Kingram Pl
Fitzwilliam Sq South
Merrion Sq East
114 •
104 •
108 •
90 •
119 • **6**
Northumberland Rd

Leeson Cl
96 •
107 •
25 •
Wilton Pl
Wilton Tce
Mespil Rd
95 •
69 •
123 •
Waterloo Rd
Baggot St Upper
Wellington Rd
Pembroke Rd
98 •

Leeson St Upper
Grand Canal
Pembroke La

267

A B C D

See North of the
Liffey Map (pp264–5)

86

1

55

35

Jervis St

Jervis La Lower

13

2

Mary's Abbey

Abbey St Upper

Capel St

Great Strand St

38

48

Swift Row

3

Arran St East

Strand St Little

50

39

36

107

The Boardwalk

Ormond Quay Lower

108

Ormond Quay Upper

Millennium
Footbridge

Grattan
Bridge

Wellington Quay

102

46

56

Liffey

101

81 Essex St East

89 10

Eustace St

16

12

100 ©

4

14

Essex Quay

20

Exchange St Lower

53

44 26

Meeting
House
Square

71

125

69

5

30 1

129 1

59

72

Dublin
Corporation
Civic Offices

Essex St West

Essex Gate

80

Scarlett Row

109

Parliament St

Crane La

Sycamore St

64

32

65

5

91

47

68

31 29

45

104

34

123

79

58

Cork's La

95

Fishamble St

37

118

Dame St

78

Dame La

119

Lord Edward St

Municipal
Buildings

City
Hall 2

11

105

85

Cork Hill

Dublin
Castle 4

Great George's St South

33

Werburgh St

Hoey's Ct

Upper
Yard

Lower
Yard

Church of the
Holy Trinity
(Royal Chapel)

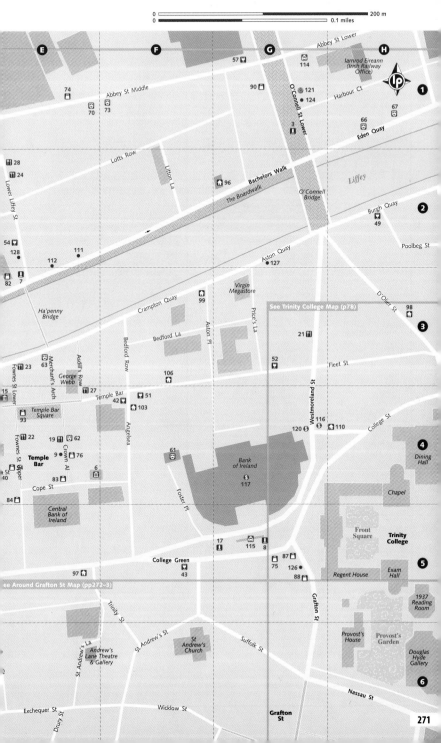

0   200 m

0   0.1 miles

E   **F**   **G**   **H**

Abbey St Lower

57

114

Iarnród Éireann
(Irish Railway
Office)

1

74

Abbey St Middle

90

O'Connell St Lower

121

124

Harbour Ct

67

70   73

66

Eden Quay

3

Lotts Row

Litton La

Bachelors Walk

96   The Boardwalk

O'Connell
Bridge

Liffey

Burgh Quay

49

2

Lower Liffey St

28

24

Poolbeg St

54

128

111

Aston Quay

127

D'Olier St

98

3

82   7

112

Crampton Quay

99

Virgin
Megastore

Price's La

See Trinity College Map (p78)

Ha'penny
Bridge

Bedford La

Aston Pl

21

52

Fleet St

Fownes St Lower

23

63

Merchant's
Arch

Asdill's Row

George
Webb

Bedford Row

106

Westmoreland St

15

27

Temple Bar

51

42   103

116

120   110

College St

4

93

Temple Bar
Square

19   62

Angelsea

61

Bank
of Ireland

Dining
Hall

22

9   76

Crown Al

Chapel

5

Fownes St Upper

40

6

83

Foster Pl

117

Front
Square

Trinity
College

84

Cope St

Central
Bank of
Ireland

17

115   8

87

75

126

88

College Green

43

97

Regent House

Exam
Hall

1937
Reading
Room

6

ee Around Grafton St Map (pp272–3)

Trinity St

St Andrew's La

St Andrew's St

Andrew's
Lane Theatre
& Gallery

St
Andrew's
Church

Suffolk St

Provost's
House

Provost's
Garden

Douglas
Hyde
Gallery

Exchequer St

Drury St

Wicklow St

Grafton
St

Nassau St

Dame St